WAR SINCE 1945

WAR SINCE 1945

Michael Carver

G. P. Putnam's Sons
New York

To those who died believing that
they fought for freedom and justice
or
just doing their duty

First American Edition 1981

Library of Congress Cataloging in Publication Data

Carver, Richard Michael Power, Baron Carver, date.
    War since 1945–

    Bibliography: p.
    Includes index.
    1. Military history, Modern—20th century.
2. Great Britain—History, Military—20th century.
I. Title.
U42.C37   1980   909.82'5   80-26914
ISBN 0-399-12594-9

Printed in the United States of America

Contents

Maps

Illustrations

Acknowledgements

The author and publisher wish to thank the following for permission to adapt maps from their books: Alistair Horne and Macmillan Ltd for a map in *A Savage War of Peace*; Julian Paget and Faber and Faber Ltd for three maps in *Last Post*; Neville Maxwell and Jonathan Cape Ltd for three maps in *India's China War*.

The author wishes to express his thanks to the staff of the Ministry of Defence Library (Army and Central) and of the Prince Consort's Army Library, Aldershot, for their unfailing courtesy and help, and to Judy Rous for her accurate and rapid typing.

Introduction

In this book I have not attempted to describe all the fighting that has taken place everywhere in the world since 1945. I have concentrated on those conflicts which have, directly or indirectly, most affected Britain. I have not concerned myself with purely civil wars, that is ones between different factions in one country in which no other nation was involved. The reader will not therefore find anything here about the Chinese Civil War, Cuba or other fighting in Central or South America, nor about Northern Ireland. All of the wars described arose as a result of the recession of imperialism, the withdrawal of the rule of the British, French and Japanese Empires. It has been a long-drawn-out and generally painful process, particularly in the case of the former French rule in Indo-China and Algeria. The story of the overthrow of colonial rule does not include the departure of the Dutch from their East Indian possessions, nor of Belgium and Portugal from Africa.

In a period when we have been inclined to think of ourselves as at peace, British servicemen, principally soldiers, have been fighting somewhere in the world every year except 1968, probably a unique year for the British regular army since its inception at the Restoration of the Monarchy in 1660.

I should have been better fitted to face the tasks before me while still serving as a senior officer, had I carried out the studies needed to write this book some time ago. I hope that it will help those who now face, or in the future will face, similar tasks, although it is an error to attempt slavishly to copy the past. History does not repeat itself, but it has much to teach us, especially about what not to do. It is largely for this reason that I have paid as much attention to the background leading up to wars as to the events of the conflicts themselves.

M.C.
1980

PART ONE

British Colonial Conflicts

Chapter One

PALESTINE

If Britain thought that her army was going to be able to sit back after VE and then VJ day in 1945, she was to be sadly disillusioned. As soon as war with Germany and then with Japan came to an end, indeed before they had done so, colonial conflicts, some but not all of which had remained dormant during the war, were not slow to raise their heads. The most immediate and the most urgent was that of Palestine.*

The origin of the problems that Britain faced there lay fundamentally in the establishment of Jewish settlements in the country towards the end of the nineteenth century and the subsequent development of the Zionist movement for a Jewish national home or state. This had from the start been opposed by the Arabs, at that time under Turkish rule. By 1914, when Turkey joined the Central Powers and found herself at war with Britain, there were 85,000 Jews settled in the country. On 2 November 1917, at a time in the First World War when things were looking pretty bleak, the Foreign Secretary, Arthur Balfour, on behalf of the British Government, wrote his famous letter to Lord Rothschild. He said that His Majesty's Government viewed with favour the establishment in Palestine of a national home for the Jewish people and would use their best endeavours to facilitate the achievement of that object, it being clearly understood that nothing should be done which might prejudice the civil and religious rights of existing non-Jewish communities in Palestine, or the rights and political status enjoyed by Jews in any other country. In that short letter Britain impaled herself on the horns of a dilemma from which she was not to be able to escape directly until 1948 and indirectly until 1956, America thereafter finding herself stuck on the horns instead.

The act of firm impalement was self-inflicted and it took the form of accepting responsibility, at the San Remo Conference in April 1920, for the administration of the country as a League of Nations mandate, confirmed in 1922 by the League Council, which agreed that Britain, as the mandatory power, should be responsible for putting the Balfour declaration into effect.

* For a general map of Palestine, see map on page 236.

This came as a final blow to Arab aspirations to independence. Britain, through Lawrence and others, had supported the Arab Revolt against the Turks, acting principally through the Hashemite family. When the British had defeated the Turks in Palestine, Syria and what was then known as Mesopotamia, the Arabs expected to rule themselves in those countries. Instead they found the British in Iraq and Palestine, and the French in Syria and the Lebanon, installing themselves as colonial powers to replace the Turks under the guise of League of Nations mandates. To add to this injury, the insult of a deliberate policy to turn at least most of Palestine into a Jewish state was the last straw.

As early as 1919, and again in 1921, there had been serious clashes between Jews and Arabs, the latter led by Haj Amin al Husseini, appointed Mufti of Jerusalem by the British High Commissioner Sir Herbert Samuel, himself a Jew, and in 1922 Winston Churchill, then Secretary of State for the Colonies, produced a new statement of British policy in Palestine, which seemed to the Jews to be backing down from the Balfour declaration. In self-defence the Jews formed their own armed forces. One was *Haganah*, a force designed for the direct protection of the settlements and linked to *Histadrut*, the labour organization. But there were those who thought that this was not enough and that an active revolutionary force should be formed to spearhead the fight for a Jewish state on both sides of the Jordan. The instigator of this movement, known as the Union of Revisionist Zionists, was Jabotinsky, a Jew born in Odessa and widely travelled in Europe. The force he formed in 1921 was later to turn into *Irgun Zvai Leumi* (or National Military Organization) and to throw off as a more extreme element *Lohamey Heruth Israel* (or Fighters for the Freedom of Israel), known by its initials of LHI or more popularly as the Stern gang. From then on there was constant rivalry between the official Zionist organization, the Jewish Agency, led by Chaim Weizmann, with Haganah under David Ben Gurion, who generally supported political action, working in co-operation with the British, and the Revisionists, who saw the British as their principal opponents. The latter's main aim was to do all in their power, without any inhibitions in the use of violence, to discredit British authority, including forcing it to take measures against the Jewish population which would antagonize them and persuade them to support the hard-liners.

There had been serious troubles in 1929 when Arabs attacked Jews and the British Police killed over a hundred Arabs in trying to protect them. Both sides accused the British of favouring the other. After each outburst of Arab violence, the Jews found the British less and less inclined to open the doors of Palestine to those persecuted by Hitler, who had come to power in 1933. They saw the prospect of Palestine, from which Transjordan had already been carved off, being established as a Jewish state receding further and further into the distance. The Arabs, on the other hand, saw a combination of Jewish immigration and natural increase as likely to result in them becoming a minority in their own country. Already between 1933 and 1936 the Jewish population had increased from 230,000 to 400,000, a third of the Arab. Spurred on by the Mufti, widespread Arab riots and attacks on Jews, combined with a general strike, broke out in that year, involving the use of British troops. The fighting went on from 1 May to 12 October. In the course of it Wingate formed his famous Special Night Squads.

The result of this was a spate of proposals for partition, culminating in the British White Paper of 1939, which proposed to limit Jewish immigration to 75,000 over the following five years, after which no further immigration would be allowed without Arab consent. This was followed by further fighting which died down when the Second World War broke out, except for continual activity by Stern and his LHI, who kept up a vendetta against the police, Stern himself being killed by a police officer in February 1942. Their principal motive, apart from an apocalyptic form of death-wish, was fear that Irgun was going the way of Haganah and would not fight to the bitter end against partition.

When it became clear in 1943 that the British were no longer in danger of losing the war and that Hitler could not win it, Irgun, now led from his place of hiding by Menachem Begin, who had arrived from Poland in 1942, became active again, spurred on by the ghastly fate of their fellow Jews under Hitler's final solution. In January 1944 they agreed to an uneasy alliance with LHI, and on 1 February Begin issued a formal and uncompromising declaration of revolt against the British administration, soon followed by explosions aimed at the immigration department and the police, resulting in some arms raids on the latter. This resort to violence was strongly disapproved of by the official Jewish organizations, while the Arabs sat on the sidelines. An attempt by Begin in August to get the support or at least the acquiescence of Ben Gurion and the Haganah failed, and in October the British succeeded in persuading Haganah to side with them. This led to a Haganah campaign against Irgun, known as The Season, which continued until April 1945. Only a fortnight after it had been agreed, without the knowledge of Irgun, LHI murdered Lord Moyne, the British Minister of State in the Middle East in Cairo, an act which cemented the alliance between the British and the Jewish Agency.

Had this alliance been maintained, the whole history of Palestine and Israel might have been different. What destroyed it was the disillusionment of the Agency and its supporters with the policy adopted by Attlee's post-war government. The British Labour party had always favoured the Jewish cause and there were strong links between it and Mapai, the strongest political party among the official Zionists. Bevin, Attlee's Foreign Secretary, appeared to be abandoning this policy in favour of a pro-Arab one for, it seemed, strategic and economic reasons; continuing to impose restrictions on immigration and proposing a partition which would have left the Jews with no more than the area proposed in 1939, and the limit of 75,000 immigrants since 1939 maintained, although the five years' time limit was extended. In the light of this, it was clearly impossible for Ben Gurion to continue to side with Britain. Irgun was able to say 'we told you so', and in August an alliance was formed between Haganah, Irgun and LHI, known as *Tenuat Humeri*, the United Resistance Movement. Its formation was closely followed by the despatch to Palestine of the 6th British Airborne Division. At this time Haganah was thought to have about 50,000 members, but most of them were tied to the static defence of settlements, only some 1,900 in the elite *Palmach* under Yigel Allon being available as a mobile striking force. Irgun probably had about 1,500 and LHI under a thousand. None of the organizations had arms for all their members or any heavy weapons.

October 1945 saw a series of explosions, Haganah alone setting off over 500, mostly aimed at the railway system. In November General Cunningham, last heard of when he had been sacked by Auchinleck from command of 8th Army in the desert four years before, replaced Lord Gort as High Commissioner and Bevin announced his policy in Parliament, including the maintenance of the immigration quota to be determined after consultation with the Arabs, for the interim not to exceed the then current monthly rate of 1,500. This was followed by a serious riot in Tel Aviv, which involved the deployment of the whole of the 3rd Parachute Brigade, a curfew being imposed which lasted for five days. In November there were attacks on police and coastguard stations and an arms raid on an RAF camp. It was now clear that Haganah, supported by the Jewish Agency, was involved and the British were getting little or no co-operation from any Jewish authority. This led to a series of massive cordon and search operations, almost the only result of which was to antagonize the whole Jewish population and range them behind the men of violence. Inevitably the security forces, the administration and the government in Britain began to treat the Jewish population as a whole as the enemy, and the accusation by the Jews that the British were favouring the Arabs became more justified, a reversal of the 1936 situation. What nobody could guess – and the British seemed to have no clear idea themselves – was whether they wished to stay for strategic reasons, playing off one side against the other, or really wanted to get out, as they were preparing to do from India. December 1945 and January 1946 saw a deteriorating situation, although British troop strength had risen to 80,000 in addition to the police, who were bearing the main brunt of attacks, and the Arab Legion from Transjordan. The country was turned into a form of military camp, the police barricaded into their Tegart fortresses, the army and administration surrounded by barbed wire, the country almost under military rule, members of the resistance forces, when caught, being tried by military courts. Arms raids continued, including a spectacular one on the RAF base at Aqir near Gaza at the end of January. This was followed in February by attacks on RAF bases in which several aircraft were destroyed.

In April 1946 the railway was a target for Irgun, a third of the hundred-man force involved being killed or captured, a pleasing success for the new Army Commander, General Sir Evelyn Barker. However it was followed by a number of setbacks, including a LHI attack on 6th Airborne Division's car park for recreational transport in Tel Aviv, in which seven paratroopers were deliberately killed. Up till then soldiers had not considered themselves to be direct targets of attack, especially off-duty. Henceforward they had to think of themselves as such and take personal security precautions at all times.

General Cunningham, the High Commissioner, and General Barker, the Army Commancer, faced an almost insoluble problem. There was no political policy, other than one of Micawberism, hoping that somehow a solution would turn up out of the discussions of the Anglo–American committee or the United Nations. American policy was itself divided. President Truman wanted a firm commitment to admit a further 100,000 Jews, while the Pentagon and the oil interests favoured a pro-Arab policy, as did the defence, foreign policy and economic interests in Britain. But there was no political solution which could even satisfy the more moderate elements on both sides and certainly not the extremists who believed in violence as the means to achieve their aim. With centuries of experience of clandestine operations behind them, especially in Eastern Europe whence most of the immigrants came, the enemy the British security forces faced was a highly sophisticated and skilled one, as well as being ruthless. Secrecy was their second nature and, as the administration and the security forces increased their repressive measures, so their support among the general Jewish population was strengthened, however much many of them might disapprove of the brutalities involved.

For the British soldier it was a frustrating sort of war. His principal activity consisted of cordon and search operations. The aim of these was to help the police find suspected terrorists or their active supporters. The police having selected their target area, probably from clues arising from some terrorist incident, the army would try to surround the area, usually in the early hours of the morning, so that nobody could move in or out of it. A separate body of troops, accompanied by police, would then search either selected or every house both for wanted persons and for arms or documents. All those who might be suspect would then be brought before a special police screening team, perhaps assisted by hooded informers. Those marked out by this process were then removed to a detention centre for further interrogation. On some occasions these operations, for instance in Tel Aviv, were executed on a colossal scale involving a prolonged curfew. This raised major practical problems for the continuation of normal life, such as the distribution of food and milk, and coping with such natural events as births and deaths. The soldier seldom saw any result for his effort, occasionally an arms find if he was lucky. The active and interesting detection work was in the hands of the police. The soldier received insults for his pains and often found his task distasteful, such as that of dealing with illegal immigrants. They arrived crammed in over-crowded hulks in filthy conditions and then had to be searched and moved, usually protesting, into other ships to be transported to Cyprus. When he was not engaged in these tasks, he was probably on guard or patrolling the railway. There was hardly ever a real military operation as such, involving active action or military skills, although he was always liable to be the target for a mine, an explosion or a shot. Most of the soldiers were national servicemen. They accepted the task with resignation, but had no great enthusiasm for it.

In June 1946 a new turn was given to the vendetta between Irgun and the security forces. Two Irgun men, captured in a raid on the army camp at Sarafand in March, were tried and sentenced to death. In retaliation Irgun kidnapped six British officers in three incidents. One escaped, two were released when the Jewish Agency voiced their disapproval of the act; the remaining three were released only when the High Commissioner commuted the death sentences to life imprisonment. Once more Irgun had succeeded in humiliating the administration. Its reaction was to carry out a massive cordon and search operation, called *Agatha*, designed to pick up leading members of the Jewish Agency, Haganah, Palmach and, if possible, Irgun and LHI. Nearly 3,000 people were picked up of whom 600, including 135 suspected Palmach men, were detained. But on 22 July Irgun went too far. A huge explosion blew up the wing of the King David Hotel in Jerusalem, in which the administration's secretariat and the army headquarters were housed. Ninety-one people were killed and forty-five injured. The British reaction was to publicize the involvement of Haganah and the Jewish Agency in these acts of terrorism. Although Irgun had carried out the operation, the United Resistance Command had authorized it; but the general revulsion world-wide made Haganah decide to opt out. Unfortunately the British failed to exploit this opportunity and imposed even stricter repressive measures on the population as a whole, including another vast cordon and search operation, which, although it screened 100,000 people, nearly 800 of whom were detained, produced very meagre results.

However violent incidents did decline while political activity increased, with yet more partition plans aired and a meeting between Britain and the Arabs in September. Nothing came of these, and towards the end of the year Irgun stepped up their activity, mostly by the use of more sophisticated electrically detonated mines on roads and railways. The British clocked up one notable success in frustrating an attempt to blow up Jerusalem railway station. In December Irgun again resorted to kidnapping, this time in retaliation for the imposition by a military court of a sentence of eighteen strokes of the cat on top of eighteen years' imprisonment on two Irgun members, caught armed when taking part in a bank robbery in Jaffa. Irgun announced that, if the sentence was carried out, 'every officer of the British occupation army would be liable to be punished in the same way'. A parachute regiment major and two sergeants were abducted, given eighteen lashes and then released, following which one of the Irgun men, who had received the sentence but was out of the country, and sixteen Arabs were granted an amnesty. This fooled nobody, the administration was humiliated again and the sentence of flogging was never imposed subsequently. Incidents continued. In January 1947 Cunningham discussed future policy with Bevin, Montgomery, then CIGS,* and Creech-Jones, the Colonial Secretary, following which another division, the 3rd, was sent out, bringing the total army strength to about 100,000. All British service and civilian families were sent home and stricter security precautions imposed both on the troops themselves and on Jews who lived near them. Another conference in London at the end of the month ended in deadlock, the Arabs refusing to consider partition. The gloomy prospect coincided with a very cold winter and a fuel crisis in Britain. The outlook was bleak and the British threw up the sponge. In February they announced that they had decided to refer the problem to the United Nations General Assembly in September, saying that there was no prospect of resolving the conflict by any settlement between the parties.

If they thought that this would ease tension in Palestine, they were to be disappointed. At the end of January Irgun had kidnapped a judge and a retired army major in retaliation for the death sentence on an Irgun man, Dov Gruner. They were released when a stay of execution was made on the understanding that Gruner would appeal to the Privy Council. This he refused to do, but others did on his behalf. The situation deteriorated in March and April with widespread Irgun and LHI attacks on British army personnel and installations, including the British officers' club in Jerusalem. Martial law was introduced, civil courts suspended and stricter curfews imposed. Two huge cordon and search operations, one in Jerusalem and one in Tel Aviv, were carried out. In spite of this, Irgun and LHI attacks continued and, in the early hours of 31 March, Irgun attacked the oil refinery at Haifa, starting a fire which lasted for three weeks. The situation was such that Bevin felt that he could not wait until September and asked the United Nations to summon a special session of the General Assembly to consider the problem.

The appeal on behalf of Gruner failed and he and three others were hanged on 17 April. Two other men, also sentenced to death, killed themselves with a grenade smuggled into them in prison in order that they might blow up their executioners with themselves. They changed their plan when a rabbi insisted that he would accompany them to the scaffold. In retaliation for this an English business man, visiting Tel Aviv, was kidnapped by Irgun and was on the point of being hanged, when they discovered he was a Jew and released him. In May Irgun brought off a dramatic break-out from the apparently impenetrable Acre prison, in which over 100 Jewish prisoners, including some fifty important Irgun and LHI men, and 171 Arabs escaped, assisted by a

* Chief of the Imperial General Staff.

daring operation from outside. However one lorry-load of escapers was intercepted by an alert group of paratroopers, guarding a bathing party of their comrades on a beach nearby, and almost all of them were killed or captured. In retaliation for the capture of five of the Irgun men who had taken part in the attack on the prison, Irgun kidnapped two British policemen, who later escaped. In June, on the day that the United Nations Special Committee on Palestine arrived in the country, a military court sentenced three of the five to death, the other two, being under age, to fifteen years' imprisonment. Almost immediately there were attempts by LHI to take hostages in retaliation. After two failures, they succeeded on 12 July in capturing two army intelligence sergeants in plain clothes. Two tense weeks followed, which included a major affair involving a refugee ship, *Exodus 1947*, which had sailed from France with 4,500 illegal immigrants on board and was intercepted at sea, leading to a general strike and a spate of attacks on the British security forces, thirteen being killed and seventy-seven wounded. Then on 29 July, the day the passengers on the *Exodus* arrived back at their port of embarkation in France in British ships, the three condemned men were hanged in Acre prison. On the same day LHI hanged their hostages in the diamond factory where they had been hidden, the bodies being removed and hung up from a tree elsewhere and booby-trapped.

And so it went on, the British press and public becoming increasingly disgusted with the whole affair and anxious to be rid of the burden of responsibility. Meanwhile all eyes were on the UN Committee, which was having great difficulty in coming up with any recommendation at all, let alone an agreed one, except that a political solution had to be found. Britain's own attitude remained enigmatic. Irgun believed that Britain would use the absence of an agreed solution, or the fact that, if there were one, nobody would be prepared to enforce it, as an excuse to remain in occupation in alliance with the Arabs. They adamantly opposed any form of partition, while the Jewish Agency accepted the principle and hoped, by lobbying, to obtain a favourable form of it. Irgun's and LHI's attacks continued while the United Nations debated. On 29 November 1947 the General Assembly voted to establish a Jewish state which it had whittled down from the partition committee's 6,000 square miles to 5,500 by excluding part of the Negev and the city of Jaffa. The mandate would end on 1 May 1948 and the process of handover of the two parts by Britain to the Jews and Arabs would start on 1 July. The end of the mandate was altered on British insistence to 1 August; but Britain then said that only she could decide when she would hand over, eventually proposing 15 May. The state to be handed over to the Jews consisted of three parts: the most northerly an enclave ten to twenty miles wide west of the Jordan north and south of Lake Tiberias, touching at one point only the central part. This was a long strip along the coast from just north of Haifa to some twenty miles south of Tel Aviv of an average width of only fifteen miles and excluding the city of

Jaffa. This strip touched at only one point the southern part, the triangle of the Negev with access to the Red Sea at Eilat. The area round Jerusalem was to be under international control.

To the Jews it seemed a totally inadequate and indefensible partition, excluding the very centre of their emotions, Jerusalem. To the Arabs, who objected to the establishment of a Jewish state in any form in their country, it appeared that about two-thirds of it was to be handed to one-third of the population. Irgun and LHI considered the United Nations to be as much their enemy as the British had been, while the Jewish Agency and Haganah took the line that they should assist a smooth handover by the British and the United Nations, seeking their help in the establishment of the new state. However all three resistance movements soon found themselves ranged on the same side against the Arabs. The latter, some spontaneously and some acting under the orders of the newly formed Arab Liberation Army, started immediately to attack Jewish settlements and traffic. The task of the British security forces changed. At first they tried to keep the peace between the two sides and maintain law and order. As the date of their departure approached, they restricted their efforts in this field, until their activity was confined solely to maintaining their own security and making sure that they would be able to depart as planned. Meanwhile the First Arab–Israeli War had in fact started – this is described in Chapter 12. The first of Britain's post-war colonial conflicts had not set a happy pattern.

Chapter Two

MALAYA

Having shaken herself free from one colonial entanglement, Britain found herself immediately faced with another, for, on 16 June 1948, a state of emergency was declared in Malaya. The events that led up to this had their origins in the Japanese occupation of the country during the Second World War. Only the Straits Settlements of Penang, with Province Wellesley opposite on the mainland, Malacca and Singapore had been directly ruled by Britain as colonies. The rest of the large, jungle-covered and lightly populated peninsula consisted of a loose federation of Malay states ruled by hereditary Sultans in a joint treaty relationship with Britain. Each had a British Resident as adviser who came under the supervision of a British High Commissioner to the Federation in Kuala Lumpur. The British had introduced the principal economic activities of the country, tin mines and rubber plantations, and had imported Chinese and Indian labour to work them. By the 1940s this labour formed a substantial element of the population, particularly on the western side of the peninsula, but they had no rights as citizens of the country outside the Straits Settlements. British rule had therefore rested lightly and, when it was swept away in a trice in January 1942 and its economic basis also eliminated by the same stroke, its authority suffered a crippling blow. The Japanese pursued an anti-British, anti-Chinese and pro-Malay policy which aggravated this, while the immigrant population found its source of livelihood removed. Large numbers of them, particularly the Chinese, were forced to turn to agriculture to keep themselves alive and established 'squatter' communities on the edges of the jungle.

The restoration of British authority in 1945 had none of the aura of victory and liberation that accompanied allied conquests in Europe. It took place after the Japanese had surrendered as an apparently undefeated army. A further complication to this unsatisfactory basis for the restoration of imperial authority was that, during the war, the only resistance movement, actively supported by the British, consisted of Chinese communists. It had called itself the Malayan Peoples' Anti-Japanese Army (MPAJA) and had its origins in the offer of the Malayan Communist Party (MCP), when the Japanese invaded

Malaya in December 1941, to co-operate with the British administration against them. A number of their members were armed and trained to operate behind the enemy lines by Lieutenant-Colonel Spencer Chapman and formed the nucleus of the MPAJA with which Force 136, the equivalent of the Special Operations Executive with Mountbatten's South East Asia Command, later established contact, provided liaison officers and delivered supplies. One of MPAJA's principal leaders was the youthful Chin Peng, whose services to the allied cause were recognized by the award of the OBE and a place in the Victory Parade in London. If all this were not enough to cause difficulties to a British administration attempting to re-establish itself, Attlee's government added a further political burden in the form of a proposed Malayan Union which would bring the Malay States and the Straits Settlements together under a firmer colonial administration, similar to that of the Settlements, and in which all the inhabitants would have equal rights. This met the aspirations of the immigrant communities, but was anathema to all Malays and particularly to the Sultans. On top of everything else Britain had therefore managed to alienate the basic population of the country. Having done so, she backed down in 1948 and thus disappointed the important Chinese element of the population who felt particularly frustrated at their underprivileged position in the country.

This was clearly a situation ripe for exploitation by the MCP, but it itself was in trouble. At the end of the war it was faced with the classic choice of whether to enter upon an armed struggle or to devote its effort to achieving its ends through political means. Its wartime alliance with the British made it difficult to turn immediately to the former and the chances of success would have been small. The position of its Secretary-General, Loi Tak, based in Singapore, was also an important factor. He had not taken part in the MPAJA and regarded them and their leader, Chin Peng, as the basis of a rival challenge to his leadership. It was not until 1948 that he came under suspicion of being an active traitor to their cause and responsible for co-operation with the Japanese in their suppression. When these well-justified suspicions began to surface early in 1948, he disappeared and was never seen again.* Chin Peng took his place and the fact that Loi Tak had favoured the political and opposed the armed struggle, while Chin Peng, backed by the widespread Old Comrades Association of the MPAJA and its clandestine resources, was naturally in favour of the latter, had undoubtedly influenced the trend in 1948 for the MCP to add violent militant action to the apparent success of its political efforts.

---

* Loi Tak was probably killed by a communist murder squad in Thailand some years later. He came from Annam and had been a French agent in Saigon in the 1930s. When his cover there had been 'blown', he was acquired by the Singapore police and acted as an agent for them; and, when the Japanese came, for them also, while maintaining his contacts with the British. He was undoubtedly responsible for two major blows against the MPAJA.

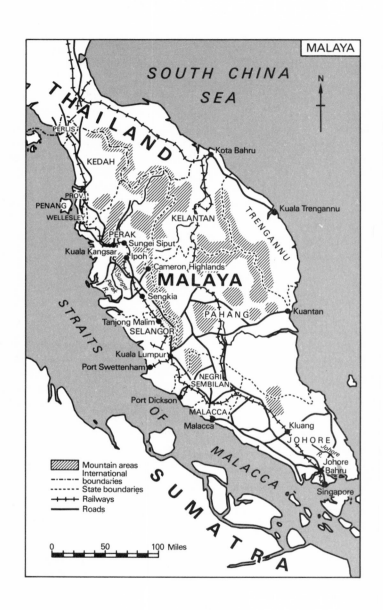

MALAYA

SOUTH CHINA
SEA

N

THAILAND

PERLIS

KEDAH

Kota Bahru

PROV.
PENANG
WELLESLEY

Kuala Trengannu

KELANTAN

TRENGANNU

PERAK ● Sungei Siput
Kuala Kangsar ● Ipoh

Cameron Highlands

MALAYA

Sungei Perak R.

Sengkia

Tanjong Malim
SELANGOR

PAHANG

Kuantan

Kuala Lumpur
Port Swettenham

STRAITS

NEGRI
SEMBILAN

Port Dickson

MALACCA
Malacca

Kluang

JOHORE

OF

MALACCA

Johore R.
Johore
Bahru

Singapore

SUMATRA

Mountain areas
International
boundaries
State boundaries
Railways
Roads

0   50   100 Miles

These had taken the form of widespread infiltration of the Pan-Malayan Federation of Trade Unions and the instigation of strikes and intimidation in mines and rubber plantations with the dual aim of ruining the economy and discrediting the government. At the same time the MCP planned to establish secretly the basis of an alternative government which would take over as the British and Malay administration and authority collapsed. By early 1948 their trade union activity was showing real signs of success, assisted by the generally low level of morale and efficiency of the police and administration, and the tendency both of the colonial government under the High Commissioner, Sir Edward Gent, and of the British Colonial Office and Government as a whole to lay at least a considerable part of the blame on the mining and plantation companies and their managers for not treating their workers properly. This view of where the blame lay was not held by the British Commissioner-General in South East Asia, Malcolm MacDonald. He held a curious position. After the end of the war a Governor-General for the British territories in Malaya and Borneo had been appointed, as well as a Special Commissioner for South East Asia, the latter responsible for the co-ordination of British government policy in all fields in the area. Malcolm MacDonald had been the Governor-General and, when Lord Killearn retired in 1948, had absorbed the responsibilities of the Special Commissioner; but he no longer had any direct authority over the High Commissioner in Malaya, who became *de facto* Governor-General of Malaya, nor over the Governors of the colonies in the area, Singapore, Hong Kong, North Borneo, Sarawak and the Pacific Islands. The military organization which complemented this consisted of a British Defence Co-ordinating Committee in Singapore, a triumvirate of the Commanders-in-Chief of the Far East Fleet, Far East Land Forces and Far East Air Force, over which MacDonald presided.

The spark which set off the declaration of a state of emergency on 16 June 1948 was the murder of three European rubber estate managers near Sungei Supit, a hard communist area in the state of Perak in north-west Malaya, shortly after the deployment of a company of Gurkha troops into the area. The reaction of the MCP, probably with foreknowledge that it was about to be banned, was to go underground, mobilize its armed forces out of the MPAJA Old Comrades Association, renamed the Malayan Races' Liberation Army (MRLA), and move them into the jungle, where secret camps had already been carefully prepared in proximity to Chinese squatter villages from which they could be supplied. They had not planned to adopt this military posture so soon and took some time to sort themselves out; but, if they were caught somewhat unprepared, the administration was even less ready.

Gent was in the middle of a row with MacDonald who, alarmed at what he regarded as Gent's complacent attitude towards the threat to British authority and its economic interests, had recommended his dismissal. Gent flew back to Britain on 28 June and was killed when the RAF aircraft in which he was travelling collided with another aircraft as it approached London. His successor, Sir Henry Gurney, who had been Chief Secretary in Palestine, did not arrive until October. The Commissioner of Police, Mr Langworthy, who had been in ill health for some time, resigned as soon as the emergency was declared and his successor, Colonel Gray, also from Palestine, where he had been Inspector-General, did not take over until August. The army commander, Major-General Boucher, had only assumed command a few weeks before, and both the officials holding the posts of Attorney-General and Financial Secretary were only temporary appointments. It is not surprising therefore that there was a lack of drive and direction on the part of the government. The general attitude was that the prosecution of the emergency and dealing with violence was the responsibility of the police, and it was for the army and the administration to provide them with whatever support they requested; but when the police asked for the support of the army in the provision of guards, the army firmly opposed what they regarded as a misuse of their limited resources. At that time the army had eleven infantry battalions available in Malaya, of which six were Gurkha, two Malay and three British, supported by one British field artillery regiment. There was a further brigade in Singapore. The Gurkha battalions had an abnormally high proportion of new recruits and the British battalions were composed largely of national servicemen, who were continually changing over. General Boucher's line was that his troops should be used for offensive operations against terrorist gangs or formed units, acting on information provided by the police. The trouble was that this intelligence was almost non-existent, responsibility for providing it being split between the police and an independent organization known as the Malayan Security Service, the head of which unfortunately was obsessed with the threat from Malay nationalist organizations with links in Indonesia. One of Malcolm MacDonald's main criticisms was of the paucity of intelligence: his other chief demand was for priority to be given to guarding mines and plantations and their managers in order to keep the economy of the country going. With the army unwilling or unable to help in this and the police gravely overstretched at a strength of only 10,000 for the whole country, the decision was taken to raise a force of Special Constables for this purpose. The initial target was for a force of 15,000: this was soon raised and 24,000 men, almost all Malays, had been enrolled in the first three months. At its peak period, in late 1952 and early 1953, the strength of the force rose to 41,000.

The initial target for an increase in regular police strength was also modest, a mere thousand men. On Gray's recommendation this was raised to 7,500. In addition to this an auxiliary police force of volunteers was raised to assist the regular police. By the end of 1948 15,000, almost all Malay, had been raised and three years later the force had expanded to a strength of 100,000. The police were therefore faced with an immense task. They had to maintain and in some cases establish their presence in the face of a terrorist challenge, often in superior strength, in order to assert the authority of government and its ability to maintain order and uphold the law. They had to adapt themselves to dealing with armed opponents, operating in formed bodies and based on the jungle. Not only was their regular force not organized, equipped or trained to do this, but they had to expand it and raise totally new auxiliary forces in large numbers, which themselves had to be organized, equipped and trained. Had ex-members of the Palestine Police not fortuitously been available, it could never have been done. They formed the essential leadership and basis for the expansion and for developing the Malayan Police into one capable of dealing with its new tasks.

At first the army adopted a somewhat aloof attitude. They took the view that their main task was to defend the Far East against a major military invasion of the Second World War type, probably originating from an alliance between Russia and the Chinese communists; and that, in any case, the defence of the base in Singapore took priority over support to the police and administration in Malaya. Unless the latter could provide information about the enemy, there was little the army could do. However Boucher did his best to tackle the problem on somewhat conventional military lines. He explained his plan at the end of July 1948 as being to break up the insurgent concentrations; to bring them to battle before they were ready; to drive them underground or into the jungle, and then to follow them there with soldiers, and with police accompanied by soldiers and supported by the RAF. His aim was to keep them permanently on the move in order to deprive them both of supplies and of recruits.

While Boucher was putting this plan into operation, Chin Peng and his colleagues were primarily concerned with forming and training their units and then attempting to establish them in areas which could form the basis of their proposed alternative government. At first they had hopes of establishing their bases in the less populated areas east of the central mountain range, but found that these areas lacked the necessary basic support from a Chinese population, the *Min Yuen*, which would provide both active logistic, administrative and personnel support for the armed units and also the political framework for the alternative government. When they concentrated their units in the more populated areas, such as Johore, they found themselves under pressure from Boucher's operations, although they suffered few actual casualties from them. Their lack of offensive action in this period led the army and the administration to adopt an unjustifiably optimistic view of the efficacy of the measures they were both pursuing. This optimism seemed to be borne out by the figures of terrorist incidents which, having averaged 200 a month from the beginning of the emergency to the end of 1948, fell to half that figure in the first half of 1949.

▸When Gurney reviewed the situation early in that year, he assumed that the communists as a militant force would have been defeated by the end of 1949 and that two years after that the police would be able to maintain order without the help of the army, the British and Gurkha element of which it might be possible to reduce as early as mid-1949, if steps to raise five additional battalions of the Malay Regiment were put in hand. His assessment was later endorsed by MacDonald who, however, still stressed the need for a much greater and more efficient intelligence effort. These views were complemented by a paper prepared for Gurney by Gray and Boucher, in which they stated that what they called 'bandit' activity had decreased; that it had been difficult for them to make any sustained large-scale and co-ordinated effort, and that the initiative had passed to the security forces. In the light of these views, it was not surprising that no plans were being considered for any military reinforcement nor any fundamental change in the conduct of emergency operations.

However the period was the lull before the storm. With Chin Peng's reorganization complete, the groundwork of his support organization laid and the heady optimism of the early days – that the economy and administration would soon collapse – dispelled, there was a steady increase in the number of terrorist incidents, until by mid-1950 they were running at an average of 400 a month. These included attacks on police stations by gangs of over a hundred strong as well as frequent ambushes on roads and railways, all serving the combined purpose of discrediting the government, intimidating the population and providing a source of arms and ammunition. In addition, and very significantly, it drove the authorities to impose restrictions and repressive measures on the Chinese population, especially on squatters and plantation labour, which tended to weld them into an alliance with the communists. By the end of 1949 it was clear that the forecasts made early in the year had been much too optimistic. General Harding, who had succeeded Ritchie as Army C-in-C in the Far East in July 1949, realized that neither the resources available to nor the methods employed by Gurney and his administration were capable of improving the situation, unless the army was prepared to give them more help, while they developed both to enable them to do so. He therefore accepted that the army would have to take over more direct responsibility and commit itself more to static tasks than it would have preferred. To do so more troops would be needed over and above the seventeen battalions to which the force available to Boucher had been increased. Above all there was a need for a better organization to direct the whole machinery of government and of operations as one whole, in contrast to one which merely did its best to co-ordinate a series of conflicting demands of varying priority, leaving it primarily to the police to take the initiative in countering the activities of the bandits, guerrillas, terrorists or whatever label was attached to the communist perpetrators of violence.

In March 1950 an additional Gurkha brigade was transferred from Hong Kong in partial response to an assessment by Boucher that he needed six more battalions in order to provide a framework of army presence all over the country to ensure that the effect of army operations, concentrated in a particular area, was not dissipated as soon as the soldiers moved on to operate elsewhere, and to provide a reserve of three battalions, permitting an opportunity for rest and retraining in rotation. This was especially necessary for the British battalions, which received a continuous trickle of partially trained national servicemen to replace those who had just learnt the skills of their trade and had to make the long journey back home before the date of their release. Both Boucher and Harding felt frustrated at the waste of military effort involved in what Harding described as 'will o' the wisp patrolling and jungle bashing' based on the slenderest of intelligence, which produced very meagre results for an immense effort on the part of a large number of soldiers. Even when there was intelligence and it was correct, the type of jungle sweep the army employed gave their opponents ample warning to slip away and await the end of that particular operation before returning, re-establishing their contacts and resuming their activities. In July Boucher's full demands were met by the transfer of another brigade from Hong Kong, 3rd Commando Brigade Royal Marines. By this time he had left and had been succeeded by Major-General Urquhart, who had commanded the 1st Airborne Division at Arnhem. The army was now keenly aware that the problem was not going to be solved by military operations alone, nor indeed primarily by them. The key lay in weaning the Chinese population away from the communists, and the basis of that must be a clear demonstration that their stake in the country was a prime interest of the administration, which had the will and the power to provide for the security of all. While the army concentrated on dealing with the armed forces of the MCP, based largely in the fringes of the jungle, the civil administration and police had to create a political, administrative and security climate which would cut off the MCP's support in the population at large. One of the principal difficulties in giving effect to this policy was to arrive at a balance between measures designed to break the link between the Chinese population and the armed men and those designed to win their 'hearts and minds'. The former involved such things as resettling squatter communities away from the jungle in what later and elsewhere came to be known as protected villages, imposition of strict curfews and control of labour, of movement, of supplies of food and medicines, and imposition of communal cooking. An early problem had been that of whether or not to provide armed guards of the Special Constabulary to Chinese-owned mines and plantations, most of whom were known to be or suspected of paying protection money to the communists. To do so was considered to be tantamount to supplying arms to the enemy: to deny them was a clear form of discrimination and could only encourage them to rely on appeasement of the terrorist gangs for protection.

In April 1950 the pressures from MacDonald and Harding, as well as from the European community, had led Gurney and the British Government to agree to the appointment of a Director of Operations to act under the High Commissioner, not just to co-ordinate but to direct all measures, civil and military, to prosecute the campaign against the Malayan Races' Liberation Army and their supporters, the Min Yuen. The man chosen was a recently retired Indian Army Lieutenant-General, Sir Harold Briggs, whose last appointment had been command of the troops in Burma before its independence. He was an excellent choice, a military commander of wide experience, endowed with clarity of mind, strength of will, sound common sense and a sensitivity in dealing with difficult personalities, whatever their race or function. His path was not smooth. His arrival in April 1950 involved treading on a number of toes; but he moved swiftly. It took him a week to analyse the problem and propose the main lines of a solution, the essential basis of which was to prove to the general population, including the Chinese element, that the government could and would provide for their security, so that they would not succumb either to the blandishments or to the threats of the communists. His plan was to clear up the country systematically working from south to north, making certain that, once the process had been completed in one area, a firm framework of sound administration and security could thereafter be maintained there. He would deal with the Min Yuen in the populated areas first, isolating the armed terrorist gangs, who would then be forced to come into the open to keep themselves supplied. On top of a basic framework deployment of soldiers to support the police all over the country, the army would provide a striking force which would deploy to each area in turn as the clearing-up process developed. Its task would be to establish itself in the populated areas and from them dominate the routes into the jungle for a distance of about five hours' travel on foot, relying principally on ambushing the routes between the terrorist camps and areas of potential supply. To put this plan into effect and direct the activities of the armed forces, the police and the administration to work together in its execution, a supreme Federal War Council was established under Brigg's chairmanship, the other members being the army and air force commanders, the Commissioner of Police and the Secretary for Defence. Similar subordinate committees were established in each state and below them at district and settlement level. A special effort was to be devoted to intelligence under the direction of Sir William Jenkin, formerly of the Indian Police.

Operations under the Briggs plan started on 1 June in the southern states of Johore, Negri Sembilan and Southern Pahang, but results were disappointing, largely because the army started its intensive operations before the administrative measures had begun to take effect in the area. Most of the army's operations were undertaken on the basis of little or no intelligence and continued to be what Harding had called 'will o'the wisp patrolling and jungle bashing'. Briggs was far from satisfied with the speed and urgency of the response he received from the government's administrative machinery, complicated by the degree of independence of the states. In a report in November he wrote: 'It becomes increasingly obvious that unless the Federal Government is placed on a war footing and the gravity of the situation is realized by HM Government, no quicker progress can be made and a still graver emergency will arise straining the morale of Malaya beyond breaking point.' He wanted the High Commissioner to put dealing with security first among his priorities, to make all matters relating to the emergency the responsibility of the Federal Government and for a greater urgency to be applied to the build-up and modernization of the police. Some measures, such as powers of conscription, were taken, but there was no dramatic change in a situation which, at the end of 1950, looked gloomy, as it did in the Far East generally, in Korea, French Indo-China and in China itself. There was certainly no sign of a shift in the government's favour in the attitude of the Chinese population. The police also had been going through a bad patch. Their rapid expansion had caused many difficulties in leadership, training, organization and morale, and there were serious differences of opinion between Briggs and Gray about how they should be used, the former fearing that delays in the development of the police organization and hesitancy on the part of Gray to employ them on new tasks before they were ready would seriously affect his plans for resettlement of Chinese squatters in new villages. There were also clashes between Gray and Jenkin over responsibility for intelligence. At the heart of many of these differences of opinion was the reluctance of the Commissioner of Police to see responsibility for operations pass out of his hands into those of the Director of Operations and his committees. However the more active the terrorists were, the greater the number of contacts between them and the security forces and the higher their casualties. In 1950, 650 guerrillas were killed, while the security forces lost under 400 men: in 1951, 1,100 guerrillas were killed and some 300 surrendered, while security force casualties rose by only about 100. There was certainly no prospect, as Gurney had originally envisaged, of defeating the communist armed men by the end of 1951, and the unpromising security situation was accompanied by growing dissatisfaction with the government on the part of all elements of the population. MacDonald and Harding, who was succeeded in May by General Keightley, had also voiced their dissatisfaction to the Colonial and War Offices respectively, Harding recommending to Slim, the CIGS, that the High Commissioner should be replaced by a General and that responsibility for all aspects of government in Malaya should be concentrated in one man, who would give priority to the emergency. Two events were to lead to his recommendation being accepted, the advent of a Conservative government to power in Britain, naturally more inclined to favour such a solution, and the tragic death of Gurney in October, ambushed by terrorists on his way up to the resort of Fraser's Hill. When the new Secretary of State for the Colonies, Oliver Lyttelton, visited Malaya in

December, he found morale low and a general atmosphere of gloom prevalent. He set about attempting to cure the malaise with vigour.

His major step was to appoint General Sir Gerald Templer as both High Commissioner and Director of Operations, Briggs retiring in December. He had tried to obtain the services of Slim himself and also considered General Sir Brian Robertson, but neither was available, and Templer, 53 years old and then GOC-in-C of Eastern Command in England, was chosen. Lyttelton also replaced Gray by Arthur Young, Commissioner of the City of London Police: Jenkin had already resigned as Head of Intelligence. A clean sweep was to be made with new brooms.

If the situation depressed the British, it was no more encouraging for their opponents, who were suffering at the time from the peculiarly bitter form of internecine struggle which seems to affect Chinese communist parties, partly ideological, partly concerned with methods and partly a struggle for power between individuals. It was to a certain, but only a limited degree a reflection of the dissensions then current in the communist world at large and among the communists in China itself, and centred round whether or not it had been right to turn to the armed struggle: if it had been a mistake, whether or not to abandon it or at least to give it lower priority in favour of preparing the ground by political action, the international atmosphere for which seemed favourable. It was also undoubtedly influenced by the growing pressure from the administration and the security forces on the Min Yuen and the failure of the armed struggle to create the conditions for an alternative government in spite of the high rate of incidents, an average of 500 a month in 1951. Although the total strength of the MRLA was now about 8,000, their casualties were heavy, over 2,000 in the year, and there had been some significant defections. A week before Gurney was killed, after a conference of the principal leaders, the Central Committee of the MCP issued new directives. On the political side emphasis was to be given to widening the area of support among the Chinese population by compromise with the bourgeoisie; to co-operation with other races and political views, with less insistence on the pure unadulterated milk of communism. On the military side, the armed forces were to work in smaller groups, operating at platoon level, and attacks were to be more selective, concentrating on ambushes. Units were to be rested, retrained and reindoctrinated. They were to be encouraged to make themselves more self-sufficient in food by growing their own within the jungle, where possible in co-operation with the aborigines. By this time the MRLA had settled down into seven areas. They were the Cameron Highlands, where Chin Peng and his more important colleagues lived; the Kuala Lumpur area, where Yeong Kuo held sway; the Raub-Bentong area, an important base for communicating with all other areas and with the outside world; Penang and Province Wellesley, under the influence of Kwok Lan in Penang; the Betong salient on the Thai border, important for east–west traffic and as a safe haven; the Tasek Bera swamp on the borders of Pahang and Johore; and the Kluang area of Johore. The communists had no radio and one of the main problems was communication between these areas. Courier was the principal means, although use was made of the civil post and telephone system.

By the time that Templer arrived in February 1952, the security forces had appreciated the need to operate more effectively in the jungle in pursuit of smaller bodies of men. In the very early days of the emergency some ex-Force 136 officers had formed what was known as Ferret Force, using Dyak trackers from Borneo; but the difficulty of keeping the force permanently in being led to its demise. Various other bodies had subsequently been formed to specialize in this field. One had been the establishment of an organization, again under ex-Force 136 officers, to contact the aborigines, wean them away from co-operating with the guerrillas and eventually win them over to operate against or at least give information about them. The police raised a large number of special jungle squads and companies, and the army, as well as resuscitating the wartime Special Air Service (SAS) as experts in this field, began to train all its battalions more effectively in jungle patrol techniques, the Gurkhas in particular concentrating on this skill and becoming very proficient at it. The SAS later specialized in working with the aborigines, the methods they employed becoming their unique stock-in-trade. Air supply was an essential form of support, if patrols were to stay in the jungle long enough to be effective, and the air force began to switch its effort from bombing to reconnaissance, supply and troop lift. The RAF was slow to develop the helicopter in this field and their early models, the Sycamore and the Whirlwind, were seriously underpowered; but the Royal Navy showed the way, encouraged by the presence far from the shore line of the Royal Marines, and by the end of the emergency in 1960 the helicopter was well established as an essential means of casualty evacuation and of moving supplies and the troops themselves.

Templer's arrival was not greeted with universal enthusiasm, MacDonald for one making public his disapproval of the concentration of authority in the hands of one man and he a soldier. The local politicians, Malay, Chinese and Indian, were also afraid that he would concentrate on security affairs and neglect the important area of political advance towards independence and the needs of the civilian population. They were soon won over, partly by the sheer drive, energy, enthusiasm and determination which Templer demonstrated from the moment of his arrival, partly because he surprised them by concentrating on just those areas which they feared he would neglect. He made clear his aim was the same as that of MacDonald, a multi-racial society which would have the confidence in itself and the ability to run its own affairs. All must co-operate in the drive forward for security and independence, for the first was the essential basis of the second. An independent Malaya must be master in its own house. Paradoxically one of the most significant moves in the political field came from the fear of the politicians that the British favoured Dato Onn's

Independence for Malaya Party. In the Kuala Lumpur municipal elections in January 1952, an alliance to fight it was formed between the United Malay National Organization, the Malayan Chinese Association and the Malayan Indian Congress, the basis of the Alliance Party formed in 1953 which brought the country to independence.

Templer was his own Director of Operations, but he delegated much of the detail to his deputy, General Lockhart, as he did on the civil side to his Deputy High Commissioner, Donald MacGillivray, who was to succeed him as High Commissioner when he left in 1954. In his two and a half years in Malaya, Templer inspired and drove all and sundry to implement to the full the Briggs plan. By then the resources to do so, in terms of numbers of soldiers, police and administrative officers and teams, trained and equipped for their tasks, were available. Army strength had risen to twenty-two battalions, a total strength of 45,000 of which 25,000 came from Britain, the remainder Gurkha, Malay and East African, later to be joined by men from Australia, New Zealand and Fiji. Templer, himself an ex-Director of Military Intelligence, placed the higher organization of intelligence on a sound, unified basis, and constant emphasis on the importance of this field was continually given priority as the results of the initial groundwork laid by Jenkin began to pay off. The New Village programme also began to make real progress, 410 of them eventually being created, and one of Templer's first and most significant acts was to get the question of land tenure settled. This was of great importance to the former Chinese squatters who had had no title to the land they had occupied.

Although major operations involving several units or even brigades still took place and were to do so for many years to come, principally in the hope of capturing important members of the communist hierarchy, the emphasis from now on was on thorough, systematic effort area by area lasting several months, at the end of which it was hoped that the area could be classified 'white', that is cleared of terrorists and one in which many of the restrictions imposed on the population could be lifted and life return to normal. This was the incentive to the population to endure and if possible co-operate with the very severe restrictions on their freedom in almost every aspect of life, which were imposed while the operations were in progress. One of the first steps forward was to select the area of operations on the basis of the communist area organization, rather than on the British or Malay administrative layout. The first phase, which could last for as long as two or three months, was devoted to intelligence: to a systematic and detailed study of the area itself, of its population and their habits, of all potential and actual links with the communists, and finally, through this, to the personalities, habits, location and contacts of the guerrillas themselves. During this phase the army would be stationed in the area, based primarily in the populated parts, familiarizing themselves with all those matters, with the people and with the ground itself. The second phase concentrated on an extremely thorough food denial programme which involved a tight degree of control of all movement of people and of merchandise of all kinds. This undoubtedly caused resentment and hardship and posed the sternest test of will on the authorities – whether or not to persevere in it at the cost of alienating the population; but it was proved to be far the most effective measure in separating the guerrillas from their support and in seriously undermining both their morale and their capability. It forced them to come out of the jungle to seek supplies or to try and exist within it on the meagre resources it could provide. In the third and final phase the army would enter the jungle on long and deep patrol operations designed to prevent the guer-rillas from developing the resources of the jungle and to make contact with them in order to kill them or force their surrender. Quick results were not expected and were not obtained; but by the end of 1953 the situation had clearly taken a decisive turn for the better. The year had seen the total number of incidents drop from 3,727 in 1952 to 1,170: more significantly major inci-dents had fallen from 1,389 to 258. This compared with 2,333 major and 3,749 minor incidents in 1951. Yet the number of terrorists killed was still round the thousand mark and surrenders had risen to 372, while security force and civilian casualties had fallen to 209 and 143 respectively, from 1951 totals of 1,195 and 1,024 and, in 1952, 664 and 632.

The improved security situation created the conditions for a dramatic step forward in the political situation with the possibility of independence looming nearer. The key to this, already mentioned, was the political alliance between the three main racially-based political parties. Early in 1955 it was announced that the first federal elections would be held in July of that year. In May the Alliance Party's manifesto proposed a general amnesty for terrorists who surrendered. This coincided with the receipt of a letter from the MCP, suggest-ing an end to the fighting and a general peace conference, but no offer of surrender on the part of the MRLA. The government's reply to this was that it was not prepared to negotiate and that, if the MCP genuinely wished to end the fighting and the emergency, they could accept the existing generous terms of surrender, an attitude which came in for some criticism from leaders of the Chinese community. Tunku Abdul Rahman led the Alliance Party into a sweeping victory, winning all but one of the fifty-two seats and receiving 80 per cent of the votes cast. From this strong position he offered an amnesty to be effective in September, and by the end of that month he had agreed to meet Chin Peng. The meeting took place at Baling in the north-east of the state of Kedah on 28 December, Tunku Abdul Rahman being accompanied by Cheng Lock Tan, leader of the Malayan Chinese community, and David Marshall, the Chief Minister of Singapore. Chin Peng was accompanied by Chen Tian, head of his propaganda department, and, for appearance's sake, by a Malay, Rashid Maidin. It soon became clear that the central issue was whether or not Chin Peng's followers would be genuinely loyal to a freely elected government of Malaya and abandon their allegiance to communism, an external influence

which the Tunku and his team considered was not consonant with loyalty to
Malaya. Chin Peng tried to dodge the issue by using the argument that neither
a Malayan nor a Singapore government could be truly independent unless it
itself had responsibility for internal security. He stated that, once they had
achieved that, the MRLA would stop hostilities and disband their armed units,
but he did not promise that they would hand in their arms or surrender
themselves to the authorities. He was hoist with his own petard when the
Tunku said that he was about to go to London where he expected to obtain the
British Government's agreement that Malaya would be responsible for its own
internal security when it became independent, which it was assumed would be
in the near future. The meeting had convinced the Tunku that there was no
genuine basis for a compromise with the communists. Chin Peng returned to
the jungle and, although there were suggestions for a further meeting in
November 1957 after independence, Chin Peng himself was not prepared to
come to it. It was clear that he did not contemplate surrender and he has
remained in the jungle ever since.

From 1955 onwards the resources of the government, both in security forces
and in the administration, were fully and vigorously deployed on the pattern
which Briggs had initiated and Templer improved. The army, with increasing
assistance from the air force, became more skilled and sophisticated in exploiting intelligence and in the techniques of jungle warfare. By this time the total
number of security forces of all kinds, including all the variations of police and
guard units, amounted to some 300,000 of which the great majority were
Malay, although the Chinese were taking an increasing part, especially in the
police Special Branch and in guarding the New Villages. The net gradually
tightened, more and more of the populated areas were declared 'white' and the
MRLA was forced back into the remote jungle. By the time of Independence (or
Merdeka) Day, 31 August 1957, the number of active terrorists had fallen to
some 1,500. In that year they had lost 540, of whom 209 had surrendered, in
addition to those who had died in the forest and whose deaths were unre-
corded. There were only 40 major and 150 minor incidents. The security forces
suffered 44 casualties of whom only 11 were killed, and civilian casualties
attributable to the emergency were only 31. The campaign was won, but not
yet over. In an attempt to eliminate the MRLA altogether, operations continued
for another three years, by which time Chin Peng and the remaining members
of his army had taken refuge in the jungle over the border in Thailand, which
has been their base ever since.

The Malayan emergency campaign has been held to be the perfect exemplar
of counter-subversion or counter-insurgency warfare. It certainly was a success story and one of which those who participated in and directed it have
every reason to be proud. The greatest credit must go to the people of Malaya
itself, who made great personal sacrifices, saw with sound sense where their
real interests lay and employed considerable political skill, imagination and

restraint in attaining their ends. To the British Government must go credit for its determination to accept its responsibilities and also for taking risks in bringing Malaya forward to independence while the war continued. Gerald Templer was the man of the hour. He arrived at the crucial moment, endowed with the qualities of intelligence, imagination, but above all of determination and drive, which made it possible to implement with success the plan which had been so soundly formulated by Briggs. A great deal of patience was needed by many different people, soldiers, police, administrators and, most of all, the humble peasants and workers, over a period of twelve years. They were all fortunate that their opponents received very little help of any kind from outside the country. Unfortunately, at the time of writing, thirty years after the declaration of the emergency, the threat has not yet been entirely removed.

Chapter Three

KENYA

Just as the situation in Malaya was taking a decisive turn for the better in the latter half of 1952, Britain found herself with a new and unexpected colonial conflict on her hands in Kenya. The Governor, Sir Philip Mitchell, after nine years in office, retired in June 1952 telling his successor, Sir Evelyn Baring: 'There really is a genuine feeling of desire to co-operate and be friendly at the present time'* and having only three months before in a public speech in London said that the general political feeling in Kenya was better than he had ever known it for many years. This complacency was surprising in view of the abundant evidence that the situation among the *Kikuyu* had deteriorated to an alarming extent, in spite of banning the secret society of *Mau Mau* in 1950. The situation in fact, later revealed in great detail by the Corfield Report,† was that a movement, of which Jomo Kenyatta was the acknowledged head, had almost succeeded in completely subverting the Kikuyu tribe to reject the government, the missions and everything European, with the eventual aim of getting rid of both Europeans and Asians from the country altogether. The movement operated through a number of different organizations, the principal one being the Kenya African Union, a legal political body, control of which had by then passed into the hands of members of the banned Kikuyu Central Association. Linked to it was the Kikuyu Karinga Education Association, the African Orthodox Church and the Kikuyu Independent Schools Association, in which the Githunguri Teachers College played an important part as the equivalent of a staff college for the movement. Mau Mau was the strong-arm paramilitary organization, combining the functions both of warrior and witch-doctor. The basic impetus behind the combined movement was mixed, varying from the frustration of the mission-educated African at finding that neither the religion nor the education which he had received changed him into the equivalent of a European, to much more primitive fears, frustrations and resentments. Fundamental to them was the impact on a tribal society, based on strict conformity

* C. Douglas Home, *Evelyn Baring*, p. 217.
† F. D. Corfield, *Historical Survey of the Origins and Growth of Mau-Mau*, Cmnd. 1030.

within the group, of contact with Western civilization, which had only reached the country in the late nineteenth century. The First World War had had a decisive effect. Large numbers of Kikuyu had been recruited, many virtually impressed, into the Carrier Corps as porters and labourers to take part in the campaign against the Germans, led by von Lettow Vorbeck in Tanganyika, and large numbers had died of disease. After the war there had been a considerable influx of Europeans and the question of land purchase or allotment, particularly in the southern part of the Kikuyu reserve bordering Nairobi, became a burning issue. It was an area which had been continuously in dispute and, although the Carter Commission in 1922 made restitution of 110 square miles, which it assessed had been erroneously allotted for European use, the accusation that the Europeans had stolen their land was widely believed and readily exploited. The Kikuyu was the largest and the most intelligent and industrious tribe and they occupied the key central area running north from Nairobi for about a hundred miles on the eastern side of the Aberdare Mountains 'facing Mount Kenya', as Kenyatta's book was called.

Kenyatta, whose real name was Kamau wa Ngenga, was born in the Kiambu District on the edge of this disputed area in 1898 or 1899, and was one of the first boarders at the Church of Scotland Mission School in Kikuyu. He was an early member of the Kikuyu Central Association, founded by Harry Thuku in 1920 to exploit Kikuyu grievances, and went to London in company with a communist, Isher Dass, in 1929, the year in which the Church of Scotland decided publicly to oppose female circumcision, a stand which aroused fierce opposition among the traditional Kikuyu and was exploited as a major grievance. In the world depression of the 1930s there was much hardship in Kenya, both European and African agriculture falling on hard times. The Second World War however brought prosperity, the demands of the forces in East Africa itself and in the Middle East providing an insatiable market. But the prosperity itself, combined with the opportunities for Africans to serve in the forces and compare the life they led there with their previous lives and also with that to which they returned after the war, provided further causes both of resentment and of disorientation. Even before the war the educated Kikuyu had begun to split into two camps, those who saw the way forward as that of co-operating with, while maintaining political pressure on, the colonial government, administration and the missions (who virtually controlled education and much of the health services), and those who opted for outright opposition, aiming at the expulsion of Europeans and Asians. Harry Thuku, after a spell in prison, joined the former group, while Jomo Kenyatta, when he returned to Kenya in 1946 after an absence of sixteen years, assumed the leadership of the latter. From then on, in spite of the fact that economically the Kikuyu were faring well and that a considerable effort was being made by the administration to develop both native agriculture and social services, the

Lari

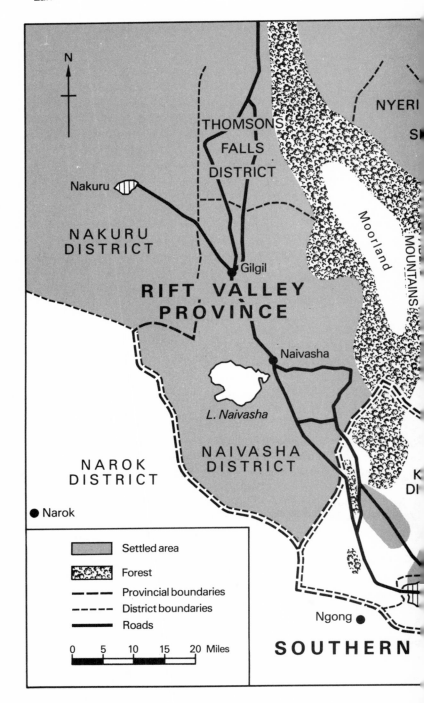

N

THOMSONS
FALLS
DISTRICT

Nakuru

NAKURU
DISTRICT

Gilgil

RIFT VALLEY
PROVINCE

NYERI

S

Moorland

MOUNTAINS

Naivasha

L. Naivasha

NAIVASHA
DISTRICT

NAROK
DISTRICT

K
DI

● Narok

	Settled area
	Forest
---	Provincial boundaries
---	District boundaries
—	Roads

0   5   10   15   20 Miles

Ngong ●

SOUTHERN

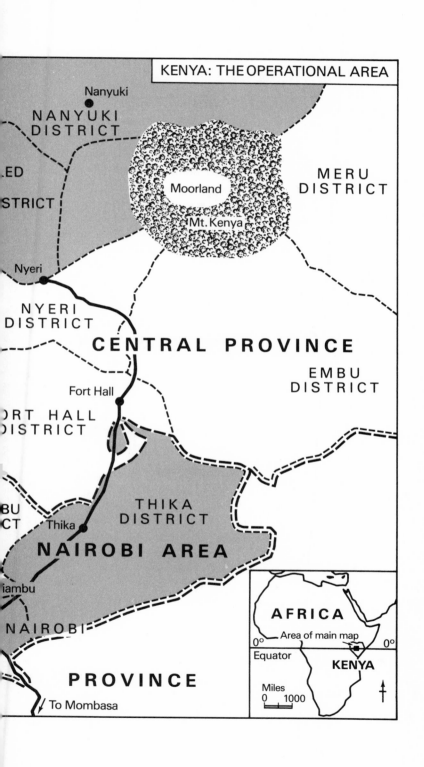

KENYA: THE OPERATIONAL AREA

Nanyuki

NANYUKI
DISTRICT

...LED

...STRICT

MERU
DISTRICT

Moorland

Mt. Kenya

Nyeri

NYERI
DISTRICT

CENTRAL PROVINCE

EMBU
DISTRICT

Fort Hall

...RT HALL
...ISTRICT

THIKA
DISTRICT

...BU
...CT   Thika

NAIROBI AREA

...iambu

NAIROBI

PROVINCE

To Mombasa

AFRICA

0° Area of main map 0°

Equator

KENYA

Miles
0   1000

tribe came more and more under the influence of Kenyatta's movement. Fortunately it did not spread to other tribes.

Although an increasing number of reports of the serious situation developing reached officials of the government in 1952 and European settlers were pressing for positive action, neither the Acting Governor, Mr Henry Potter, nor the Colonial Secretary, Oliver Lyttelton, thought it necessary that Baring should take up his appointment any earlier than was planned, at the end of September: this in spite of a detailed report by the Commissioner of Police, dated 14 July, in which he said: 'I am forced to the conclusion . . . that something in the nature of a general revolt among the Kikuyu people against European settlement and the policy of the Government has been planned and that the plan has already begun to be put into effect.'* The trouble was that the report was made to John Whyatt, who combined the post of Attorney-General with that of Member of the Legislative Council for Law and Order, being much more concerned with Law than with Order. This was only four days after a long debate in the Council in which the European Elected Members, led by Michael Blundell, had voiced their anxieties and called on the government to take measures to improve the situation, to which both Whyatt and the Member for African Affairs, Mr Davies, had replied in complacent tones. Two weeks later Kenyatta held a mass meeting organized by the Kenya African Union at Nyeri, attended by some 25,000 Kikuyu, which nearly got out of control and at which the crowd cheered at every mention of Mau Mau. In August Kikuyu leaders who supported the government, Chief Warukiu, Harry Thuku and Eliud Mathu, a nominated member of the Legislative Council, organized meetings to try and influence Kikuyu opinion against Mau Mau, but murder, oathing,† intimidation and boycott of government activities increased.

Baring arrived on 29 September and immediately started a tour of the affected areas. He was shaken by all he heard and saw. Everywhere he went he was told by the Africans working with or for the government that the situation was almost out of control and that, unless he took immediate steps against Kenyatta and his principal supporters, not only would their lives be at risk, but the government would lose control of the Kikuyu altogether. Any inclination he might have had to hesitate was dispelled on 9 October by the cold-blooded murder of the respected Chief Warukiu. That day he sent a long telegram to Lyttelton in which he outlined the situation and recommended the declaration of a state of emergency and the arrest of Kenyatta and his associates. He concluded by saying that, if he did not do this,

---

* Corfield, p. 141.

† The Mau-Mau enforced allegiance by initiating members of the Kikuyu tribe in ceremonies of a particularly disgusting nature. Kikuyu who had been subjected, generally by intimidation, to these ceremonies felt that they had 'sold their souls to the devil', and were therefore totally committed to the Mau-Mau cause.

(i)   the chiefs, headmen, Government servants and missionaries among the Kikuyu who still support us will cease their support and may well be killed;

(ii)   the trouble will spread to other tribes who are more warlike than the Kikuyu and who provide the men for the Kenya Police...

(iii)   there will be reprisals by Europeans...*

He believed that, if he took these measures, indoctrination of tribes other than the Kikuyu would cease (attempts to subvert the *Embu, Meru* and *Wakamba* had started) and that, even among the Kikuyu, there were sufficient centres of resistance and so many followers of Mau Mau who had joined from fear alone that the position could be regained. His recommendations were accepted and, allowing for time to make the necessary preparations, including the despatch of a British infantry battalion by air from the Middle East, a state of emergency was declared on 20 October 1952 and orders signed to detain 183 known leading members of Mau Mau, including Kenyatta: eight were already under arrest for other offences.

The army in Kenya was totally unprepared for anything of this nature. In 1950 an attempt had been made to set up a joint internal security intelligence committee to provide warning of such a situation, but the army had soon opted out of it. The headquarters of East African Command in Nairobi (Lieutenant-General Cameron) came under GHQ Middle East (General Sir Brian Robertson) and Cameron himself had been the chief administrative staff officer to the latter, a post to which he was by nature and experience better suited than to dealing with an internal security emergency. The command extended to all military units in Kenya, Uganda, Tanganyika and Mauritius and was still engaged in handing over those in northern Rhodesia and Nyasaland to the newly-formed Central African Federation. The only combat troops were African, infantry battalions of the King's African Rifles (KAR) of which Kenya normally had three, Uganda one and Tanganyika one, one company of which was in Mauritius. Additional battalions from Kenya and Tanganyika had recently been raised in order to provide battalions for Malaya. The only other force was the Kenya Regiment, a part-time volunteer infantry battalion of Europeans. The pick-up operation was carried out successfully without any resistance at 5 a.m., two and a half hours before the Lancashire Fusiliers arrived in RAF Hastings at the RAF station which also served as Nairobi's airport. They then drove round Nairobi looking warlike, while the KAR supported the police.

Cameron took the lofty view that, as the Governor was also Commander-in-Chief, the Brigadier of the KAR brigade in Nairobi should advise him about military support and provide it, while he, Cameron, attended to the affairs of his command as a whole. The Royal Navy chimed in with an opportune visit

* Corfield, p. 275.

by HMS *Kenya* to Mombasa, 300 miles from the nearest Kikuyu. Settler morale was raised, but quickly dashed again by the murder within the first two weeks of one of the most respected Kikuyu chiefs, Senior Chief Nderi, and of Eric Bowyer, the first European settler to be killed. He lived alone on a small isolated farm with his African servants, both of whom were killed, slashed with pangas, the local universal cutting tool, while he was in his bath. The first reaction of the government was to concentrate on defensive security measures and to plan a major expansion of the police force. It was also decided to raise a Kikuyu Home Guard to serve both as a local security force and as a resistance movement around which Kikuyu could rally in opposition to Mau Mau. The army was to back up the police, the British battalion in the European settled areas, and the KAR in the reserve, where the Tribal Police operated under the orders of the administration, the Colony Police serving under the Commissioner in the towns and European settled areas. There was no real plan of campaign nor any offensively directed operations, for, as usual, there was little or no information on which to base them. Baring realized this, and in November, seeing that, in spite of the measures taken, the situation was deteriorating with more murders of Kikuyu who supported the government, he asked Lyttelton both for expert advice on the organization of intelligence and for the appointment of a Director of Operations in the rank of Major-General, a proposal which Cameron approved. He got his Major-General, but only after flying to London and pleading with Churchill, then Prime Minister. He was 'Loony' Hinde, and a very valuable asset he was to prove, but for inscrutable reasons of military protocol he was only allowed to be styled as Chief Staff Officer to the Governor. In response to his other request Sir Percy Sillitoe, head of the Security Service, was sent out, reviewed the situation and rapidly recommended a concentration of the separate bodies involved in collection and assessment of intelligence, both in the police and in the administration, and measures to link their work with the security forces; but there was a long way to go and many obstacles to overcome before the intelligence organization began to function satisfactorily.

None of the measures had begun to show any effect by January 1953 when, following a run of murders of loyal Kikuyu, a young European farmer named Ruck, his wife and 6-year-old son were brutally murdered on their farm on the Kinangop plateau in the Rift Valley. The murder contained all the elements which naturally incensed the settler population. The Rucks were typical of the best of the settler community and had always treated their labour well. Yet their own Kikuyu staff, in this case farm employees not domestic staff, were involved, whether willingly or not is not known, and they were killed in a particularly brutal and nauseating fashion. The upshot was a march by Europeans on Government House in Nairobi, only dispersed by the courage, good sense and eloquence of two of the European Elected Members of the Legislative Council, Michael Blundell and Humphrey Slade.

It was into this atmosphere that Hinde was pitchforked on his arrival at the beginning of February. He was struck by the contrast between the demand of the settlers for more drastic action by the government and the fact that they appeared to continue to live their normal carefree lives. His brother was a settler near Nanyuki, below Mount Kenya, and was able to keep him in touch with settler opinion, which was of considerable value to him. He set about trying to establish a pattern of organization similar to that devised by Briggs in Malaya, but found himself up against many obstacles. Provincial Commissioners and District Officers, who had traditionally been left to run things their own way, were jealous of their authority and reluctant to share it with police, military or anybody else. Hinde himself exercised no executive authority, except over the operations of the army, until in April his appointment was changed from that of Chief Staff Officer to the Governor to that of Director of Operations. One of the awkward issues was that of the participation of the European settlers in the security organization. They wished to have a say both in policy and in its execution; but to incorporate them into the governmental machine when the natural Colonial Office reaction was to blame the troubles on the lack of political progress for the African, much of the responsibility for which they could lay at the door of the Europeans, appeared to be a move in the wrong direction.

The organization for the prosecution of the emergency, which Hinde set up, consisted of two tiers of committee. At the top was the Colony Emergency Committee, presided over by the Governor and attended by Hinde, the Commissioner of Police and the senior members of the administration. Two of the European Elected Members of the Legislative Council, Blundell and Havelock, also attended. Subordinate to this large and unwieldy body was Hinde's own Director of Operations Committee, almost equally large and consisting of representatives of the army, police and administration. Below this again, Provincial and District Emergency Committees were established. The defects of the organization lay in a diffusion of authority and responsibility for action. General Harding, Chief of the Imperial General Staff, who had visited the colony in February 1953, soon after Hinde had arrived, sensed this and persuaded Churchill and Lyttelton to appoint a more senior General, Sir George Erskine, as Commander-in-Chief with full executive powers over the army and RAF and over the police in respect of emergency operations. At first it was considered that he would replace Hinde as Director of Operations, but Baring fortunately pressed that Hinde should stay as Erskine's deputy in this field. Cameron also stayed on for a time, somewhat to Erskine's embarrassment, as his deputy for all matters in East Africa not connected with the emergency. A further result of Harding's visit was the despatch of a British infantry brigade headquarters, the 39th, with two battalions. They arrived in April, but Erskine himself did not reach the colony until June, by which time the situation appeared to have deteriorated further, one incident in particular causing grave concern, the Lari massacre at the end of March. One of both Baring's and Hinde's priorities had been the build-up of the Kikuyu Home Guard, and the Lari massacre was an operation designed by Mau Mau to intimidate Kikuyu who might be inclined to support the government. Even before it, it was the Kikuyu who were suffering most at the hands of Mau Mau. By mid-February 177 of them had been murdered since the emergency had been declared, compared with nine Europeans and three Asians. After dark on 26 March, a day on which unfortunately the company of the KAR which was normally stationed in the area had been moved away to support the police who were expecting trouble at a prison south of Nairobi, nearly a thousand Mau Mau surrounded the village of Lari north-west of Nairobi at the southern end of the Aberdare Mountains, a village which had a vigorous Kikuyu Home Guard and a large number of Kikuyu loyal to the government. The Mau Mau plan was to detail a group to make for each hut known to house loyal Kikuyu, tie a cable round it so that the door could not be opened, soak it with petrol and set fire to it. Others stood by to kill with pangas any who tried to escape. Although the police had been tipped off by an informer eight days before that an attack was planned, the 150-strong Kikuyu Home Guard detachment, armed at that stage only with spears and pangas themselves, was away patrolling the nearby forest. It was not until the fires had been raging for some time that any help reached the village in the form of a detachment of Tribal Police, led by the local chief. By that time 200 huts had been destroyed, 84 Kikuyu, two-thirds of them women and children, killed and 31 grievously wounded. A thousand cattle had been slashed. In the event the massacre had the opposite effect to that intended. It led both to the decision to equip the Kikuyu Home Guard with firearms and to a fuller realization of the bestiality of Mau Mau methods, which rallied more Kikuyu to the government. However this was offset by a major exodus of Kikuyu from the settled areas back into the reserve, as a result partly of expulsion by their employers and partly of their own fears of retribution against them by Europeans. Landless, disgruntled and unemployed, they provided a fertile recruiting ground for the Mau Mau, more and more of whom were now based in the forests.

When Erskine arrived in June, he realized that the major fault lay in the lack of any clear plan of campaign. The army available to him consisted of 39th Brigade with three British battalions and 70th (East African) Brigade with five KAR battalions, an armoured car company and a heavy anti-aircraft battery, as well as the Kenya Regiment, in all some 7,000 soldiers, half British and half African. He also had a flight of RAF Harvards, training aircraft which could drop 19 lb bombs. Information about his Mau Mau opponents was still at this stage very vague. The current estimate of the total organized in gangs, based on the forests but operating in the reserves and settled areas adjacent to them, was 8,000; but it was later found to have been an underestimate, the true figure being nearer 12,000 of whom only about 1,500 had firearms, other than home-made ones which were often more dangerous to the firer than to the target, although useful for intimidation. In general they were organized in three groups. Those recruited from the Nyeri and Fort Hall districts and based in the Central and Northern Aberdares under Dedan Kimathi; those from the area south of them surrounding Nairobi under Stanley Mathenge, and a group based on Mount Kenya under 'General China'. The gangs were supported in the reserves, in Nairobi itself and in the settled areas by a 'passive wing' of about 30,000 out of a total Kikuyu population of a million and a quarter. The European population at that time, excluding British service personnel and their dependants, was 42,000. By the end of the year, when a further British infantry brigade, the 49th, had arrived with two more battalions as well as an engineer regiment, the strength of the security forces had risen to 10,000 soldiers, 21,000 police and 25,000 Kikuyu Home Guard. In prohibited areas, generally the forest, they could shoot at sight. In what were called 'special areas', generally the Kikuyu reserve, they had the right to fire only on those who did not stop when they were challenged. They had the right to question and search and, if suspicious, to arrest and hand the suspect over to the police.

There were four different areas to consider, the native reserves, the forests of the Aberdares and Mount Kenya, the European settled areas (principally the Nanyuki–Nyeri areas between the Aberdares and Mount Kenya in the north, the Rift Valley and the coffee and sisal growing area north of Nairobi) and Nairobi itself. Erskine decided to deal with the Kikuyu reserve first, while simultaneously driving rough roads into the forest to make it possible for soldiers to operate from within it, instead of entering it only from the fringe bordering the reserve or the settled areas, a method which had hitherto proved fruitless. From the time of his arrival until March 1954 he concentrated army operations in the districts of Fort Hall and Nyeri, leaving the minimum number of troops elsewhere, where the strength of the Home Guard was gradually built up and more effective security measures imposed, such as guarding of stock, control of firearms, food supplies and movement and evacuation of isolated farms and houses. This policy was unpopular with the settlers, who disliked many of the restrictions and felt that their interests and security were being given second place. This, the lack of any evidence of a real improvement in the situation and dissatisfaction with Baring, whom the settlers thought weak and indecisive and whose health was deteriorating under the strain, led to increased pressure from the Europeans for greater participation by them in the conduct of the emergency. European civilian casualties in fact were still very small, only sixteen killed and five wounded by the end of the year, compared with 613 loyal Kikuyu killed and 359 wounded. Mau Mau on the other hand had lost 3,064 killed and over a thousand captured, while the astonishing figure of 156,459 suspects had been arrested of whom 64,000 had been brought to trial. The Colonial Office was not prepared to give way to the pressure for greater participation in government by the Europeans without it being accompanied by more participation by Asians and Africans also. The outcome was what was known as the Lyttelton Constitution, which introduced six elected members of the Legislative Council as ministers, three European, two Asian and one Arab, and the nomination of five Africans as under-secretaries. The idea had originated with Blundell and he and Lyttelton had a difficult time getting the other European elected members to accept the presence of Asians and Africans in the government. Had they realized that Lyttelton had undertaken that, at the elections which would replace this nominated government and which he had promised the Africans would take place six months after the end of the emergency, Africans would be directly elected to the Legislative Council, they might well not have accepted even the very limited advance introduced by the Lyttelton Constitution. Lyttelton himself, accompanied by Harding, had come out to Kenya in February 1954 to negotiate its introduction. While there he and Baring accepted another of Blundell's proposals, of much greater significance to the conduct of the emergency, the establishment of a small War Council, with full executive authority in all matters concerned with the emergency, to replace the two existing committees. Its membership was restricted to Baring, Erskine, Blundell and the deputy Governor, Sir Frederick Crawford, but normally attended also by the Minister for Defence, a recently created post held by an official, Richard Turnbull, and the Minister for African Affairs, another official, Edward Windley. A further significant step was the appointment of George Mallaby as secretary. He came from the Cabinet Office in London and was served by a small joint military and civilian staff. These changes brought about an immediate and dramatic change in the firmness, speed and efficiency with which emergency business was conducted. At last it was directed, not just co-ordinated. Serious consideration had been given to Baring's dismissal and to the installation of Erskine as Governor in the Templer mould; but, although Baring was clearly in need of a rest, Lyttelton decided to keep him, sending him off on leave for three months, Crawford acting in his place.

Changes also took place in the police at this time with unhappy consequences. A parliamentary delegation, which had visited the colony early in the year, had unanimously pressed Lyttelton to appoint a new Commissioner of Police. He appointed Arthur Young, recently returned to the City of London Police from his time with Templer in Malaya, and unfortunately gave him the impression that Baring was unlikely to return to the colony after his sick leave. Young interpreted his main aim as to free the police from their subordination to the administration, in so doing replacing the Tribal Police in the reserves by Colony Police, subordinate to him. This had been the recommendation of a commission in 1952, and Young considered it to be the only method by which the African population could be brought to look on the police as friends and not agents of a repressive government. His attitude led to a direct clash, with himself and Whyatt, the Attorney-General, on one side, and the administration on the other. The quarrel came to a head at the end of the year when the former pressed charges of illegality and brutality against some of the loyal Kikuyu chiefs and others. Baring, whose return in June coincided with Young's arrival, sided with the administration. Young resigned and Whyatt went as Chief Justice to Singapore, replaced respectively by Richard Catling and Eric Griffith-Jones, both from Malaya (Catling, ex-Palestine Police) and both more prepared to co-operate with the administration, which they did most effectively during the emergency and for many years afterwards.

While these changes were being discussed and introduced, Erskine was concerned with two important developments in the security field. He had decided that his next target area must be Nairobi itself. Operations in the reserve had shown that the Kikuyu population of the city was the main base of the passive wing and source of supply to the gangs in the forest. A vast cordon and search operation, named *Anvil*, was planned for April, in preparation for which detention camps had to be secretly constructed, the largest at Mackinnon Road near Mombasa, site of an abortive attempt to build a military stores base as an alternative to that in Egypt. While this was being planned, General China, the Mau Mau leader on Mount Kenya, was captured. After long talks with Ian Henderson of the Police Special Branch, a fluent Kikuyu speaker, he was persuaded to try and induce his followers to surrender. A long exchange of letters between China and his subordinates was set in train. By the end of March this had led to plans for a meeting between representatives of the government and Mau Mau leaders near Nyeri; but, as a result of differences of opinion among the latter, they failed to turn up. Meanwhile the planned date of *Anvil*, 24 April, was approaching. After Henderson and a colleague, Bernard Ruck, had gone into the forest to try and contact them and sort things out, a meeting was fixed for 10 April, but a clash between the army and a large gang in the reserve outside the forest not far away convinced the Mau Mau, who included 'General' Gatamuki, believed to be opposed to the surrender, that it was all a trap, and nobody turned up at the rendezvous. Gatamuki himself maintained that he had been willing to surrender and that 2,000 of the total of 5,000 Mau Mau in the Mount Kenya area were assembled there for that purpose. Unfortunately two of China's principal lieutenants, Tanganyika and Kaleba, who had previously been captured and were helping the surrender negotiations, escaped in the confusion and rejoined their gangs in the forest. When the story became generally known, it led to severe criticism from the Europeans.

All the attention of the security forces was now directed on Operation *Anvil*, which started on 24 April and lasted for two weeks, five battalions and large numbers of police being employed. While the army surrounded the African location of the city, the police moved in to search the area and remove all Kikuyu, Embu and Meru for screening, making extensive use of hooded informers. In subsequent days other parts of the city were similarly surrounded and combed. By 8 May 30,000 Africans, out of an estimated Kikuyu population of Nairobi of 65,000, had been screened. Of them 16,538 were detained and 2,416 returned to the reserve. The operation continued at a lower level of intensity for a further two weeks. The first immediate evidence of its success came in a dramatic fall in the crime rate, but it was not long before it was realized that it had proved to be the turning-point of the whole emergency, destroying the effectiveness of the passive wing both in supporting the gangs and in intimidating the rest of the Kikuyu population. From then on a very large proportion of the able-bodied Kikuyu male population, who were not actively supporting the government in the Home Guard and other organizations or were not in gangs in the forest, were languishing in detention camps. The administration of those remaining, particularly in Nairobi and the adjoining reserve in Kiambu district, was tightened up and the ability of terrorists or their supporters to move freely in the reserve greatly restricted. One of the major measures contributing to this was the vigorous pursuit of a policy of villagization in the Kikuyu reserve. This was desirable not only as a method of breaking the links between the terrorists and the population, but also as part of a general plan to improve native agriculture by a concentration of holdings and the application of terracing to counter erosion. Baring's main interest lay in this direction and he applied much of his personal effort to pushing the scheme forward and furthering a campaign to convince the Kikuyu that it was in their own interests, a campaign which was successful and of lasting benefit to the country's agriculture.

Erskine had intended to switch his effort into the forests in the latter half of 1954, but the need for troops and police to assist the administration and the Kikuyu Home Guard in *Anvil* and post-*Anvil* operations, in order to impose a tighter control of the population, forced him to postpone this until the beginning of 1955, when the weather would in any case be more favourable, January and February normally being dry months. Until then the RAF were given a free hand to bomb suspected terrorist hide-outs in the forest with the squadron of Lancasters brought in for the purpose to reinforce the two squadrons of Harvards. The principal sufferers from the bombing were the large game animals, particularly elephant and rhino, and they in turn became the principal threat to soldiers operating in the forest. The Mau Mau terrorists found no great difficulty at this stage in avoiding both the enraged animals and the British and African soldiers, who were not yet very skilled in jungle craft. During this period also the intelligence organization began to get into its stride. The police and army intelligence had been brought together under the Head of Intelligence, John Prendergast, with army intelligence officers integrated into the Police Special Branch, both at the centre and at province and district level. One of their most promising developments had been the use of captured Mau Mau terrorists who were persuaded to turn against their former comrades, not merely as informers but as active infiltrators in what came to be known as pseudo-gangs. Led by Kikuyu-speaking Europeans disguised as Africans, most of them from the Kenya Regiment, they formed teams masquerading as Mau Mau gangs in order both to contact the latter and to identify their suppliers and supporters. It was clearly essential to avoid clashes between the security forces and the pseudo-gangs and, as this technique developed, a certain rivalry built up between the two, particularly as the operations of the one had to be restricted in order to permit freedom of movement to the other.

When Erskine began to consider his plan to switch effort to the forests at the turn of the year, he realized that the major sweep by large forces of soldiers crashing through the forest was not likely to be effective. His general plan was to allot sectors of the forest to units, within which they would combine static and patrol operations to find and eliminate the gangs, who would be kept permanently on the move. If they attempted to escape from the forest into the reserve or the settled area, they would be intercepted at the forest edge by the Kikuyu Home Guard and Tribal Police, manning a ditch full of bamboo spikes which the native population had been impressed to construct. Units were to be reorganized to select and train their best soldiers to form Forest Operating Companies, each of three tracker/combat teams. Each team, led by a British officer or NCO consisted of eight soldiers (Africans in the KAR), a radio operator, an interpreter (for British Battalions), three African trackers, a tracker dog and a patrol dog. Each of the five British battalions was to produce one of these companies: the four Kenya KAR battalions were to produce two companies between them, and the Uganda and Tanganyika battalions and the East African motorized squadron were each to produce one tracker/combat team. In addition each battalion was to produce a 'Trojan' team of five soldiers, led by a Swahili-speaking NCO from the Kenya Regiment, available to follow-up at very short notice hot information provided by the local military or field intelligence officers attached to the Police Special Branch.

This organization was introduced for Operation *Hammer* which began in January 1955 under Hinde's direction in the Aberdare Mountains, starting in the moorland above the tree line and gradually working down to the forest edge, supply being maintained primarily by air. The area was too great to cover in one operation and it assumed the character of a sweep, although a more sophisticated one than had been previously attempted, and it was not too difficult for terrorists to escape to a part of the forest which was not being subjected to intense operations. The results were disappointing, only 161 Mau Mau being accounted for. Effort was then switched to Mount Kenya in Operation *First Flute*. Here it was possible to allot sectors to each unit and leave them there to conduct systematic operations in slower time, and the results were more rewarding. Concurrently with these operations, Erskine was persuaded by Prendergast to let Henderson try and negotiate a surrender through the pseudo-gang contacts. This began in February, aimed at detaching Stanley Mathenge and his followers in the southern Aberdares from Dedan Kimathi. The attempt nearly succeeded, but Kimathi got wind of it and threatened reprisals against Mathenge's followers. Although it failed in its main aim, it succeeded in sowing the seeds of a permanent rift between the followers of each.

Erskine left in April 1955, handing over to General Gerald Lathbury. Over 5,500 Mau Mau had been accounted for in the previous twelve months, the total of those active in terrorist gangs having been reduced from about 12,000 to 5,000. The Kikuyu reserve was under tight control, as was the Kikuyu population outside it in the towns and settled areas. Intelligence had improved dramatically both in quantity and in accuracy. The back of the rebellion had been broken, but at the cost of imposing very severe restrictions on the Kikuyu population, a large number of whom were in detention camps, and irksome ones in the rest of the colony, which many farmers and business men complained affected their livelihood and profitability. Lathbury appreciated that the task of eliminating the smaller and more scattered gangs that survived was henceforth one which required more skilled and sophisticated methods than had been employed hitherto; and that, if they were to be successful, the restrictions both in the reserves and outside them had to be maintained. His general plan was to leave the task of finding the gangs and pursuing them in the forest more and more to specialized units like the pseudo-gangs, and to give the soldiers the task of operating on and from the forest edge, the KAR in the reserves and the British battalions in the settled areas. He himself devoted a considerable effort to improving relationships with the European community in order to persuade them to continue to accept restrictions which were unpopular and which they felt should no longer be necessary.

One more major operation on the *Hammer–First Flute* pattern was launched in July 1955, named *Dante*, in the forest backing Kiambu district. Its immediate results were not impressive, but the toll of terrorist casualties continued. By the end of the year twenty-four out of the fifty-one principal terrorist gang leaders had been killed, most of them in pseudo-gang operations, and the total active gang strength reduced to about 2,000. By this time the Kikuyu population could see clearly that the government was winning and they were prepared to turn out in large numbers to sweep the forest edge to find terrorists who lay up there in order to obtain food. Success snowballed in 1956 and by the second half of the year the terrorists were split up into small gangs almost permanently on the move within the forest, while life outside it was returning to normal. The climax came when Dedan Kimathi himself, wounded in a clash with one of Henderson's pseudo-gangs, was found and killed by a Tribal Policeman at the forest edge on 17 October 1956. Stanley Mathenge was never traced. In the following month the army was withdrawn from operations, four years after it had started, and, although the emergency was not formally brought to an end until 1960, the active war against Mau Mau was over. During this war 10,527 of them had been killed, 2,633 captured, 26,625 arrested and 2,714 had surrendered. Some 50,000 of their supporters had been detained. Mau Mau had themselves killed 1,826 and wounded 918 African civilians, killed 32 and wounded 26 Europeans, killed 26 and wounded 36 Asians. Casualties inflicted on the security forces were 63 Europeans, 3 Asians and 534 Africans killed, 102 Europeans, 12 Asians and 465 Africans wounded. It had taken 10,000 British and African soldiers, 21,000 police and 25,000 Home Guard four years to defeat a rebellion limited to one tribe, which had no support of any kind from outside and a very limited supply of firearms. The cost of the emergency was assessed at £55 million, borne equally by the British and Kenyan Governments. Although in terms of the resources devoted to it by the British Government it could have been regarded as little more than a sideshow, it had a profound effect in persuading influential Conservative political figures in Britain to bow to the wind of change in Africa, and had brought about a radical transformation in the attitudes of the different races in the colony towards each other.

Chapter Four

CYPRUS

It was fortunate for Britain that her colonial conflicts followed in succession. If they had all struck her simultaneously, she would have been hard put to it to cope with them, even with national service running at a call-up period of two years, as it was in the 1950s, providing her with an army of about 400,000 men from Britain. In addition she recruited substantial numbers of soldiers overseas, Gurkhas, Malays, East Africans and others. The Mau Mau insurrection in Kenya had broken out just as the situation in Malaya was being brought under control. The troubles in Cyprus erupted in the spring of 1955 just as the tide had clearly turned in Kenya.

There had been significant differences both in the origins and in the nature of the insurrections in Malaya and Kenya. There were considerable differences also between them and that which faced the colonial government in Cyprus. In the latter the political motive, although, as in the case of others, it embraced the aim of getting rid of British colonial government, was for union with Greece, *enosis*. This had been the aspiration of the majority of Greek Cypriots, including the independent Orthodox Church of Cyprus, ever since Greece herself had been liberated from the Turkish yoke in 1832. Hopes of it had been raised on various occasions. In 1878, when Britain, in agreement with Turkey and in order to support her against the threat posed by Russia, then almost at the gates of Istanbul, had taken over the administration of the island. Then in 1914 when, as Turkey had joined the Central Powers, Britain unilaterally annexed the island, the suzerainty of which, as of Egypt, had legally remained that of the Ottoman Empire: indeed in 1915 Britain had offered Cyprus to Greece, if she would join France and herself in defending Serbia against Bulgaria; but the price was too high. Hopes were dashed again in 1923 when, after Greece's humiliating defeat at the hands of Mustafa Kemal in southern Turkey, the Treaty of Lausanne recognized British annexation of the island as a colony. Between the wars, and notably in 1931, agitation for *enosis* was kept alive both by the Church and by the mainland Greek schoolmasters introduced with British agreement to teach in the Greek Cypriot schools, just as nationalist feelings among the Turkish Cypriots were nurtured by school-

masters imported from Turkey, imbued with the fervour of Ataturk's successful revolution. Between 1939 and 1945 Cyprus, for the first time since 1878,
lived up to the purpose which had justified British presence, that of a *place
d'armes*, not for any strategic contribution it might make, but for fear of it being
occupied by Britain's enemies. Moreover considerable numbers of Cypriots,
both Greek and Turkish, served in the British forces in the Middle East and
this, together with Britain's support of Greece in 1941 and her intervention
there in December 1944, again raised hopes that Britain would be favourably
inclined towards *enosis*, particularly as the first post-war government in Britain
was a Labour administration, expected to favour release from colonial rule.
These hopes were to be disappointed and, as those who favoured *enosis* saw the
Italian Dodecanese islands pass to Greece (as Crete had done in 1908), the
British depart from Palestine and the French from Syria and the Lebanon, and
pressure for release from colonial rule mount world-wide, they applied themselves to the methods of bringing pressure themselves.

The two leaders of this campaign were Archbishop Makarios III, elected
Archbishop of the Cyprus Orthodox Church and Ethnarch of the Greek
Cypriots in June 1950 at the age of 37, and a retired colonel of the Greek Army,
George Grivas, then 52. Makarios had been born Michael Mouskos, son of a
poor shepherd of Ano Panayia in the district of Paphos in the south-west of the
island. Grivas was the second son of a prosperous, pro-British seed-merchant
from Trikomo in the north-east corner, the Karpas or Panhandle. Both had
been pupils of the Pancyprian Gymnasium in Nicosia, a fertile seed-bed of
Greek nationalist fervour. There are conflicting accounts of when they first
met, but it was certainly in Athens either in 1942 or 1946. Mouskos was then
priest at the church of Saint Irene in a fashionable suburb of Athens. In 1946
Grivas, who had organized and commanded an extreme right-wing private
army to fight the communists, known by the Greek letter x or KHI, which had
gained an unsavoury reputation for atrocities, was an embittered man, as he
had been excluded from the post-war regular Greek Army. They met again in
Athens in 1949 and in March 1951, when Makarios paid his first visit to
Athens as Ethnarch and hatched plans for an anti-British campaign with a
committee formed there by the brothers Loizides. As a result of that meeting,
Grivas was co-opted to the committee and in July 1951 went to Cyprus to
assess the situation and devise a plan, spending several months there. His
reconnaissance led him to favour a guerrilla campaign based on the mountains. Makarios argued against this. The British were all in the towns, and a
campaign of sabotage against the government installations and activities,
which is what Makarios had in mind, would have to be centred there. Grivas
had much grander ideas, visualizing an island-wide movement of resistance
and revolt, about which Makarios and other church leaders were sceptical.
Makarios saw a campaign of sabotage as a means of pressure to persuade the
Greek Government, then headed by Venizelos, to support his campaign in the

international field, especially in the United Nations. However Venizelos showed no sign of doing this, but hopes were pinned on his opponent, Field-Marshal Papagos, who had shown sympathy and who came to power in November 1952.

By that time Grivas had paid another visit to the island to finalize his plan, based on a guerrilla organization in the mountains in the centre of the island and in the northern range, supplemented by sabotage teams in the towns. These were to be formed from the youth movements, which, on Grivas's advice, had been founded by the Archbishop, OXEN (Young Peoples Christian Orthodox Union) and the more militant PEON (Pancyprian Youth Organization), the latter led by Stavros Poskottis. He also made contact with an official of PEK, the Greek Cypriot Farmers' Union, Andreas Azinas, who was to become the principal organizer of his arms supplies. When Grivas returned to Athens in February 1953, Azinas, a graduate of Reading and Salonika universities, became his principal representative on the island, able to travel all over it on his PEK business without arousing suspicion. It was he who brought Gregoris Afxentiou, a reserve officer in the Greek Army, into the organization which was to be called EOKA (*Ethniki Organosis Kuprion Agoniston* – National Organization of Cypriot Fighters). Before he left the island, Grivas had submitted his plan to Makarios. Its aim was not to expel or to defeat the British, but to draw the attention of international public opinion by harassing them. This should continue until the United Nations had been seized with the problem and *enosis* brought about by diplomatic means. The methods to be employed would be sabotage of government and military installations, surprise attacks by highly mobile guerrilla units on British forces, and the organization of passive resistance by the population. Grivas recognized that the main weight would have to be on sabotage, as the country was not capable of absorbing large guerrilla forces. Sabotage groups were to be organized for every town and district, using time-bombs, explosive and mines. Grivas himself would determine their action and supervise their formation. An intelligence organization would be set up to observe British military movements and installations. Any Cypriots who acted as British agents would be severely dealt with. He laid great emphasis on organizing public support, which should include a boycott of everything British, and on encouragement to students to participate in disturbances. As soon as he got back to Athens, he set about organizing the arms supplies without which his plan could not be implemented. Most of them were obtained without much difficulty from sympathizers in the Greek Army and the first load was successfully smuggled ashore north of Paphos on 25 March 1953, Makarios having reluctantly given his approval while on a visit to Athens at that time.

He had found Papagos unwilling to support anything other than diplomatic action, and, although Makarios was still in favour of preparing a campaign of sabotage, he was reluctant to authorize anything that went further than that.

Eighteen months later the atmosphere had changed. Anthony Eden, then British Foreign Secretary, had rebuffed Papagos with words that appeared to rule out *enosis* in any circumstances, and in June 1954 it had been announced that, as a result of negotiations with Egypt, the British Army and Air Force headquarters, with all the garrison and communications necessary to support them, were to be transferred to Cyprus from the Suez Canal zone, while the base there was to be converted to a civilianized organization. Britain and the United States were both at this time much concerned with the potential Russian threat to the Middle East and intent on creating a political and military barrier of states in the area to oppose it. Turkey played an important strategic part in this and there was much concern to find ways to bolster the position of those who might be prepared to lend their support, notably Nuri es Said in Iraq and the young Hussein in Jordan. Having abandoned Palestine and now about to move out of Egypt, the only British *place d'armes* left in the area was Cyprus. Greece was not entirely unsympathetic to the British attitude and had suggested at one stage a solution by which Britain should lease bases in Cyprus and in Greece itself, but Eden curtly dismissed this suggestion also. In November 1954 Papagos changed his tune and raised the question in the UN General Assembly, while Grivas, having been refused a visa, was smuggled back into the island after a very rough voyage via Rhodes in the caique *Siren*, which had brought in the arms the year before. He was followed by the caique *St George* which dumped its load of arms in the sea, when its master thought that its arrival had been spotted.

The United States had supported Britain in persuading the United Nations not to adopt a resolution on the Cyprus issue. As a result, Papagos gave Makarios the green light to go ahead with his plans, and the latter chose 25 March, the anniversary of Greek independence, for the start of the campaign. Grivas wanted to start earlier, but the interception of a further load of arms in the *St George* on 25 January reconciled him to further delay. Meanwhile Makarios was preparing the ground with inflammatory speeches and sermons. At a meeting on 7 March he and Grivas agreed that the date should be shortly after Greek Independence Day, when the British might be expecting trouble, and on 29 March they fixed the night of 31 March as the time, Makarios still insisting that action should be limited to sabotage of military installations which would not cause casualties, and that Grivas's favoured guerrilla groups elsewhere should remain quiescent.

Grivas had made good use of the four months he had spent on the island, hidden in two different houses in the suburbs of Nicosia. To lead the sabotage group in Famagusta he had recruited Gregoris Afxentiou, who had succeeded in recovering considerable quantities of explosive which the British had dumped in the sea off Salamis in 1946. Another important recruit was Polycarpos Georgadjis, a young clerk in the office of the Cyprus Chamber of Commerce, who developed contacts among acquaintances serving in the police and with the administration and the services. He acted as Head of Intelligence in Nicosia, Evangelos Evangelakis being in charge of the group in the city, in which Markos Drakos was a prominent leader. Stavros Poskottis, the head of PEON, was in charge in Larnaca and Notis Petropouleas, an ex-army sergeant, in Limassol. Grivas himself adopted the *nom de guerre* of Dighenis, a legendary Greek hero of the Byzantine age.

The bombs went off soon after midnight. In Nicosia they were mostly successful, the principal damage being inflicted on the transmitter of the Cyprus Broadcasting Corporation and minor damage to the Secretariat building and the army barracks, which housed the headquarters of the Commander-in-Chief Middle East, General Keightley. Afxentiou had failed in Famagusta and had fled to his home village of Lyssi with the police on his trail. Poskottis had been more successful in Larnaca, but he and his group had been arrested. Petropouleas in Limassol had started two hours late, by which time the police were on full alert. Although he had successfully attacked two police stations and a power plant, some of his men had been caught and they had dropped petrol bombs outside the houses where all their explosives were kept, so that the police found them all. After this muddled start, explosions continued while recruiting was intensified, including a number of Greek Cypriot policemen who joined Georgadjis's intelligence organization. The manufacture of home-made explosives was also developed. The trial at the beginning of May of those caught smuggling arms in January led to an intensification of EOKA activity, culminating in an attempt by Markos Drakos on Empire Day, 24 May, to assassinate the Governor, Sir Robert Armitage, by placing a bomb near where he was to sit at a charity film performance in aid of the British Legion. Fortunately for him and those near him the film ended earlier than Drakos had calculated, and the bomb went off five minutes after they had left. In a report to Makarios at the end of the month, Grivas explained that he saw the campaign as designed to last until October, when the Cyprus question was again due to be debated by the United Nations. His aim was to disperse, fatigue and irritate the British, while not being so active as to run the risk of suppression by them before October. His plan was to operate in three phases. The first would include acts of sabotage in the towns and on communication centres with simultaneous attacks on police stations, particularly in the mountain areas, in order to force the British to disperse their forces. The second phase would give emphasis to surprise attacks in mountainous areas on police stations and army camps. If these were successful, the third phase would be a general uprising of youth in militant demonstrations all over the island, supported by the general populace. All of this would be orchestrated to suit diplomatic and political activity by the Archbishop.

Grivas need not have worried about the possibility of his movement being suppressed by October. The forces available to the Governor were very

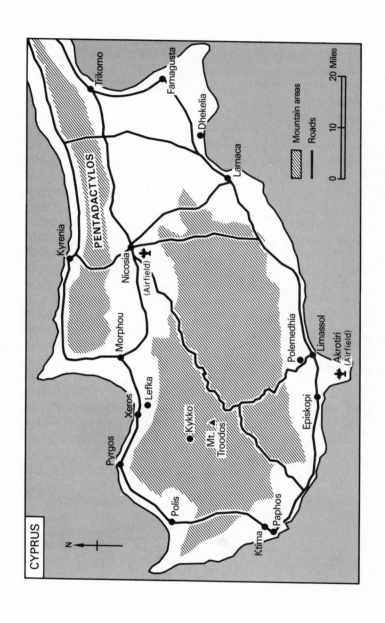

CYPRUS

N

Trikomo
Famagusta
Dhekelia
Larnaca
PENTADACTYLOS
Kyrenia
Nicosia
(Airfield)
Morphou
Polemedhia
Limassol
Akrotiri
(Airfield)
Lefka
Episkopi
Xeros
Kykko
Mt.
Troodos
Pyrgos
Polis
Ktima
Paphos

Mountain areas
Roads

0   10   20 Miles

limited. The organization and morale of the police were not attuned to such a threat. A new Commissioner, Robins, had arrived in November 1954, but had not been able to make much headway on a limited budget, ranking low in the colony's list of priorities. Special Branch was headed by a British officer and had a total strength of thirty-seven, much of its attention being devoted to watching the communists of AKEL (Progressive Party of the Working People). The army had only two infantry battalions, an engineer regiment and an artillery regiment in the island, in addition to the recently arrived GHQ Middle East, with its large supporting signal and administrative tail, more of a liability than an asset in those circumstances. The engineer regiment and one of the battalions were employed on construction of the new bases at Dhekelia, between Famagusta and Larnaca, and Episkopi near Limassol. Brigadier Ricketts, with a small district headquarters, was in command.

The situation deteriorated throughout the summer of 1955, notable incidents being the murder of a key Greek Cypriot policeman, Constable Poullis, the wounding of a British soldier in an explosion in a bar in Famagusta and the explosion of bombs at the houses of General Keightley and another senior officer. On 30 June Eden, now Prime Minister, announced that the Greek and Turkish Governments had been invited to a conference on 'questions concerning the Eastern Mediterranean, including Cyprus', but there was no mention of representation of the Cypriots themselves. In July the Governor introduced a number of security measures, including detention of those suspected of being members of an organization responsible for the attempted overthrow of the government by violence, and a ban on persons under twenty-one carrying firearms. Under this order Evangelakis and Drakos were picked up in Nicosia and detained in Kyrenia castle, and Grivas decided to move from Nicosia into the mountains. Lennox-Boyd, the Colonial Secretary, came out to discuss matters with the Governor on 19 July. As a result both of his visit and of one from the CIGS, Field-Marshal Harding, reinforcements were sent to the colony, arriving in September, two Royal Marine Commandos from Malta and two infantry battalions from the Suez Canal zone. In that month and in October bomb explosions increased in number, the British Institute in Nicosia was set on fire and wrecked and there were more attacks on British service personnel, an RAF officer being wounded and a soldier of the Royal Scots dying of his wounds when a grenade was thrown at his vehicle, the first British soldier to die at the hands of EOKA. Six days after Constable Poullis had been killed on 28 August, Michael Caraolis was arrested and charged with his murder. Georgadjis, who had ordered him to do so, was later picked up with two of his assistants who were carrying arms. No evidence could be produced against Georgadjis, who was detained and sent to join Afxentiou and Drakos in Kyrenia castle, from which they escaped in September, joining Grivas in the mountains.

Meanwhile events outside the island were having an influence within it. At the Tripartite Conference, Harold Macmillan, now Foreign Secretary, had proposed a joint Anglo–Greek–Turkish study of how to make gradual progress towards self-government for Cyprus. When a constitution had been agreed and Cypriot representatives elected under it, they would themselves participate in the government; but sovereignty would rest with Britain 'for the foreseeable future'. This was followed by a bomb attack on the Turkish Consulate in Salonika, in retaliation for which anti-Greek riots took place in Istanbul and Izmir. Turkey had made clear that, if there was any threat of Cyprus becoming independent or of *enosis*, she would call into question the Treaty of Lausanne which recognized Greek sovereignty over the islands close to Turkey in the Aegean.

On 21 September the steering committee of the UN General Assembly, under pressure from America, Britain and Turkey, again rejected a Greek appeal for discussion of the Cyprus problem. It was clear that there was not going to be any quick and easy way out of the impasse and Eden, who was anxious to show himself to the right wing of the Conservative party as a worthy successor of that indomitable imperialist Winston Churchill, was in no mood for concessions. He turned to Field-Marshal Harding, about to relinquish the post of CIGS and end his active career, to achieve for Cyprus what Templer, who was about to succeed him, had done for Malaya. Reluctantly Harding accepted and arrived in Cyprus on 3 October 1955 as Governor and Commander-in-Chief, his predecessor, Sir Robert Armitage, slipping away into the shadows.

As soon as he arrived Harding acted with energy and speed on two fronts. On the security front he set out to create an organization on the pattern that Briggs had introduced in Malaya, welding together army, police and administration, improving the organization, strength and training of all three, with high priority given to intelligence, and infusing them all with a sense of urgency and clear direction through two principal deputies, Brigadier George Baker for operations and George Sinclair, a provincial commissioner from the Gold Coast, on the civil side. On the political front he immediately began negotiations with Makarios, trying to persuade him that the overall threat was one of international communism and that this should determine everyone's general attitude towards the position of Cyprus; and that, if Makarios would co-operate with the British Government in a gradual move towards self-government for the island, the strategic position would change, removing the obstacles which for the present the British Government saw to any rapid steps in that direction. He made clear his determination to use all the resources at his disposal to stop intimidation and terrorism and appealed to the Archbishop for his co-operation. Makarios went no further than to promise to 'use his influence' to prevent disorders as long as he and Harding were engaged in discussions. In reply he made three demands, or 'suggestions' as he called them: that the British Government should recognize the right of the people of Cyprus to self-determination as 'the indispensable basis' for a solution; once they had, he would be willing to co-operate in framing a constitution for self-government and in putting it into immediate operation; finally that the timing of the grant of self-determination would be discussed between the British Government and the representatives of the Cypriots elected by that constitution. When, after a series of meetings between 4 and 11 October, it became clear that Harding could not move beyond Macmillan's proposals to the Tripartite Conference, Grivas set off another round of explosions and attacks on service personnel and installations, including a successful raid on a store in Famagusta harbour containing British arms and ammunition. Harding was reinforced with a complete British infantry brigade, bringing the total army strength to 12,000. The RAF had 2,000 men on the island.

Soon after their arrival a major operation took place in the hills south and east of Kyrenia, in which 1,700 men from five units took part, leading to the capture of a number of EOKA activists and some arms finds. Towards the end of November Grivas stepped up activity in Famagusta and Nicosia and in the mountains. The Post Office in Nicosia was blown up, bombs thrown into bars frequented by the services and the first of the murders perpetrated by Grivas's execution squads of off-duty servicemen, the pattern of which was to become sickeningly familiar. The victim was a sergeant in Nicosia. A time-bomb was also set off in a sergeants' mess and the climax came on 26 November at the annual dance of the Caledonian Society in the Ledra Palace Hotel. Harding had been expected to attend and an EOKA employee of the hotel, who controlled the main light switches, turned them off and then threw grenades at what he assumed was the Governor's table, wounding five people including the daughter of the Director of Intelligence. Harding's reaction to this increase in EOKA activity was to declare a state of emergency, introducing very severe penalties for offences connected with the emergency, conferring wide powers of arrest and search on the security forces, widening the causes for which people could be detained and tightening control of the press. EOKA kept up the tempo in December, prompting Baker into organizing a major operation in the mountains to catch Grivas himself, named *Foxhunter*, which was preceded by a search of all the monasteries. Although a small quantity of arms and ammunition was found, EOKA had been tipped off by their friends in the police and the large amount of supplies kept at Kykko monastery and elsewhere had been removed and distributed to safe houses. Grivas, who was suffering from violent toothache and a heavy cold and sore throat, was forced to abandon his hide-out above Spilia and narrowly avoided capture as he made his way over the mountains, protected by Afxentiou, to an alternative hide-out near Kakopetria. Although the Marines failed to catch their fox, they caught one important guerrilla leader, Remos Kyriakides, younger brother of the Bishop of Kyrenia. His group was based on Kykko, and it was with them that Grivas had taken refuge when he first moved to the mountains.

A few days later Markos Drakos was nearly accounted for also. He and his group ambushed an army landrover on the coast road between Xeros and Pyrgos. In it were Major Brian Combe of the Royal Engineers and his driver, Lance-Corporal Morum, the latter being killed instantly. Combe managed to drive the vehicle forty yards on into a ditch by a small hill. From there he engaged his ambushers with his sten-gun, removed his driver's and used that, shouted a message on two occasions to passing vehicles to get help, and all the time kept his opponents under fire. In fact he had killed one, Haralambos Mouskos, a cousin of the Archbishop, and wounded the other three. Help finally came. But the least badly wounded, while pretending to negotiate surrender, managed to escape: it was Markos Drakos. Sympathy for EOKA, and particularly its support by the Church, was made evident in the hero's funeral given to Mouskos. The cortège wound its way at funeral pace the thirty miles from Lefka to Nicosia, acclaimed by crowds with Greek flags at every village, at least a thousand people attending the funeral at the Phaneromeni Church in Nicosia at which the Bishop of Kitium sang the dead hero's praises.

January 1956 saw the arrival of five more battalions, followed in February by the armoured cars of the Royal Horse Guards, the Blues, bringing the total number of army units engaged in emergency operations to fourteen. They were organized in four brigades, 50th Infantry Brigade in Nicosia with two battalions, 51st Brigade in Famagusta with five, 3rd Commando Brigade Royal Marines in Limassol with three and 16th Parachute Brigade with two, in reserve with unbrigaded units. The Parachute Brigade had been sent to Cyprus as a general reserve for the Middle East, but was available to Harding if not required for other operations. This added up to about 17,000 troops. At the same time the RAF sent more Sycamore helicopters to supplement the few they had reluctantly allowed to be diverted from their search-and-rescue role to support the army. They had proved invaluable, although under-powered and with a very limited lift capacity when operating in the mountains.

Although the measures which Harding had introduced on his arrival were beginning to get into gear and he now had a considerable force at his disposal, his campaign was still in an embryo stage, while that of Grivas was coming to full fruition. Harding's plan had been to give priority to the security of towns and of the communications between them. Clearing up EOKA in the countryside would have to wait until life could be lived normally and government authority reign unchallenged in and between the centres of population. Minimum force was the rule, but, if the security forces were attacked, no matter what the odds, they were to fight it out, an order which Major Combe had set a splendid example in obeying. On the other hand no commander was to embark on an operation without having at his disposal or on call the resources to see it through. In a report on security to the Colonial Office at the end of 1955, Harding said that he was satisfied that he was working on the right lines, but warned that it would take time and a great deal of effort both in Cyprus and in Britain to set up a fully effective organization. During January

1956 Harding held a series of secret meetings with Makarios, centring round a formula which the British Government had reached after discussion with Greece, based on one suggested by Harding in October. Known as 'the double negative', it began by stating that it was not HMG's position that the principle of self-determination could never be applied to Cyprus, but went on to state that there were strategic reasons why it could not be granted at that time. It said that Britain had offered 'a wide measure of self-government now', and that, if the people of Cyprus would participate in constitutional development, Her Majesty's Government would 'work for a solution which will satisfy the people of Cyprus within the framework of the Treaties and Alliances to which the countries concerned in the defence of the Eastern Mediterranean are parties'. HMG would be prepared to discuss the future of the island with representatives of the people of Cyprus 'when self-government had proved itself a workable proposition and capable of safeguarding the interests of all sections of the community'. In the course of these discussions some amendments were made in the hope of making them more palatable to Makarios, and by the end of January Grivas was getting sufficiently concerned that Makarios might give way that he stepped up his activities again, adding violent and widespread riots by students and schoolchildren to explosions and shootings, as a result of which many of the schools were closed. The murder of a Turkish Cypriot policeman added inter-communal rioting to the general mayhem. Harding had tried to force Makarios to condemn the use of violence in writing, while the latter dodged the issue and raised new ones, such as the form of the constitution itself, an amnesty for EOKA and the responsibility for internal security. Harding envisaged it remaining with the Governor, while Makarios saw the latter as becoming no more than a sort of constitutional monarch. Britain's line over the constitution was that this could only be discussed with 'all sections of the community at the appropriate time'. Makarios played for time and found considerable support among a wide circle of Greek Cypriots for the view that he should cautiously accept the invitation to discuss constitutional issues further. However he realized that Grivas would not like this. The latter had recently distributed a pamphlet demanding immediate self-determination and warning the Archbishop that EOKA would not accept any agreement he made with Harding and would continue the struggle 'unless and until criminals and torturers among the Security Forces had been punished'. Makarios went secretly to meet him at Kykko monastery, the arrangements being made by Loulla Kokkinou, a secretary in the Cyprus Transport Corporation who, with her two sisters, headed the women's side of EOKA. Grivas refused to accept any solution in which the British retained responsibility for internal security, and considered their proposals as too vague and uncertain to be pursued. All he would agree to was to suspend operations while Makarios continued negotiations with Harding. He kept his promise until the eve of talks between Lennox-Boyd, Harding and Makarios on 1 March, when nineteen bombs went off at various points in the island. Makarios was furious and in later years maintained that it had wrecked favourable chances of agreement. It is difficult to accept that view, as the two sides were still far apart, the unresolved issues being the responsibility for internal security, the demand by Britain for a written condemnation of violence by Makarios and the latter's demand for an unconditional amnesty for EOKA men and women detained or imprisoned. Neither side would budge and Harding, by now convinced both by the way Makarios shifted the argument to new issues as soon as agreement looked near on old ones, and by the evidence which came to light from Grivas's diaries, recently discovered, that the Archbishop was in close league with EOKA (if he did not even perhaps direct it), came to the conclusion that, as long as he was in Cyprus, whether free or restricted in some way, terrorism could not be effectively dealt with nor any real progress made. He was supported in this by the British Government and, on 9 March, as he was about to fly to Athens, Makarios was picked up and, with the Bishop of Kyrenia, the latter's secretary, Ioannides, and the priest of the Phaneromeni Church, Papastavros, was flown by the RAF to Mombasa and taken from there by the Royal Navy to 'restricted residence' in the Seychelles.

Everyone had expected a violent reaction to his deportation, but it was slow in coming, perhaps because Grivas feared that widespread activity at this time could involve him in excessive losses. Opposing Harding's 17,000 troops, EOKA had a very small force of armed men. According to Grivas's own account he had 7 groups totalling 53 men in the mountains, 47 groups totalling 220 men in the main towns, 2 groups within the British bases of Episkopi and Polemidhia, and 75 groups of part-time terrorists totalling 750 men, armed only with shotguns, in villages all over the island. He had to consider his future strategy and conserve the resources to implement it. There had been one incident four days before Makarios was deported which would have caused a severe reaction had it been successful. A time-bomb was placed in an RAF Hermes transport aircraft due to fly servicemen and their families back to England. It was discovered twenty minutes before take-off and defused. One of the first signs of a resumption of hostility was an attempt on the life of Harding himself, which he was lucky to escape. One of the Greek Cypriot staff of Government House, Neophytos Sofokleos, placed a bomb under his mattress, timed to explode at 2 a.m. When Sofokleos failed to turn up next day and the Greek Cypriot staff refused to turn out the bedrooms, suspicion was aroused and Harding's soldier servant found the bomb. It exploded five minutes after it had been removed in a dustpan to the bottom of the garden. The murder of a British police sergeant off duty led to severe measures being taken against shops and houses near the scene of the crime. A further and important blow against the police occurred in April when Superintendent Kyriakos Aristotelos, known as Kyriacoudi, for long a sharp thorn in EOKA's flesh, was killed when visiting his wife and new-born child in hospital. Further severe measures, including collective punishments, were imposed, and on 10 May Michael Caraolis and Andreas Demetriou, condemned for the murder of Constable Poullis, were executed, the first EOKA men to be hanged. Grivas immediately announced that two British Army deserters, Hill and Shilton, who had fallen into the hands of EOKA, had been hanged in retaliation. At first the authorities threw doubt on this; but it was later discovered that they had been killed, although not at the same time. In May the total of British soldiers killed, apart from these two, reached thirty. The same month saw serious inter-communal riots and the introduction of identity cards for the whole population.

Harding realized only too clearly that mere repression was no solution to the problem and, with Makarios out of the way, he applied himself to a fundamental review of policy. His conclusion was that it was essential to reach some agreement about the future international status of the island. To attempt to make progress towards self-government before that had been agreed, if only for an interim period of five or ten years, was pointless and even dangerous. The British Government took a different view and on 12 July announced that, as international agreement could not be obtained for the present, they intended to proceed forthwith with the development of internal self-government and that Lord Radcliffe was to start immediately to study and recommend a constitution. A fortnight later Nasser nationalized the Suez Canal and the attention of Ministers was diverted into other channels, while Harding's military campaign against EOKA suffered diversions of effort to provide forces, support and security for the operations mounted from Cyprus and Malta against Egypt. The Royal Marine Commandos returned to Malta and the Parachute Brigade was taken off operations to brush up their parachute training. Before this happened, two major operations, known as *Pepperpot* and *Lucky Alphonse*, had taken place in the mountains. *Pepperpot* lasted from 17 to 28 May and was directed by Brigadier Butler, commanding the Parachute Brigade. Beside his own two battalions he had a Royal Marine Commando, part of another, two infantry battalions and the armoured cars of the Blues, some 2,000 soldiers in all. The main target was Grivas. Baker had noticed that an area of some twenty miles by twenty miles, centred on Kykko monastery and the village of Kambos, had remained free of incidents, although there had been many on the periphery. He guessed that Grivas was somewhere near Kykko, if not in it, and planned to infiltrate the soldiers as secretly as possible from all directions, dropping a few by helicopter and others from trucks which continued on their way. The whole area was to be combed by ambushes and patrols, while police and army intelligence teams followed up any clues gained from their captures or discoveries. Grivas realized that a major operation was imminent and split up his groups over a wider area than they normally occupied. He also ordered diversionary operations all over the island, including a spate of bombings, carried out in Nicosia by schoolgirls under the command of Loulla Kokkinou. Grivas, accompanied by Antonis Georghiades, kept permanently on the move and nearly lost his life over the side of a steep cliff. When the operation finished on 28 May, seventeen hard-core terrorists had been captured, several of them prepared to turn informer almost immediately. Four complete groups had been captured and many suspects held for screening and interrogation. Fifty-two weapons of various kinds, ammunition, food, clothing and other stores completed the haul. After a pause of ten days, Operation *Lucky Alphonse* began, concentrating on a smaller area round Kykko in the search for Grivas and for Markos Drakos's group. It very nearly succeeded in its first aim. Sergeant Scott of the 3rd Parachute Battalion, leading a patrol back to his platoon base near the village of Ayia Arka, saw a group of five men by the side of a stream thirty yards away. He opened fire and they fled into the undergrowth, abandoning their belongings. It was Grivas, Georghiades and three companions. They hid in the undergrowth a few hundred yards away until it was dark two hours later, and were not found, although a tracker dog was used and a soldier came within forty feet of them. Georghiades had left his boots behind and Grivas his Sam Browne belt, spectacles, beret and diary, which he had been writing up and which included an account of his movements for the previous three weeks. After various adventures and taking refuge in two monasteries, Grivas abandoned the idea of trying to join up with Afxentiou's group and decided to leave the mountains and take refuge in Limassol. He summoned EOKA's Limassol leader, Haji Miltis, to meet him near the village of Saittas and was driven by him to Limassol, where he was taken to the house of Dafni Panayides, where an underground hide-out already existed. While he was thus escaping, one of Butler's battalions, the Gordon Highlanders, suffered a severe blow when two platoons were caught in a forest fire, started by mortar bombs, in which twenty-one soldiers died and fourteen were badly burned. *Lucky Alphonse* came to an end on 23 June. So much information had come to light incriminating Kykko monastery as a supply centre for EOKA that it was decided to close it down as a monastery and subject it to a detailed and thorough search, an act which was hailed in Greece and elsewhere as desecration. July saw an increase in street murders in Nicosia, where Nicos Sampson was now controlling the execution squads in a particularly vicious and ruthless campaign, one of the victims of a bomb thrown into a restaurant being the American Vice-Consul, William Boteler. Grivas published his regrets at what he called a 'tragic error'. Many of the targets of the execution squads were Cypriots suspected of being informers.

Under pressure from the United States, the Greek Prime Minister, Constantine Karamanlis, appealed to Grivas to call a truce to allow diplomatic activity to be resumed in search of a solution. Grivas reluctantly agreed and on 17 August EOKA distributed pamphlets announcing that it was suspending operations in order that Cypriot demands, as set out by Makarios, could be discussed: meanwhile EOKA would 'stand guard, ready for more sacrifices, knowing that it has all the moral and material backing necessary'. The announcement raised everybody's hopes. It was a week before Eden's government responded. Their answer was to offer surrender terms, giving EOKA three weeks to give themselves up with their arms: they could then individually choose either to be exiled for life to Greece or stay in Cyprus and be detained. Those suspected of specific acts of violence could face trial and the penalties of conviction. Grivas rejected the terms defiantly on the following day, 23 August. Four days later the British published extracts from Grivas's diaries which had been discovered buried in Nicosia and in Lyssi, revealing the complicity of Makarios, Grivas's ruthless orders to his subordinates and his adverse comments on many of them. For a man obsessed with secrecy and expert at it, it was astonishing that he should commit so much to paper, apparently foreseeing the need to justify himself in the eyes of posterity. Suspecting a Nicosia watchmaker, Andreas Lazarou, of having betrayed the whereabouts of the diaries, he had him murdered.

About this time Nicos Sampson organized two dramatic rescues of EOKA men in custody, both when they were visiting the hospital in Nicosia for treatment. His first rescue was aimed to snatch Koutsoftos, who was under sentence of death, but they took the wrong man, a mainland Greek, Karedemas, who had been on the caique *St George*. The other was Polycarpos Georgadjis. Grivas, joined again by Georghiades, had moved into a new hide in September on the edge of Limassol, below the house of Marios Christodoulides, a clerk in a branch of the Ottoman Bank in the British base of Episkopi. In that month he ordered an increase in the activities of execution squads, British servicemen and police being among the targets. But they were not the only ones: a British journalist, Angus MacDonald, and a customs official, Patrick Kaberry, and his wife were also victims. The ambush of the latter between Lefkoniko and Kyrenia led to an operation in the northern mountain range aimed at the EOKA group responsible, led by Sozos and Christofi. It was called *Sparrowhawk I*. Butler was again in charge with four battalions, armoured cars, a battery of searchlights and naval launches off shore. It lasted for the first ten days of October and led to the capture of the two men, twenty-nine other terrorists and several arms caches. It was immediately followed by *Sparrowhawk II* on the western end of the range, which lasted for five days with practically nothing to show for it. A week after it, a time-bomb exploded when two football teams of the Highland Light Infantry at Lefkoniko turned on a tap for a drink. The whole village was searched and the accusations of the brutality with which this was done led to an inquiry. Butler had already been switched to his old *Pepperpot* stamping ground, the targets again being Markos Drakos and his 'Sky' group. With his two parachute battalions, three infantry battalions and an artillery regiment employed as infantry, the whole area was covered by observation posts, patrols, ambushes and intelligence teams, while curfews were imposed, no movement being allowed outside villages by day or within them by night. In the middle of the operation, 28 October, Butler and his parachute battalions were whisked away to take part in Operation *Musketeer*, the attack on Port Said.

In spite of appeals from Karamanlis and others to observe a truce before the Cyprus issue came before the UN General Assembly, Grivas saw the entanglement of Britain in the Suez affair as a golden opportunity for intensified EOKA activity. November as a result was a bad month with 416 incidents of all kinds, bombs, ambushes and shootings, in which forty people were killed, twenty-one of them British. But with the end of the Suez operation, Harding had eighteen battalions or their equivalent available, a force of some 20,000 men with which to pursue a few hundred terrorists in an island only 60 miles by 140 and with a population of about 450,000 Greek and 100,000 Turkish Cypriots and some 8,000 others, Maronites and Armenians contributing 3,000 each. Of equal significance, the police had been greatly strengthened and their efficiency raised under the direction of a new Commissioner of Police, Geoffrey White, who had served with Harding in Trieste in 1945, and the intelligence organization had also immensely improved, profiting from the captures in operations earlier in the year. The tide was about to turn dramatically, and in two major operations in the mountains in January 1957 Drakos and Afxentiou were killed, their groups broken up and Georgadjis recaptured. Nicos Sampson and other important EOKA leaders in Nicosia had also been picked up, and the ring broken of customs officials in Limassol implicated in smuggling arms despatched from Greece by Azinas.

In the political field Radcliffe's constitutional proposals had been published and had received a favourable response from the British and Turkish Governments. Neither Greece nor the Greek Cypriots were prepared to show their hand in the absence of comment from Makarios, who took the line that, being out of touch with Cyprus, he could not express any views. The United Nations debated Cyprus again in February and passed a resolution, agreed between the British and Greek Governments, calling for a renewal of discussions. Under political pressure from Greece and military pressure from the security forces in Cyprus, Grivas, still undiscovered in his hide-out in Limassol, distributed a pamphlet on 14 March 1957 stating that 'in compliance with the spirit of the UN resolution and in order to facilitate the resumption of negotiations between Britain and the real representative of the Cyprus people, Archbishop Makarios, EOKA declares that it is ready to order the suspension of operations at once if the Ethnarch Makarios is released'. It took the British Government a week to decide its response, Lord Salisbury resigning in disgust when it was agreed to accept the offer, although Makarios would not be allowed to return to Cyprus until the Radcliffe constitution had been implemented and was working. An attempt to extract a condemnation of violence from him as a condition of his release brought an equivocal answer, which was nevertheless considered acceptable. The previous offer of safe conduct out of the island for EOKA men who surrendered was renewed, but none took advantage of it.

In the two years since the EOKA campaign had started, they had killed 203 people, of whom 78 were British servicemen, 9 British police, 16 British civilians, 12 Cypriot policemen and 4 Turkish civilians. They had set off 1,382 bomb explosions. 51 of their members had been killed, 27 imprisoned and 1,500 detained.

Makarios went to Athens and, while political and diplomatic activity proceeded, Harding's men continued to try and track down EOKA leaders and Grivas overhauled his organization, Azinas developing a new arms smuggling route through an EOKA man in the post office at Ktima. In November Sir Hugh Foot replaced Harding as Governor, but little progress was being made in the search for a solution. It was the Turks who were now proving difficult, demanding partition of the island if it were to become independent, and tension between the two communities increased, erupting into riots and attacks by one community on the other.

In this situation Grivas decided to renew action, and in March 1958 gave orders for an anti-British economic boycott, enforced at the point of the gun. On 1 April, third anniversary of the start of EOKA's campaign, he ordered a general strike, followed by a week of riots in the streets and in detention camps and prisons. The army was called in to support the police and prison staff, provoking a threat from Grivas to renew full-scale activity. This was followed by the murder of a British Special Branch interrogator and a spate of bomb attacks. Foot's reaction was to try and arrange a meeting with Grivas, but the latter suspected a trap. He agreed to a temporary halt in operations, but said that he would order a general attack unless what he called 'measures against political prisoners' ceased. Georgadjis at this time had escaped again and made contact with Georghiades, who was looking for a new hide-out for Grivas behind the Armenian cemetery in Nicosia. The latter was finding it difficult to control affairs from Limassol and was at odds with Makarios, who wanted him to call off the boycott which was unpopular with many Greek Cypriots. The Archbishop was also concerned at the tendency of EOKA to become an anti-Turkish organization.

June 1958 saw a major step forward in the political field as Macmillan, who had succeeded Eden as Prime Minister, reduced the demand for British military facilities and produced a plan which associated the Greek and Turkish Governments with the British, and with Cypriot Ministers, in the government of the island, with two separate Greek and Turkish elected assemblies, for an interim period of seven years. Turkey rejected it and there were rumours of a Turkish invasion, which sparked off a series of intercommunal riots. The British now found themselves standing between the violent men of both communities, although Grivas accused them of being in league with the Turks.

This led to EOKA attacks on British soldiers, and in July the situation seemed to have reverted to what it had been two years before. In August the Turkish Prime Minister, Menderes, decided to change his tune and to support the British plan, and Macmillan announced that he would go ahead with it. Makarios feared that he would be left out, and in September announced that he abandoned the demand for *enosis* and would accept an independent re-public, a switch of policy which had the support of the Greek Government, but which led to a breach with Grivas that was never healed. His proposals were almost immediately rejected by Britain, and a fresh outbreak of violence, including the cold-blooded killing of two British soldiers' wives in Famagusta, hit the island. It continued until February 1959 when, at a conference in London, agreement was reached between the British, Greek and Turkish Governments, reluctantly accepted by Makarios, on the proposals for an independent republic, excluding two British Sovereign Base Areas at Dhekelia and Episkopi, which in the event were to come into effect in 1960. Makarios considered that, if he had not accepted them, Turkey would have forced partition on the island, as she was eventually to do fifteen years later, having never at heart accepted the integration of the two communities and fearing the presence of a hostile island so close to her southern coast. Grivas was furious, but had no alternative but to accept Makarios's decision. The Archbishop returned to Cyprus on 1 March 1959, received by wildly enthusiastic crowds. On 9 March he and Grivas met and on 13 March EOKA handed in a sufficient number of arms to satisfy the authorities. On the following day Grivas, whose whereabouts had become known to the British authorities some weeks before, was flown by the Greek Air Force to Athens, where he was immediately granted the rank of General. The EOKA campaign was at an end, but the troubles of Cyprus were not.

Chapter Five

ADEN

Britain's departure from her military base in the Suez Canal zone and the subsequent Suez affair had its repercussions on the far side of the canal as it had, in the case of Cyprus, on the near side. She was greatly concerned with the threat to her oil and other interests in the Middle East, not only directly from Russia and indirectly from communism, as she had been for some time, but also from Arab nationalism, fomented and encouraged by Nasser, now seeking revenge for the events of 1956. She was at pains to bolster the position of Arab rulers, great and small, with whom she had treaty relationships, and the ability to support them and her own interests with military force was regarded as an essential element in this policy. The Sovereign Base Areas of Cyprus were designed to serve this end north and west of Suez. Beyond it, the choice fell on Kenya as the main base for troops and stores, with Aden as a forward staging post to support intervention in the Persian Gulf. Soon after the army had been withdrawn from operations in Kenya in 1956, work started on the construction of a cantonment and base for an infantry brigade near Nairobi. The need to provide for military intervention in the Gulf was reinforced by the events of 1958, when the revolution in Iraq came as a severe setback to British policy, although the subsequent intervention by the United States in the Lebanon and Britain in Jordan appeared to justify that policy, as did the rapid deployment of a sizeable force to Kuwait in 1961, when it was threatened by Iraq. By then, however, it was becoming apparent that Kenya was not a suitable choice for a base. It had been selected on the assumption that it would remain a colony for about a decade after the end of the emergency, or that, if it became independent earlier, the base could be maintained under some arrangement similar to that arrived at in Malaya or Cyprus. By 1962 it was becoming clear that neither of these assumptions was valid, and it was decided to transfer the brigade and other facilities to Aden, which already contained an important RAF base and the newly established headquarters of the Joint Service Commander-in-Chief Middle East. A new cantonment was to be built west of the bay near the BP refinery at Little Aden to replace that just being completed in Kenya, to be ready to receive the brigade in 1964. It was an inauspicious time at which to put one's money into those barren rocks and to state, as the 1962 Defence White Paper did, that British forces would be stationed there 'permanently'.

Britain had established herself in that desolate spot, described by Kipling as 'like a barrick stove that's not been lit for years', in 1839, when Captain Haines of the Indian Navy (who died in a debtor's prison in Bombay) was sent by the Government of Bombay to acquire it from the Sultan of Lahej in retaliation for the maltreatment of the crew and passengers of a ship that had been wrecked there. It was subsequently used as a coaling station and until 1937 was administered by the Government of India, the mixed population of immigrants from the surrounding area and elsewhere in the Indian Ocean growing up round the port's activities and living in the town built inside the crater of the extinct volcano which had created the natural harbour. The hinterland was rugged in the extreme and populated by wild and primitive Arab tribes, whose main activity was fighting one another and extracting money from or plundering caravans which passed through their area on their way to the Yemen. Farther to the east along the coast, the Hadramaut, of which Mukalla was the centre, had in the past seen prosperous and civilized days with strong links with Sumatra. No attempt was made either by the Indian Government or, after 1937 when responsibility was transferred to the Colonial Office, by the British to administer or develop this area. Following a policy similar to that applied to the north-west Frontier of India, treaties were made with the tribal leaders, sweetened by periodic gifts of arms, and they were left to their own devices. Only if they transgressed the rules by fighting each other too much, plundering travellers or attacking His Britannic Majesty's representatives was punitive action taken against them. This was applied by the RAF, who, after due warning, would bomb their houses and fields, while the inhabitants and their flocks retired to the safety of nearby caves until it was all over. For the immediate security of airstrips and posts up-country, a force was raised in 1928 by the RAF, mainly from the Aulaqi tribe to the east of Aden, known as the Aden Protectorate Levies. Two other forces were raised by the Colonial Office, one of 500 armed police, known as Government Guards, recruited locally in each state of the Western Aden Protectorate, the hinterland west of Aden and up to 250 miles east of it, and the Hadrami Bedouin Legion in the Eastern Protectorate, which stretched another 400 miles along the coast to the border with Muscat. The ruler of each state within these protectorates raised his own Tribal Guard.

· Aden itself was run as a Crown Colony and had a small locally raised force to police the population of 220,000 within its small area of thirty square miles. The only threat to Aden and the British presence there, apart from dissension between the tribes of the Western Protectorate, lay in the claim of the Yemen to the area of the Western Protectorate and to Aden. This claim had been maintained since the Yemen became independent of the Ottoman Empire in

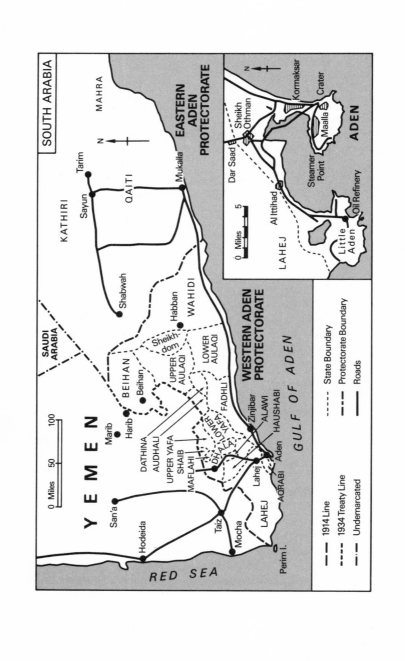

1919, and, although supposed to have been settled by the Treaty of Sana'a in 1934, continued to be a matter of dissension, the Yemen objecting to any attempt by Britain to extend her influence into the hinterland.

Aden and its associated protectorates did not escape the general ferment in the Arab world in the 1950s, and Britain sought, as she did elsewhere, some solution which would produce a viable state that could stand on its own feet in close association with herself. In outlook, composition and interest Aden colony and the Sheikhs and Sultans of the protectorates had little in common, other than a sensitivity to the accusation that association with Britain ran counter to the current tide of Arab nationalism. While the trade union movement in Aden, led by Abdullah al Asnag, sympathized with Nasser's blend of socialism and Arab nationalism, and aimed at throwing off the colonial yoke in favour of independence, the Sheikhs and Sultans wanted to see which way the wind would blow. They had no wish to be subordinated to the townsmen of Aden. If they could be certain that Britain would stay and uphold her position against subversive threats from within and without, they would maintain their association, but saw no great need to combine together to do so. If, however, Britain's presence and power were not to be maintained, it would be prudent for them to align themselves more closely with their neighbours to the north, the Yemen or Saudi Arabia. Britain's concept, first adumbrated in 1954, was to form a federation of as many as possible of the states of the two protectorates and, having done so, to link it with Aden itself. The various rulers were hesitant, but by 1960 ten of the seventeen states of the Western Protectorate had joined and formed the Federation of Amirates of the South, the Government consisting of the rulers, served by officials working from a new capital built at Al Ittihad, a small Arab village half-way between Aden and Little Aden on the border between the colony and the Western Protectorate. All but one of the rulers of the Western Protectorate finally joined, but the three of the Eastern Protectorate never did. To this Federation were transferred the Aden Protectorate Levies, renamed the Federal Regular Army (FRA), then consisting of four battalions with British officers, the plan being to hand over to Arab officers as soon as possible. By 1965 all four battalions were commanded by them. The Government Guards and Tribal Guards were also transferred to the Federation and together formed the Federal National Guard.

The first blow to this somewhat flimsy structure came in 1962 when, after the death in September of Imam Ahmed, ruler of the Yemen, his son Badr was overthrown by Colonel Sallal in a republican revolution supported by Egypt. Abdullah al Asnag, and his Peoples' Socialist Party in Aden, welcomed this and demanded the union of Aden with the Yemen, echoed by radio propaganda from the latter calling on the people of Aden and the protectorates to rebel against Britain and her puppet, the Federal Government. The rulers immediately turned to Britain to suppress both the internal and the external threat and were disappointed that the only response was to appoint a British Colonial Police officer as Director of Security in Aden and Hassan Bayoomi, a distinguished and courageous Arab member of the Aden Government, as Ministerial Adviser on security to the High Commissioner to the Federation, Sir Kennedy Trevaskis. However in November the British Parliament supported the government in resolving not to recognize the new regime in the Yemen, to continue to support the Federation and to merge Aden colony with it, which it proceeded to do in January 1963. During 1963 relations deteriorated with the Yemen, where Egyptian troops had been deployed to support Sallal against the ousted Royalists, who were helped by Saudi Arabia. Egyptian organized propaganda was stepped up from the radio stations of Sana'a and Taiz, a new subversive organization being based at the latter, known as the National Liberation Front. On 14 October it announced that it was launching a full revolutionary struggle which would include the use of violence. On 10 December a grenade was thrown at the High Commissioner, a member of his staff and several Ministers of the Federal Government when they were about to board an aircraft at Aden to fly to London for a constitutional conference. Fifty-three people, including Sir Kennedy, his aide-de-camp and some of the Ministers were wounded, an Indian woman killed and Trevaskis's assistant, George Henderson, died of his wounds a few days later. The Federal Government declared a state of emergency throughout the Federation, including Aden State (as it was now called), closed the frontier with the Yemen, arrested 57 members of the Peoples' Socialist Party and deported 280 Yemeni subjects as 'undesirables'.

Subversion was not confined to Aden itself. Throughout 1963 trouble had been brewing in the hinterland adjoining the Yemen border and especially on the ancient caravan route leading into the Yemen through Dhala, eighty miles north of Aden. In the area astride this route, known as the Radfan, the Quteibi tribe had levied tribute or protection money from the passing traffic, and tended to shoot those who would not pay it. Not only had the traffic dried up, but in 1961 they had wounded a British officer in this way, as a result of which they were sternly ordered to desist and punitive action was taken. The final insult was the replacement of their protection money racket by official Federal Government customs and dues. They were therefore a ready source of subversion by the Yemenis, who supplied them with arms and ammunition and trained them in their use, requiring them only in return to stir up as much trouble as possible, which they proceeded to do. The Federal Rulers demanded action. 'Air control' would not suffice and was by now disapproved of as internationally embarrassing. A 'hearts and minds' programme of development would not produce results quickly and in any case could not be embarked upon without military protection. The newly appointed Commander-in-Chief, General Sir Charles Harington, therefore decided to despatch a punitive expedition, using three of the four battalions of the Federal

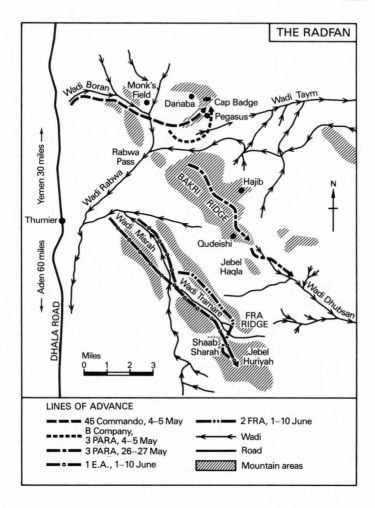

THE RADFAN

Wadi Boran
Monk's Field
Danaba
Cap Badge
Pegasus
Wadi Taym
Rabwa Pass
Wadi Rabwa
BAKRI RIDGE
Hajib
Thumier
Wadi Misrah
Qudeishi
Jebel Haqla
Wadi Tanate
Wadi Dhubsan
FRA RIDGE
Shaab Sharah
Jebel Huriyah

Yemen 30 miles
Aden 60 miles
DHALA ROAD

N

Miles
0   1   2   3

LINES OF ADVANCE

━ ━ ━ 45 Commando, 4–5 May
▪▪▪▪▪▪ B Company, 3 PARA, 4–5 May
━ ▪ ━ 3 PARA, 26–27 May
━ o ━ 1 E.A., 1–10 June
━ ▪▪ ━ 2 FRA, 1–10 June
← ← Wadi
━━━ Road
▨▨▨ Mountain areas

Army, supported by a troop of British tanks, a battery of light artillery and a troop of engineers. The RAF would use its Hunters in close support and misuse its Shackleton Maritime Patrol aircraft as bombers, the Royal Navy supplementing with six Wessex helicopters the small RAF force of twin-rotor Belvederes. There had been opposition to this decision from several quarters. Brigadier Lunt, commander of the FRA, feared it would disrupt his programme of Arabization and training, and that, once launched, it would turn into a permanent commitment, a view shared by political advisers. If it were to be followed by a 'hearts and minds' development campaign to try and prevent a recurrence, neither the plan nor the resources for such a campaign existed, and it would require a military presence to get it going. However something had to be done to demonstrate to friend and foe alike that Britain meant business, and Operation *Nutcracker*, hastily organized on a shoe-string, was launched on 4 January 1964 with the aim of occupying high ground overlooking the Wadis Rabwa and Taym, a few miles east of Thumier on the Dhala road, where there was a convenient air-strip capable of taking the cumbrous but manoeuvrable Beverley transport aircraft. Once established on the high ground, a road was to be constructed along the Wadi Rabwa. The operation was successfully completed by the end of the month, and the FRA remained there until March. By then the strain on them was beginning to tell, affecting their ability to carry out effectively their normal task of patrolling the frontier. They were therefore withdrawn, having suffered five killed and twelve wounded.

No sooner had they left than the Quteibi armed men reoccupied their old positions and destroyed the new road. Egyptian propaganda hailed the withdrawal as a defeat and the renewal of trouble was encouraged by flights of Yemeni aircraft over the border, including, on 13 March, an attack on a village in the state of Beihan. Its ruler, a tough, independently-minded member of the Federal Government, demanded action, if he were to be expected to believe in British assurances of support. On 19 March, therefore, the Federal Government invoked their treaty and asked officially for British retaliation. A protest to the Yemen having only resulted in a further raid, the RAF retaliated on 28 March against the Yemeni fort at Harib, which immediately became the subject of protests of brutal aggression even in the British press and led to a debate in the UN Security Council on 9 April. Attacks on the Dhala road increased and it was decided that further military action would have to be taken, but that it was beyond the capability of the FRA alone and would have to be undertaken primarily by British troops. As before, doubts were expressed as to the effectiveness of such an operation and about its implications for the future, but, once again, something had to be done if the federal rulers were to be persuaded to stay on the British side. Cobbling together a brigade headquarters from the resources of Aden garrison under Brigadier Hargroves, the Commander of Middle East Land Forces, Major-General Cubbon, gave him a Royal Marine Commando with a company of the 3rd Parachute Battalion, two battalions of the FRA, the same guns and sappers as before, a squadron of armoured cars instead of a troop of tanks and the same air support, but without the invaluable naval Wessex helicopters which were not available. A further British infantry battalion, 1st East Anglian, would become available a few days after the operation had started. The political aim of *Radforce*, as it was called, was 'to bring sufficient pressure to bear on the Radfan tribes to prevent the tribal revolt from spreading, to reassert our authority, and to stop attacks on the Dhala Road' by pursuing the military aim of 'ending the operations of dissidents in the defined area', a vague enough objective. The method proposed was a rather more ambitious dose of the same medicine as before, extending the heights to be seized to an important feature a few miles north-east of the Rabwa Pass. This was to include a parachute drop by night to follow a night advance by the Royal Marines up the Wadi Boran to reach the high ground before daylight. Logistic support, particularly water supply, of the troops on the way to and when established on the heights was a major problem. The shortage of helicopters was sorely felt.

The first move in the operation was the flight at last light on 29 April, in three army Scout helicopters, of an SAS troop to a point from which they would make a night move to mark the dropping zone for the parachute company. Unfortunately their lying-up position was discovered and they were hotly engaged throughout 30 April by some fifty tribesmen. Only the brilliant efforts of the RAF Hunters saved them; but they were unable to mark the dropping zone and a second troop, attempting to fly there directly, was shot up and had to return, the original troop commander, Captain Edwards, and his radio operator having been killed. The parachute drop was therefore cancelled. The marines however had been successful and were on their objective overlooking the Danaba basin by dawn on 1 May. The next problem was how to capture the hill on the far side, known as Cap Badge, which had been the objective of the parachute drop. Hargroves decided that 45 Commando, with the parachute company, should move on foot to attack this during the night 4/5 May, when they had been relieved by 1st East Anglian. In spite of delays, they were successful and were established on top of the feature by dawn, but the parachute company had run into trouble and, after a march lasting eleven hours, were still in low ground east of their objective when day broke. Again RAF Hunters came to the rescue and the reserve company of the marines was flown by helicopter to help. After ten hours' fighting, in which two of their men were killed and six wounded, the tribesmen withdrew and the weary company struggled up the steep hillside to reach its objective.

In the following week *Radforce* patrolled the area overlooked by its positions on the heights, on 11 May handing over to a regular brigade headquarters, the 39th, flown out from Northern Ireland, commanded by Brigadier Blacker. For the next two weeks steps were taken to ease the logistic supply problem, and the demands on helicopters for it, by developing tracks for motor transport and strips for light aircraft, reducing the number of troops in the forward positions and making use of camels, donkeys and cable lifts. Operations were to be restricted to air action until the force was ready to extend the area under its control by the occupation of two important ridges running south-east from the Wadi Rabwa, the eastern one called Bakri Ridge, terminating in Jebel Haqla, the other astride the Wadi Misrah to Jebal Huriyah. By the end of the month the force available to Blacker would amount to seven battalions, three British infantry, one parachute, one Marine Commando and two FRA, the artillery having been supplemented by a section of medium guns. By that time also the Wessex helicopters of HMS *Centaur* would be available.

The aim was again vague and was expressed as:

(a)   to demonstrate to the dissidents the ability of British troops to penetrate into their territory, and to invade even those areas of particular prestige value to the tribes;

(b)   to provoke the dissidents to fight and so to suffer casualties which would lower their morale.

The main operation was preceded by an armoured 'show of force' up the Wadi Misrah on 19 May. This was of doubtful value. There were a number of delays, the terrain proving rougher than expected, heavy rain produced a flash flood and the force was withdrawn as it got dark, no doubt interpreted by the enemy as an admission of failure. Three days before this a patrol of the 3rd Parachute Battalion found that the Bakri Ridge was unoccupied and Blacker ordered them to seize it, although he had not planned to start the main operation for at least another five days. They met no opposition until they reached the southern end of the ridge after an advance of some six miles, on 23 May. After a full-scale attack with air and artillery support, they drove the enemy out of what had clearly been one of their principal bases, at Qudeishi. This success was followed by an advance beyond the ridge down into the Wadi Dhubsan, considered to be an area of 'particular prestige value' and likely to be strongly defended. It involved occupying Jebel Haqla which overlooked it. By this time rain and low cloud were restricting flying both by helicopters and fixed-wing aircraft. The advance began on the night of 25 May and led to a fierce battle in the wadi on 26 May. Fortunately the full scale of air and artillery support could be developed and by the end of the day the battalion had reached the far end, having lost one man killed and seven wounded, believing that they had killed six of the enemy. They had nearly lost their commanding officer, Farrar-Hockley, when his helicopter overshot the front line, was shot up and forced to land, fortunately just behind his forward troops.

The final objective of Blacker's plan was the Jebel Huriyah, 5,500 feet above sea level. The advance towards this on both sides of the Wadi Misrah, a few miles west of where 3rd Parachute Battalion had been operating, was led by 1st East Anglian, supported by 2nd Battalion of the FRA and the armoured cars of 4th Royal Tanks. It began on 30 May and met little or no opposition until 7 June, as 2nd Battalion FRA neared Jebel Huriyah itself, when a body of some fifty tribesmen fired on them from across the valley. The latter were subjected to every form of fire, from air, artillery and infantry, and, when 2nd FRA attacked the position at first light next day, they found it deserted. 1st East Anglian were taking no chances and laid on a full-scale attack on Jebel Huriyah on the night of 10/11 June, meeting no opposition. Thereafter, Brigadier Blair, who had succeeded Blacker, settled down to occupying the area, a task which became the responsibility of 24th Brigade when it moved to Little Aden from Kenya towards the end of the year. The Radfan was not again to be the scene of major operations, although it remained a commitment for another two and a half years.

Meanwhile Aden itself had remained comparatively quiet, but it was to prove the lull before the storm. One factor which roused the storm was the announcement by the British Government, of which Alec Douglas Home was Prime Minister, in July 1964 that Britain intended to maintain her military base at Aden, but would grant independence to South Arabia not later than 1968. The second was the result of the General Election in October, which returned a Labour government. The latter was expected to be more sympathetic to those opposed both to the retention of a British military base and to the concept of a federation in which the rulers of the Protectorate would predominate, the federation being unlikely to survive without the British military presence. This expectation was to prove correct. The rival contenders for power could now see that they had a maximum of four years in which to stake their claims and establish their positions. There were three rival contenders for power in opposition to the Federal Government and the British who supported it. First in the field had been the South Arabian League (SAL), founded in 1951 by Mahomed al Jifri, member of an influential family in the state of Lahej, which lay west of Aden, bordering the Yemen south of Taiz. They aimed at an independent South Arabia, separate from the Yemen. Jifri himself was exiled in 1956 and lived in Cairo. Their influence declined with the rise of Abdullah al Asnag's Peoples' Socialist Party (PSP), based on the trade union movement in Aden, which aimed at the incorporation of Aden and the Western Protectorate into the Yemen. Its support came almost wholly from those who lived in Aden, both original inhabitants and immigrant workers, a large proportion of whom came from the Yemen. These two organizations formed an uneasy alliance in February 1965 under the title of the Organization for the Liberation of the Occupied South (OLOS). In principle the two movements sought to achieve their aims by political action and were considered respectable political parties by sympathizers both in Britain and elsewhere, who viewed the Federation as one more example of Britain's attempts to protect her own interests by bolstering up a puppet government of reactionary hereditary rulers. The third movement, the National Liberation Front (NLF), made no bones about being prepared to use violence to gain its ends, the destruction of the Federation, the removal of the British and the establishment of a Marxist-orientated state with close links both with the Yemen and with Egypt. It was based in the Yemen and drew its support in Aden and the Western Protectorate primarily from immigrants and from those in the Protectorate who were not full members of the local tribes. Its leader was Qahtan Asshabi. When, in January 1966, OLOS and NLF unexpectedly joined forces to form the Front for the Liberation of Occupied South Yemen (FLOSY), SAL broke off, as they were opposed to Egyptian domination, being themselves linked to Saudi Arabia. They ceased to have any influence thereafter in Aden or the Western Protectorate, concentrating their activity on the Eastern Protectorate. The alliance did not in practice last long and in December 1966 NLF broke away from FLOSY and began to fight for power against it, at the same time weakening its links with Egypt, which transferred its support to the ex-PSP element of FLOSY and helped form its own militant off-shoot, PORF (The Peoples' Organization of Revolutionary Forces).

The NLF's terrorist campaign in Aden opened up at the time of the visit of the new Labour Colonial Secretary, Anthony Greenwood, in November 1964. Over a period of six weeks there were eleven incidents in which two British servicemen were killed and thirty-four wounded. Action to counter the campaign was greatly complicated by the plethora of organizations with divided responsibilities and loyalties. In the civilian field the High Commissioner, Sir Kennedy Trevaskis, had since 1963 combined the posts of a sort of Governor-General of the Federation and Governor of Aden, but each had its own government institutions and police forces with a degree of self-government, until that in Aden was suspended in September 1965, when its Chief Minister, Abdul Mackawee, who had come to power in May of that year and had actively supported the PSP, was dismissed. On the military side, the organization was even more complex. At the apex was the Commander-in-Chief Middle East, for almost all the time General Sir Charles Harington. He was responsible to the Chiefs of Staff in London for all British military activities in the Middle East, east of Suez, and in East Africa, exercising this responsibility through a Rear-Admiral, a Major-General and an Air Vice-Marshal, all of whom had their headquarters alongside his in Aden. In Aden colony itself a brigadier was responsible for military operations, while the commander of the 24th Infantry Brigade in Little Aden concerned himself with British military activities in the Western Protectorate in co-operation with the commander of the FRA, another British brigadier who, for reasons of availability of accommodation, had his headquarters and some of his troops inside Aden colony. As terrorism was stepped up in 1965, this fragmentation of responsibility, with the most senior officers living at the centre of the troubles but not theoretically being directly responsible for action to counter it, added to the difficulties basically caused by the British Government's hesitation in acceding to the demands of the federal rulers that subversive activity in Aden and across the border from the Yemen should be firmly and decisively suppressed.

Trevaskis left in January 1965 and the unfortunate man who had to struggle with the problem as High Commissioner was Sir Richard Turnbull, who, as the last Governor of Tanganyika, had brought that country to independence in amicable co-operation with Julius Nyerere. One of his first tasks was to appoint Abdul Mackawee, a member of the PSP, as Chief Minister of Aden, as he was bound to do constitutionally, Mackawee having the support of the majority of the members of the Legislative Council. He proceeded to cause as much trouble as he could and to obstruct measures designed to improve security in the colony, which was deteriorating. Strikes, riots and demonstrations became weekly, if not daily, occurrences, grenades were thrown into British service and government buildings and facilities, and a cold-blooded murder campaign instituted against the Police Special Branch. In June Turnbull declared a state of emergency, widening his powers of detention and proscribing the NLF, all these measures being opposed by Mackawee.

In pursuance of its aim to incorporate Aden into the Federation, the British Government proposed to despatch a two-man constitutional commission, in the persons of Sir Ralph Hone and Sir Gawain Bell, to visit Aden and the Federation in July, before holding a constitutional conference in London in August. Mackawee refused them permission to land in Aden. Their visit was accordingly postponed and this was seen by the federal rulers as weakness on Britain's part and a sop to Mackawee, whose obstructive attitude made certain that the London Conference proved fruitless. It was followed by two serious incidents, the murder on 29 August of a British Police Superintendent in the Aden Crater, and ten days later that of the respected British Speaker of the Aden Legislative Council, Sir Arthur Charles. Further murders and attempted murders of police followed, and on 17 September a grenade was thrown at a party of 73 British schoolchildren at the airport, about to fly back to Britain after the holidays, injuring five of them. It was after this, and a good deal of argument with London, that Turnbull dismissed Mackawee, suspended the Aden Government and imposed direct rule by himself, greatly simplifying and strengthening the security organization. This act led to strikes and riots; and in October Turnbull took the unprecedented step of calling in the Federal Regular Army and Guard to help the British Army deal with demonstrations in the crater which defied the curfew he had imposed. In the same month he arrested a number of PSP leaders and banned two of their newspapers. By the end of the year there had been 286 terrorist incidents in Aden, causing 237 casualties.* Although the troubles of Aden had dominated 1965, minor operations up-country continued, primarily concerned with keeping open the Dhala road against attempts of infiltrators from over the Yemen border and their sympathizers to stop or interfere with its use. The casualty list arising from these came to 350, 81 killed and 269 wounded, 10 and 61 respectively being from the British force, most of them from 24th Brigade.

---

* Paget, *Last Post*, p. 135. Details were:

	Killed	Wounded	Total
British Security Forces	6	78	84
Local Security Forces	13	8	21
British civilians	2	31	33
Local nationals	14	85	99
Total	35	202	237

1966 was in fact to see the end of all hopes of a peaceful and stable solution to the problems of South Arabia with the announcement by the British Government in February 1966 that they no longer proposed to maintain defence facilities in South Arabia after granting independence in 1968. The best interpretation that could be placed on this body-blow to the Federation was that it was delivered in the belief that it was the continuation of British military presence which provoked the hostility of Egypt, the Yemen, like-minded Arab nationalists and their anti-colonial supporters in the United Nations: the worst, that it was a gesture of despair and abdication similar to those which had preceded British departure from India and Palestine. Whatever the motive, the result was to undermine the Federation and open the door to a struggle for power which would increase in intensity as the date of withdrawal approached. In 1966 therefore there was an intensification of terrorist activity, with the nationalist organizations acting together with the support of the Yemen and of Egypt, who by now had some 60,000 troops in that country. Terrorist incidents organized by the NLF, strikes and riots became ever more frequent. As the Aden Police began to think about what the future held for them, they became decreasingly willing to take action or give information, and the British Army assumed greater responsibility for internal security, Major-General Willoughby, Commander of Middle East Land Forces, being appointed as Security Commander. In this situation intelligence began to dry up, in spite of the efforts of John Prendergast, who had successfully headed the intelligence machine both in Kenya and in Cyprus. The security forces had to rely for their information largely on what they could extract from terrorists whom they had arrested or captured. The methods they employed to do this led to protests from Amnesty International, a visit by a Turkish doctor representing them, and subsequently an inquiry ordered by the British Government. This was carried out by Mr Roderic Bowen QC, who, in December, reported that 'speaking generally, they [military personnel and police] discharge their duties with great restraint'. The use of similar methods in Northern Ireland in 1971 was to cause rather more fuss.

By the end of the year the annual list of incidents had risen to 480, causing 573 casualties.* Up-country operations similar to those of the previous year had continued, more emphasis being devoted to air attack in support of both the British and the federal armies, but also as a punitive measure to be

---

* Paget, p. 264. Details were:

	Killed	Wounded	Total
British Security Forces	5	218	223
Local Security Forces	2	8	10
British civilians	6	19	25
Local nationals	32	283	315
Total	45	528	573

employed on its own. Troubles extended to the Eastern Protectorate also, and in October the Irish Guards were hastily deployed for a short operation in the Hadramaut. British casualties for the year in the Protectorate totalled 111.

1967 sounded the death-knell of British plans for a solution based on a merger between Aden and the Federation in an independent South Arabia, accompanied by a crescendo of political activity in the United Nations and of military and anti-military activity in the streets of Aden. In the background of this cacophony could be heard a dirge in diminuendo, as hopes died and fears deepened among the federal rulers and their supporters, and a clash of percussion instruments in June when the Six-Day War between Israel and her Arab neighbours broke out. The year opened with continued riots in Aden, under cover of which terrorists shot at British troops deployed to deal with them. By now the Aden Police restricted their activity to normal police work and the British Army had taken over the primary responsibility for dealing with internal security in the colony. NLF and FLOSY had split apart at the end of 1966 and it was not long before they began to fight each other at the same time as both aimed their blows at the British and both organizations worked by threats and by persuasion to win over the various forces of the Federation, who were being hurriedly merged, reorganized and developed in the faint hope that they would be able to assure the security of the Federation when Britain abandoned it at a date not yet firmly fixed, but 'not later than 1968'. The first major challenge came on Federation Day, 11 February, eighth anniversary of its foundation. Major demonstrations had been planned by NLF and FLOSY, but with four British battalions deployed in advance into the small area of Aden itself, trouble was nipped in the bud, the High Commissioner narrowly escaping death or injury when a mine was discovered on the helicopter pad at Al Ittihad before he was due to land there for the anniversary celebrations. Trouble continued for four days, while a curfew was imposed, in the course of which sixty-six attacks were made on the British troops. A fortnight later a bomb exploded in Mackawee's house, killing three of his sons and three other Arabs. The NLF denied responsibility and blame was laid at the door of SAL, leading to attacks on their followers. In the next few months the centre of activity tended to move to two villages on the edge of the colony, Sheikh Othman and Al Mansoura, through which passed the roads leading into the colony from the Protectorate. The nationalist movements waged a battle to impose their control over these areas, directed as much against each other as against both the British and the Federal authorities.

This struggle had taken place against the background of increased political activity from outside. In March George Thomson, then a Minister in the Foreign Office, had proposed to the Federal Government that the date for independence should be in November 1967 and that, as a deterrent to an attack on them from the Yemen, a naval carrier force would remain off-shore to provide air support for six months thereafter. Being realists, the rulers rejected the offer and demanded not only that independence should not be granted before the spring of 1968, but that it should be accompanied by a defence agreement under which British troops would remain in Aden indefinitely to support them. In this they had the backing of the Conservative opposition in Britain. Thomson was followed by another government emissary in April, Lord Shackleton, who conceded that independence could be postponed until January 1968, but could make no concession over the continued stationing of troops. The rulers were non-committal in their reply. April also saw the visit of a three-man United Nations mission, instructed by a General Assembly resolution of February 'to recommend practical steps for implementing previous UN resolutions on South Arabia'. The mission, a Venezuelan, an Afghan and a citizen of Mali, arrived on 2 April, to be greeted not only by torrential rain but by a major attempt by NLF and FLOSY to demonstrate that they and only they had the right to be recognized as the representatives of the people and *de facto* wielders of power. In spite of a major deployment of troops, there was a large number of incidents, a total strike and a fierce battle at Sheikh Othman. The mission refused to recognize or visit the Federal Government, met with a hostile reception from the NLF and FLOSY inmates of the Al Mansoura detention centre, which they insisted on visiting, and then retired to sulk in their hotel. They demanded the right to make a broadcast, but when the Federal Government, who owned the broadcasting facilities, demanded to see the text and saw that it did not accord them recognition, it refused permission. On 7 April they left in a huff, and the situation calmed down. During their visit there had been 280 incidents in which 18 British servicemen had been wounded and 8 terrorists killed.

Lord Shackleton's visit, which followed that of the UN mission, was the precursor of a change in the post of High Commissioner. With scant courtesy Sir Richard Turnbull was abruptly replaced on 20 May by Sir Humphrey Trevelyan, who had been British Ambassador in Egypt at the time of Suez and made no secret subsequently of his disapproval of that adventure, and then Ambassador in Iraq at the time of the 1958 revolution there. George Brown, the Foreign Secretary, had decided that a policy of opposing Egyptian influence in the Middle East was a mistake and had placed his faith on mending his fences with Nasser, with whom he felt he could establish good relations. Trevelyan's appointment was intended as a means of implementing this policy, Turnbull having been associated with repression of Egypt's protégés. His mandate was to attempt to establish relations with the nationalist movements and bring together a caretaker government, including both them and the federal rulers, to which power could be transferred with the benevolent approval of Egypt, the Yemen and other Arab countries. Two events were very soon to shatter any hopes of this, slender as they were in any case; the Arab–Israeli Six-Day War and the mutinies in the federal forces. The two were not unconnected.

In the Six-Day War from 3 to 9 June Egypt, and to a lesser extent her allies, Syria, Jordan and Iraq, suffered a humiliating defeat, one of the chief factors in which was the virtual elimination of her air force at the start. Nasser was reluctant to admit that this had been caused by the Israeli Air Force alone and concocted the accusation that both the United States and Britain had been involved. As evidence of this he cited the presence off Aden of a British aircraft-carrier, sent there from the Far East when the British Government was contemplating naval action to ensure free passage of Israeli ships through the Straits of Tiran to Eilat. The war had set back George Brown's hopes of a reconciliation with Egypt and had aroused anti-British feelings in much of the Arab world, including Aden, where rumours were rife that Britain was on the point of taking some drastic military action.

It was in this atmosphere that trouble broke out within the federal forces. It will be remembered that the origins of the Federal Regular Army and the Federal Guard had been different, the former tending to be dominated by the Aulaqi tribe. The recent merger of the two did not remove, indeed it accentuated, the rivalry between them. At the same time they could sense that the days of the Federation were numbered. They were as anxious to be on the winning side as the contestants for power were to win them over to their cause. Aden also had its Armed Police, a para-military body whose task of backing up the normal police in times of disorder had been for the present largely taken over by the British Army. They also were a target for subversion by the rival parties.

The spark that set off the worst disorder Aden was to see was the selection by the Federal Government of an Aulaqi, Colonel Nasser Bureiq, to succeed the British Brigadier Dye as the first Arabian commander of what was now called the South Arabian Army. He was clearly a political choice, not being very competent in the military field. His selection was resented by several senior officers, particularly those who had formerly been in the Federal Guard. On 16 June four senior non-Aulaqi colonels lobbied their brother officers in protest and complained directly to the Federal Minister of Defence. As a result they were suspended from duty and a rumour spread that they had been arrested and dismissed. Some young soldiers in a camp of the South Arabian Army on the edge of the airfield in Aden mutinied in sympathy, attacking the officers' mess and releasing prisoners from the guard room, letting off some shots as they did so and setting fire to some buildings. Order was soon restored by their Arab officers and NCOs, no British troops being involved. However the shots were heard in the neighbouring South Arabian Police Camp, whose inmates leaped to the conclusion that the British were firing on their comrades in the army. They then mutinied, seized weapons from their armoury and manned the camp perimeter to defend themselves against an assumed attack. At this juncture a British army truck, bringing soldiers back from range practice, drove along the road a hundred yards from the camp. It was fired on, eight

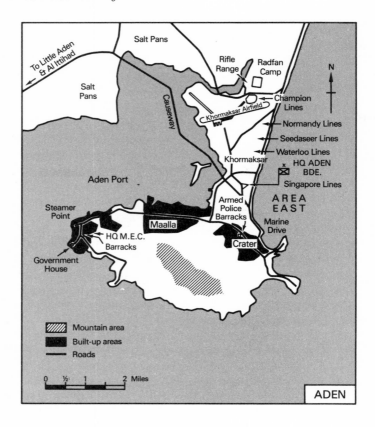

being killed and eight wounded, as were two vehicles which came along soon afterwards, in which two Adeni policemen and a British employee of the Public Works Department were killed. The mutineers then opened fire on the nearby Radfan camp, which housed a British battalion, killing one of its officers.

When the federal authorities heard what had happened, they immediately asked for British help in suppressing the mutiny. The 'stand-by' company of the King's Own Border Regiment, supported by a troop of armoured cars, was told to secure the guard room and main armoury of the South Arabian Police camp in Champion Lines, but not to fire on Arab forces unless it was absolutely necessary. Soon after they had left Radfan camp, they came under fire, one soldier being killed and eight wounded. In the face of sporadic rifle and machine-gun fire, they completed their task by 12.20 p.m., having hardly opened fire at all themselves. A further attempted mutiny by the South Arabian Police at Al Ittihad was quickly brought to a stop as a result of resolute action by the Federal Minister for Internal Security, Sultan Saleh of Audhali.

By then, however, the trouble had spread to the barracks of the Aden Armed Police in the crater area of Aden. A rumour spread that the British were firing on Arab soldiers and were on their way to attack them. Their commander was away and the 140 policemen present rushed to the armoury, seized weapons and manned the walls and roof of their barracks. The British battalion responsible for the crater was the Northumberland Fusiliers. They did so from positions on the edge, dominating the two roads that led into it, through the Main Pass and Marine Drive. They found a number of road-blocks in the main road that ran through the town and, as they removed them, they noticed that the Armed Police, whose barracks they passed, did not look friendly. The patrol commander, 2nd Lieutenant Davis, reported this by radio and was told by his company commander to leave the area. This he did by the Main Pass, which involved returning to his camp by a roundabout route in the course of which radio contact was lost. His company commander, Major Moncur, having heard no more from him, feared that he was in trouble and decided to go himself with a sergeant-major and two men of his own company and also Major Malcolm and two soldiers of the Argyll and Sutherland Highlanders, who were due to take over from the Fusiliers in a few days' time. As this party approached the Armed Police barracks, they came under a fusillade of fire, all but one man, Fusilier Storey, being killed. He was eventually rescued by a senior Arab police officer. When 2nd Lieutenant Davis got back to camp, he tried to contact Major Moncur by radio and, unable to do so, set off in two armoured cars to find him. When he saw the burning vehicles and the bodies beside them, he dismounted with three men and sent the armoured cars back to get help. He and his party were never seen again. A further casualty that day was a helicopter, taking an observation party to a post on the rim of the crater. It was shot at, the pilot wounded and the aircraft set on fire. However the pilot and his two passengers, although all hurt, were safely rescued, one of them, Fusilier Duffy, earning the Distinguished Conduct Medal for his gallantry. Three attempts were made during the rest of the day to reach the bodies near the Armed Police barracks, but all were abandoned in the face of heavy fire from small arms and anti-tank weapons.

It was not clear to Trevelyan and Admiral Le Fanu, who had succeeded General Harington, until quite late in the evening what the situation was either in general or in the crater itself. They were faced by conflicting demands. Maintenance of their own authority and of the morale of the British forces argued for a major operation to be promptly undertaken to restore order in the crater, rescue the bodies of the British soldiers and find out what had happened to Davis's party. However this would almost certainly lead to further fighting against the Aden Armed Police, which would not only cause damage and casualties to the inhabitants of the crowded crater, but almost certainly spread to the rest of Aden and the Protectorate, becoming a direct clash between the British Army and the federal forces, of whose loyalty there was at that moment considerable doubt. The lives of about a hundred British officials and others within the Protectorate would be at risk. It was therefore decided to wait for a week and hope that the pot would simmer down, a decision which was unpopular with the British Army and resented in particular by the Argylls, who were spoiling for a fight to avenge the death of Major Malcolm and the two soldiers with him. Their commanding officer, Colin Mitchell, had no hesitation in making his own views known. A fortnight later they re-entered the crater in a skilfully planned and executed operation in which hardly a shot was fired. By that time also, as part of a previously agreed plan to hand over operations in the Protectorate entirely to the federal forces, all British troops had been withdrawn from up-country into the cantonment of Little Aden or to Aden itself.

The British had re-entered the crater, but the federal authorities had been totally discredited. From July until the British finally left at the end of November, the Federation gradually collapsed, while attempts were made both by Britain and by the United Nations to form a broadly-based caretaker government. They failed, while NLF and FLOSY fought it out, competed for the support of the Federal Army and Police and pursued the active subversion of the tribal areas themselves. By the end of August it was clear that the NLF was winning, but the fight between them and FLOSY continued throughout September, in which month the British handed over Little Aden to the South Arabian Army and withdrew into the restricted perimeter of Aden colony. Early in October they pulled their horns in further, handing over Sheikh Othman and Al Mansoura and manning a shorter perimeter across the peninsula three miles north of Khormaksar airfield. The beginning of November saw fierce battles between the NLF and FLOSY in these villages, ending in victory for the NLF, after which the South Arabian Army transferred their allegiance to that movement, renaming themselves the Arab Armed Forces in Occupied South Yemen. Several of their senior officers and some Aulaqi soldiers, who were pro-FLOSY, left and returned to their tribal areas. After a burst of violence in Aden, designed to elicit a reply from the British Government to the NLF's demand to be recognized as the only representatives with whom the transfer of power should be negotiated, Britain agreed to open negotiations. She proposed to begin them on 16 November in Geneva and leave Aden six days later. This was too soon for the NLF, and 30 November was agreed on as the day of independence. Supported by a strong naval task group from the Far East, including an aircraft-carrier, a commando carrier with one Royal Marine commando deployed ashore, and an assault landing ship, the remaining garrison of 3,500 men was evacuated over the previous five days, the last troops leaving at 3 p.m. on 29 November.

In the eleven months of 1967 there had been over 3,000 incidents, in which the casualty list totalled 1,248, 369 of them among the British forces.* Since 1963, 57 British servicemen had been killed and 651 wounded, and there was nothing to show for it. It had been a sorry story, which left a bitter taste in the mouths not only of all the British armed forces who had served there in that time, but also, perhaps even more so, of the British officials, especially those who had devotedly served the cause of the Federation. There was no doubt that the rulers, their supporters and most of their tribesmen had been left in the lurch, as had also the more reasonable and law-abiding of the inhabitants of Aden. They had trusted in Britain's word, and they had been let down and abandoned to their fate at the hands of a motley crew who had come to power through violence and the support of external influences, in no way through any form of democratic process. Aden had been yet one more of those places which successive governments and chiefs of staff had regarded as of 'vital interest' to Britain and yet had been abandoned with hardly a fight. Little wonder that soldiers, airmen, marines and the few sailors involved asked themselves and each other what they had been fighting for; and officials, devoted as much to the Arab cause as they were to Britain's interests, whether their devotion had been worth the effort and the sacrifice.

The motives that lay behind the policy pursued were, as has already been noted, mixed. The Foreign Office contained Arabists of two schools, those who maintained that the preservation of Britain's interests lay in accommodation with the Arab Awakening; that a policy based on military intervention in support of traditional rulers was out-dated and bankrupt, and that the events in Iraq had proved it beyond doubt. In their eyes, the sooner Britain abandoned its military presence, the better: they believed that the whole attitude of the Arab world to Britain would then change and her oil interests would be more secure. The rival school believed that recent events in the Middle East, in Egypt and Iraq in particular, made it more important than ever that Britain should stand up and be counted with those who remained true supporters and to whom she was bound by treaty. The real centre of British interest lay in the oil-bearing small states on the shores of the Persian Gulf. They would be more influenced by such a stand than by association with movements led by the town-bred Arabs of the Awakening. Between these two diametrically opposed views lay the traditional Colonial Office desire for a gradual and stately progress through nominated and then elected councils to limited and finally

---

* Paget, *Last Post*, p. 264. Details were:

	Killed	Wounded	Total
British Security Forces	44	325	369
Local Security Forces	5	43	48
British civilians	9	31	40
Local civilians	240	551	791
Total	298	950	1,248

full self-government, based on the Westminster pattern, and the hard-headed realists who saw that, with India gone, the whole pattern of relationships east of Suez had fundamentally changed: this, combined with the need to pull in defence horns, for reasons both of finance and manpower, dictated the abandonment of a policy of military commitments in that vast area. Finally a Labour government, as anxious as its Conservative predecessor to economize on defence, was politically inclined to favour a movement which was anticolonial, opposed to hereditary feudal rule, professed socialism as its political creed and was likely to have the approval of the United Nations. In the end nobody gained, least of all the inhabitants of Aden and South Arabia.

Chapter Six

━━━━━━

BORNEO

At the same time as Britain had been conducting in South Arabia one of the least satisfactory of her colonial conflicts, she had been engaged in a very different conflict farther east, the outcome of which counter-balanced the depressing course of events in Aden. Starting with a revolt in Brunei in 1962, it turned into what was euphemistically known as 'confrontation' with Indonesia. Wars in those days tended to be classified as general, limited or cold. 'Confrontation' was a very limited form of limited war.

The revolt in Brunei and the subsequent confrontation with Indonesia had a common origin in opposition to the proposal to create the Federation of Malaysia, conceived jointly by Britain and Malaya. Duncan Sandys, who in 1962 added responsibility for the Colonies to his existing ones as Commonwealth Secretary, saw it as a way for Britain to divest herself of her direct responsibility for affairs in South East Asia, while retaining her essential strategic needs in association with a friendly independent nation, which would be anti-communist. Tunku Abdul Rahman, Prime Minister of the newly independent Malaya, saw the extension of Malaya to absorb not only Singapore but also Sabah, Brunei and Sarawak in North Borneo as a means of balancing the Chinese population (particularly desirable if Singapore was to be absorbed) with a larger number of people of generally Malay stock, as well as adding the considerable natural resources, notably oil, of North Borneo to those of Malaya. However there were those both within and outside the territories involved who were opposed to the proposal. Lee Kuan Yew in Singapore accepted it, realizing that at least it represented the first step towards getting rid of British colonial rule and hoping that it would open up greater opportunities for Singapore and its people. The Sultan of Brunei had no wish to share with his neighbours the lucrative income he derived from the Shell Company's exploitation of the oil on his coast or to accept any form of control from Kuala Lumpur. Under pressure from Britain he had recently introduced party politics into his diminutive state, which had been a British protectorate since 1888. The area of the country, shaped like a tooth with its roots in the Fifth Division of Sarawak, was only 2,226 square miles, much of which was jungle. Of the population of 85,000, half were Malay, a quarter Chinese and the rest native Dyaks. The Malays and Chinese lived near the coast. To the Sultan's dismay, the first elections, held in September 1962, had resulted in an overwhelming victory for the party opposed to his personal rule, the *Partai Ra'ayat*. Although not against the federation in principle, they were only prepared to accept it if the territories of Sabah and Sarawak were first united to form one state with Brunei, under whose suzerainty they had originally been. The then Sultan of Brunei had granted the territory of Sarawak to the famous James Brooke in 1841, basically because he was unable himself to control it and the pirates who operated from it. His exercise of suzerainty over Sabah had virtually disappeared at that time. Britain had assumed a very light form of responsibility for it in 1891, when the North Borneo Company had acquired the right to operate there, primarily to extract timber, as a result of a deal with the Sultan of Sulu through the agency of a shady Austrian Count. After the whole area had been liberated from Japanese occupation in 1945, both Sarawak and Sabah had been administered by Britain as normal colonies.

But the main opposition to the formation of Malaysia came from outside, from Sukarno in Indonesia. He had grandiose ideas of a major Malay federation, Maphilindo, which would incorporate Malaya, Singapore, Borneo and the Philippines into a greater Indonesia of which he would be the head. The formation of Malaysia as an independent pro-Western federation would frustrate his ambition. He therefore began to organize opposition to the concept and to give direct help to those who were prepared to fight against it. One of these was a 34-year-old citizen of Brunei of mixed Arab and Malay parentage, named Azahari. Under the Japanese occupation he had been sent to the occupied Dutch East Indies for his education and there joined the Indonesian revolutionaries who fought against the Dutch return. He had come back to Brunei in 1952 and, when the *Partai Ra'ayat* had started its campaign for a more liberal, democratic constitution, he had formed a secret army to support them, known as *Tentera Nasional Kalimantan Utara* (TNKU) – the North Kalimantan National Army, Kalimantan being the name given to the whole island of Borneo by Indonesia, to which the greater, southern part belonged.

The result of the election in Brunei and the promised support of Indonesia persuaded Azahari to make a bid to overthrow the Sultan and install himself as leader, employing TNKU to seize power by an armed revolt. Azahari appointed Yassin Affendi as the operational commander of TNKU's 150 fully-trained men, backed by some 4,000 supporters, the latter armed only with shotguns, pangas or spears. The only warning that anything of this nature was afoot came from the newly arrived British Resident at Limbang in the Fifth Division of Sarawak on the south-east border of Brunei. He was Richard Morris, an Australian, and almost as soon as he arrived, he received information that something was brewing. He passed this on to his superiors in Kuching, who reported it to

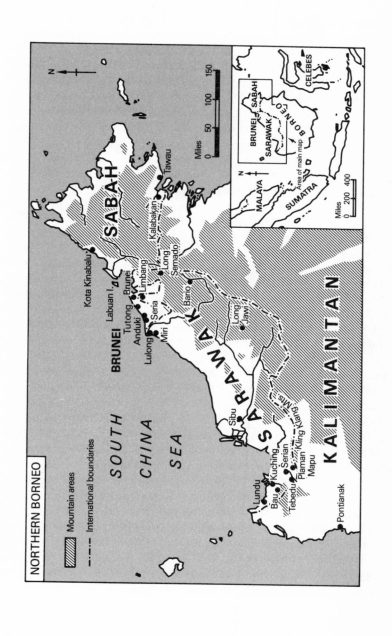

NORTHERN BORNEO

Mountain areas
International boundaries

SOUTH
CHINA
SEA

BRUNEI
Kota Kinabalu
Labuan I.
Tutong Brunei
Anduki Limbang
Seria
Lulong
Miri

SABAH
Kalabakan
Tawau
Long
Semado
Bario

SARAWAK
Long
Jawi

Sibu
Mts
Kling Klang
Serian Plaman
Bau Kuching Mapu
Tebedu
Lundu
Pontianak

KALIMANTAN

N

Miles
0   50   100   150

BRUNEI SABAH
BORNEO
SARAWAK

Area of main map

CELEBES

MALAYA

SUMATRA

N

Miles
0 200 400

Kuala Lumpur and to Singapore, headquarters of the Commander-in-Chief Far East, Admiral Sir David Luce. His headquarters had only begun to operate that month, the three service commanders in the Far East having previously acted together under the chairmanship of a civilian, the Commissioner-General for South East Asia, but with no joint operational headquarters. They had not taken kindly to the imposition above them of a joint service Commander-in-Chief and the relegation of their own titles to that of Force Commanders. Luce had been the naval Commander-in-Chief and was to hold the new post only until April 1963, when he was due to head the navy as First Sea Lord, handing over to Admiral Sir Varyl Begg.

In response to the warning, Sir Claude Fenner, Inspector-General of the Malayan Police, visited Sarawak, but could find no firm evidence of any serious uprising. Luce saw him on his way back and told his chief of staff to brush up the contingency plan for intervention in Brunei to support the police. This provided for flying two companies and a small headquarters to Brunei with appropriate support, one company for the town of Brunei itself, the other for the Shell oilfield area of Seria, eighty miles west along the coast. A last minute warning came to Morris in Limbang on 6 December, and next day to his colleague in the Fourth Division at Miri, on the far side of Brunei and the site of part of the Shell oilfield. He was John Fisher, who happened to be the brother-in-law of Major-General Walter Walker, Commander of the 17th Gurkha Division, based in Malaya and the principal operational formation in the Far East. Both Morris and Fisher were warned by local contacts that a rebellion was due to start on 8 December. The Sarawak Government was immediately told and they passed the information on to the Police Commissioners in Brunei and Sabah, who placed their police on alert.

The warning was correct, and at 2 a.m. TNKU in Brunei town attacked police stations, the Sultan's palace, the Prime Minister's and the British Resident's houses and the power station, the last of which they captured. They had also got hold of the acting High Commissioner, Mr Parks, but he was rescued by the Police Commissioner, Mr Outram, who acted throughout with great courage and presence of mind. His police managed to recapture the power station and generally re-establish control of the vital points in Brunei itself during the day. He was reinforced at midday by a platoon of the North Borneo Police field force, flown in from Jesselton by the RAF stationed on the nearby island of Labuan.

When the first news of the revolt reached Luce's headquarters in Singapore at 4 a.m., 1/2nd Gurkha Rifles, stationed there, were placed at forty-eight hours' notice to move to implement the contingency plan. This notice was shortened to readiness to move at 4 p.m. that day, but, as the urgency of the situation became apparent, they were told to move immediately to the airfield at Seletar, the other side of Singapore island, and move as soon as aircraft became available. It was unfortunately Saturday morning and it took some time for the RAF to get three Beverley transport and one Hastings ready. They finally took off at 2.45 p.m. Singapore time. Fortunately the rebels had failed to occupy the airfield at Brunei, although they had tried to block the runway, and the three Beverleys were diverted directly there, the Hastings, which could not land there in any case, going to Labuan and the men it carried being ferried by light aircraft from there to Brunei. By this time it was dark and Major Lloyd-Williams, in command of the force, had not got enough men, one and a half companies, ready for action before 11 p.m.

The situation described to him by Outram was that the latter's police held the most important places in Brunei town, but had not been able to clear the rebels from many other points between them. Farther along the coast, at Tutong and the oilfield area at Seria, the rebels appeared to be in control. Lloyd-Williams attempted to enter and clear Brunei in the dark, but this led to confusion and a number of casualties, and he decided that he must wait for daylight. Meanwhile he sent Major Lea and half a company off down the coast road to try and restore the situation at Seria. They ran into rebels half-way there at Tutong and were unable to get any farther, although they succeeded in gaining control of Tutong itself. Lloyd-Williams managed to establish complete control of Brunei town by 9 a.m. on 9 December, twenty-four rebels having been killed and the remainder disappearing into the countryside. Soon after this, his commanding officer, Lieutenant-Colonel Shakespear, arrived with another company, which was flown on to occupy the oilfield areas at Lulong and Miri, just over the border in Sarawak. He was followed by Brigadier Glennie from Luce's staff with an *ad hoc* joint service headquarters to command the operations of all three services.

The crisis point was now Seria, where the rebels were established with employees of the Shell Company and their families as potential hostages. 1/2nd Gurkhas had enough on their hands already, and it was decided to employ The Queen's Own Highlanders, standing by for action in Singapore, to recapture it. The commanding officer, Lieutenant-Colonel McHardy, and the first troops arrived early in the morning of 10 December. Glennie stressed the urgency of acting quickly and, after a personal reconnaissance from the air, McHardy decided to attack from east and west simultaneously, flying one company of ninety men in a Beverley straight into the grass airfield at Anduki, just east of the oilfield area, and one of sixty men in five Twin Pioneers into an airstrip ten miles farther west. This bold plan, put into action at 3 p.m., was entirely successful, and, although the Beverley was shot at and one Twin Pioneer bogged for a time, all the aircraft flew off again safely. No great progress was possible before dark and the operations on 11 December cleared the area from both ends, gradually identifying and isolating the places where an estimated 200 rebels were holding out and had hostages with them. Action that was too violent and precipitate could put their lives at risk. By the afternoon of 12 December the Highlanders had achieved their aim. The hostages were rescued unharmed and most of the rebels had fled into the surrounding jungle, the Highlanders themselves not having suffered a single casualty.

While McHardy's men had been regaining control of Seria, the Royal Marines had attacked Limbang, just over the Sarawak border on the far side of Brunei, where some 200 rebels had captured the police station, the gaol, which held two leading TNKU members, and the Residency, where they took Richard Morris and his wife prisoner. After a short stay in the gaol, they and six other hostages were moved to a room in the hospital, which the rebels also occupied. 42 Royal Marine Commando had been flown from Singapore to Brunei as a further reinforcement and had one company available on the morning of 11 December. There was no airfield at Limbang and the assault would have to be made up the tidal mouth of the Limbang River. The problem was to find suitable craft. Two Ramp Cargo Lighters were available at Brunei. They were not designed as assault craft, but for the transfer of stores ashore, but they had a ramp forward and, with some modification to give protection to the crew, could serve the purpose. The crews of the naval minesweepers worked flat out to convert them and get them ready, and they also provided the crews to man the craft. Piloted by the Brunei State Marine Officer, they threaded their way down the Brunei River and up the Limbang in the dark, approaching Limbang itself at first light on 12 December. After a short sharp exchange of fire, the marines landed and had soon recaptured the police station and released the hostages unharmed. Sporadic fighting continued for the rest of the day and the remaining rebels fled during the night, leaving fifteen dead behind. The marines lost five men killed and several more wounded or injured.

The rebellion had now been decisively defeated and the task transformed into one of rounding up those who had fled into the hinterland. By now British troops were pouring in, supported by helicopters both from the navy's commando carriers and from the RAF. A second Royal Marine Commando, 40, was sent to Kuching, where it was joined by the armoured cars of the Queen's Royal Irish Hussars, and the 1st Green Jackets had been sent to the Fourth Division of Sarawak to look after the important oilfield there. From this area, on the initiative of the Resident, John Fisher, the Ibans and other tribes of the mountainous jungle were organized to give information of and to cut off any TNKU stragglers who might try and make their way up the river valleys to cross the border into Indonesian Kalimantan. The man who took charge of this was Tom Harrisson, then curator of the Sarawak Museum. He had first come to the area on an archaeological and anthropological survey as an undergraduate before the Second World War. He had been dropped into the country by parachute in the closing stages of the war to organize resistance to the Japanese and knew the area and the tribes better than any other European. He did more than any other to build up a spirit of co-operation and trust between them and the British and Gurkha soldiers who were to operate in the jungle over the next three years. The deployment of troops into western Sarawak round Kuching was a precautionary measure against the threat of an uprising similar to that in Brunei. There was a large communist element among the Chinese population there and it was feared that they would seize the opportunity to subvert the government. The Governor of North Borneo, as Sabah was then called, was also concerned that the large immigrant Indonesian population of Tawau, in the extreme south-east of the colony, could also cause trouble, and a company of Gurkhas was sent there.

The situation was therefore well under control and only mopping up operations needed when Major-General Walter Walker arrived to take over from Glennie on 19 December, thirsting to see action. He had been on a trek in Nepal after having paid his annual call as Major-General Brigade of Gurkhas on the King, an interview that was later to land him in some very hot water. He had hurried back, determined to put into effect all the experience he and his Gurkhas had gained in Malaya, and indeed in the jungles of Burma before that, and also to prove that the plan the British Army had recently revealed to him for a severe reduction in their numbers was misguided. By the time of his arrival, 40 rebels had been killed, 1,897 'hard-core' detained and 1,500 'soft-core' returned to their homes. Mopping up was to continue for the next three months, made more difficult by the exceptionally heavy rain which caused widespread flooding and made river crossing dangerous.

Walker was convinced that the failure of Azahari's revolt, Azahari himself having fled to Indonesia, would force Sukarno to intervene directly to frustrate the formation of Malaysia, due to come about later in the year. He therefore resisted any premature return of headquarters or troops to Singapore or Malaya and was glad to find his views supported by the new Commander-in-Chief Far East, Admiral Begg. The first sign that he was correct in his judgement came on Good Friday, 12 April, when the police station at Tebedu, on the Sarawak border south of Kuching, was attacked, two policemen being killed. At first it was not certain whether the attackers had come over the border or were local Chinese communists, as the latter were strong in the area; but evidence left behind by the raiders proved that they were Indonesian soldiers disguised as TNKU. The Sarawak Government was taking no chances and set in hand emergency measures, ordering the surrender of all firearms, even though licensed. Fearing opposition to this, more troops were flown in to help pick up a total of 8,500 shotguns. Confrontation had begun.

Both sides had their reasons for using this term and for pretending that it was not a war. Neither wished it to develop into full-scale hostilities, covering air and sea as well as land and extending to the whole territory on the one hand of Indonesia and on the other of Malaya and Singapore, the latter being separated from Indonesian islands by only a few miles. Sukarno wished to let it be thought internationally that resistance to Malaysian federation was the will of the people and that their aspirations were for a united Kalimantan within Indonesia. It did not suit his book for it to be seen as aggression, based on his desire for expansion. Australia, at the other end of Indonesia and anxious about his attitude towards Papua and New Guinea, was also concerned to avoid finding herself at war with him. This pretence that it was not a war was to cause a number of difficulties, but on the whole was as much in Britain's and Malaysia's interest as it was in Indonesia's. Shipping through the important straits and waters surrounding Indonesia was not interfered with, although there were some tense periods when Britain, in order to assert the right of innocent passage, sailed her warships through them.

The frontier from west of Kuching to Tawau was about a thousand miles long, for the most part following the watershed in jungle-covered mountains rising to 8,000 feet. Away from the coast, the country was almost entirely jungle, the huge trees forming a canopy up to 200 feet above the ground, except where they had been felled to provide clearings for cultivation. Once cultivation was abandoned, a thick secondary jungle grew up, very difficult to penetrate. Rivers were the main routes of movement and, when they ceased to be navigable in their upper reaches, paths naturally followed them. The coast was covered with thick mangrove swamps, the cultivated areas lying between them and the hills. Most of this was in the west of Sarawak, which was divided into five administrative divisions, numbered from west to east. To cover the whole of this vast area Walker had only five battalions. He was determined that they should not just act defensively and saw that the two key elements in his plans must be the provision of intelligence – he must know when raiders crossed the border and where they were heading – and mobility – he must be able to place his forces ahead of or behind them, making use of the most effective jungle tactic, the ambush. The answer to the former lay in the development of Harrisson's force. This was achieved through the wide-spread deployment of small SAS teams maintaining contact with local tribesmen, who acted as their eyes and ears. Initially the tribesmen were organized as a uniformed force, called Border Scouts. This in fact restricted their employment and invited retaliation. When British and Gurkha troops were themselves deployed in the frontier area, they ceased to be a uniformed organization and worked closely with the SAS, while not recognizable as their helpers if they came across Indonesian patrols. The answer to mobility was the helicopter.

The four months following the Tebedu raid in April 1963 were quiet ones. Yassin Affendi and the few remaining TNKU leaders in Brunei were captured in May, and in June Tunku Abdul Rahman agreed that he would attend a meeting with Sukarno and President Macapagal of the Philippines in August; also that a United Nations team should visit Sarawak and North Borneo to report on whether their populations wished to join Malaysia or not. But, as the date for the creation of the federation, 16 September, approached, Indonesian cross-border activity increased. In August there were two major raids, one in the First Division and one in the remote Third, each consisting of some sixty men. Both were effectively dealt with, the first by Marines and the second by Gurkhas. The United Nations team having reported favourably and the Secretary-General, U Thant, having commented that 'it is my conclusion that the majority of the peoples of the two territories wish to engage with the peoples of the Federation of Malaya and Singapore in an enlarged Federation of Malaysia', the latter was proclaimed on 16 September. The British Embassy in Djakarta was attacked and burned, and Indonesia refused to recognize Malaysia, who in turn broke of diplomatic relations both with her and with the Philippines, whom she suspected of siding with her. An intensification of Indonesian activity was not long delayed. At the end of the month a party of 150 raiders crossed the border in the Third Division and attacked a small post at the village of Long Jawi. It was manned by six Gurkhas, three policemen and twenty-one Border Scouts: one of each was killed and the rest forced to withdraw. The operation to restore the situation took the whole of October and was one of the first in which extensive use was made of dropping ambush parties down into the thick jungle by helicopter. The first men generally roped down from the hovering helicopter, and then set about felling trees with power-saws in order to create a hole through which the helicopter could descend. The naval Wessex helicopters from the commando carriers took to this new task with enthusiasm, and were soon permanently based ashore.

The handover of responsibility for Sarawak and Sabah (as North Borneo was now to be called) from Britain to Malaysia brought about a change in the organization responsible for operations, as it did of course for administration. Hitherto the Director of Operations, as Walker was styled, had had to deal with three separate and independent administrative authorities, the Government of the Sultan of Brunei and the Governors of Sarawak and North Borneo. Each state had had a separate Emergency Committee, of which Walker was chairman. For operations and all military matters he had been directly responsible to the Commander-in-Chief Far East, a position which had caused some friction with the Commander Far East Land Forces, for much of which Walker's dictatorial and uncompromising attitude was responsible. In fundamentals the position did not change, except that the British Governors of Sarawak and Sabah stepped into the background as Deputy High Commissioners, the State Mentri Besar taking their place as the chief executive of the state administration. Their separate police forces became subordinate to the Inspector-General of the Malaysian Police, Claude Fenner. At Federation level two committees were formed, a National Operations Council, chaired by the Tunku, and subordinate to it, a National Operations Committee, chaired jointly by the Chief of the Malaysian Armed Forces Staff, General Tunku Osman, and Fenner, Admiral Begg being in fact the most important member. This was the body from which Walker officially now received his orders and he normally attended its meetings in Kuala Lumpur. Initially there was some rivalry between Fenner and Walker about responsibility for operations, Fenner regarding the campaign as analogous to that in Malaya; but by this time it was clearly not an internal subversive movement, but an externally directed war, and Walker won his argument for responsibility to remain in his hands.

Malaysian responsibility was to be outwardly and visibly complemented by participation in operations. One Malay battalion and an armoured car squadron went to Sarawak's First Division and another to Tawau in Sabah. The latter was clearly a danger spot. Many immigrant Indonesians were employed in timber felling there, and the island forming the southern arm of the bay was half in Sabah and half in Kalimantan. At the end of December a party of 128 Indonesian Marine Commandos crossed the frontier in four groups. After dark on the twenty-ninth, two of these groups attacked posts held by the Malay Regiment and the Police at Kalabakan, taking them by surprise. Eight Malaysian soldiers were killed and nineteen wounded. Walker immediately sent a Gurkha battalion to deal with the situation. By the end of February, 96 of the 128 raiders had been killed or captured. It had been a severe shock to the Malayan soldiers, but it taught them a lesson and thereafter they paid more attention to security and alertness. It had also clearly undermined Sukarno's claim that the revolt was an internal matter. In the same period there had been other incursions across the Sabah border farther west.

January 1964 saw a short period of cease-fire. Following an appeal by U Thant, Sukarno agreed to a truce starting on 25 January, while the Foreign Ministers of Malaysia and Indonesia met in Bangkok. The talks broke down and thereafter the Indonesian Army took full responsibility for operations in Kalimantan, and abandoned the pretence that the soldiers and marines in its special units were 'volunteers', helping local insurgents. The first sign of this was the incursion early in March of a considerable body of Indonesian soldiers, who occupied a position on the important Kling Klang ridge just inside the border of the Second Division. They were dislodged by a skilful attack by 2/10th Gurkhas, who were responsible for the whole Division. Further incursions into this area were made by even larger bodies of men, one over 200, and the battalion was successful in dealing with all of them. At about the same time similar incursions had been made into the extreme west of the First Division, successfully dealt with by the Royal Marine Commandos.

Walker now had to adapt his tactics to the new Indonesian methods. The latter, instead of sending over raiding parties, who would return over the border after carrying out their planned attack, appeared to be intent on establishing bases over the Sarawak border with forces of a hundred or two hundred men. From these they would intimidate the natives and carry out operations, while bringing about a *de facto* expansion of Indonesian territory. This could clearly not be tolerated, and it was no longer sufficient to hold the main forces back from the frontier, relying only on small detachments in contact with the tribesmen for information. The latter had to be supported by the actual presence of British or Gurkha troops, who must dominate the jungle by offensive patrolling. The concept was an obvious one, but its implementation in practice more difficult. There were severe limitations not only on the troops available, but even more so on the ability to supply them in the area near the frontier. The key was the helicopter and there were never enough of them. The Indonesians were operating in bodies of up to 100 men. Patrols and their bases had to be strong enough to stand up to forces of this size, although they need not be as large as that to do so. The conclusion to which this led was that the right size of base was one that could hold a company, but be defended by a platoon for long enough to be reinforced either by its absent patrols returning or by additional troops being flown by helicopter to help. Patrols sent out from the base would normally be of platoon strength. Given the area to be covered, this, together with the need for reserves, determined the number of troops required. The bases, which could not be concealed, were strongly fortified with dug-outs, wire, obstacle belts of sharpened bamboo, known as *panjis*, anti-personnel mines and later various devices to detect enemy movement. At a later stage each base was to contain one light field gun. Most of them had a light aircraft strip nearby as well as a helicopter pad. They were generally sited on high ground with the water supply pumped up from the nearest stream. If one of the jungle patrols came across signs of an incursion in its area, other forces from its battalion reserve would be helicoptered in to intercept and ambush the enemy, either on his way to his presumed objective or on his way back over the border. The latter was generally more rewarding as it was easier to predict the route he would take. The number of helicopter landing points near the frontier was continually being increased. This policy could not be implemented overnight and its development was continuous. It had however made a start when, in June 1964, further political talks took place, this time in Tokyo, between the Tunku, Sukarno and Macapagal. Again they got nowhere, and were soon followed by further Indonesian incursions into Sarawak, of which there were thirteen in July, resulting in thirty-four attacks.

Walker expected a significant increase in Indonesian activity, which, linked to the still serious Chinese communist threat in Sarawak, demanded, in his opinion, an increase in the number of troops as well as freedom to operate over the border into Kalimantan. There was some resistance initially to this, partly from fear of its leading to escalation both in the numbers involved on both sides and in the scope of the 'confrontation' generally, partly from anxiety about the international implications and partly from a suspicion that Walker was pressing for an increase as part of his campaign to frustrate the intention of the authorities to reduce the size of the Brigade of Gurkhas. It then stood at 16,000, 6,000 above the figure agreed with Nepal when India became independent in

1947, an increase agreed as a result of the Malayan emergency. The army authorities in Whitehall had been planning to reduce it to about 6,000 when the Brunei revolt took place. Walker had been confidentially warned of this and had deliberately leaked the information to the King of Nepal, to the anger of the authorities in Whitehall.

Walker's demand for an increase in troop strength was supported by the Commander-in-Chief, Begg, and his case was strengthened in August when the Indonesians launched an attack from Sumatra across the Straits of Malacca on the mainland of Malaya. On 17 August a flotilla of small craft landed 100 men on the mainland north-west of Singapore, following it up with a parachute drop, meant to be of nearly 200, aimed at Labis, sixty miles farther north. The latter was reduced to 100 men, one aircraft returning to base with engine trouble and another never being heard of again. Neither operation achieved anything, but it was not till the end of October that almost all of them were rounded up. Some remained in hiding for many months later. Other attempts were made over the next six months to raid Malaya and Singapore, but the measures taken to frustrate them were successful and they were never more than a nuisance.

The Labour government, which came to power in Britain in October 1964, was determined to show itself resolute in pursuing the campaign, and Walker received support from the new administration, in which Denis Healey was Defence Secretary and Mulley Army Minister. Mountbatten, the Chief of the Defence Staff, also backed Walker's demand for reinforcements. By the end of the year he had eighteen British battalions, eight of which were Gurkha and two Royal Marine Commandos: he also had three Malay battalions. He had five batteries of light artillery, two squadrons of armoured cars and four of engineers, a force of some 14,000 men, almost all in combat units. Thanks to the helicopter and air supply, the tail remained very slender. His principal demand, as ever, was for helicopters, which could so dramatically extend the capability of the troops available. He had sixty naval and air force troop-and-supply carrying helicopters, and forty small army ones for reconnaissance and liaison. His command organization was also revised to handle the large force. Originally, from his joint service headquarters in Brunei, he had commanded directly two brigade headquarters, 99th Brigade covering Sabah, Brunei and the eastern divisions of Sarawak, and 3rd Commando Brigade, responsible for West Sarawak. This had later been extended to three brigade areas, East, Central and West, 99th Brigade, after a spell back in Malaya, replacing 3rd Commando Brigade in West Sarawak. Now in 1965 a further brigade sector, Mid-West, covering the Third Division, was added, 52nd (Gurkha) Brigade headquarters coming out from England to take responsibility for the Central sector, covering Brunei and the Fourth and Fifth Divisions. Walker found that he could not also continue to be responsible for the multifarious day-to-day administrative needs of the soldiers. He had already handed over command of

17th Gurkha Division, the headquarters of which had returned to Malaya, and the job of Major-General Brigade of Gurkhas to Major-General Peter Hunt. Hunt and his headquarters were now brought over to Labuan to take over the task, where they were joined by Walker's headquarters which remained entirely responsible for operations and intelligence, not an easy position for Hunt, but one which he filled with an astute blend of firmness and understanding.

Walker's other demand, for permission to carry the war over the border, was more controversial. It would be even more likely both to escalate the war and to arouse international and some domestic opposition. But, after the Indonesian attack on Malaya, permission was given to operate up to 5,000 yards beyond the border, provided that each individual operation was personally approved by the Director of Operations himself and that the strictest secrecy was observed about the fact that the border had been crossed. As time went on and these operations, which were given the code-name *Claret* and were always based on information obtained either from interrogation of prisoners or from other sources, produced more and more rewarding success, and also as their secrecy was maintained, permission was obtained to operate more deeply, finally up to 20,000 yards and with large bodies of men. The aim of these operations was almost invariably to ambush bodies of men, or those supplying them, while on the move either on foot or by boat. Ambushes of the latter were generally the most rewarding and must have severely affected the morale of the Indonesian soldiers.

Maintaining secrecy about these operations posed many problems. Knowledge of them was restricted to the minimum and special *Claret* operations rooms were kept separate. Not only did this cause staff and public relations problems, but it was also a test of morale. If soldiers were wounded or killed, there might be difficulty in getting them back. In fact the bodies of some who were killed had to be left behind. Recognition of the efforts of the soldiers involved had to be restricted or falsified. The one VC of the campaign was awarded to Lance-Corporal Rambahadur Limbu of 2/10th Gurkhas for an action which took place in November 1965 just over the frontier south of Bau in the First Division, and the details of exactly where it had occurred had to be concealed. Fortunately the Indonesians co-operated in this deception of the world's public, probably because they did not wish to admit that operations were taking place more and more inside Kalimantan and less north of the border.

When Walker handed over to Major-General George Lea on 12 March 1965, the tide had turned very clearly in favour of the alliance between Britain and Malaysia. Incursions north of the border were less frequent and, when they did occur, seldom achieved anything. The Chinese communists in Sarawak and the dissidents in Brunei were well under control, the majority of them locked up. Most of the practical difficulties and problems of operating in the remote jungle-covered mountains in all weathers had been solved, and methods of doing so were being improved all the time. More Malayan troops were being deployed and their commanders assuming more responsibility. Perhaps most important in Walker's eyes, none could doubt the outstanding contribution made by his Gurkha soldiers. Within months of his departure, Begg left also, replaced by Air Chief Marshal Sir John Grandy. Lea was no stranger to the jungle, having commanded the SAS in Malaya; but he was a very different character from Walker, just as determined, but less abrasive and readier to appreciate the point of view of others. Not long after he had assumed command, he found it unnecessary to have a separate land force commander and Hunt and his headquarters returned to Malaya. Six weeks after his arrival, Colonel Supargo, subordinate to General Panggabean commanding all forces in Kalimantan, demonstrated to Lea that he could still strike a sharp blow north of the border. The 2nd Parachute Regiment had recently arrived and one of its companies was occupying a base at Plaman Mapu, in the south-east corner of the First Division. Most of the company was out on patrol, leaving only the headquarters, a weak platoon and the mortar section in the base under the command of the company sergeant-major. At 5 a.m. on 27 April they were suddenly attacked by almost a whole Indonesian battalion, two companies of which had closed up to the base undetected during the night. A fierce battle ensued, compared by some to the defence of Rorke's Drift in the Zulu War of 1879. CSM Williams, himself wounded in the face, and his paratroopers, two of whom were killed, fought gallantly. After three attacks in an hour and a half had been driven off, the Indonesians began to withdraw, harried by the rest of the battalion, having, it was believed, suffered about thirty casualties.

The problem of relieving the Gurkha battalions, who had been continuously engaged, and those British units which were based in the Far East on three year tours with their families, had by now become an urgent one, and it was fortunate that the Australians and New Zealand Governments agreed that their battalions in 28th Commonwealth Brigade, based in Malaya, could take their turn, as the British battalion in the Brigade already had, in operations in Borneo. When they did, they served in West Brigade in Sarawak.

August 1965 produced what appeared at first to be a set-back to Britain's policy over Malaysia, the expulsion or secession of Singapore from the Federation. The crux of the issue lay in the differing views of the Tunku and of Lee Kuan Yew about the real purpose and future of the Federation. The Tunku saw it as a means of preserving Malaya as a fundamentally Malay state, at the same time expanding its resources and, while profiting from the energy and diligence of the large Chinese population, making certain that it did not dominate nor gain control politically. Lee Kuan Yew viewed it from exactly the opposite angle, as developing into a state in which political influence, exercised through political parties, would control affairs, removing powers from the antiquated Malay states. He saw the Chinese population, with their skills and energy, as achieving the status of political power by normal democratic means, which their numbers and their individual skills justified. The incorporation of Singapore in Malaysia, and the prospect of Lee Kuan Yew's Peoples' Action Party spreading its influence among the Chinese population within Malaya, seemed to the Tunku and his fellow Malays as a clear threat. Reluctantly Lee accepted that his future and that of his people and party would have to be restricted to an island the size of the Isle of Wight. The first reaction of some of those in Sabah and Sarawak, who had not been much in favour of federation from the start, was to try and follow Singapore's example; but a rapid visit to both by the Tunku, with the strong support of Britain, helped of course by the presence of all the forces in Borneo, stifled this potential opposition.

Fortunately for Britain, Malaysia and Singapore, Indonesia was in no state to profit from this apparent split in the ranks of her opponents: she was having her own troubles. On 1 October a coup took place in Djakarta, in which several pro-communist officials, including Doctor Subandrio and the chiefs of staff of the navy and the air force, seized power, stating that they did so to pre-empt a coup planned by the army to overthrow Sukarno. This event was followed by months of confusion in which fighting between communists and their opponents broke out all over the country. It was not finally resolved until 12 March 1966, when the army prevailed over the pro-communist elements and General Suharto replaced Sukarno as the real ruler of the country. While this had been going on, it was inevitable that the Indonesian direction of 'confrontation' in Borneo should falter, while Lea's operations over the border claimed ever greater success. For some months after Suharto's accession to power, it was not clear what attitude his team would take to 'confrontation'. As the army was now firmly in power, it was thought by some that it would intensify the war. But in May a team of Indonesian officers flew to Kuala Lumpur to initiate discussions, and, after a meeting between Tun Razak, the Tunku's deputy, and Adam Malik, Suharto's Foreign Minister, in Bangkok in June, preparations were set in hand to bring 'confrontation' to an end. In July Suharto stripped Sukarno of all his powers, and on 11 August 1966 a peace agreement was signed and hostilities, which had practically ceased already, came to an official end.

For Britain, and indeed for Malaysia for whom it achieved much, it had been a cheap war. At its peak 17,000 servicemen of the Commonwealth had been deployed at one time in Borneo with 10,000 more available in Malaya and Singapore. Casualties had been 114 killed and 181 wounded, a high proportion Gurkha. There were also 36 civilians killed, 53 wounded and 4 captured, almost all of them local inhabitants. It was estimated that 590 Indonesians had been killed, 222 wounded and 771 captured. It had lasted for nearly four years and had clearly and decisively achieved its aim of preventing

Indonesia, or any other outside influence, from strangling Malaysia at birth. If it seemed to have involved a deployment of British defence effort out of all proportion to her interests in the three territories directly concerned, Sabah, Brunei and Sarawak, that must be balanced by an appreciation of the contribution it made to the future stability of the area and to the development of a policy which enabled Britain to reduce its military commitments in the future without prejudicing her interests. In so many other conflicts of a similar kind, there had been a tendency to act with too little too late. From the start of the revolt in Brunei, apart perhaps from some faltering on the first day, this was not a fault which could be attributed to the British Far East Command. Fortunately the Commander-in-Chief had resources to hand, notably soldiers in Walker's 17th Gurkha Division, with extensive and recent experience of the right kind in Malaya. In the Royal Marine Commando Brigade, with its associated commando carriers and squadrons of naval helicopters, he also had an invaluable force, keen to justify its existence. In addition he had RAF resources adequate for the task, although more helicopters would always have been welcome. Being far from Whitehall, where Mountbatten, presiding over the Chiefs of Staff, was keen to prove the value of his newly-established joint service organization in the Far East, he had more freedom of action than most commanders had enjoyed in similar circumstances. Skill, courage and resource the soldiers, sailors, marines and airmen had in plenty. Other factors were also in their favour. Unless things went badly wrong, Indonesia had little hope of winning over the inhabitants of Northern Borneo to its side. Logistically, Britain had a large base conveniently placed with a safe and easy sea and air line of communication to the points of entry in Northern Borneo, which were much nearer to the frontier than those which Indonesia had in the south of the island. Although the forces available to Indonesia were very large numerically, the problems of deploying them and supporting them up to and over the frontier severely limited the numbers they could actually produce in the critical area. Finally the political ferment in Djakarta brought to an end a 'confrontation' which might have continued almost indefinitely, and could have imposed a severe burden on Malaysia and Britain alike. How much the commitment to confrontation and the frustration of the army at its failure contributed to the coup which brought it to an end, it is difficult to say. But that it was a campaign which was both skilfully fought and well directed at every level, there can be no doubt; and it did much to counterbalance the depressing experience in Aden which was to come to an end fifteen months later.

PART TWO

French Colonial Conflicts

Chapter Seven

INDO-CHINA

Britain was not alone in facing post-war colonial problems; the Netherlands and France had theirs also, both being faced immediately with the problem of reasserting their authority in the area occupied by the Japanese, in France's case in Indo-China. The problems that faced her in doing so were complicated by the events of the war and the way in which it came to an end, in addition to the inherent problems of the country.

French missionaries and traders had established themselves in Indo-China in the eighteenth century. After France had lost her hold in India at the end of that century, and as the British extended their activities eastward to Malaya and China, the French developed their activities in what was then known as Annam. These were resisted by the Annamese, a people basically of Indonesian origin, who had settled in the coastal areas and the deltas of the Red River and the Mekong, driving the original inhabitants back into the hills. In the north, later to be known as Tonkin, this brought them into direct conflict with the Thai people, who had spread southward from southern China. Over the centuries Chinese domination of Tonkin fluctuated until the beginning of the fifteenth century, after which China left the Annamese in *de facto* control, while maintaining the *de jure* position that both Tonkin and Annam itself were her subjects. In the south the Annamese profited from the weakness of the Khmer people, based in Cambodia, who had originally inhabited the Mekong delta. A series of disastrous wars between them and Siam had weakened them to a degree which allowed the Annamese to impose their rule on the fertile area of what was later to be called Cochin-China.

On the pretext of protecting their missionaries and traders, the French had been militarily involved in Annam since 1847. After a short war in 1863, France occupied part of Southern Annam, extending it in 1867 and declaring it in that year to be the French colony of Cochin-China, at the same time establishing a protectorate over Cambodia. In 1884 she went further, Cambodia being incorporated as a colony and Annam and Tonkin declared to be French protectorates, in spite of protests from China. In 1892 Laos was also declared a protectorate, and in 1897 direct French rule of Tonkin was established after an agreement in 1894 with China delimiting the frontier.

Resistance to the imposition of French rule had been widespread and was initially centred on the Annamese imperial family and the mandarins and scholars who served it. The Japanese victory over Russia in 1905 did much to stimulate it and there was a serious revolt in 1916. The motives behind the resistance were mixed. First came resentment of a proud people, who had for centuries maintained their independence, culture and control of the country against rival powers. Second was the resentment of those who had previously been privileged and respected wielders of power and influence at being thrust aside and made redundant by foreigners, whose activities were directed towards their own enrichment. Finally the impact of Western civilization destroyed the structure of society, both at the higher level and at the lower, where it was based on a communal system in which the village elders held sway. The impact of Western capitalism was felt more keenly in Cochin-China, where rubber-growing and other forms of crop were introduced which replaced simple native agriculture and turned the peasant into a landless labourer. At the same time the French attached great importance to the introduction of their culture. Young Vietnamese (as the Annamese called themselves) who received a French education soon came to contrast the *égalité*, *fraternité* and *liberté*, which they were taught to regard as the first principles of society, with what the French practised in their country. The idea of applying these principles to Indo-China itself was not restricted to the educated *élite*. France had recruited large numbers of men from Indo-China to serve both as soldiers and as labourers in France in the First World War. When they returned home, they resented being treated as second-class citizens and were susceptible to the appeal of communism, propagated by Russia.

In 1892, eight years after France had declared Tonkin a protectorate, a boy called Nguyen Ai Quoc (Nguyen The Patriot) was born there, later to become famous as Ho Chi Minh. He had left his country as a merchant seaman in 1914, and at the Versailles Conference in 1919 was to be found presenting a list of Vietnamese grievances and a demand for independence in accordance with Woodrow Wilson's Fourteen Points. He was at Tours in 1920 when the French Communist Party broke away from the Socialist Party, and it was as their delegate that he went to Moscow in 1923 for the Congress of the Peasant International. He stayed on there, and in 1925 went to China, where he studied the work of Sun Yat Sen. In Canton he formed the Association of Vietnamese Revolutionary Youth from Vietnamese who lived there, sending its members back into Vietnam to form revolutionary cells.

The year 1927 saw Chiang Kai-shek turn against the communists in China, and Quoc returned to Moscow, while his Revolutiuonary Youth Association moved its headquarters to Hong Kong. He joined them there in 1930, engaged in attempts to weld together the different communist parties active in Indo-

China into one covering Vietnam (i.e. Tonkin, Annam and Cochin-China), Laos and Cambodia. The communists were not the only revolutionaries. In 1927 a non-communist Vietnam Nationalist Party (*Viet Nam Quoc Dan Dong* or VNQDD) was formed in Hanoi. It attempted an uprising in 1930, which failed, and its leader, Nguyen Thai Hoc, was executed. Its organizers fled to China, where they were financed and supported by Chiang Kai-shek. The VNQDD's attempted revolt was followed in 1931 by widespread communist-inspired troubles, sparked off by conditions of famine in many parts of the country. It was ruthlessly suppressed and Quoc's organization thrown into disarray, Quoc himself being arrested by the British in Hong Kong. He was soon released and quickly disappeared from view. In the following year the young Emperor Bao Dai returned from his education in France to his imperial capital of Hué and appointed as his Chief Minister a young mandarin of 32, widely respected for his honesty and ability, Ngo Dinh Diem. Diem soon discovered that he was powerless, the French holding the real reins of power and restricting Bao Dai and his imperial government to little more than ceremonial functions. He therefore resigned and was succeeded by Pham Quynh, who sought in vain to gain for Vietnam a status similar to that of British Dominions under the 1931 Statute of Westminster.

In Cochin-China, a colony administered as if it were part of France, the Communist Party was allowed to exist as a legal political party. It was led by Tran Van Giau, who maintained links with the French Communist Party and the Comintern, while keeping up a running fight with a Trotskyist party, led by Ta Thu Thau. Rival political influence was exercised in their own areas by two semi-religious sects, the *Cao Dai* and the *Hoa Hao*. Cao Dai was a local imitation of Catholicism with ingredients of several other religions. Originating in Saigon and growing to a strength of 300,000, its influence began to wane after its founding 'pope' died in 1932, and its centre moved to Tay Ninh near the Cambodian border west of Saigon. Hoa Hao was a modified form of Buddhism, which had a strong following in the southern part of the Mekong delta.

There were therefore strong elements resistant to French rule when war broke out in Europe in 1939 and France fell in 1940. General Catroux, the Governor-General of Indo-China, was immediately faced by a demand from the Japanese, then at war with China, that the use of the Haiphong-Kunming railway through Tonkin to supply Chiang Kai-shek should cease and that a Japanese mission should be accepted to supervise this. Catroux had only 60,000 soldiers in the whole country, two-thirds of whom were locally recruited. Cut off from outside help, he had no alternative but to agree, as a result of which he was dismissed by Pétain and replaced by Admiral Decoux. In September Japan increased her demands to the use of airfields, the stationing of troops and transport facilities, including the passage through Tonkin of a division which was in difficulties over the border in China. Decoux hesitated, whereupon the Japanese attacked French posts near the frontier, bombed Haiphong and landed troops there who began to march on Hanoi. After two days' fighting, in which 800 Frenchmen were killed, Decoux gave way. The communists in Cochin-China thought that this was the time to rise and throw off the French yoke, but they miscalculated both their own strength and French weakness and were soundly trounced. Driven underground, they lost touch with fellow communists in the rest of Indo-China. The next blow to French authority came from Siam, whose forces crossed the Mekong and invaded Cochin-China. Fighting continued until March 1941, when the Japanese stepped in to stop it, forcing the French to cede one province of Cambodia and two of Laos to Siam, as Thailand was then known.

Meanwhile almost all of those nationalists who wished to eject the French had taken refuge in southern China and were dependent on Chiang Kai-shek. Quoc had resurfaced in the Chinese province of Kwangsi, where the local war lord, Chang Fa-kwee, although officially serving the Kuomintang, was not unsympathetic to the communists, whom he later joined. The Indo-Chinese communists held a congress in Kwangsi in May 1941, at which important decisions were taken. Representatives of other nationalist organizations attended and it was decided to form a political party to work for independence, to be known as The League for the Independence of Vietnam or *Viet Nam Doc Lap Dong Minh Hoi* (*Viet Minh* for short). Partly to accommodate non-communist nationalists and partly to avoid trouble from the Kuomintang, no mention of communism appeared in the title and there was some vagueness as to whether Vietnam included Laos and Cambodia or just the territory of the old Annam, i.e. Tonkin, Annam and Cochin-China. Having settled the political aspect, the congress turned to the military. It decided that guerrilla bands should be formed to operate against the French over the border in the province of Cao Bang in north-west Tonkin, a hilly jungle area suitable for such activities. The man chosen to plan and execute this was a young schoolmaster from Hanoi, who had already been imprisoned by the French for his subversive communist activities, but had escaped in 1939, Vo Nguyen Giap. His first act was to establish a network of agents and informers based in the mountains of northern Tonkin and spreading out its tentacles into the Red River delta. Having done this, he went off to join Mao Tse-tung's army in China, where he attended a course at their political and guerrilla warfare school. When he returned to Kwangsi province late in 1942, he found that Quoc had been imprisoned by Chiang Kai-shek in the hope that the latter's protégés, the VNQDD, would oust the communists from control of the Indo-Chinese nationalist movement. In October 1942 Chiang had summoned a meeting of all the non-communist elements and made them form The Vietnam Revolutionary League or *Viet Nam Cach Menh Dong Minh Hoi*, generally known as *Don Minh Hoi*. Long before this, in December 1941, Japan had widened her war with China by her attack on the US Navy at Pearl Harbor, followed by that on

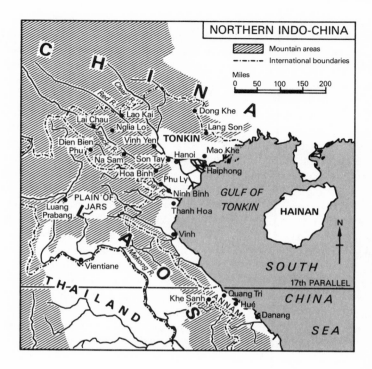

Malaya and Singapore, extending her activities and demands on the French administration in Indo-China as she did so. This lowered the morale and authority of the latter even further.

In 1943 there were important developments. Quoc was released from prison and appointed head of Dong Minh Hoi. This was when he changed his name to Ho Chi Minh and it appears that the reason for his doing so was to attempt to conceal from Chiang Kai-shek that he was the same man as the Nguyen Ai Quoc who had been imprisoned for his communism. The motive for his release was that the Americans, their allies and the Kuomintang depended for their information about Japanese activities in Indo-China on the Indo-Chinese nationalists. Those in the Dong Minh Hoi produced nothing, and the Governor of Kwangsi province, Lun Sun, who was responsible for providing the information, realized that only Giap's organization could produce it. Giap's *quid pro quo* was the release of Quoc, who took the name of 'The Enlightened One' or 'He who enlightens' as he stepped out of jail. Giap by this time had extended his guerrilla activities throughout Tonkin, establishing a secondary base south of the Red River delta, his intelligence and other activities becoming complicated by the presence of agents of de Gaulle's Free

French, who had been parachuted in and were reporting to a French mission with Chiang Kai-shek. His strength was increased in 1944 and training improved. In October Ho Chi Minh joined him, and by the end of the year the Viet Minh guerrillas had established their influence throughout Tonkin.

By then the Americans had recaptured the Philippines and there could be no doubt but that the Allies would win the war. Fearful of an allied attempt to invade Indo-China, the Japanese increased their forces there and on 9 March 1945 gave Decoux an ultimatum, demanding that all French troops be confined to barracks and placed under their command. Faced with superior force on the spot, most of the French succumbed, although those on the northern border of Tonkin resisted. The garrison of Lang-son was one of them, and when General Lemonnier and the civilian Governor, Monsieur Auphelle, refused to order them to surrender, they were beheaded. Some 6,000 troops, many of them under command of General Alessandri, made their way through the mountains to the Chinese Nationalists, where they were coolly received and interned, the Americans with Chiang Kai-shek, on instructions from Washington, giving them the cold shoulder. In this situation everyone was jostling for power and influence. Chiang hoped, if not actually to absorb Indo-China, at least to establish there a regime friendly to him. The Americans aided and abetted him in this, being in any case far from keen on the preservation of any colonial regime, least of all one which would boost support for de Gaulle, of whom Roosevelt had always disapproved. While Britain, as a matter of principle, had to support the restoration of colonial rule in the Far East, she was certainly not prepared to give any priority to saving Indo-China for France. In the eyes of the Free French, the French administration there was tainted with the stigma not only of the general collaboration of the Vichy regime with the Axis, but also with its own local collaboration with the Japanese, who themselves were by now concerned primarily with their own survival.

The body best placed and organized to exploit these rivalries and the situation created by the Japanese overthrow of the French was the Viet Minh, and Ho Chi Minh and Giap immediately took advantage of it to replace French authority with their own. As long as this did not interfere with their military requirements, the Japanese put no obstacle in their way. Locking up the French meant locking up the Free French agents and sympathizers with them, and the allies suddenly found contacts which the latter had made and the information derived from them cut off. They turned instead to the only other source, the Viet Minh, who welcomed American support, which appeared to be – and was – opposed as a matter of policy to the restoration of French rule, at any rate in the north. Ho Chi Minh moved quickly and the Japanese allowed him to take over the administration of Tonkin, although formally entrusting Bao Dai with the responsibility both for Tonkin and Annam. They left the administration of Cochin-China to a coalition of the nationalist parties and sects, the Cao Dai, Hoa Hao and Tran Van Giau's communists.

Ho Chi Minh and Giap looked forward to a period of at least several months while the war against Japan continued, the French remained locked up and they received increasing support from the American Office of Strategic Services, who now favoured them over their rivals. The Potsdam Conference had agreed that Chiang Kai-shek's Kuomintang should occupy Indo-China down to the 16th degree of latitude, that is all of Tonkin and two-thirds of Annam, including the capital of Hué, as well as Laos. The British would occupy the southern half. The occupying powers would disarm the Japanese, and the question of the future status of the whole area was left open for negotiation. De Gaulle did not accept this and was already preparing an expeditionary force to reassert French authority. The explosion of two atomic bombs on Japan on 6 and 9 August 1945 and her subsequent surrender took all but a very few by surprise. Nevertheless the Viet Minh moved quickly. By 20 August they were in control of all of Tonkin and Northern Annam, except for the main cities, and by the end of the month they held these also. Bao Dai accepted the *fait accompli*, abdicated and moved to Hanoi to join Ho Chi Minh's government, which also included members of the VNQDD, until he left the country six months later. On 2 September Ho Chi Minh proclaimed the existence of the Democratic Republic of Vietnam.

The Nationalist Chinese soon swept into the north, disarmed the Japanese and handed over or bartered their military equipment to the Viet Minh. This made it possible for Giap to increase his forces to a strength of 31,000. Preoccupied with the state of affairs in their own country, the Chinese allowed the Viet Minh to establish their authority and do their best to administer the whole country north of the 16th parallel, much of which was suffering from a state of famine, due to a poor rice crop in the spring and flooding in the summer rains, caused by failure to maintain the dykes.

South of the parallel, a force of British and Indian troops under General Gracey had arrived in Saigon by air from Rangoon on 12 September. Gracey was told that his only task was to disarm the Japanese and that he was not to get involved in keeping order. However he found Saigon in a state of chaos. The prisons had been opened and their inmates, armed with captured Japanese weapons, were looting and robbing without restraint, while Giau's communists were seizing the opportunity to acquire weapons both from disarmed French and Japanese. Gracey had to restore some sort of order and at first employed Japanese troops to help him. Within a few weeks a small number of Free French troops arrived, sparking off massive communist-inspired demonstrations, which Gracey only brought under control with Japanese help. He had already released all the French whom the Japanese had locked up, but he had not given the soldiers back their arms. However, on the demand of the Free French, he did so. On 23 September the latter seized all public buildings from Giau and his supporters and forcibly dispersed demonstrators who protested against it. Two days later Giau struck back, killing or kidnapping 450 Frenchmen. Gracey's troops intervened and disarmed the French again, although leaving them in possession of the public buildings.

In October General Leclerc arrived with a division of colonial infantry, replacing Gracey's British and Indian troops. He quickly cleared up Saigon and by February 1946 had re-established French authority over the whole of the area up to the 16th parallel, although in practice it was limited to the towns and the roads between them. Giau, who hitherto had regarded himself as independent of Ho Chi Minh, was forced to join forces with him, dispersing his less well armed guerrillas into the countryside. However, instead of cultivating the support of the peasants, he antagonized both them and his allies, the Cao Dai, Hoa Hao and Binh Xuyen, another private army with extensive contacts in the underworld of Saigon, by adopting a scorched earth policy in the face of Leclerc's attacks. Ho Chi Minh therefore got rid of him and replaced him with a hardened old revolutionary, Nguyen Binh. The latter's method of winning support was based much more on intimidation and terrorism than on 'winning hearts and minds'.

In November 1945 Admiral d'Argenlieu, who was also a member of a Catholic monastic order, had arrived in Saigon as High Commissioner for the whole of Indo-China, determined to reassert French authority over the whole area, not helped in this by the resignation of de Gaulle in January 1946. Meanwhile, north of the 16th parallel, Ho Chi Minh's hopes had begun to fade. Although he was firmly established in control of Tonkin and most of Annam, he received little support from Chiang Kai-shek, whose interest was limited to having a buffer state between him and the French. The Americans had also withdrawn their support in the face of French protests. He therefore decided to negotiate with the French, proposing that the three territories, Tonkin, Annam and Cochin-China, should be united and granted independence as Vietnam under his leadership. While negotiations were pursued, Giap could strengthen his army, eliminate rivals and build up nation-wide support. France would have none of this and instead negotiated with Chiang Kai-shek for his withdrawal from the north in return for opening up the Haiphong–Kunming railway, the abandonment of French concessions in China and some adjustment of the frontier. An agreement was reached in February 1946, but the Chinese were slow to withdraw. This led to a clash when French troops landed at Haiphong on 6 March, but they established themselves there and, in spite of protests from Ho Chi Minh, entered Hanoi ten days later. From this position they came to an agreement with him. The French accepted provisionally and in principle a republic of Vietnam as part of an Indo-Chinese Federation within the French Union (as the Empire had been renamed) with its own government, administration and armed forces. In return Ho Chi Minh agreed that a maximum of 25,000 French troops could move into the north and reoccupy certain garrisons and posts on the frontier with China and elsewhere, no single garrison to have more than 800 men. These garrisons were to be progressively withdrawn over a period of five years. Ho Chi Minh and Giap had great difficulty in persuading their followers to accept the return of the French, and Giap certainly regarded it as only a temporary truce. The French took the same view. They used it to build up their forces as quickly as possible, and their part of the bargain was never ratified by the French Government, who refused to announce that they accepted an independent Vietnam. As the Chinese began their withdrawal in May, both the French and Giap's men followed them up closely, eyeing each other with deep suspicion. Negotiations dragged on both in Indo-China and in August and September at Fontainebleau. When he returned empty handed in October, Ho Chi Minh agreed with Giap that the only way to get rid of the French would be by armed force with full popular support, and that they must work to that end. Ho Chi Minh favoured maintaining a cease-fire for as long as possible while the Viet Minh built up both its military and its political strength; but Giap feared that the longer they waited, the more would the French build up their strength and extend their grip.

Elsewhere the French were doing just that. Cambodia had declared itself independent in March 1944, but Leclerc had completely re-established French rule early in 1946. In Laos he had to wait until the Chinese withdrew, leaving groups of guerrillas of a Laotian independence movement active in the north of the country. D'Argenlieu was meanwhile working hard to re-establish Cochin-China as a French colony independent of Annam and Tonkin.

After the failure of the Fontainebleau Conference, tension rose in the north, the spark which set light to it being the French decision to take over the customs at Haiphong, partly because they knew that Giap was bringing arms in through the port. This led to fighting in November between the French Army, now commanded by General Valluy, and Giap's men, when the former seized a boat carrying arms for the latter. A French cruiser bombarded the Indo-Chinese quarter of Haiphong, allegedly killing 6,000 people and wounding many more. They cleared Viet Minh troops from the town and by the end of the month had moved on and taken control of Hanoi. Viet Minh uprisings in other towns also failed, and by the end of March General Valluy had established control of most of the Red River delta, while a force from Tourane on the coast of Annam had relieved the isolated French garrison of Húe. Ho Chi Minh and Giap withdrew into the hills north of the Red River delta and prepared for a long guerrilla war, Giap's main force of regular troops, the Chuc Luc, being still about 30,000.

There was a year of stalemate in 1947. Valluy thought that he could defeat the Viet Minh if he were given another division. He was promised it, but it was diverted instead to deal with trouble in Madagascar. Nevertheless by the end of the year he had a total of 100,000 men under arms, just over half of whom were French, the rest being Foreign Legion, Algerians, Moroccans and Tunisians. In addition he had locally recruited levies. A new High Commissioner, Émile Bollaerts, was sent to replace d'Argenlieu and to pursue a more conciliatory policy towards the nationalists, to which Valluy was opposed. Bollaerts envisaged a coalition of nationalist parties forming a government of an independent Vietnam within the French Union, but he had very little freedom of action. He tried to form a grouping round Bao Dai, then in Hong Kong, which he hoped could negotiate an agreement with the Viet Minh. Bao Dai's problem, apart from lack of unity, authority and enthusiasm among his potential or actual supporters, was that he could only compete against the Viet Minh for popular support if he demanded a degree of independence from France which she was not prepared to concede, and the avoidance of which was her only purpose in supporting him. If the French had been prepared to concede that, they would have dealt with Ho Chi Minh and ignored Bao Dai.

The stalemate continued in 1948. The Viet Minh was gradually strengthening its hold all over the country and building up its forces. An integrated political and military organization was established based on six zones, three covering Tonkin, two Annam, north and south of Húe, and one Cochin-China. The main guerrilla base was still in the Viet Bac, the mountains north of the Red River delta, with the second main base in Tonkin south of the delta. In Annam the Viet Minh controlled most of the country, the French being restricted to the towns of Hué and Tourane and the main coastal road. In the south the Viet Minh were based on four areas, an important one being the Plaine des Joncs, a swampy region north of Saigon. The bulk of Giap's regular forces were concentrated in the Tonkin bases. Elsewhere he was building up regional forces of part-time soldiers who, at this period, bore the brunt of operations against the French. This took the form of constant harassment by ambushes and surprise attacks against small bodies of men. These forces were supported in every way by larger numbers of militia, who had little military training and few or no firearms, but provided information, gathered and delivered supplies, passed messages, recruited and provided guards. Giap was still in the stage defined by Mao Tse-tung as 'guerrilla warfare', although in some areas verging on that of 'protracted warfare'. The French made little headway in operations against the Viet Minh, who dispersed and disappeared into the jungle or the general population, while they themselves suffered a continuous drain of casualties.

After a final attempt to involve the Viet Minh in negotiations with Bao Dai in April, the French Government agreed to the formation of a provisional government of Vietnam of which Bao Dai was the titular head, the Chief Minister being General Nguyen Van Xuan, a Vietnamese serving as a regular officer in the French Army, who had little popular support. However, in setting up the government, France had at last conceded the principle of the unity of the three territories of Vietnam. It did them little good, as it soon became apparent that the French had no intention of handing over the real reins of power, which they intended to continue to keep in their hands through the retention, indeed the further recruitment of large numbers of Frenchmen in the administration and the armed forces of the country. It was not until May 1949 that the French National Assembly finally approved the union of the three territories. Xuan resigned and Bao Dai, unable to persuade anyone to succeed him, resigned as Emperor and assumed the position of Head of State himself, Monsieur Pignon replacing Bollaerts as High Commissioner.

The military situation, in spite of an increase in troop strength to nearly 150,000, was still unsatisfactory. General Revers, Chief of the French General Staff, reviewed the situation in May 1949 and made some drastic recommendations. He proposed that the frontier garrisons in Tonkin, vulnerable to the presence of Giap's army behind and around them, should be withdrawn, concentrating in the Red River delta, which should be pacified and placed under an indigenous administration. The same policy should be pursued in the Mekong delta. A strong independent Vietnamese army should be built up quickly and more French instructors and more and better equipment provided. When these measures had been completed, a counter-offensive against the Viet Minh could be launched. In the interim period, further French troops would be needed to implement the plan. The Viet Minh got hold of a copy of this plan and broadcast extracts from it, which contributed to its rejection by the French Government. As a result things continued as before, the French forces being scattered all over the country, mostly in static posts guarding roads and rivers, incapable of and unwilling to embark on offensive operations.

Later in the year the whole situation was changed by Mao Tse-tung's decisive victory in China, bringing his forces right up to the frontier of Tonkin. Militarily and politically this changed the balance decisively in favour of the Viet Minh, and in January 1950 Ho Chi Minh announced that his was the only representative government of Vietnam, being recognized as such by China, Russia and most of the communist bloc. In reaction to this, the West recognized Bao Dai's government, the Americans significantly coming down off the fence and deciding that, now clearly faced by the threat of international communism, Indo-China qualified for military aid. This saw the start of a long tussle between France and the United States about how this should be applied, the United States wishing to provide it direct to Bao Dai's administration and to Laos and Cambodia, while the French insisted it should be channelled through them.

Giap now definitely turned to protracted warfare, almost to the final stage of 'mobile warfare'. He started with an attack in February on the isolated battalion garrison of Lao Kai on the Red River near the Chinese frontier. Outnumbering it five to one, he captured it after a short fight. In the next three months he was busy absorbing supplies of guns and mortars from China and training his men in their use. In May he struck at another battalion garrison in the north-east at Dong Khe. He captured it, but the French counter-attacked with a parachute force and took it back. The rains then set in and neither side did very much until they finished in October. By then Giap had nearly doubled the strength of his regular forces and formed five divisions, four in the Viet Bac and one, the 320th, in the South Delta base. By the end of the year three of them had been equipped with field and anti-aircraft artillery and mortars.

Giap's opponent, now General Carpentier, was not so fortunate. His government had proposed that his forces should be reduced, as fewer volunteers were forthcoming and the French Government, bedevilled all this time by internal dissensions, refused to contemplate ordering conscripts to Indo-China. They hoped that the Americans would provide equipment of all kinds which would make somewhat smaller forces more effective than the largely static scattered garrisons which absorbed so much manpower. But the Americans had both political and military reservations. They did not believe that a primarily French force, designed to preserve a French presence, however indirectly, could win the war. In any case they had ingrained political inhibitions about supporting it. They were above all anxious to prevent the spread of communism and tended to believe that this could only be done by granting independence and giving sufficient support, political and military, to a non-communist independent government to enable it to defeat its communist rivals both politically, in terms of being seen to have won independence, and militarily by having a strong and effective army of its own, independent of French command. American military support was therefore never as whole-hearted as the French hoped.

Once the rains were over, Giap returned to the attack on French garrisons near the frontier. Dong Khe was the first to fall after a fierce two-day defence by the Foreign Legion. He then successfully ambushed other garrisons, who were trying to evacuate the frontier area, and the relief column sent to help them. By the end of October he had forced the French to abandon the whole area and had inflicted very heavy casualties on them. Giap's victory caused near-panic among French civilians in Tonkin, who saw the area under French control reduced to that of the delta south of the Red River, apart from some enclaves on the coast. General Carpentier had lost 6,000 men, most of them taken prisoner with all their equipment. Before this the total strength of the forces under his command had risen to 152,000 of whom 65,000 were French. This did not include some 120,000 Vietnamese serving in Bao Dai's army, in partisan forces or as militia on the government side. Since 1946 his French soldiers had suffered an average of 2,500 casualties a year, including a total of 800 French officers, equalling the output of St Cyr over that period. Vietnamese casualties on the government side had averaged 7,500 a year.

French morale sank to an all-time low. Marshal Juin, the new Chief of the French General Staff, came out to help restore it, and Carpentier and Pignon were dismissed amid mutual recriminations between the soldiers and the politicians. The shock, however, spurred the French Government to greater efforts to support the military in Indo-China. Marshal de Lattre de Tassigny, one of France's most brilliant soldiers, was sent out to combine the posts of High Commissioner and Commander-in-Chief. He swept through the military hierarchy with a new broom, cancelled plans for the evacuation of French families and applied himself to the development of an offensive strategy, for which he had been given a free hand. This was an adaptation of the plan which Carpentier had evolved, but not been allowed to put into effect. While placing greater emphasis on the rapid build up of an indigenous Vietnam army, he planned to hold securely the vital areas, the Red River delta, Tourane and Hué in Annam and the more important areas of the Mekong delta; and to form mobile groups, supported by air attack and airborne troops, who could rapidly concentrate to counter-attack any Viet Minh attack. The first test of this came in January 1951, when two of Giap's divisions attacked Vinh Yen on the Red River, forty miles north-west of Hanoi, overrunning most of the garrison. De Lattre took personal command of the counter-attack. The battle lasted for five days and casualties were heavy on both sides. Giap had employed 22,000 men to attack the garrison of 6,000, increased by the counter-attacking force to 10,000. It is estimated that he lost 6,000 killed and 8,000 wounded: only 600 were taken prisoner. Many of the casualties resulted from napalm attacks by the French Air Force. De Lattre was left in possession of the field, but realized that it had been a close shave. His reaction was to put a great effort into improving the defences of the delta on what was called the 'de Lattre line', in order to free more troops to form mobile groups for counter-attack, and to develop special forces of Indo-Chinese, led by French, to carry out offensive patrols into the areas occupied by the Viet Minh.

Giap, having retired to lick his wounds, struck again in March near the coast east of Hanoi at Mao Khe with one division. The French were slow to react, suspecting it to be a diversion, but, when they did, the combination of paratroops, a considerable concentration of artillery, air attack and the intervention of a naval support force was successful in defeating the attack. Giap's 316th Division withdrew, suffering some 3,000 casualties over five days of fighting. French morale had received a significant boost. Giap now realized that, in aiming to recapture Hanoi and Haiphong, he had pitched his hopes too high. His next blow was aimed at the Catholic-dominated area on the Day River on the south side of the delta. The main target was the town of Phat Diem, with diversionary attacks on Ninh Binh and Phu Ly higher up the river. They were to link up with operations by Viet Minh regional forces within the delta itself. The attack was to be launched at the end of May when the rains would have started. Not only would this aid surprise, but it should also limit the ability of de Lattre's air and mobile troops to intervene. The French reacted quickly and strongly, their naval force on the river being particularly effective. Giap had spread his forces over a wide area and, being a Catholic area, he received no support from, indeed was opposed by the local population. After three weeks of inconclusive fighting, he withdrew to lick his wounds once more.

It was clear to Ho Chi Minh that Giap had turned too soon to mobile warfare, and that he should return, as the Chinese had advised, to guerrilla warfare. Some scapegoat had to be found, and, illogically, as he had merely been engaged in attempting to contain French forces in Cochin-China by guerrilla tactics, Nguyen Binh was summoned north to be dealt with. On his way he ran into a French patrol and was killed. Honour was satisfied by this. The vendetta was called off, but it opened the way for the Viet Minh to extend and strengthen their influence in the south. The rainy season was given over to a thorough shake-up of the whole Viet Minh organization, political and military, communications being greatly improved, the regular divisions equipped and trained with heavier weapons and considerable attention paid to the development of the supply system. De Lattre was also hard at work on his plan, strengthening his defences, forming more mobile groups and improving Bao Dai's army, for which conscription had now been introduced, a measure which was far from popular and may well have been counter-productive as far as hopes of increasing political support for Bao Dai's administration were concerned and led to difficulties with the Cao Dai, Hoa Hao and Binh Xuyen.

In spite of his experiences earlier in the year, Giap opened the campaigning season in October with another attack, on Nglia Lo, an isolated garrison of 700 men in a fertile plain among the jungle-covered hills between the Red and Black Rivers about a hundred miles north-west of Hanoi. Giap's 312th Division attacked on 3 October. French reaction was swift: an air attack, combined with a parachute drop of three battalions, one to reinforce the defenders and two behind the attacking troops, defeated the Viet Minh and drove them back into the hills. The success of this action encouraged de Lattre to maintain these garrisons in key areas which controlled the few roads along which the Viet Minh might be supplied from China. Buoyed up by the victory, de Lattre decided to strike back at Hoa Binh, a communication centre twenty-five miles west of the de Lattre line on the Black River. On 14 November three parachute battalions dropped and captured the town with no difficulty. They were reinforced by two columns, one coming up the river and the other, a large one of eight mobile groups, up Route Coloniale 6. Having done so, five battalions were left there and four more were deployed to guard the two routes, the mobile forces being withdrawn. Giap realized that this offered him a good opportunity to counter-attack, but he took his time. He deployed all six of his regular divisions into the area, intending to use three of them in a counter-attack. This he launched on 9 December with an attack on one of the posts guarding the river approach, at Tu Vu. It was completely successful and was followed up during January with further attacks which forced the French to abandon the river supply route. Giap then turned his attention to the road, which became the scene of fierce fighting, absorbing the efforts of all the French mobile reserves available in the delta. They managed to open up the road again, but keeping it open absorbed so much effort that the maintenance of the garrison at Hoa Binh became an unacceptable drain on their resources.

De Lattre had returned to France on 20 November and died there on 11 January 1952, having already lost his only son in the fighting at Phat Diem the previous year. He was succeeded by General Salan, who had to take the unpalatable decision to withdraw from Hoa Binh and the whole area between it and the de Lattre line.

The rainy season of 1952 coincided with a lull in the war in Korea, in which the Chinese were now involved. As they were receiving plentiful supplies of Russian equipment, as well as manufacturing their own, they were able to pass on to Giap both their old supplies of captured Japanese weapons and also American equipment taken in Korea, the latter having the advantage that much of it was common to that used by the French. These supplies made it possible for Giap to improve the equipment of his five infantry divisions and significantly that of his 351st Heavy Division. By the middle of 1952 he probably had some 110,000 regular troops, 75,000 men in regional forces and 120,000 active in village militia.

Salan also received more equipment, principally from the United States, the most significant being Dakota transport aircraft to replace his ancient captured German JU52s. Although the strength of his forces had fallen from 192,000[*] to 174,000, he had hoped for further reinforcements, but none were forthcoming and he had to pin his hopes on the growth of the Vietnam National Army. Although its strength was nominally over 100,000, only one of its planned four divisions had been formed and most of its forty battalions were still under French control. They reluctantly agreed to increase the target to six divisions and to hasten the hand-over of forces to Bao Dai, under pressure from the Americans, who threatened to cut off supplies if they did not. The lack of suitable material to train as officers and the high rate of desertion among conscripts were among the reasons for French reluctance to move more quickly in this field.

Giap took the initiative at the end of the rainy season in mid-October with a renewed attack on Nglia Lo and other garrisons on the ridge between the Red and the Black Rivers. This surprised Salan, who had been expecting an attack in the Red River delta. The French were outnumbered and their paratroopers suffered heavy casualties in an attempt to rescue the garrisons as they withdrew. It was a severe reverse for Salan, who tried to counter it with a thrust up the valley of the Clear River from the north-west tip of the de Lattre line.

[*] 51,000 French, 18,000 Foreign Legion, 25,000 North Africans, 56,000 Indo-Chinese, 42,000 other native auxiliaries.

Thirty thousand troops were used in this attempt to block one of Giap's principal supply routes from China and strike at one of his main base areas. As in the case of the Hoa Binh operation in 1951, the French reached their objective without difficulty, capturing a large haul of stores and equipment; but their troubles started as they tried to maintain their position at the end of a hundred-mile-long narrow corridor with only one road, on both sides of which Giap gradually closed in. Keeping his forces supplied absorbed the whole of Salan's air transport fleet and on 14 November he decided to withdraw all the way back to the de Lattre line. In the process of doing so, one large column was ambushed and suffered heavy casualties, French losses for the whole operation amounting to 1,200. To counterbalance this failure, the French successfully held Na Sam in the Thai highlands on the route leading into Laos against an attack a week later by Giap's 308th Division. Little fighting took place in the north after this, Giap keeping his forces in the highlands astride the Red and Black Rivers, Salan switching his effort to improving the situation in Annam and the Mekong delta. He succeeded in clearing several areas, but, as soon as his forces had done so and moved on, the Viet Minh resumed their sway.

In April 1953 it suddenly became apparent to the French that Giap's concentration in the Thai highlands was aimed, not at a renewal of attacks in the Red River delta, but at an invasion of Laos. This immediately threatened the French garrison of Sam Neua in north-east Laos. Salan, having initially ordered its reinforcement, decided to evacuate it instead, and the garrison was involved in a running fight with Giap's 316th Division as it withdrew. By the end of the month his 312th Division was on the outskirts of the royal capital of Luang Prabang, while his 308th was threatening Vientiane. The hurriedly reinforced French position in the Plain of Jars was surrounded, its maintenance once more absorbing all Salan's air transport resources. While Salan was wondering what to do next, Giap withdrew almost all his forces north again as the rains began. He had forced Salan to dance to his tune, even if there were no very concrete gains to show for his venture.

Salan was now discredited and was succeeded by General Navarre, who assumed command at the end of May 1953. He found the situation in the Mekong delta tolerable, although large portions of it were under the control of the Cao Dai, Hoa Hao and Binh Xuyen rather than of either the French or Bao Dai's armed forces. In Annam French control was still limited to the areas immediately round Hué, Tourane and Nha Trang. Although the coast road was open, it was dangerous to use it and most supplies moved by sea. In Tonkin the de Lattre line was absorbing the bulk of his 175,000 soldiers, only seven mobile groups and eight parachute battalions being available for offensive or counter-offensive operations. In spite of this, Giap had three independent regiments operating within the de Lattre line, two battalions in Hanoi itself. His regular force of six divisions numbered 125,000, supported by 75,000 regional troops and by now perhaps a quarter of a million militia. Bao Dai's

Vietnam National Army's nominal strength had risen to 150,000 but nothing like that number could be put into the field.

Navarre's plan was to try and avoid major engagements in the next campaigning season, October 1953 to April 1954, while he built up a mobile force of six or seven divisions with American equipment. Meanwhile the Vietnam National Army could progressively relieve French forces of static defensive tasks and there would be a major expansion of light battalions, capable of infiltrating areas dominated by the Viet Minh. He was confident that, although he might lose control of Annam, he could retain both delta areas until launching an offensive in the 1954/5 campaigning season. This plan was not received with enthusiasm either by the French Government or by the Americans. The former was reluctant to provide the French reinforcements which it entailed. By now the Indo-Chinese War was thoroughly unpopular in France and troops could only be found either from Algeria or at the expense of NATO at a time when great pressure was being brought to bear to persuade France to accept the rearmament of Germany. The Americans were already dissatisfied with what they considered the ineffectiveness of French military action in Indo-China and viewed with dismay Navarre's proposal to do nothing for a year. However, after a visit to France, he extracted ten more battalions and a half-hearted promise of support from the United States. During the rainy season Navarre concentrated on training the Vietnam National Army and carried out two effective operations, one in Tonkin, which resulted in the destruction of large stocks of Viet Minh supplies, the other to clear the coast road in Annam. He attempted, without success, to eliminate Viet Minh forces within the de Lattre line, which had been increasing as Giap infiltrated them in from outside. The latter's major effort had been the improvement of road communications between his Thai highland bases and China.

When the rains finished, Navarre expected Giap to attack in the Red River delta, and, when he did not, decided to try and draw him by an attack on Phu Ly on the Day River. It was successfullly resisted by Giap's 320th Division without any help from elsewhere, a rebuff for Navarre, who was faced with the alternatives either of striking against Giap's main base area north of the delta or of interposing his forces between Giap's and Laos. If he did neither, the initiative would pass once more to the Viet Minh. The former could involve considerable casualties, setting back his plans to increase his mobile forces. He therefore chose the latter and selected Dien Bien Phu, a centre of communications just over the border in Laos, as the best place for his purpose, dropping three parachute battalions there on 20 November to start building a strong defensive base. Having put his money on Dien Bien Phu, he evacuated other garrisons on the approaches to it, one effect of which was to withdraw support from the light mixed French and Indo-Chinese special units based on them. An attempt by Navarre in February to extend his hold on Annam met with failure and absorbed more of his precious reserves. While he was doing this, Giap made another rapid incursion into Laos, once more threatening Luang Prabang and straining Navarre's air transport fleet in moves to counter it.

By the beginning of March 1954 the garrison of Dien Bien Phu had been increased to twelve battalions with supporting artillery, which included four 155 mm. medium guns, and ten light tanks flown in and assembled on the spot. Six fighter-bombers were based on the airstrip in the middle of the main position, which was overlooked from the surrounding hills. There was a second strip near the detached position, known as *Isabelle*, four miles to the south. Navarre was confident that it could withstand an attack by up to three Viet Minh divisions, and, when Monsieur Pleven, the French Minister of Defence, and General Ely, the Chief of the French General Staff, visited it in February, they saw no reason to disagree. By the end of that month Giap's forces were closing in all round, and by 13 March, when he launched his attack on the outlying positions north of the main ones, he had elements of five of his divisions concentrated around the position, amounting in total to the equiv- alent of four divisions. After four days of bitter fighting, in the course of which an additional battalion had been parachuted in, the three outlying positions in the north had been lost and the perimeter restricted to the main position, apart from *Isabelle*. One result was that the airstrip could no longer be used either for casualty evacuation or for supply, which henceforward was restricted to paradrop. Every available aircraft was thrown in, particularly to try and counter Giap's artillery, but it was very well concealed, guns being sited singly and constantly moving position. Anti-aircraft units from Red China were moved down, while on the French side civilian aircraft were for a time employed to drop supplies.

At the end of the month the Viet Minh carried out a series of mass attacks on the main positions. They made some inroads, but failed to effect any serious penetration and suffered very heavy casualties, but successfully held French counter-attacks. For almost the whole of April they systematically sapped and burrowed their way forward to the edge of the French positions all round the perimeter in the manner of an old-fashioned siege operation. The French reinforced the garrison with another parachute battalion, but were having difficulty in dropping supplies inside the restricted perimeter. On 22 April the rains came and what had been a dust-bowl turned into a sea of mud. Navarre hoped that this would bring an end to Giap's attacks, although it seriously restricted the air support he could give to the 16,000 of his best soldiers tied up in this remote base. The French in desperation turned to the Americans to seek the direct intervention of their air power, even to the extent of employing a nuclear weapon; but this was not to be, the British under Churchill strongly objecting to Truman to any question of using a nuclear weapon. On 1 May, that Socialist festival, Giap began his final assault which continued for six days. At midday on 7 May 1954 his men broke through to the centre of the position and all was over. It had cost him over 20,000 casualties, 8,000 of them killed. The French had lost 7,184 men killed, wounded or missing, and 11,000 were marched off into captivity. Of the total of nearly 20,000 men involved, only 3,000 were French. Six thousand of the garrison had been Indo-Chinese. Of the thirteen infantry battalions, seven had been parachutists, mostly of the Foreign Legion, three North African and three Indo-Chinese.

The day that Dien Bien Phu fell saw the opening of the Geneva Conference, called to wind up both the Korean and the Indo-Chinese Wars. Although France had signed a declaration for the complete independence of Vietnam, Laos and Cambodia on 28 April, she was still haggling over details. Meanwhile fighting continued, General Ely replacing Navarre on 3 June, his aim being to withdraw through Haiphong in as orderly a fashion as possible. On 21 July an armistice agreement was signed at Geneva, under which the French were to evacuate the country down to the 17th parallel within a hundred days, handing it over to Ho Chi Minh. South of that line, the country would be handed over to a Government of South Vietnam, of which Ngo Dinh Diem, returned from the United States, was to be the head. All this was to be supervised by an international commission provided by India, Poland and Canada and was to be the prelude to elections throughout Vietnam in two years' time. French troops were also to leave Cambodia, but they were allowed to retain two bases and a training mission in Laos. It was the best that the French Prime Minister, Mendès-France, could achieve, anxious as he was to be relieved of this burden which was poisoning the political atmosphere of France itself.

There are those who suggest that, if the French had fought their campaign in a different way, if they had followed the pattern which the British did in Malaya, they could have succeeded. But conditions were very different. Ho Chi Minh and Giap had established their position, certainly in Tonkin, in far greater strength politically and militarily than Chin Peng in Malaya. The great majority of the people resented the return of the French, whose presence was much more oppressive in the main delta areas than that of the British in Malaya. Hopes of restoring French authority throughout Tonkin were very slender even before the Chinese communists reached its frontier. Thereafter the attempt to do so was hopeless, but into it France poured all her military effort. Successive French Commanders-in-Chief had all come to the same conclusion: that the solution lay in creating an indigenous army which could take over the role of static defence, while, with equipment provided by the Americans, they created a reserve of French units, mobile both by air and on land, to counter Giap's regular forces and take the offensive to regain control of the country. But the resources to implement their plans were slow in coming and, before they could develop their strategy, they were forced to react to Giap's initiative. His widespread control of the countryside freed his regular forces to concentrate on keeping the initiative in his hands. Having learnt his lesson in 1951, he was careful thereafter to limit his offensives to objectives where the balance of advantage lay in his favour.

Had France been content to grant real and immediate independence to Tonkin and Annam and concentrated her effort on maintaining her influence in Cochin-China, spreading from there into Cambodia, she might well have been successful. But to have done so would have been a very bitter pill to swallow, just as she was trying to re-establish her position in the world after the humiliations of the Second World War. It would have had repercussions all over her empire, and in Asia in particular it would have been hailed as a victory for communism. As it was she suffered the worst of all worlds and her army became embittered with her politicians, with consequences that were to be seen later in Algeria. America took on the burden of opposing communism in Vietnam and was in the end to be no more successful than France in doing so, in spite of her overwhelming military power. France's Indo-Chinese War was the start of a long, stark tragedy.

Chapter Eight

ALGERIA

If France can have been said to have had any good fortune in her colonial problems, one stroke of luck was that she was able to wash her hands of Indo-China just before she faced an equally intractable problem in Algeria, which was to have greater repercussions in France itself. Algeria was France's Ireland, almost as closely linked to the homeland as Ireland had been to Great Britain until 1922, and with the same problem of a minority population implanted by colonialization.

The original inhabitants were the Berbers, 'natives' or '*barbari*' as they were named by the Romans who settled on the coast, a name perpetuated by the Arabs who overran the coastal area in the eleventh century AD and drove the Berbers back into the mountains, at the same time converting them to Islam. In the sixteenth century the Turks established their rule, which was so lightly imposed that a century later the Deys and Beys they had appointed became a law unto themselves, falling under the domination of their mercenary soldiers, the Janissaries. This was the age of the Barbary corsairs, whose depredations caused the European powers and even the United States to consider action against them. In 1830 France decided to intervene, partly to bolster the unpopular regime of Charles X, the pretext being retaliation for the insult inflicted on her consul three years before, when, in an argument about money owed by the French Government under Napoleon to Jewish traders in Algiers, the Dey of Algiers had struck him in the face with a fly-whisk.

Within two years of invading the country, the French found themselves with a war on their hands, the resistance to them led by Abd el Kader. The French under Marshal Bugeaud waged a bitter and relentless campaign against him for fifteen years. In 1847 he surrendered and retired to exile in Damascus. In the following year the French Second Republic declared the whole of Algeria to be an integral part of France itself, dividing it into three departments, an act as fateful in its consequences as the 1801 Act of Union uniting the Kingdoms of Ireland and Great Britain. By that time France had already initiated a policy of colonization, about 40,000 Frenchmen having been settled among the three million Arab and Berber inhabitants, mostly in the coastal Arab-inhabited areas. Resistance developed as this colonization proceeded on lands taken over from the Turkish state domains, expropriated as 'under-utilized' or purchased from its existing owners, settlers coming not only from France, the German occupation of Alsace and Lorraine in 1871 leading to an influx from there, but also from Spain, Malta and Corsica. By 1870 the number of settlers, known as *pieds noirs*,* had risen to 100,000 and they demanded a say in how the country was run – hitherto it had been administered almost wholly by the army. This led to a form of representative government, dominated by the *pieds noirs*, but in which the Muslim inhabitants were represented separately through a colonial administrative system, of which the officials were almost exclusively French or *pied noir*. Opposition to the growing presence and influence of the latter led to troubles with the Kabyle, people of Berber origin who lived in the mountains east of Algiers, which was not finally suppressed until 1881.

The grievances and resentments inescapable in such a colonial situation were all present. The best land was taken either by settlers or by large organizations, although they also reclaimed and developed land that had never been used before. The Compagnie Génévoise was the most prominent. The result was that crops were raised on a large scale, turning the simple peasant into a landless labourer. The more the land was developed, the greater the contrast between the life of the original inhabitants and that of the settler, who acquired special privileges and treated the former as a second-class citizen. At the same time, as in Indo-China, the missionary zeal of the French to impart their culture, a zeal shared by the anti-clerical liberal, the church and the army each in their own fashion, created the expectation among a class of educated native Algerians that they would be treated as equals by the French. This expectation, as in Indo-China, was shared by the tens of thousands of Algerians who served in the French armed forces, particularly in the First World War. The influences of the Second World War, the humiliation of France, the second humiliation of the Vichy regime in Algeria itself, the liberation by the Allies with the expectation raised both by de Gaulle's Brazzaville declaration in January 1944 that it was French policy 'to lead each of the colonial peoples to a development that will permit them to administer themselves, and later to govern themselves' and by the American desire to see an end to colonialism, all created a fertile seed-bed for the idea of an Algeria in which the non-European inhabitants would at least have equal rights with the French and *pieds noirs*, whatever might be the form of its association with France.

By 1945 the movements favouring this had coalesced into three principal groups. First the *Ulema*. This was a puritanical Islamic movement led by

---

* The origin of the term is disputed. Some derive it from the black leather shoes of the French Army: others from the disparaging view of the metropolitan French that the *colon*'s feet were burnt black by the sun. Alistair Horne, *A Savage War of Peace*, p. 30.

Sheikh Ben Badis, a Berber from Constantine descended from a family that had been influential in political and religious affairs for centuries. The movement resisted the spread of French culture and called for a return to strict Mohammedanism, expressing its creed as 'Islam is my religion, Arabic my language, Algeria my country'. Second was the movement led by Messali Hadj, who, born in 1898, served in the French Army from 1914 to 1918 and founded in 1927 the *Étoile Nord-Africaine*. This was also a nationalist Islamic movement, but was based on proletarian socialism and favoured more extreme revolutionary methods than the *Ulema*. Messali's call for a revolution to bring independence to all three French North African countries (Morocco and Tunisia were protectorates), based on universal adult suffrage, led to the banning of his movement and his imprisonment or exile. As a result it underwent several changes of name, through the PPA (*Parti Progressiste Algérien*) to, by 1945 the MTLD (*Movement pour le Triomphe des Libertés Démocratiques*). The third, in contrast to the other two, was in favour of an association with France. Ferhat Abbas was the acknowledged leader and his movement was later to be known as the UDMA (*Union Démocratique pour le Manifeste Algérien*). He also came from Constantine, his father, a simple peasant's son, having risen to be a *caid*, a local governor, and a companion of the Legion of Honour. Abbas was educated at a French Lycée in Constantine and at Algiers University, became a pharmacist, married a French wife after having divorced his Muslim one, and served in the French Army in the Second World War, although not as an officer. After the failure in 1936 of the Blum–Violette proposals for making Algeria a truly integral part of France and all its inhabitants equal French citizens, he became disillusioned and switched to favouring an independent Algeria, although still in association with France.

These were the movements which had an influence in bringing about the tragic events of VE day, 8 May 1945, at Sétif, eighty miles west of Constantine, which were to have a profound influence in leading, nine years later, to the outbreak of what Alistair Horne has aptly called 'A Savage War of Peace'. Supporters of Messali Hadj planned to exploit the ceremony to celebrate victory by a huge demonstration flourishing banners calling for his release and for a free and independent Algeria. The police were ordered by the sub-prefect to seize the banners. In the struggle shots were fired by both sides, the police were overwhelmed and the demonstrators ran wild. For five days Muslim extremists attacked Europeans all over the area, killing, raping and mutilating, leaving 103 dead and 100 wounded. By then the army had been called in, and in savage retaliatory operations, which included summary executions, dive-bombing of remote villages and naval bombardment of the small town of Kerrata, at least 500 Muslims were killed. In addition the *pieds noirs* took their own revenge, the casualties from which have been estimated at such varying figures as 1,300 and 50,000, the most generally accepted total being about 6,000. One man who was profoundly affected by the savagery of this revenge

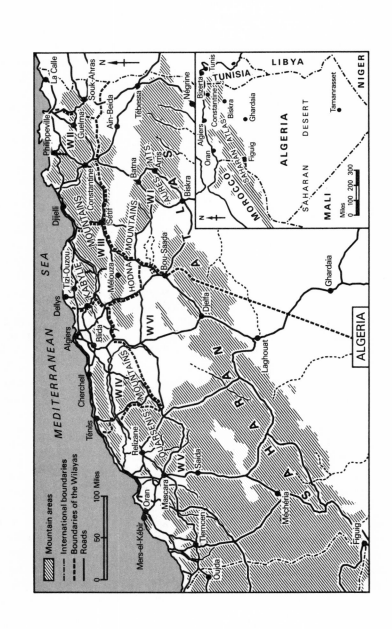

was a sergeant of the 7th Regiment of Algerian Tirailleurs, decorated for bravery in a regiment that had a high reputation for courage among the Free French, many of whose soldiers came from the area round Sétif. His name was Ben Bella. Another aspect of the *pied noir* revenge for Sétif was the participation in it of the Algerian communists. The PCA (*Parti Communiste Algérien*) had close links with the French Communist Party, at that time reflecting the glory of its participation in the resistance and the liberation of France, and its members labelled the Muslim outburst at Sétif and after as fascist-inspired. They were not to be forgiven for this by Messali, Abbas and those who later joined the ranks of the nationalists.

Reaction to Sétif was not however entirely negative. It prompted the French Government to propose reforms giving concessions to the Muslims in terms of representation, rights and recognition of Arabic as an official language in addition to French, although the system was to be retained by which French and Muslim representatives were separately elected, so that the minority European population of about one million had equal representation with the Arab and Berber population, then nearing nine million and increasing at the rate of a quarter of a million a year. The Europeans considered that they had a right to at least this say in the affairs of the country, in that they had developed it and created its wealth, which they continued to do, and made the major contribution in the form of taxation to the services provided for the whole community. The proposals satisfied neither the *colons* nor the nationalists and only just scraped through the French parliament. The elections for the new Algerian assembly, held in 1948, were conducted in a blatantly fraudulent manner, resulting in government-favoured candidates for the Muslim seats gaining 55 seats, Messali's MTLD 9, Abbas's UDMA 8 and Independent Socialists 2, in contrast to a forecast that, if they had been fairly and freely conducted, MTLD would have gained 60. In further elections held in 1951 this rigging was carried to a fine art, the total nationalist vote being reduced to a total of eight. By the time of the second election the extremists among the nationalists were beginning to get the upper hand. Prominent among them were Ben Bella and Belkacem Krim. Ben Bella headed a militant splinter group from the MTLD, known as OS (*Organisation Spéciale*), which began to prepare for armed action. After a poorly executed bomb raid in 1950, the police broke up OS and Ben Bella was arrested and imprisoned, later escaping and making his way to Cairo, while Messali was exiled to France. Arguments about whether or not to support OS and a policy of militancy led not only to a split between MTLD and UDMA, but to a division within the MTLD, led by the more extreme element who objected to its domination by Messali. Belkacem Krim, a Kabyle Berber, had also served in the army and, like Abbas, was the son of a *caid*. On demobilization he joined the MTLD and, when summoned to appear in court for organizing a political strike, took to the mountains of Kabylia and began to form an armed resistance movement with another Kabyle, Oman Ouamrane.

As the climax of the battle of Dien Bien Phu was approaching in April 1954, the extremists came together to form a new body, the CRUA (*Comité Révolutionnaire d'Unité et d'Action*) headed by the *'neuf historiques'*: Ait Ahmed, another son of a Kabyle *caid*; Ben Bella, Ben Boulaid, from the wild Aures area in the south-east, like Ben Bella a highly decorated ex-army warrant officer; Ben M'hidi from Oran; Rabah Bitat, from the area round Algiers; Mohamed Boudiaf, head of the MTLD in France; Mourad Didouche, his deputy; Mohamed Khider, based with Ben Bella and Ait Ahmed in Cairo; and Belkacem Krim. The fall of Dien Bien Phu and its aftermath spurred CRUA on to advance their plans to strike while France, as they saw it, was at her weakest. After attempts to enlist the support of the other nationalists had failed, the decision was taken at a meeting in Switzerland in October 1954 to start military action on 1 November, All Saints Day, observed by the French as a holiday. CRUA was to change its name to the FLN (*Front de la Libération Nationale*) and Ben Bella and his colleagues were to seek political and military help from Nasser and the Arab League. The affairs of the movement were to be controlled by a committee, consisting of the External Delegation (Boudiaf in France, Ben Bella, Ait Ahmed and Khider in Cairo) and the Internal Delegation, formed from the nominated leaders of the six regions, or *Wilaya*, into which they divided Algeria. They were:

Wilaya	I	The Aures Mountains:	Ben Boulaid
	II	North Constantine:	Mohamed Didouche
	III	Kabylia:	Belkacem Krim
	IV	Algiers, and to south and west of it:	Rabah Bitat
	V	Oran and the west:	Ben M'hidi
	VI	The desert area south of the Atlas Mountains:	no commander designated

The Wilaya commanders were to be responsible for all political and military matters in their area and were to have a free hand in raising armed forces, which were to be known as the ALN (*Armée de Libération Nationale*), and in deciding how they should be employed. In principle they would follow the Viet Minh pattern. As arms became available, regular forces, called *Moujahidines*, would be formed, supported by *Moussebilines*, part-time soldiers without pay or uniform, rather more akin to the militia than to the regional forces of the Viet Minh, and the *Fidayines*, local supporters who acted as couriers, supply-carriers, informers and guards. At the start the total number of armed men was probably not more than 3,000, the principal limitation being the supply of weapons. Apart from shotguns, they were limited to those stolen or obtained by devious means from the French, some during the Second World War, and some smuggled in. The *Moujahidines* were to operate in small bodies of four or five and their targets were to be public installations, the private property of the *grands colons*, French military personnel and police, and Muslims who worked for or collaborated with the French authorities. European civilians, especially women and children, were not to be attacked for fear of a reaction similar to that of Sétif. As soon as attacks had been carried out, the fighters were to withdraw. The explosives needed were made within the Muslim quarter of Algiers, the Casbah, and at Souma, thirty miles away, under the direction of Bouadjadj, chief of the Algiers area. The tightest secrecy was observed to conceal the preparations both from the French and from the other factions of the MTLD. This was successful, although, as All Saints Day approached, warnings that something was afoot had reached the Head of the Security Service, Jean Vaujour, the Governor-General, Roger Léonard, and the Commander-in-Chief, General Cherrière, known as 'Babar' from his elephantine figure. The warning had been passed on to François Mitterand in Paris, Minister of the Interior and as such responsible for Algeria; but none of them suspected a major outbreak of violence.

The area chosen by the FLN for its main attack was the desolate and remote area of the Aures Mountains in the south-east. Here Boulaid with some 150 men was to attack targets at Biskra, Batna, Arris and Khenchela and the lead mine at Ichmoul. The timing of his attacks was ill-co-ordinated, with the result that, in several cases, the police were already alert. Nowhere could they have been said to have been successful, apart from some damage from explosions, but one incident was to have wide repercussions. With the connivance of the driver, they ambushed a bus south of Arris in order to kill a loyal *caid*, Hadj Sadak. Also on the bus were two French schoolteachers, Guy Monnerot and his wife, returning from their honeymoon. In shooting Sadak, they also wounded the Monnerots, the husband dying before they were rescued. ALN attacks in the rest of the country were no more successful, all the planned attacks in Algiers itself failing, as did attacks by Bitat's and Ouamrane's men, their total haul of weapons coming to no more than ten. Ben M'hidi's men in Oran were even less successful, eight of them being killed. Only Belkacem Krim had had any significant success, the damage his men caused to barracks, gendarmeries and cork and tobacco warehouses being assessed at 200 million francs. The attacks were accompanied by a proclamation by the FLN, broadcast on Cairo radio, inviting the support of all Algerian patriots to gain national independence through the restoration of an Algerian state, based on the principles of Islam, preserving all fundamental freedoms, without distinction of race or religion. This would be achieved internally through 'political house-cleaning', externally by internationalizing the problem, the pursuit of North African unity in an Arab–Islamic context, seeking help through the United Nations and sympathizers of liberation. The struggle would be long, but they were prepared to negotiate with the French on the basis of the latter's recognition of Algerian sovereignty, 'one and indivisible', and the release of all political prisoners. In return for this, French cultural and economic interests would be recognized, as would the rights of the French as individuals, provided that they chose either to be treated as foreign nationals or as Algerians on a basis of equality. An ambitious programme for a movement in its infancy, but one from which they were never to waver and which, nearly eight years later, they were to achieve.

The limited results of the ALN attacks and the ease with which they were dealt with gave the French authorities a false impression of what they were faced with. The demands of Morocco and Tunisia for independence had appeared both more urgent and more real than those of the handful, or so it seemed, of nationalists, clearly divided among themselves, in Algeria. The attacks came when Mendès-France and his government were in a weak position, dependent on the votes of those who supported the *pieds noirs*. Mendès-France and Mitterand, in order to survive, made forthright statements, refusing any sort of negotiation or suggestion that the position of Algeria could be akin to that of Tunisia and Morocco. 'Algeria is France,' said Mitterand in the Assembly, 'and who among you would hesitate to employ every means to preserve France?'

Léonard had to decide what he would do to satisfy the demand from all sides for immediate and effective action. Although 'Babar' Cherrière had 57,000 soldiers in Algeria, he could only muster 3,500 for active operations. It was decided that the army's task was to clear up the Aures, while the police rounded up the MTLD, most of whom had not been involved with and were opposed to the FLN. Cherrière's forces were unsuited to the task, neither trained nor equipped for it, being road-bound conventional forces. Their heavy-handed tactics of searching all villages and wreaking their revenge on those which they suspected of harbouring the ALN, who ambushed or attacked them, played into the hands of the FLN by antagonizing the population, while their soldiers shivered in the bitterly cold mountains, ill-prepared for spending a winter in those surroundings. The effectiveness of the French Army's operations was radically improved by the arrival of the 25th Airborne Division, led by General Ducournau, fresh from Indo-China. He moved his division into the Aures and, at the end of November, had a successful battle in which twenty-three of the ALN were killed, among them the celebrated Belkacem Grine. This was a severe blow to FLN morale there, but they did not give up, retiring farther into the mountains in an exceptionally hard winter, Ben Boulaid himself being killed in February. Belkacem Krim was also having a difficult time keeping his forces together in Kabylia. In Algiers Bitat and Bouadjadj were arrested and their organization broken up, while Didouche in Constantine had been killed. In spite of these successes, the rebellion continued and pressure on Mendés-France to institute more drastic measures increased. His solution was to send as Governor-General Jacques Soustelle, a brilliant man of 43, who had been head of de Gaulle's secret service in the war. Mendès-France intended that he should overcome the pressure of the *grands colons* and find a solution that would satisfy Algerian Muslim aspirations. Before Soustelle could leave, Mendès-France fell from power; but his successor, Edgar Faure, confirmed his appointment, the new Minister of the Interior being his old colleague in the resistance, Bourgès-Maunoury.

Soustelle, whose sympathies lay equally with Muslim liberals and the 'poor whites' among the *pieds noirs*, attempted to follow a liberal policy of advancement for the Muslims, but he was foiled by the opposition of the *pieds noirs* and the growing support for the FLN. The latter resulted partly from intimidation, partly from reaction to the punitive measures of the administration, police and army, and partly from disillusionment at the failure of the French authorities to make any real headway against the overpowering pressure of the *colons*. The latter increased rather than diminished as the FLN concentrated their activities more and more on brutal murders of Muslims who supported the authorities, the *Beni Oui-Oui*, as they called them. The army seemed incapable of preventing these and attacks on *colon* property, farms, vineyards and stores, although its strength had been increased to 100,000 and it was inflicting increasing casualties on the ALN. Soustelle did his best to stop the army from indulging in reprisals, but was frustrated by Cherrière, who condoned them and ordered a policy of collective punishments to include bombing of villages suspected of harbouring terrorists. Soustelle's political solution was to promise 'integration' of Algeria with France, as unpopular with the *pieds noirs* as it was with those Muslims who sought an independent, Arabic-speaking, Islamic state.

As 1955 wore on the situation deteriorated, the FLN gathering support throughout the country and increasing the number and brutality of its attacks both on individuals and on property. Soustelle was becoming disillusioned, and the Philippeville massacres in August completed the process. In a mood of desperation at the losses the FLN had suffered at the hands of the French Army all over the country, Youssef Zighout and Ben Tobbal, who had taken over the leadership of Wilaya II, the North Constantine region, decided to reply to Cherrière's policy of collective punishment by a collective reprisal against Europeans at Ain Abid, twenty-four miles east of Constantine, and El Halia, a mining centre near Philippeville. Seventy-one European men, women and children were brutally murdered, as were fifty-two 'loyal' Muslims, including Ferhat Abbas's nephew. Immediately one of Ducournau's parachute regiments from Philippeville took its revenge, the official figure of the 'insurgents' killed by them being 1,273, although there is no doubt that many more Muslims who were not directly involved were also killed, the FLN putting the figure as high as 12,000. From this time on the hope of reconciliation between the *pieds noirs* and the Algerian nationalists finally faded, and the brutalities on both sides increased. If Soustelle had any hope left, it was dashed by Faure's decision to resign and submit to elections. These were held on 2 January 1956, the Communists and Poujadists making significant gains and the Socialist

Guy Mollet taking office. A month later Soustelle left Algiers in an emotional scene in which tens of thousands of the *pieds noirs* hailed him as their saviour. The replacement for him, nominated by Mollet, was the 79-year-old General Catroux, unpopular with the *pieds noirs* both for proposing reforms as the wartime High Commissioner and for, in their eyes, selling out to nationalists in Syria and Morocco. When Mollet visited Algiers in February, he met with such a hostile reception from the whites that he cancelled his selection and appointed instead one of his Ministers, Robert Lacoste. He had brought with him a reinforcement of parachute troops, commanded by a general of whom much was to be heard later, Jacques Massu.

At this time, despite many setbacks and much internal quarrelling, the FLN had gained significantly in strength. The regulars of the ALN, the Moujahidines, were now between 15,000 and 20,000 strong, in spite of losses which, including the Moussebilines also, had amounted to some 3,000. In return for this, they had killed 550 men of the security forces and at least as many civilians, and had inflicted damage on nearly a thousand farms and vineyards. They had won over and absorbed most of Messali Hadj's MNA (Mouvement Nationaliste Algérienne) based in Algeria, as well as the communists, whom they had emasculated, and had tempted a significant number of soldiers to desert the famous *Tirailleurs*. New leaders had taken the place of those who had been killed or captured, prominent among them being Ramdane Abane, who ran Algiers in co-operation with Ouamrane and Krim, who had moved there from Kabylia, where his place was taken by Mohamedi Said and the fanatical and cruel Ait Hamouda, known as Amirouche. Externally the FLN's international position had been greatly strengthened by the attendance of its delegation at the non-aligned conference at Bandung. The year 1956 was to bring more success in the political field, notably the accession of Ferhat Abbas and the UDMA after a meeting with Ben Bella in Switzerland in April. The accession of these new supporters, the existence of serious internal conflicts between the Wilayas and within them, notably in the Aures, and differences of opinion between the internal and external leaders led to the convening of a conference in the Soummam valley in the Kabylia Mountains in August. The moving spirit was Abane, although Ben M'hidi officially presided. The external leaders were to have been smuggled in, but were left stranded in the Libyan capital of Tripoli, the conference taking place without them and before they realized it had done so. Its result was a decision to tighten up the whole organization, improving collective leadership at the top, centred on the CCE (*Comité de Coordination et d'Exécution*), consisting of Abane, Krim and Ben M'hidi, joined later by Ben Khedda and Saad Dahlab, both ex-MNA. This committee acted on behalf of the CNRA (*Conseil National de la Révolution Algérienne*), a body consisting of thirty-four representatives elected from all the Wilayas, which was to meet at regular intervals. Strict rules were drawn up regulating every aspect of the revolution, and a policy laid down from which

the FLN was never to deviate: that there should be no cease-fire before independence was recognized; that the whole of Algeria must be included, and that
there was to be no dual citizenship for the *pieds noirs*. On the military side ranks
and pay were laid down from private soldier to colonel, and the organization of
military units was defined from the section of 11 men up to the battalion of 350,
although in practice the backbone of the organization was to remain the
company, or *katiba*, of 110 men.

These accretions of political strength had not been matched by success in
the military field: indeed, it was to a certain extent the military setbacks which
had necessitated a strengthening of the organization. The French
Commander-in-Chief, now General Lorillot, had instituted a new system,
quadrillage. Instead of punitive columns ranging the country, the army was to
maintain a presence everywhere, co-ordinating its information and action with
that of the police and administration, what the British called 'framework'
operations. The trouble was that, in such a vast country, this absorbed a great
deal of manpower, and, even with 200,000 men, few were left over for offensive
operations or as a reserve. To support the regular forces, the French employed
Muslim auxiliaries to a total of 180,000, of which 26,000 were organized in
special operational units, known as *harkis*. These auxiliaries were a frequent
target of terrorist attack. Complementing their security forces, a widespread
programme of civil development was instituted, based on teams of SAS (*Section
Administrative Spécialisée*). These were detachments, led by junior army officers
who could speak Arabic, which devoted themselves to winning the 'hearts and
minds' of the populace by helping them with every form of development. They
achieved a great deal and were effective in countering the influence of the FLN,
to whom they were a frequent target. Unfortunately this policy was accompanied by a repressive one of moving the population from scattered and
isolated villages in areas dominated by the FLN and concentrating them in
camps near the army garrisons, where conditions were generally far from good
and in some cases disgraceful. Mollet had also taken a significant decision to
increase the strength of the army in Algeria to 500,000 by recalling reservists
and lengthening conscript service to twenty-seven months. As the results of
this increase became effective, a major offensive by the French in April and
May had inflicted heavy casualties on the FLN, some 6,000 out of an estimated
total of 18,000 Moujahidines being killed in these operations. Between 1 April
and the end of the year the total reached 13,899 insurgents of all kinds. Many of
them had been at the hands of the *élite* forces, the parachutists and the Foreign
Legion, serving under a number of famous commanders, of whom Massu was
the chief. The ferocity of the fighting, one brutality being revenged by another,
was continually on the increase and *les paras* made their own distinctive
contribution to it. One notable occasion had been their revenge for the ambush
of twenty-one young reservists near Palestro in May. Many of them had been
killed after they had been captured and revoltingly mutilated. It was an event

which shocked France and brought home the realities of the war to the public more than anything else.

But in October the parachutists found themselves diverted to take part in the Suez operation, which took place in November and which, for France, was closely connected with events in Algeria. The French had consistently exaggerated the support that Nasser had given to the FLN. Although Ben Bella and his colleagues were based in Cairo and were given propaganda support by Cairo radio, they had received very little in the way of either financial or material help. But on 14 October a ship, the *Athos*, flying the flag of the Sudan, was intercepted by the French Navy and found to contain arms and ammunition for the FLN, loaded in Alexandria. Eight days later an Air Maroc aircraft, piloted by a French reservist officer, flying Ben Bella, Khider, Ait Ahmed, an Algerian professor and an American journalist to Morocco to negotiate for more arms, was diverted to Algeria and its occupants arrested, the FLN leaders being imprisoned in France. This intelligence coup, or act of piracy, whichever one likes to call it, was organized by the French Army. Whether or not either Lacoste or Mollet were aware of it beforehand, has not been established; but whichever is the case, they did not dare face the unpopularity in France and in Algeria which releasing those kidnapped and disowning the action of the military would have involved, the imminence of the Suez operation complicating matters. General Lorillot, who had authorized although he had not instigated the operation, was a disillusioned man and at the end of the year was succeeded by General Salan, who arrived in December and within a few weeks was the subject of two incidents. The first was a plot by some of the military and their sympathizers to carry out a coup and replace Lacoste by the Commander-in-Chief. The second was more serious, a bazooka attack on his office just after he had left it. It killed his *chef de cabinet* and was the work of an extreme *pied noir* group who regarded Salan as responsible for the loss of Indo-China and intended to replace him by his deputy, General Cogny. His first real trial was to be the Battle of Algiers, an event which was to have a decisive effect on the future of the country.

The origin of the tense situation that had developed in Algiers by this time lay in the reaction of the FLN back in June 1956 to the first executions by guillotine of condemned FLN terrorists. In revenge Abane announced that 100 French would be indiscriminately killed for every member of the FLN executed, and he had given orders to the 29-year-old Saadi Yacef, in charge of operations in Algiers since the arrest of Bitat, to kill any European male between the ages of 18 and 54. Between 21 and 24 June Yacef's men shot down forty-nine civilians in random attacks. Unofficial groups of *pieds noirs* replied in kind with a bomb explosion inside the Casbah which killed seventy Muslim civilians. This set off a bombing campaign by the FLN on the orders of Ben M'hidi, now responsible for the general direction of FLN affairs in the Algiers area, Yacef acting as his operational commander. It took several months to build up the organization to conduct it, women playing an important part. By the end of September Yacef was ready for the first blow. Three young Muslim women, disguised as *pied noir* girls, led by Zohra Drif, placed two bombs in different cafés frequented by *pied noir* youth, and one in the Air France terminus. The last failed to explode, but the others, although they only killed three people, wounded fifty, most of them very badly cut by flying glass. After this more murders and explosions took place, culminating in the shooting on 28 December of the Mayor, Amédée Froger, by a 26-year-old FLN member of the underworld, Ali la Pointe. *Pied noir* rage was now at boiling point and Lacoste sent for the recently arrived Salan and Massu, who had brought back his 10th Parachute Division frustrated from Suez. Lacoste said that, as the police could no longer control the situation, Massu would have a free hand to restore order and ensure the defeat of the FLN. It was a fateful step down a road which would lead in a very different direction from that of Lacoste's own aim, a negotiated settlement which would establish a *loi-cadre*, a bill of rights for the Muslims in an Algeria associated with France.

Massu and his chief of staff, Colonel Yves Godard, an expert in intelligence and undercover operations, went to work with all the intense determination that was characteristic of them both: Massu a direct, uncomplicated man of immense energy, drive and determination; Godard a more subtle, intellectual figure, but equally intense. Massu's four regimental commanders were all men of fire and fury, the one responsible for dealing with the centre of the rebellion, the Casbah, being the legendary Colonel Bigeard. A week after receiving his orders, Massu brought his regiments into Algiers and began his preparations. The moment for action came with the FLN call for a general strike on 28 January 1957. Ben M'hidi had announced this to coincide with the opening of a session of the United Nations General Assembly, part of the agreed policy of internationalizing the conflict. The response to the strike among Muslim shopkeepers, workers and schoolchildren was almost total; but Massu quickly retaliated, forcing open the doors and shutters of the shops so that their owners were faced with the choice of operating them or being looted. The threat of force by Bigeard's paras outweighed intimidation by Yacef's men, and, as the days went by, the strike became less and less effective. It was supported by a bombing campaign, once more targetted against places frequented by *pied noir* youth, the bomb carriers being again girls, one of them a European. Casualties were 15 killed and 105 wounded. Bigeard's paras had now imposed a tight hold on the Casbah and intelligence from various sources, some obtained by brutal methods, was accumulating. The net began to close round Yacef and his bomb makers and carriers, culminating on 19 February in the discovery of his main bomb factory. The CCE was now a very worried body of men and, after much deliberation, decided to leave the city, Yacef remaining in charge. Ben M'hidi was reluctant to go and, before he had done so, he was tracked down on 25 February by the paras who were on the trail of Ben Khedda. A fortnight later it was announced that he had committed suicide in his cell, but there were suspicions, which subsequent revelations have done nothing to dispel, that he met his death at the hands of a 'special section' of the paras. This triggered off a controversy about the use of torture by the paras, which was later to have a decisive influence on the attitude of the public in France to events in Algeria. There is no doubt that torture was employed, although never officially condoned, the paras justifying it on the grounds that the FLN themselves employed the most brutal methods both against their opponents and, even more so, against fellow Muslims who did not support them, and that the need to extract information in order to defeat them was overriding. One of the most telling accusations against the FLN was the massacre in May at Melouza in southern Kabylia of 300 peasants, supporters of Messali Hadj's MNA. All the males over the age of 15 had been rounded up, herded into houses and the mosque, and slaughtered in brutal fashion. But it was the growing evidence of the use of torture and secret killing by the French Army and Police, aided and abetted by the revengeful *pieds noirs*, which finally persuaded the people of France to wash their hands of Algeria in disgust.

However, at this stage the French Army, the authorities in Algeria and the *pied noirs* were rejoicing in the feeling that at last the tide had turned, that the FLN had been defeated and that victory had been gained by men who, unlike the shilly-shallying politicians of France, were prepared to meet force with force and ruthlessness with ruthlessness. The CCE split up, Abane and Saad Dahlab heading west for Morocco, Ben Khedda and Belkacem Krim, now the only survivor of the original nine, east for Tunis, narrowly escaping capture as they did so. Bigeard took his paras back to the area of Wilaya II in which the ALN were posing a serious threat. Its collective leadership under the direction of Si Sadek, who had replaced Ouamrane when he moved into Algiers, had stepped up its activity in order to try and take pressure off the city. In May one of his colleagues, Si Azedine, had ambushed a Spahi unit and killed sixty of them, following this up with an ambush of a *Tirailleur* battalion, in which ten men were killed and many others deserted to the ALN. Intelligence reported that Si Sadek was moving two of his companies to join Azedine and Bigeard moved quickly to intercept them, deploying his men by helicopter and night march to occupy the high ground near the mountain village of Agounnenda, dominating the valley through which Azedine's men were moving. A fierce battle was fought from 23 to 26 May, Azedine losing 96 dead and 9 taken prisoner, Bigeard 8 dead and 29 wounded; but he only recovered 45 weapons and the bulk of the FLN forces escaped.

Yacef meanwhile was still biding his time in Algiers. The city had been quiet since the end of February 1957, but in May two parachute soldiers were shot after they had left a cinema. In retaliation the paras went into a Turkish bath, suspected of being a FLN hide-out, and shot everybody in it, some eighty Muslims, many of them beggars who spent the night there. Yacef thereupon

decided to renew his bombing campaign and on 3 June placed some small
bombs in the base of lamp standards near bus-stops, timed to explode in the
rush-hour. Casualties were 8 dead and 90 wounded, half of them Muslims.
This was followed on 9 June by a large bomb placed under the orchestra
platform of the Casino, crowded with Europeans on a Sunday evening. The
appalling scene, with 8 dead and 95 wounded, triggered off a wave of indis-
criminate *pied noir* attacks on Muslims all over the city. Although 200 Europeans were arrested by the police, only four were detained and they were soon
released. Bigeard and his paras were brought back to the city to hunt down
Yacef, employing every form of undercover means, including the use of turncoats, known as *bleus* from the workers' dungarees in which they were clothed.
It was not until 24 September that the net finally closed and Yacef and Zohra
Drif were taken from their hide-out in the Casbah, their whereabouts having
been revealed under torture by one of his couriers. Two weeks later Ali la
Pointe and two of his colleagues were also tracked down and, when they
refused to surrender, were blown up with the house in which they were hiding.
The Battle of Algiers was finally at an end and Massu and his paras were
acclaimed by the *pieds noirs* as heroes and saviours.

Before this, important developments had occurred in the political field, both
in the FLN's external branch and in France. The FLN's military setbacks in
Algiers and in the countryside, combined with the effectiveness of the SAS in
attracting Muslim 'hearts and minds', were serious factors on the debit side of
the FLN account. On the credit side could be set resentment at the measures
taken to resettle the population in FLN-dominated areas and the hardships to
which it gave rise, revulsion at the brutalities perpetrated both by the *pieds noirs*
and the security forces, and growing support outside Algeria itself, notably
among the 400,000 Algerian workers in France, who had initially tended to be
under the influence of the MNA. However the situation could not be regarded
by the FLN as anything but very serious, and this led to dissension at the top,
partly between the military leaders and the politicians, partly reflecting the
struggle between the internal and external leadership. It culminated in a
meeting on 27 July 1957 in Cairo. At an earlier meeting in Tunis Ramdane
Abane, always insistent on the primacy of the political arm, had been highly
critical of Boussouf, head of Wilaya v, and his deputy Boumedienne, whom he
accused of antagonizing the population by their tyrannical and ruthless
methods, and had complained that the Wilaya leadership generally was
allowed too much freedom and was falling into the hands of the military. At the
meeting in Cairo a new CCE was formed of five 'colonels' and four 'politicals'.
The colonels were Krim, Boussouf, Ben Tobbal, Ouamrane and Mahmoud
Chérif; the politicals Ferhat Abbas, Lamine Debaghine, Abdelhamid Mahri
and Abane, with an inner council consisting of the five colonels and Abane as
the only political. But Abane's criticism had been too much for the colonels. It
was not until the following May that it was publicly announced that he had

died 'on the field of honour', while engaged on an important mission to Algeria. The story given out was that he was killed while he and his bodyguard were trying to cross the frontier, but in fact he was killed in Morocco, to which he had been lured in December in the company of Krim and Chérif, on the orders of Boussouf, an act which thereafter was itself to be a source of dissension between the colonels.

In France the political situation had deteriorated. In spite of the victories of the army in Algiers and outside it, no solution to the country's problems was in sight. The *pieds noirs* were even more strongly opposed to any political concessions to the Muslims, let alone to the FLN. They demanded a policy of inflexible toughness. Lacoste's aim, supported by Mollet's Socialist government, which was dependent on Communist support, for a devolution of power in Algeria to elected assemblies in each of the eight provinces, appealed neither to the FLN nor to the *pieds noirs*, and would have depended on the support of European and Muslim moderates, the ranks of both of which had been drastically thinned. On 27 May Mollet's government fell, to be succeeded after three weeks by one headed by Bourgès-Manoury. He in turn fell when the *loi-cadre*, introducing Lacoste's proposals, was defeated in the National Assembly on 30 September, Soustelle making a significant intervention to block it. A general strike of Europeans in Algiers on 18 September, although firmly suppressed by Massu and his paras, had undoubtedly also contributed to its defeat. After six weeks of juggling Felix Gaillard succeeded in forming another left-wing government which just managed to get an emasculated *loi-cadre* through the Assembly.

Both the military and the political struggle now switched to the border with Tunisia. Since Bourguiba had acquired independence his country had become the FLN's external base, to the intense annoyance of the French, who still based their navy at Bizerta. They watched with growing anger and frustration the FLN organizing and training their forces and receiving supplies of arms not merely with the connivance of Bourguiba, but apparently with his active support, at least politically. All this with impunity. One reaction to this was the creation of the Morice line, named after Gaillard's Minister of Defence. It was a fence erected the whole length of the frontier, electrified at 5,000 volts, sown with mines and supplemented with detection devices. The population on the Algerian side had been removed and a hightly sophisticated reaction system developed to meet attempts by the FLN to break through it. From mid-1957 onwards they made continuous attempts to do so, responding to appeals from the Wilaya to come to their support, of which hardly any were successful and in which they suffered heavy casualties. Frustration at the security provided for the FLN forces in Tunisia led in February 1958 to an incident, which, like the use of torture, was to have more profound consequences than its military instigators had foreseen. In January a strong FLN force of some 300, with, so the French alleged, Tunisian Army support, had crossed the frontier and ambushed a French patrol, killing fifteen of them and capturing four. A few days later a French reconnaissance aircraft was shot down by machine-gun fire from the Tunisian village of Sakiet, across the border in the same area. In spite of French warnings, another aircraft was shot at and hit on 8 February, but managed to land west of the Morice line. Three hours later a squadron of French Air Force bombers attacked Sakiet in force, killing eighty people, including women and children, and hitting a school and a hospital. There was an international outcry and Bourguiba immediately demanded the withdrawal of all French forces from Tunisia and accused France before the United Nations Security Council of aggression. Britain and the United States offered their 'good offices' as mediators in the dispute, clearly hoping that this could lead to the opening of negotiations between France and the FLN. Gaillard accepted the offer, bringing down on his head a load of criticism from the right, the army and the *pieds noirs*, who already suspected him of being prepared to surrender France's possession of the valuable oil and gas fields in the Algerian Sahara, which had just come on stream, and were furious that he and Lacoste had refused to accept responsibility for the bombing of Sakiet, insisting that it had been a military decision in which they had not been consulted. Gaillard's government fell on 15 April, leading to yet another period of political juggling while the ship of state drifted this way and that.

Behind the scenes a number of different factions were manœuvring in order to ensure that the result was not yet another weak left-wing government. They included Gaullists who wished to bring the General back for the sake of France. Such were Chaban-Delmas, Delbeque and Debré, who saw an opportunity to use Algeria as a means to this end. Others were Gaullists who wished to use de Gaulle to save Algeria for France: Soustelle was their leader, supported by Sanguinetti, a *pied noir*, and Biaggi, a Corsican. Then there were the *pieds noirs*, of whom the key figures were Alain de Sérigny, owner and editor of the Echo d'Algers, Pierre Lagaillarde, a fanatical law student at Algiers University, recently returned from his service as a reserve parachute officer but appearing in his parachute combat uniform, and Jo Ortiz, a tough café proprietor. They wanted to use the army to establish a *pied noir* government independent of Paris. Finally there was the army itself, frustrated, angry and determined no longer to tolerate a shilly-shally left-wing government that might treat with the enemy. A key figure linking the others to the army was Colonel Thomazo, dubbed *Nez-de-cuir* from a leather patch covering his nose, in which he had been wounded at Cassino. Their plots were cooking when, on 9 May, the FLN announced that they had executed three French soldiers, who had been in their hands for eighteen months, for torture, murder and rape.

This was the spark that lit the fire. That day Salan sent a message to the Chief of the Armed Forces Staff, General Ely, stating that the army would not tolerate a government which abandoned Algeria and requesting him to bring this to the notice of the President. It was clearly an ultimatum. Accompanied by two other generals and the admiral commanding the French Mediterranean Fleet, he showed the telegram to Lacoste and warned him that he would lay a wreath on 13 May in memory of the three soldiers, at which he expected a turn-out of all the *anciens combattants*. Lacoste was being pressed by Sérigny to form a Committee of Public Safety, and to avoid these pressures he quietly slipped away 'to report to the President' in Paris, where the political negotiations had resulted in agreement for Pflimlin to form a government, an eventuality which Sérigny's 'Group of Seven', Soustelle and the army were all determined to resist.

At 6 p.m. on 13 May, in front of a large crowd of *pieds noirs*, Salan was due to lay his wreath. Two hours beforehand Lagaillarde had begun to harangue the crowd, and by the time that Salan, accompanied by Massu, arrived, they were worked up and greeted him with 'The army to power' and 'Massu to power'. After he had left, Lagaillarde led an attack by the crowd on the nearby offices of the government, while the police fired a few ineffectual rounds of tear-gas and the army was conspicuous by its absence. Lacoste's besieged deputy telephoned for instructions and was told by Lacoste that on no account should anyone fire on the crowd. Apart from that, he gave no guidance, Pflimlin not yet having been installed. Salan and Massu were soon both on the scene and, after discussion with Lagaillarde and others, Salan went out on to the balcony to be greeted with insults and demands for Massu. The latter, after a short discussion with Salan, went out and announced that he had formed a Committee of Public Safety and read out a hastily compiled list, which included Lagaillarde and three of his supporters who happened to be at hand, the two senior parachute colonels present, Trinquier (who had succeeded Bigeard) and Ducasse, Massu's Chief of Staff, and also Colonel Thomazo, who had turned up. Massu then reported his action to Lacoste and to President Coty in Paris. At the instigation of the Gaullists, these messages were followed by one from Salan saying that 'the responsible military authorities esteem it an imperative necessity to appeal to a national arbiter with a view to constituting a government of public safety': no mention of General de Gaulle, but a clear hint.

In spite of this, or perhaps because of it, Pflimlin was accepted on 14 May by the Assembly by 280 votes to 126 and proceeded to adopt an ambivalent policy, telling Salan that he supported his actions, but deciding to cut off supplies from France to Algeria. Next day, a public holiday, Salan appeared on the balcony in Algiers again, this time to applause, organized by Thomazo, and, at the end of a speech saying that 'What has been done here will show the world that Algeria wants to remain French,' he added a rather muted 'Vive de Gaulle' to his 'Vive l'Algérie Française'. De Gaulle himself had remained enigmatically silent, but, in reply to Salan's call, announced that 'in the face of the trials that again are mounting toward it, the nation should know that I am ready to assume the powers of the Republic'. This statement was received with wild enthusiasm in Algiers, in which crowds of Muslims participated in an unprecedented gesture of fraternity with the *pieds noirs*, which was as fleeting as it was inexplicable. De Gaulle now began a calculated game of playing hard to get. He was determined to come to power only on his own terms, invited constitutionally and not swept to power on the back of the army or of any political faction; nor was his return to be solely to solve the Algerian problem, but to save France herself. As the days passed and Pflimlin hesitated, Salan and Massu planned Operation *Resurrection*. Using the transport aircraft which General Challe, Ely's deputy, had transferred to Algeria (for which he was placed under house arrest) and in collusion with parachutists and other sympathizers in France, they planned to seize Villacoublay airfield and from there key points in Paris itself. De Gaulle was able to pose as the saviour of democracy from the threat of a military coup, and Mollet's Socialists deserted Pflimlin in his favour. Salan having for a second time threatened to execute this plan if de Gaulle were not installed, President Coty on 29 May announced that he had called on him, and on Sunday 1 June de Gaulle returned to the National Assembly, which he had left twelve years before, and was accepted by 329 votes to 222, with a mandate to rule by decree for six months, sending the Assembly on leave for four of them, and to submit a new constitution at the end of it. Not a word about a policy for Algeria.

On 4 June de Gaulle arrived in Algiers and was given a rapturous welcome by European and Muslim alike, in spite of suspicion from the harder line *pieds noirs*, who had been supporters of Pétain during the war and objected to de Gaulle's Brazzaville declaration. He made a number of Delphic utterances which could be and were interpreted by their recipients to mean that he supported their cause, at the same time harping on the need for reconciliation. Two phrases were of special significance: the 'I have understood you' with which he greeted the crowd from the balcony of the government building in Algiers and the statement that there was only one category of inhabitant in Algeria, 'Frenchmen in the full sense – *à part entière*'. His own plan, however, was not what the *pieds noirs* or the army had in mind. It was, firstly to establish France's firm authority over Algeria and the army there; secondly to seek peace with the rebels on a formula which would retain an association with France, and finally to strengthen the military effort to ensure that the enemy's operations did not obstruct progress or affect his decisions. Had he cashed in quickly on the initial enthusiasm with which he was received, he might have won the Muslim population away from the FLN, who, at that time, were at their lowest ebb, defeated in the field and split by internal dissension. But his first priority was France itself and he had only six months in which to sort it out before he faced the parties. At the end of September he held a referendum on his constitution throughout the French Union, which was to be followed by elections in November. If any part of the Union rejected it, all connection with

France would be totally severed. All Algerians, male and female, voted on a single electoral roll and, in spite of attempts by the FLN to boycott it, 79·9 per cent of the electorate turned out and 96·6 per cent voted '*Oui*', although there was still no indication of what de Gaulle's policy for Algeri was to be. On 3 October, on a visit to Constantine, de Gaulle announced a massive programme of development, including distribution of land to Muslims, raising wages to the equivalent of those paid in France, and major advances in education and openings for employment in the administration. One thousand detained rebels would be released on Armistice Day, 7,000 on New Year's Day 1959 and 5,000 on Bastille Day. Capital sentences would be commuted. Three weeks later he announced his '*paix des braves*', an offer to the FLN to negotiate under an amnesty, although the wording could be interpreted to mean that surrender was expected. Soustelle and the hard-liners saw it in the first light, as a capitulation to the FLN, who however took the opposite view and promptly rejected it through the mouth of the former moderate, Ferhat Abbas. From then on the adherents of '*Algérie Française*' were to become increasingly suspicious of de Gaulle, who, they considered, had owed his advent of power to them.

While he had been developing his political programme, de Gaulle had been quietly purging the army, posting suspected officers away from Algiers and ordering the forces to withdraw from political activity. In December it was Salan's turn. Hoping to succeed Ely, he was instead side-tracked into the largely honorific post of Military Governor of Paris. His responsibility as Governor-General was given to a technocrat, Paul Delouvrier, and that of Commander-in-Chief to the Air Force General Challe, a tough, rugger-playing, pipe-smoking, straightforward and very able officer. Delouvrier was given only the vaguest of instructions, while Challe was told to crush the ALN in order to give de Gaulle complete freedom of action. This Air Force General planned and executed a more effective campaign than any of his army predecessors. Working on the same principles as Briggs had done in Malaya, he concentrated his forces, land and air, in each Wilaya in turn, starting from the west and working eastwards, crushing the ALN and driving the remnants towards the Morice Line, and, when he had done so, following the concentrated military operations, which he personally directed in the field, with a concentration of effort and resources on development. Under the previous *quadrillage* concept, military effort had been dispersed over seventy-five districts, each of which tended to act independently, largely in reaction to FLN activity. Salan's mobile reserve, out of 500,000 troops, had never numbered much more than 15,000, almost exclusively parachutists and Foreign Legion. Challe reduced the numbers employed on *quadrillage* and created a reserve equivalent to two divisions, liberally supplied with helicopters and supported by old-fashioned but effective ground-attack aircraft. He had also increased the number of *harkis*, loyal Muslims organized in special units, from 26,000 to 60,000, insisting on a guarantee to them that Algeria would remain French.

Reliable figures of the strength of the ALN, when he began his campaign in 1959, are hard to come by. At the beginning of 1958, the French estimated that the ALN had 30,000 Moujahidines, and the same number of Moussebilines, and claimed to have inflicted over 25,000 casualties on them by August, while the FLN maintained that they had increased their overall forces within and outside Algeria from 40,000 to 100,000. By the end of 1959 the French estimated that they had reduced the forces of all kinds that the ALN could put into the field inside Algeria to 15,000. They had also eliminated a large number of the principal leaders, including Amirouche. The largest in scale and the most effective of Challe's operations was carried out in July in the Grand Kabyle Mountains, both parachute drops and amphibious landings by marines being employed. The operation, known as *Jumelles* (Binoculars), continued until October, 3,746 of the rebels being killed, captured or wounded and the ALN forced to split up into small parties. By that time the FLN themselves admitted that, in one form or another, including desertions, they were losing 500 men a day. By the end of the year Challe had only the area of the Aures to deal with, when other events intervened.

September 1959 saw important developments: a recurrence of the FLN bombing campaign, a declaration by them that they had formed a government in exile, the GPRA (*Gouvernement Provisoire de la République Algérienne*), and, most significant of all, a speech by de Gaulle on 16 September, following immediately after a visit to the army in Algeria, during which, although stating that a solution could not lie in military success alone, he had given nobody, not even Challe, an inkling of the bombshell he was about to launch. This lay in the words: 'I deem it necessary that recourse to self-determination be here and now proclaimed.' The Algerians would be able to choose between three options: complete secession, which would entail the rupture of all relations with France; integration with France, or self-determination, which he described as 'the government of Algeria by the Algerians, backed up by French help and in close relationship with her'. He made it clear that the last was the one he preferred and expected the Algerians to choose. It would be based on a federal form of government which gave safeguards to minorities. He appeared to envisage a referendum within Algeria and not a negotiation with the external GPRA, which, after an internal revolt at the end of 1958, in which four 'colonels' were executed, was firmly in the hands of the hard-liners, the secretive and grim Boumedienne having achieved the key position of Chief of Staff of the ALN. But it was a step away from '*Algérie Française*' which Challe and his men felt as a betrayal of the victory they were on the point of achieving. While the French and the international public hailed it as a statesmanlike pronouncement, Challe wrote to de Gaulle's Prime Minister, Debré: 'One does not propose to soldiers to go and get killed for an imprecise final objective

... One can thus only ask of soldiers of the army of Algeria today that they die in order for Algeria to remain French.'* From then on elements in the army, notably three parachute colonels in key positions, Argoud, Gardes and Godard, were in league with Soustelle and with the *pieds noirs*, among whom Lagaillarde and Ortiz led rival factions, to oppose the policy. The spark which set this explosive mixture alight was an interview given by Massu to a German journalist, in which he severely criticized de Gaulle and said: 'Myself, and the majority of officers in a position of command, will not execute unconditionally the orders of the Head of State.'† De Gaulle demanded his instant dismissal and, in spite of arguments from Debré, Ely, Challe and others that it would have a catastrophic effect in Algiers, he insisted.

The result was as Challe had foreseen. Ortiz and Lagaillarde, separately and in opposition to each other, brought their men out in thousands on to the streets and erected the traditional barricades, Lagaillarde in the University and Ortiz in the middle of the city. Reluctantly Challe brought in the 10th Parachute Division from operations in Kabylia, while he negotiated without success with Ortiz, who was in league with the parachute colonels. On 24 January 1960 a police operation was ordered to try and move Ortiz's men out of the centre to the outskirts of the city, just as it was getting dark. They were fired on by Ortiz's men and then viciously attacked by an assortment of weapons, while the parachutists took three-quarters of an hour to cover the 600 yards to come to help them, by which time 14 had been killed and 123 wounded. This started a week in which de Gaulle fulminated at Delouvrier and Challe that order must be restored, while the latter hesitated to order troops to fire on fellow Frenchmen, knowing that they might not be obeyed. They finally decided to move out of Algiers together, before perhaps becoming hostages themselves, after Delouvrier had made a speech which appeared to support 'the faith that Algeria should remain French' and offer a compromise to the rebellious *pieds noirs*. In response, de Gaulle, dressed in uniform, made perhaps the greatest broadcast speech of his life. He emphasized his authority and the need that it should be respected: he reiterated that 'the Algerians shall have free choice of their destiny'; he made an ambiguous appeal to the *pieds noirs*, denying that giving the Algerians a free choice meant abandoning them; he gave a firm warning to the army, and finished with an emotional and eloquent appeal, saying that, if he were to yield to those 'who dream of being usurpers, France would become but a poor broken toy adrift on the sea of hazard'.‡ For another two days, while the rain poured down, the barricades held out and de Gaulle impatiently ordered Delouvrier and Challe to clear them away; but they preferred to avoid a direct confrontation. Ortiz disappeared and Lagaillarde was arrested, as were other *pied noir* leaders, several

* Horne, *A Savage War of Peace*, p. 347.
† Horne, p. 357.
‡ Horne, p. 368–9.

senior army officers were removed and Gardes's controversial 5th Bureau, officially psychological warfare, closed down.

Challe's military campaign had been interrupted and he was not allowed to stay and finish it off, leaving on 23 April for a senior NATO appointment, being succeeded by a reliable, pedestrian gunner, General Crépin, a solidly loyal Gaullist. Pleading unfamiliarity with the situation, he postponed the resumption of major operations until July 1960. These took place in the Ouarsenis Mountains in Wilayas IV and V, and it was not until October, a year after the end of Operation *Jumelles*, that operations in the Aures Mountains started. By then negotiations with the FLN had tentatively got under way. These had taken two forms. One, known as Operation *Tilsit*, resulted from contacts with the ALN leaders, headed by Si Salah, in Wilaya IV, who had been very hard hit as a result of the operations by the *bleu* turncoats. It developed to the stage that Si Salah and two colleagues were flown to Paris to meet de Gaulle himself, after they had told his personal emissary, Bernard Tricot, that they were disenchanted with the external leaders and wished to negotiate a cease-fire. De Gaulle told them that he was about to make an appeal to the GPRA to discuss one and that, if they rejected it, he would then turn to Si Salah, who should contact the other Wilayas and try and bring them in. This he did in a broadcast on 14 June. After painting a glowing picture of Algeria's potential prosperity with its oil and gas, he offered the GPRA 'an honourable end to the fighting that drags on', to the dismay of the army in Algeria and even more so of Colonel Jacquin and those who had developed Operation *Tilsit*. On 20 June the GPRA announced that 'under certain conditions' they accepted the invitation and would send a delegation to France. Next day Jacquin escorted Si Salah and four colleagues to Wilaya III to contact ALN leaders there. Three of them were executed on the orders of the GPRA, Si Salah himself and his one remaining colleague being later killed by the French in the course of operations. Many later expressed the view that de Gaulle had made a fatal error in not seizing the opportunity offered to him by Operation *Tilsit* to undermine the standing of the external leaders. Instead, the public invitation to them and their acceptance of a meeting recognized them as the body with whom he was to negotiate the future of Algeria. The meeting, held at Melun from 25 to 29 June, never got past deadlock over the issue of who was to represent both sides, the GPRA insisting on the release of Ben Bella and those captured with him and on French representation being at ministerial level. De Gaulle broke off the talks, having undoubtedly suffered a severe rebuff.

French public opinion was now crystallizing between the two extremes: on the right, those, like Soustelle, who saw that de Gaulle was prepared to sacrifice Algeria and were determined to fight him at all costs; on the left, those who were so opposed to the war that they were prepared openly to encourage French conscripts to disobey or desert. Although the majority would not go so far as the left-wing intelligentsia, they were undoubtedly on de Gaulle's side in wishing to free France from its entanglement. Before the Melun Conference Salan had reached the statutory retiring age of 60 and initially attempted to settle in Algeria. In September he returned to France and in October went on to Spain, to which Lagaillarde and his colleague Susini escaped, when on bail awaiting trial. From there Salan plotted with the retired Generals Jouhaud and Faure and others, both in Algeria and elsewhere. In spite of the army's successes in the previous year, the 'smallpox chart', showing the distribution of terrorist incidents, continued to provide an ugly rash all over Algeria, and from July onwards FLN activity in Algiers itself, which had been quiescent since the Battle of Algiers three years before, came alive again with a spate of bombing incidents. The military and political authorities maintained that the internal security situation was not deteriorating, but the *pieds noirs* refused to accept that. They, and important elements in the army, headed by Colonel Dufour's 1st Regiment of Foreign Legion Parachutists (1st REP), were in touch with Salan and his group in Spain, as well as with the retired General Zeller in France and with political leaders in Algeria and France, seeking a leader to rally all those who were prepared to fight de Gaulle. Their efforts were intensified after a broadcast by de Gaulle on 4 November 1960, in which he went further than before, not only saying that he had 'embarked on a new course leading to an Algerian Algeria . . . an emancipated Algeria which will have its own government, its own institutions, its own laws', but talking of 'an Algerian Republic'. This last phrase was the final straw for his opponents and even for some of his supporters, Debré, his faithful Prime Minister attempting to resign. The loyal Delouvrier also could stand no more and resigned, considering that his attempts to implement the plan which de Gaulle had announced at Constantine in 1959 had been finally undermined by its author. De Gaulle took the opportunity to change the leadership in Algeria, Delouvrier being replaced by Jean Morin, another official, formerly prefect of Haute-Garonne, but given less independent responsibility. This rested with Louis Joxe, created Minister of State for Algeria in Paris. Crépin, whose loyalty was being strained by the pressures to which he was subjected from the army, was to be replaced by General Gambiez, a loyal Gaullist then commanding the Oran sector and described by Alistair Horne as 'looking more like a country curate than a fighting general'.*

While de Gaulle's opponents were seething with rage at his latest speech, he made the rash decision to pay a personal visit to Algeria. Dufour, who had been posted away from 1st REP after encouraging his divisional chaplain, at the funeral of ten of his men killed in an ambush, to say: 'You died at a time when, if we believe the speeches we hear, we no longer know why we die',† deserted and plotted with Jouhaud and a key figure, Captain Sergent, serving in 1st REP, and with the *pied noir* private army, the Front de l'Algérie Française

* Horne, p. 424.
† Horne, p. 427.

(FAF). When de Gaulle arrived in Algeria, there was to be a general strike accompanied by incidents all over the city, which would provoke the calling in of the army to reinforce the police. The army would then not only seize control of Algiers, but de Gaulle in person. Their plan was frustrated by de Gaulle, when he arrived, avoiding Algiers altogether. Partly by chance and partly by calculated security measures, he evaded at least four attempts on his life. While he was visiting other places, Algiers was reduced to chaos by the *pied noir* FAF, leading to a Muslim reaction, the extent and impressive organization behind which surprised the FAF, the army and the police, who had been the main target of the FAF. All three now found themselves side by side against the Muslim mob, and both sides took savage revenge on each other. De Gaulle left a day before he had planned, with no illusions about the real state of opinion among the communities in Algeria. Any hope of a solution based on the support of the moderates in both communities had totally disappeared. From then on he saw even more clearly than before that the only way for France to shake itself free was a negotiation with the FLN.

His opponents appreciated this and sought all the more intensely for a leader who would use the army to save Algeria for France. Their choice fell on General Challe, embittered at what he believed to be the failure to exploit his victories and the prospect of abandonment of the loyal Muslim *harkis*. He felt that his honour was bound up with those Frenchmen and Muslim Algerians who had fought, and many of them given their lives, under his command. He had resigned in January 1961, after de Gaulle had held a further referendum on the question: 'Do you approve the Bill . . . concerning the self-determination of the Algerian population?' and received a 75 per cent '*Oui*'. In Algeria 40 per cent of Muslim voters had abstained, and in Algiers itself the *pieds noirs* had contributed to a 72 per cent '*Non*'. Almost immediately afterwards Georges Pompidou was deputed by de Gaulle to establish secret contacts with the FLN. These led in March to the announcement that official talks were to be held in Evian on 7 April, and that, in order to show good intention, the army in Algeria would observe a unilateral truce. On 31 March Joxe, leading the French delegation, announced that the MNA, as well as the GPRA, would take part, whereupon the latter refused to participate. The plotters saw this as a chance to strike while the army was infuriated by the truce and before the talks could be got going. Under great pressure, on 12 April Challe agreed to accept the leadership of the various factions, whose ideas varied from a coup which, supported by the armed forces, would first seize control of Algeria and then bring about the fall of de Gaulle's government in France, to those who, like Challe himself, saw a seizure of control in Algiers as a means to force de Gaulle to change his policy. They gave little thought to what would follow, and their plans for the coup were hastily made and ill-co-ordinated.

In the evening of 20 April Challe and Zeller left France in a French Air Force aircraft, provided by the *pied noir* Air Force General Bigot with the connivance of the Chief of Staff of the Air Force, General Nicot. Having arrived at Blida instead of Algiers, where they were awaited and to which they flew on, they found that 1st REP had postponed action for twenty-four hours, which Challe spent checking the plans and the loyalty of those they depended on. Shortly after midnight 21/22 April, 1st REP set out to cover the twenty miles from their barracks to Algiers, on the way capturing General Gambiez, who had driven off, as a result of a warning from Morin, received from the loyal General Simon at Tizzi-Ouzou, to find out what was afoot. Morin also managed to alert Paris and many other key command headquarters, before he was himself captured in his office. From then on things began to go wrong for the plotters. Once again, as in 1940 and on many subsequent occasions between then and 1945, French officers, particularly the senior ones, were faced with an agonizing decision as to where their loyalty and duty lay. Some, like General Gouraud in the key sector of Constantine, wavered to and fro under pressure: others, notably General Pouilly at Oran, remained staunchly faithful to the Head of State. De Gaulle's most effective allies proved to be the conscript French soldiers. On 23 April, dressed in his uniform as a *général de brigade*, de Gaulle made another of his emotional and highly effective appeals to the French nation, with the words: 'The nation defied, our strength shaken, our international prestige debased, our position and our role in Africa compromised. And by whom? Alas! Alas! Alas! by men whose duty, honour and *raison d'être* it was to serve and obey.' With great force and vigour he forbade all Frenchmen, and especially soldiers, to give them aid and appealed to all Frenchmen to help him. The conscript soldiers in Algeria, all with their transistor radios, heard and responded to this appeal. Neither the cause for which they served there, and some of them actually fought, nor the life they led held much attraction for them. With many of the officers wavering and Pouilly in Oran bravely facing Challe and his colleagues, jealous of the arrogance of the paras and the publicity they received, the rank and file began to frustrate the intentions of the rebels. By the end of Monday 24 April Challe, surrounded by bickering colleagues, now including Salan, flying in from Spain as impeccably dressed as ever, saw that the game was up. Next morning, while Salan, Jouhaud, Dufour and the others slipped away to carry on the struggle under the banner of the OAS (*Organisation Armée Secrète*), Challe flew to Paris to surrender, expecting to face the firing squad. Two days later 1st REP was disbanded, the legionnaires having blown up their barracks and fired off all their ammunition.

It was both victory and defeat for de Gaulle. He had asserted his authority and had his countrymen behind him. He could now save France by getting rid of Algeria; but with the army shattered by its experiences, from which it was to take long to recover, he held no cards in his hand as he entered negotiations with the FLN, a far cry from his aim that the army should crush the enemy in order to give him freedom of action and decision. The negotiations were to drag on, while the war became one between the OAS and the FLN within

British Colonial Conflicts

The explosion at the King David Hotel, Jerusalem, in July 1946
(*Imperial War Museum*)

A ship with illegal Jewish immigrants at Haifa in August 1946
(*Imperial War Museum*)

A train derailed by terrorists in Malaya, 1951 (*Imperial War Museum*)

opposite: British SAS troops with aborigines in the Malayan jungle, 1954 (*Imperial War Museum*)

A British infantry jungle patrol in Malaya, 1953 (*Imperial War Museum*)

A patrol of the King's African Rifles in the Kenyan forest, 1955
(*Imperial War Museum*)

A Mau Mau terrorist under interrogation in Kenya, 1955
(*Imperial War Museum*)

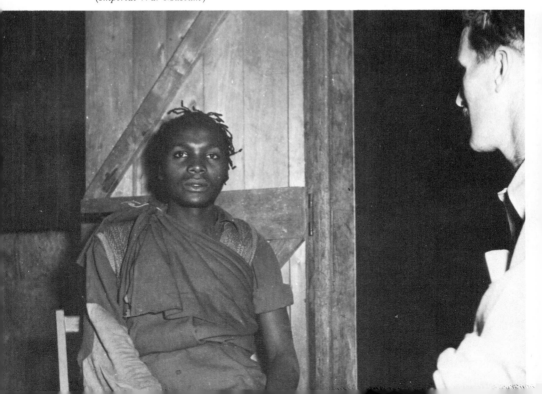

Grivas (third from right) with Markos Drakos (in civilian cap) and other EOKA leaders. This photograph was found with Grivas's diaries (*Popperfoto*)

below: British infantry react to a terrorist incident in Cyprus, 1956 (*BBC Hulton Picture Library*)

below right: Royal Marines in the Troodos Mountains of Cyprus, 1956 (*BBC Hulton Picture Library*)

Royal Marines overlook Wadi Taym in the Radfan, May 1964 (*Imperial War Museum*)

A British armoured personnel carrier patrols the Aden Crater in April 1967
(*Popperfoto*)

Gurkhas prepare to embark in Royal Navy helicopters, Sarawak, 1964 (*Imperial War Museum*)

British infantry patrol a Sarawak village, 1965 (*Imperial War Museum*)

French Colonial Conflicts

above left: French infantry in Indo-China, July 1953 (*Keystone*)

left: Waiting for the next attack. Dien Bien Phu, March 1954 (*Keystone*)

above right: Pay-day for the Algerian Liberation Army in the Atlas Mountains, 1957 (*Popperfoto*)

right: Pied noirs stone the police in Algiers during de Gaulle's visit to Algeria in December 1960 (*Camera Press*)

American Adventures

above left: US Marines landing at Inchon, Korea, in 1950 (*BBC Hulton Picture Library*)

left: US infantry pass a knocked-out Russian-made T34 tank of the North Korean army, 1950 (*BBC Hulton Picture Library*)

above right: US Marines fire mortar as a supply helicopter takes off, Vietnam, 1968 (*Keystone*)

right: US Army fire-base in the Central Highlands of Vietnam, 1971 (*Keystone*)

Conventional Clashes

left: Indian troops in Kashmir, 1948 (*Popperfoto*)

above right: Sikhs of the Indian Army dig in on the Tibetan frontier, 1962 (*Associated Press*)

below: An Indian patrol on Panggong Lake, Ladakh, 1962 (*Keystone*)

India's Russian-made T55 tanks in East Pakistan, 1971 (*United Press International*)

above right: Israeli infantry on the march in the War of Liberation, 1948 (*Popperfoto*)
right: Israeli tanks on the Golan Heights in the Six Day War, June 1967 (*Keystone*)

Egyptian crossing of the Suez Canal in the Yom Kippur War, October 1973 (*Keystone*)

Algeria, centred on the cities where most of the *pieds noirs* lived, especially Algiers and Oran. The aim of the OAS was twofold: to destroy the FLN's internal army and to cause such a breakdown of security that the authorities would have to call in the army to take control. They still hoped that the army would then rally to their side. But as the savagery increased on both sides, the army turned increasingly against the OAS and their *pied noir* supporters, no longer hesitant to fire on Frenchmen. Meanwhile the unfortunate Joxe had to abandon one negotiating position after another, fighting hard for France to retain some rights to the oil and gas of the Sahara, but eventually having to submit to the demands presented by Belkacem Krim on behalf of the GPRA, which had never conceded anything. Finally, on 18 March 1962 agreement was reached on a cease-fire. Power was to be handed over to a Provisional Executive, French forces were to leave Algeria within three years, but France would be allowed to retain her naval base at Mers-el-Kebir and make use of other installations in Algeria and the Sahara for a period. The FLN promised to guarantee the rights of Europeans and take no action against the *harkis*. This was confirmed by yet another referendum on 8 April with a 90 per cent '*Oui*'; but the OAS had already reacted violently, now fighting not so much against the FLN as against the army and the police. Jouhaud was arrested on 25 March, Salan on 20 April, but Dufour fought on, an attempt being made by his men to assassinate de Gaulle. As the violence and reaction to it by the ALN intensified, the *pieds noirs*, faced, as it had been said, with a choice between 'the suitcase and the coffin', chose the suitcase in overwhelming numbers. By the time that independence finally came on 4 July 1962, 1,380,000 Algerians, some Muslim, had left for France, 50,000 for Spain, 12,000 for Canada, 10,000 for Israel and 1,550 for Argentina. Only 30,000 Europeans stayed. In the seven and a half years of war European civilian casualties in the 42,000 acts of terrorism amounted to some 10,000, of which 3,200 were killed or never accounted for. The French forces, which had included over 100,000 Muslims, had lost 17,456 dead and almost 65,000 wounded or injured. The French estimated that they had killed 141,000 of the FLN, that another 12,000 had died in the internecine fighting, that the FLN had killed 16,000 Muslim civilians and that another 50,000 could never be traced. To these figures must be added the *harkis* and other Muslims loyal to France killed after independence, of which estimates vary from 30,000 to 150,000, and those who died of starvation or disease as a result of the enforced concentration of population by the French, and the 4,300 Algerians killed in France. Estimates of the total Muslim Algerian deaths vary from 300,000 to one million, the latter officially adopted by the government of Boumedienne, who, resting his power on the army he had formed and kept intact in Tunisia, ousted his rivals in 1964, some of them, like Belkacem Krim, paying with their lives.

Could the issue have been different? Could Algeria have been saved for France? Given the fundamental divergence of aim between the Muslim nationalists and the *colons*, it is doubtful if any compromise between them could have been maintained for long. The *pied noir*, particularly the less well off, was not prepared to be treated on a basis of equality with the Muslim Algerian, and the latter would not in the end be prepared to accept anything else. It is doubtful if a solution involving association with France, based on the support of the moderates in both camps, would have lasted for long. If de Gaulle had given first priority to Algeria, when he came to power in May 1958, and acted quickly, cashing in on his general popularity at that time, he might have won the initiative away from the external leaders of the FLN, and, with a military campaign intensely pursued at the same time, as Challe was to execute the following year, it is possible that a settlement with some of the nationalists could have been reached; but, even if that had been achieved, it is unlikely that it would have lasted. By the time of Operation *Tilsit* two years later the chances were even slimmer.

But de Gaulle's first priority was to cleanse the political Augean stables of France herself and to lay the foundations of a new France, looking to the future. He had no love for the *colons*, *grands* or *petits*, and was prepared, for the sake of France and her army, to sacrifice Algeria and the interests of its inhabitants, white and brown. This he did, and millions suffered in the course of his brutal surgical treatment. However, many more might have suffered over a longer period, if he had not acted as he did.

After the Challe offensive the army had every right to feel that it had achieved a victory; but by that time the external leaders of the FLN had won enough political support in the world at large, added to the distaste of the French public for the war and the methods used to prosecute it, for them to be able to survive, as long as the military operations in Algeria were sufficient to keep the *pieds noirs* dissatisfied with the French authorities. In Maoist terms the ALN never got to the stage of 'mobile warfare', hardly for long to 'protracted warfare'. For almost all the time 'guerrilla warfare' was all they could achieve, but it was enough. Boumedienne's army, by force of circumstances kept intact in Tunisia, was the tool with which, after independence, he asserted and maintained his personal supremacy over his rivals. The grim lesson of the story appears to be that the ruthless hard-liner, who is prepared never to compromise and is willing to wait, wins in the end.

PART THREE

American Adventures

Chapter Nine

KOREA

Korea's geographical situation was bound to make her, down the centuries, a meeting place of rival powers. A peninsula jutting out from the Manchurian mainland to within 125 miles of the coast of southern Japan, her northern frontier on the Yalu River was only 500 miles as the crow flies from Peking. When Russia extended her sway to the Pacific in the nineteenth century, her border touched that of Korea near Vladivostock. For many centuries it had been a vassal state of the Chinese Empire, in practice enjoying a degree of autonomy, similar to that of Annam, under its own king. Japan began to try and displace Chinese influence in the 1870s. In 1894 this resulted in a short war between China and Japan in Korea, in which China was defeated. As a result she recognized the independence of Korea. Japan had demanded cession of the Laotung peninsula with Port Arthur at its apex; but Russia, at that time building the Trans-Siberian railway to Vladivostock, brought pressure to bear on China to refuse and, instead, to cede Formosa, now known as Taiwan. Russia herself had designs on Korea, and the rivalry between her and Japan on this issue led, after Japan had made sure by the Anglo–Japanese Treaty of 1902 that Britain would not intervene against her, to the Russo–Japanese War, of which the first act was the attack on Port Arthur on 9 February 1904. It was through Korea that Japan advanced to defeat the Russians at the Battle of Mukden the following year, and in the Tsushima Strait, between Korea and Japan, that Admiral Togo sank almost every ship of the Russian Baltic Fleet, which had set sail from Leningrad in October of the year before in a vain attempt to save the besieged Port Arthur, which had already fallen when the fleet had only got as far as Madagascar.

Japan annexed Korea in 1910, imposing a form of colonial government until 1942, when she declared it to be an integral part of Japan itself. During this period she had developed its industry, including mining and the hydro-electric power required for it. Most of this was concentrated in the north, the long peninsula, running south for 500 miles, being largely devoted to agriculture, the more fertile area being on the western side of the mountain range which ran the full length of the eastern side of the country. Japan's oppressive rule met with two separate movements of resistance. One was based on the old-fashioned regime and led by a descendant of the ancient royal family, Lee Sung-man, better known by the westernized form of his name, Syngman Rhee. He had instigated a rebellion against the Japanese in 1919, which had been brutally repressed. He had fled to Shanghai, where he set up a provisional government in exile, and later went to the United States. The other was based on the Korean Communist Party, formed in 1925. Its leader was Kim Sung-chu, who took the name of a renowned early hero of resistance to the Japanese, Kim Il-sung. In the 1930s Kim Il-sung II operated an ineffective resistance movement based in Manchuria and at some stage went to the Soviet Union, where he is said to have served in or been trained by its army.

It is hardly surprising, therefore, that Russia took a considerable interest in what was to be the status of Korea after the end of the Second World War. Stalin had agreed that 'in due course Korea should be free and independent'; but, in return for a promise to sign a treaty of friendship with Chiang Kai-shek, had extracted one from Roosevelt that 'the wrongs' done to Russia by the Treaty of Portsmouth, which had ended the Russo–Japanese War in 1905, should be put right, hoping thereby to regain the southern Sakhalin Islands, which he did, and also to re-establish the pre-1904 Russian position in Manchuria and Mongolia. At the Potsdam Conference in July 1945 after the defeat of Germany, the commitment to an independent Korea was reaffirmed, and it was decided that, when the war against Japan came to an end, the Russians would be responsible for disarming the Japanese down to the 38th parallel of latitude, about half-way down the peninsula, just north of Seoul, and that the Americans would do the same in the southern half. Japan's sudden collapse, after the atomic bombs on Hiroshima and Nagasaki on 6 and 9 August 1945, found the Russians better placed to implement this agreement than the Americans. On 8 August their troops had entered Manchuria, and on 12 August, two days before Japan capitulated, they crossed the Yalu to enter Korea with an army of 100,000 men under General Chistiakov. The nearest US troops were at Okinawa, 600 miles away. It was not until 8 September that the first of them, under the command of General Hodge, landed at Inchon. They found the country already firmly divided, as Germany had been, the nine million Koreans north of the 38th parallel, with almost all the industrial resources, cut off from the twenty-one million to the south, and a puppet government, led by Kim Il-sung, installed at Pyongyang. He and the Russians immediately began to propagate the idea that it was solely due to American imperialism that the country was divided.

The foreign ministers of Britain, America and Russia agreed to set up a joint commission of the Russian and American military administrations in Korea to make recommendations for the establishment of a single government, but with the proviso that the country would not become independent for five years. Meanwhile those nations with China would act as trustees. This was opposed

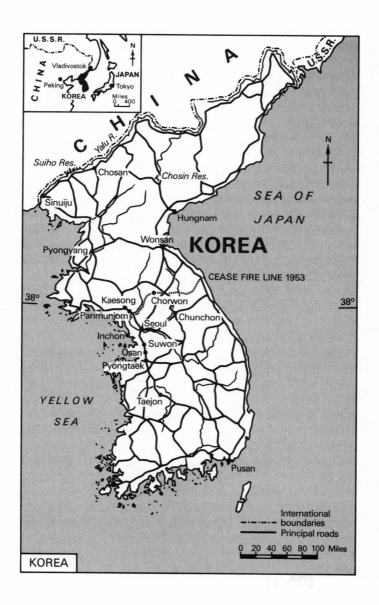

KOREA

by all the Korean nationalists except the communists, with the result that the Russians demanded that the joint commission confer only with them. The Americans could clearly not accept this, and throughout 1946 and 1947 no progress was made, while the Russians steadily built up North Korean armed forces. In 1947 the United States referred the matter to the United Nations General Assembly, which resolved that elections should be held throughout Korea in the spring of 1948 and appointed a commission of nine to arrange them. The Russians refused to allow the commission into the north and the election was therefore confined to the south, the deputies forming the National Assembly which resulted, choosing the aged Syngman Rhee as the first President of the Republic of Korea. The communists responded by proclaiming a Peoples' Democratic Republic of Korea in the north and named Kim Il-sung as its first Prime Minister. At the end of the year, 1948, the Russians withdrew their own forces, leaving behind a strong North Korean army.

The United States had deliberately not built up similar forces for Syngman Rhee, limiting them to a gendarmerie for border control and reinforcement of the police for internal security in emergency. No heavy weapons were therefore supplied. This policy was based partly on a well-meaning concept of the real needs of the Koreans and partly on distrust of the use that Syngman Rhee might make of them. Any other policy would have raised serious domestic political difficulties. It inevitably meant that the new Republic would have to depend on support from America for its external defence, when the last of the American occupation troops left, as they did, in June 1949. In defining her policy in what we call the Far East, after Mao Tse-tung had ousted Chiang Kai-shek and gained control over all mainland China in 1949, the United States was to face a permanent dilemma between giving sufficient assurances of support to encourage the nations surrounding China to stand up to the threat of communism, and at the same time avoiding such a commitment that it would both over-commit herself and tend to make the indigenous people feel that they need do little themselves. It was this dilemma which Dean Acheson, then US Secretary of State, faced when, in January 1950, he defined the American defence commitment as running along the Aleutians to Japan and then via the Ryuku Islands to the Philippines. 'So far as the military security of other areas in the Pacific is concerned,' he went on to say, 'it must be clear that no person can guarantee these areas against military attack. But it must also be clear that such a guarantee is hardly sensible or necessary within the realm of practical relationship.' In May the Chairman of the Senate Foreign Relations Committee, Senator Connally, said that Russia could seize South Korea without US intervention, as Korea was not 'very greatly important'. The risks of doing so cannot then have seemed very great to the Russians, particularly if it was largely carried out by proxy. Arguments for acting were produced by the growing development of the Republic both economically and politically. New elections in May 1950 had returned a sizeable opposition to Syngman Rhee and there were reasons to believe that, as a result, the United States might be more generous in its aid, and that a strong and viable democratic state could be established in the near future. If North Korea struck quickly, its military superiority, backed by Russia, should be able rapidly to overrun the country and face the world with a *fait accompli*. Mao's China was too wrapped up in its own problems to raise any serious objection. Kim Il-sung's Commander-in-Chief, General Chai, had a combat army of 90,000 men, producing seven infantry divisions and an armoured brigade equipped with some 200 Russian T34 tanks, supported by 2,000 guns, including medium artillery, and an air force of 210 Russian aircraft. The South Korean (ROK) army was of much the same size, the combat element of 65,000 men producing eight small divisions, but with no tanks or aircraft and artillery limited to ninety short-range field guns. These two armies faced each other on the 38th parallel, as Chai moved the forward elements of his divisions into the area five to ten miles north of the frontier, from which the population had been permanently removed, supporting a public demand by Kim Il-sung for elections to be held throughout the whole country.

Although the CIA had expected further communist agitation in South Korea against Syngman Rhee's government, assisted by saboteurs infiltrated from the north, nobody seems to have considered that there was a serious threat of a direct invasion. When it came at 4 a.m. on Sunday 25 June 1950 (2 a.m. 24 June in Washington), it took everyone by surprise. The main assaults were on either side of the Imjin River on the two roads converging on Seoul, and on Chunchon just west of the mountains. Subsidiary attacks were made on the isolated Ongjin peninsula on the west coast and on the east coast, both down the coast road and from the sea, south of the frontier. The ROK forces offered limited resistance, and by the evening of 26 June the authorities in Seoul, Tokyo, where General MacArthur was in Supreme Command, and in Washington were seriously alarmed. President Truman ordered MacArthur to use US naval and air forces to evacuate US personnel and summoned a meeting of the UN Security Council, which called for a cease-fire and withdrawal of North Korean forces. The Soviet Union had been refusing to attend the Security Council since January in protest at the continued occupation of a permanent seat by Nationalist China. As a result, neither on this occasion nor on the subsequent ones, in which the Council recommended members to assist the Republic of Korea, was she able to exercise her veto. By the following day, 27 June, Seoul was threatened by a converging attack from north and north-east. The population began to stream south, while efforts were being made to move a ROK division north to deliver a counter-attack. Chaos was caused when the vital bridge over the Han River was prematurely demolished, and on 28 June the city fell to the invaders. In response to a signal from MacArthur on 26 June, giving his estimate that 'a complete collapse is imminent', Truman had authorized him to employ US naval and air forces to support the ROK Army.

The news of the fall of Seoul led to the adoption by the Security Council of the US-sponsored resolution recommending 'members of the UN to furnish such assistance to the ROK as may be necessary to repel the armed attack and to restore international peace and security in the area'. MacArthur flew to Korea and toured the front himself on 28 June. Impressed by the flood of refugees and the demoralized state of the ROK Army, he reported to Washington that 'the only assurance for holding the present line and the ability to regain later the lost ground is through the introduction of US ground combat forces' and went on to say that he proposed, if authorized, to move a regimental combat team there as soon as possible and 'provide for a possible build-up to a two-division strength from the troops in Japan for an early counter-offensive'. On 29 June Truman gave him the authority he asked, and, as two North Korean divisions crossed the Han at Seoul, another pushed down the central route and a fourth along the east coast, 406 men of Lieutenant-Colonel Smith's 1st Battalion 21st Infantry from the US 24th Division, pulled from their comfortable beds in Japan, flew into the airfield of Pusan, the port at the southernmost tip of Korea, on 1 July.

MacArthur had four divisions, three infantry and one cavalry, acting as infantry, as occupation troops in Japan. They were at 70 per cent normal strength, had few support weapons, only light M24 (Chaffee) tanks and the last thing that any of their soldiers expected to do was to fight: a relaxed life, the tedium mitigated by the delights of occupation forces, was what they expected and were enjoying. But the senior NCO's and officers were experienced men and the 24th Division's commander, Major-General Dean, was a tough soldier. His task was a pretty hopeless one. With an exiguous force and little hope of a rapid build-up, he had to move 200 miles against a stream of refugees and demoralized ROK soldiers in a country of primitive communications, of which few of the inhabitants could speak his language. His own troops were ill-equipped and trained for the task, materially, physically and mentally. Everything depended on the presence of US forces strengthening the morale of the ROK forces. It is to their credit that, at first and in most cases, they struggled manfully to cope with their task. But as one attempt after another to stem the tide of the North Korean advance failed, their own morale began to suffer and, as Dean's forces built up, the new arrivals became infected with the defeatism which is an inescapable aspect of a chaotic withdrawal. At the end of the first week of July, it was clear that the enemy was not going to be held in the north and that a defensive position would have to be established farther south. Acting on a report from Dean, MacArthur reported to the US Chiefs of Staff that the situation was critical, assessing that it was not just an indigenous North Korean invasion, but 'a combination of Soviet leadership and technical guidance with Chinese Communist ground elements'. It had developed into a major operation, and he requested that a further four American divisions with appropriate support be despatched to him 'without delay and by every means of transportation available'. He had already been given a brigade of US Marines and, as a result of this request, another division was ordered to his command from the United States.

MacArthur had already decided that he must use all his available combat troops from Japan under Lieutenant-General Walton (Johnny) Walker, Commanding General of the US Eighth Army, a tough, determined and highly professional soldier, who had commanded a corps in Patton's Third Army in north-west Europe. Walker established his headquarters in Korea on 13 July and four days later assumed command of the ROK Army as well, giving him a force of 58,000 Koreans and 18,000 Americans. Dean's 24th Division had been joined by Kean's 25th, whose main task was to secure the Pusan area, while Dean delayed the enemy's southward advance and the 1st Cavalry Division was brought ashore at Pohang on the east coast and moved west to join hands with him. Walker persuaded Dean to try and hang on to the important road centre of Taejon in order to make this link-up possible, but in doing so Dean himself and many of his troops were cut off, the remnants withdrawing through the 1st Cavalry into what was to become the Pusan perimeter, the south-east corner of the country, eighty miles north to south and fifty miles wide, east of the Naktong River. By 1 August the the US strength of Walker's army had increased to 47,000, including nearly 5,000 Marines, while its ROK strength had decreased to 45,000. It faced a North Korean army of some 70,000, several thousand of whom were South Koreans impressed to replace the heavy casualties it had received in its unskilful but gallant attacks, as well as at the hands of the US Air Force.

There had been anxious moments before the perimeter was firmly established, on both flanks and at the key north-west corner town of Taegu, and there were several attempts by the North Koreans during August to break through: but in some bitter fighting they were all held, although some ground was lost in the extreme south-west corner, in the defence of which the newly-arrived British 27th Infantry Brigade took part. The British contribution, including a significant naval one, was the largest of all those sent by the fifty-three of the fifty-nine members of the United Nations who had voted for the resolution of 27 June: twenty-one sent military units, of which five limited them to medical ones. In terms of military effectiveness they added nothing very significant to the US and ROK forces, and their presence complicated the administration of the force; but politically their involvement was of the greatest help to the United States. Chiang Kai-shek had offered a sizeable force and MacArthur strongly recommended in public that it should be accepted, the first of the open political disagreements he was to have with Truman.

By September Walker was firm and secure, in possession of a port in Pusan which could guarantee the supply of his force. As far back as 10 July Mac-Arthur had pressed for the release to him of the 1st Marine Division, having already decided, although he did not reveal it, that his counter-offensive was to be based not on a return slog up the length of the country, but, on the pattern of his victories in the Western Pacific, on an amphibious assault. Bradley, then Chairman of the Joint Chiefs of Staff, at first turned the request down, but MacArthur persisted, saying that he must have them by 1 September, and was successful: accordingly, on 19 July, Truman authorized the call-up of Marine reservists. While Walker was fighting ding-dong battles to hold the Pusan perimeter in August, MacArthur was planning a daring and risky counter-stroke, a landing at Inchon, the port of Seoul. Everybody but he himself opposed the plan. The tides were terrific, over thirty feet between high and low water, the latter leaving miles of mud flats in the approaches to Inchon. There were hardly any suitable beaches and many of the assaulting troops would have to land directly into the port itself. The area in which supporting ships could be deployed was restricted to narrow channels with strong currents, in which they would have to anchor, like sitting ducks. There were only two or three days in the month when tidal conditions made landing possible at all.

MacArthur overrode all objections and was triumphantly vindicated on 15 September when the Marines struggled ashore with the support of a devastating naval bombardment and carrier-borne air attacks. All their landings were successful, and on 17 September the 7th Infantry Division began to land and push through them. On the previous day Walker began to try and break out of the Pusan perimeter, following an abortive ROK attempt to land a guerrilla force behind the enemy lines on the east coast. Progress was at first disappointing and MacArthur began to contemplate a further landing at Kunsan, farther south on the west coast in October, in order to loosen things up. However a few days later the prospect looked brighter, and on 22 September MacArthur and Walker agreed to scrap the idea of withdrawing some of the latter's divisions for this purpose and to concentrate on breaking out to join up with the Inchon landing. Thereafter the North Korean collapse came quickly, perhaps brought about by an order to withdraw because of the threat from Inchon. Whether or not it was intended, it almost immediately became a rout, accompanied by the wholesale slaughter of prisoners and South Korean civilians. It was during the fighting that led to the break-out that one of the battalions of the British 27th Infantry Brigade, the Argyll and Sutherland Highlanders, lost eighty-nine men, sixty as a result of an attack by the US Air Force, owing to confusion about which hill they had taken, caused, it was said, by the enemy using captured marker panels. On 26 September the troops of the 1st Cavalry Division made contact with those of the 7th Infantry near Osan, forty miles south of Seoul and scene of the first action in which US troops had been involved almost three months before. A fierce battle was then in train for Seoul itself, in which the Marines blasted their way straight through the city, while two other divisions, one ROK and the other US, outflanked it. On 28 September it fell, and next day MacArthur, in a dramatic ceremony, handed it over in ruins to Syngman Rhee.

Ever since August, when the Soviet Union had returned to the Security Council to take the chair, acrimonious argument had been going on there, Russia, represented by Malik, subsequently backed up by Communist China in the person of Chou En-lai, accusing the United States and her allies of imperialist aggression, and the latter countering with accusations of Russian and Chinese involvement in North Korean aggression. These arguments had reached a high pitch at the time of the fall of Seoul, which inevitably raised the question of whether or not MacArthur was to be allowed to move his forces north of the 38th parallel. In spite of great pressure brought by the Soviet Union, both in the Security Council and in the General Assembly, to convince the waverers like India that to do so would be overt aggression against North Korea, MacArthur was authorized by the US Chiefs of Staff on 27 September to move north of the dividing line 'to carry out the destruction of the North Korean Armed Forces', but with the limitation that only ROK forces should be used, unless there were indications that Russian or Chinese forces were entering the country. On no account was he to cross the Yalu River into Manchuria, and, if he were to approach it, only ROK forces were to be used. The US Government was determined to avoid an escalation of the conflict into a general one between the West and the two major communist powers, fought in an area which was of no real vital interest. Her allies were even more determined to avoid it. MacArthur was intolerant of these hesitations. He now felt that he must strike while the iron was hot. Rhee ordered his units to move north of the parallel on 1 October; MacArthur therefore felt free to move US forces also, although Chou En-lai, on 2 October, announced that, if they did so, Communist China would enter the war. This warning was repeated after the first US troops crossed the line on 7 October, the day after such action had received the approval of the UN General Assembly. It was not long after this that intelligence reports began to reach MacArthur and Walker that Communist Chinese troops in Manchuria were moving towards the Yalu River. When Truman met MacArthur on Wake Island on 15 October, ROK troops had already reached Wonsan, eighty miles north of the parallel on the east coast. MacArthur, contrary to Walker's wishes, had insisted on withdrawing the Marine and 7th Divisions to embark them for an amphibious attack on the port, and they were hanging about off the coast, waiting for the mines to be cleared from the approaches, when the ROK 1st Corps captured it.

Truman found MacArthur in optimistic mood, saying that he believed that all formal resistance in North Korea would be over by Thanksgiving Day (23 November) and that Walker's Eighth Army would be back in Japan by Christmas. In reply to a question about the possibility of Communist Chinese intervention, he said that they only had 100,000 to 125,000 men on the Yalu River and no air force. 'Now that we have bases for our Air Force in Korea,' he said, 'if the Chinese tried to get down to Pyongyang, there would be the greatest slaughter.' Next day the first Chinese began secretly to infiltrate into

Korea across the Yalu. But MacArthur's optimism appeared justified. On 21 October Pyongyang fell and the North Korean Army began surrendering *en masse*, the total of prisoners taken reaching 135,000. On 24 October that veteran division of the campaign, the 24th, with the British 27th Commonwealth Brigade, crossed the Chongchon River forty miles farther north, heading for Sinuiju and the Suiho Dam on the Yalu, seventy-five miles farther on. Two days later the ROK 6th Division reached the Yalu to the east of them at Chosan, where, a few days later, they were to be sharply counter-attacked by the Chinese, fleeing in disorder. In spite of this, there was a general mood of great optimism and a confidence that, in spite of the obvious presence both of the Chinese Army and of their Air Force, they were intent only on securing the Manchurian border.

This complacent mood did not last long. By 5 November MacArthur was giving a public warning that he was faced by 'a new and fresh army', which had already operated east of the Yalu, and that it was 'a matter of gravest international significance'. His warning appeared to have had the effect intended, as the Chinese, although remaining east of the Yalu in most of the area, drew back and made no contact with MacArthur's forces for three weeks. MacArthur asked for and was refused permission to bomb the Yalu bridges and Chinese bases and concentrations of troops over the border. Russia had already stated that, if the US Air Force attacked airfields in Manchuria, her air force would retaliate. MacArthur was ordered to clear the area up to the Yalu (which in his opinion involved dealing with some 60,000 Chinese troops east of it) and then to make preparations for elections to be held throughout the country under UN auspices. MacArthur made his plans for this, General Almond's 10th Corps (including the Marine and 7th Divisions, which had carried out the landings at Inchon and had been intended to repeat the performance at Wonsan) operating directly under his command to clear the north-east corner of Korea up to the Russian frontier near Vladivostock, while Walker's Eighth Army closed up to the Yalu. D-day for this was to be the day after Thanksgiving, 24 November, and Walker's troops, ill-prepared for the bitter cold of a Korean winter, were none too keen to resume operations, when they had been told to expect to be out of the country by Christmas.

The lull in operations was a classic case on the part of the Chinese General Lin Piao of *reculer pour mieux sauter*. His army was itself preparing to attack all along the line. He had sixteen divisions facing, in Walker's Eighth Army, four US and four ROK divisions, and the British Commonwealth and Turkish brigades. Beyond a gap of over fifty miles was Almond's 10th Corps of three US and two ROK divisions with a British Royal Marine Commando group, opposite which General Chen Yi had another fourteen divisions. In all, MacArthur had 205,000 men in his land forces facing 300,000 Chinese nominally under command of Kim Il-sung, but actually under the Chinese General Peng Teh-huai at Mukden. But MacArthur's forces were dispersed over a wide front, totally unprepared to meet a counter-offensive, which almost everywhere took the form of attacks *en masse* through the hills on either side of the valleys in which the road-bound US and ROK forces were crammed head to tail. The main thrusts of both Chinese field armies were made in the hilly country in the centre of the front, where the Chinese gained greater advantage from their tactics. Their strategic aim was to outflank Eighth Army from the east and 10th Corps from the west, pressing them back against the coast and leaving the centre free for a push down the spine of the country.

After four days of fighting, Eighth Army was retreating everywhere, many of its formations forced to withdraw as they were outflanked. The 2nd US Division, withdrawing from the Chongchon River towards Sunchon on 1 December, found itself cut off in a narrow five-mile-long defile. In spite of intense air operations in support, only 3,000 men succeeded in escaping, the British 27th Brigade helping to open up the southern end of the pass. The whole of 10th Corps was in danger of being cut off in the north-east corner, and on 30 November MacArthur ordered it to withdraw to Hungnam and embark from there to reinforce the vital south-east corner of the country. He hoped to stop the rot in the neck of Korea on the line Pyongyang–Wonsan, but Walker was unable to form an effective defence there and the North Korean capital fell on 5 December. MacArthur thereupon decided to make a clean break and stand on the 38th parallel. He was helped in this aim by the Chinese pausing for their supplies to catch up, a necessity for them every four or five days, the period for which each soldier carried his personal rations. By 13 December the Eighth Army was back on the Imjin River and 10th Corps had begun its evacuation from Hungnam, the 1st Marine Division, with remnants of the 7th, having fought a fierce and intense battle to break out southwards from the area of the Chosin reservoir, where they had been surrounded by General Sung Shin-lun's Ninth Field Army. Fighting in ice and snow, the Marines had beaten off attacks by greatly superior forces and, having evacuated over 4,000 of their own casualties by air, fought their way grimly southwards to join up with the US 3rd Division, defending the Hungnam bridgehead. In all they suffered 7,500 casualties, including many of the British Royal Marine Commando Group, half of them from frostbite, and claimed to have inflicted 37,500 in return. This gallant fight had made it possible for the rest of 10th Corps to get safely back to the bridgehead. The evacuation was successfully completed on Christmas Day, 105,000 troops, 91,000 refugees, 17,300 vehicles and 91,000 tons of stores being taken off while the bridgehead was held.

On Christmas Eve General Walker was killed in a traffic accident and was succeeded by General Mathew (Matt) Ridgway, wartime commander of the 82nd US Airborne Division and at the time serving in the Pentagon. He took over as his army withdrew over the 38th parallel, at last taking under its command 10th Corps as it did so, bringing it up from Pusan, to which it had been ferried, to plug gaps in the centre caused by the collapse of demoralized

ROK divisions. They left behind the Marine Division in central southern Korea to deal with a force of North Korean troops who had been carrying on guerrilla warfare in the area since they had been cut off after Eighth Army's break-out from the Pusan perimeter in September 1950, and had been joined by others who had broken through the front in the mountains. Ridgway found himself unable to hold the line under renewed Chinese pressure, especially on his western flank, and withdrew again, Seoul, Inchon and the important airfield of Kimpo falling to the Chinese on 4 January, as the floating bridges over the nearly frozen Han River were blown again, floods of refugees fleeing south once more, this time in bitter winter weather. Ridgway finally formed a firm defensive line in mid-January, running due east from Pyongtaek, where it was seventy-five miles south of the 38th parallel, to the coast some forty miles south of it.

In an attempt to stem the tide, MacArthur had demanded the bombing of targets in Manchuria and, once again, reinforcement by Chinese Nationalist troops. Both were refused and he began to sulk, taking the view that his country, its President and Chiefs of Staff had lost the will to win, and having no sympathy for their view that to run the risk of confrontation with Russia and China in the Far East was to be faced, in Omar Bradley's words, 'with the wrong war in the wrong place at the wrong time with the wrong enemy'. NATO was in its infancy and the defence of Western Europe in no state to face a Soviet threat there. There was even a suggestion that atomic bombs should be used, lent credence by a statement by Truman in a press conference. In a question about taking 'whatever steps are necessary to meet the military situation', he was asked 'will that include the atomic bomb?', to which he replied: 'That will include any weapons we have.' When further pressed, he said: 'There has always been active consideration of its use. I don't want to see it used.' This brought strong protests from the British Labour party and Prime Minister Attlee flew to Washington on 3 December and extracted a more pacific announcement from the President, although he did not persuade him, as he had hoped to do, to buy off Communist China by supporting its admission to the United Nations. Even if Truman had himself been inclined to that, which he was not, the pro-Chiang lobby was too strong. However, many of America's allies and others in the United Nations were not as resolute, and ever since the retreat began in early December, there had been pressure for cease-fire talks with Communist China. These were fortunately vetoed by the Soviet Union and publicly rejected by China. This and the stabilization of the front in Korea in mid-January brought a slackening of the pressure for a cease-fire, although the pessimism engendered by the course of the war had led the US Chiefs of Staff and administration to consider where their strategic priorities lay. In a message to MacArthur in late December, the Chiefs of Staff had said that they believed that Korea was not the place to fight a major war, but that a successful defence was nevertheless of great importance, if it could be accomplished without incurring serious loss. He was directed to defend successive positions, but it was left to him to decide if an evacuation was necessary in order to maintain the defence of Japan, which was of higher priority. They wished to avoid a situation in which the Chinese could permanently deploy a superior force against him. MacArthur reacted strongly to this apparently defeatist view with a proposal that the war should be widened by attacking China herself elsewhere, blockading her coast, bombing the mainland and supporting Chiang Kai-shek in taking the offensive against them. This would take the pressure off Korea, which must be defended. The Russian threat to Europe was not an imminent one. Additional forces deployed to Korea would later be available for Europe, and by then better trained for war. The Joint Chiefs replied with arguments, such as the need to convince allies, notably the British with their interests in Hong Kong, which were not likely to appeal to MacArthur, and reiterated their directive that the primary considerations were the safety of his troops and the defence of Japan. 'Should it become evident in your judgement', they signalled on 9 January 1951, 'that evacuation is essential to avoid severe losses of men and material, you will at that time withdraw from Korea to Japan.' MacArthur's reply was an angry demand for clarification of their policy. He refused to accept responsibility for deciding whether or not evacuation was necessary, and ended his message with the question: 'Is it the present objective of US political policy to maintain a military position indefinitely, for a limited time, or to minimize losses by the evacuation as soon as it can be accomplished?' After a meeting of the National Security Council on 13 January, Truman sent him a long, detailed message, clearly and patiently explaining all the advantages to be gained from a successful resistance in Korea, but setting out also the wider factors that had to be considered, above all the need to mobilize world-wide support for a general policy of resisting Russian pressures elsewhere. Unfortunately, on the very day that he wrote this, the UN General Assembly passed a resolution calling for an immediate cease-fire in Korea, with guarantees that the truce would not be used to screen military build-ups and that it would be used to arrive at decisions on the basis of a permanent settlement. All 'Non-Korean' troops would be withdrawn 'in appropriate stages' and the country would be administered by the United Nations during the truce. A special agency, including Russia, Communist China, Britain and the United States, would settle Far Eastern issues, such as the future of Formosa (Taiwan) and the admission of Communist China to the United Nations. This was passed by fifty votes to seven, the US representative casting his vote with the majority when he saw that it had overwhelming support. This produced a storm of protest, which subsided when Chou En-lai countered it with a proposal which was so clearly unacceptable that it amounted to a flat rejection. In an attempt to cash in on this, the United States tried to persuade the General Assembly to brand Communist China as an aggressor in Korea; but it was not until 1 February that she succeeded in persuading her allies to support it, and then only on being given an assurance that the war would not be extended beyond Korea. By then the clouds of gloom, which had darkened the strategic scene, had begun to lift.

When Ridgway stabilized his line in mid-January, he had some 365,000 men in three US and three ROK corps and the air situation had been improved by the arrival of the first F104 Sabres, which quickly established their superiority over the Russian MIG15s flown by the Chinese. Ridgway's forces now included units of fifteen nations, the British having produced a second infantry brigade, the 29th, which had reached the front in time to take part in the fighting round Seoul. At this time the only other nation to provide more than a battalion was Turkey, who contributed an infantry brigade. These units were integrated into US divisions, all of which also included several thousand South Koreans, officially enlisted into the ROK army, but fully integrated into American units. This had the interesting effect of bringing about the integration also of American black soldiers, who hitherto had always served in separate units. Ridgway also raised a Korean Service Corps for labour and similar duties behind the front line, an important one being the provision of porters to supply troops deployed well off the few roads. From west to east Ridgway had deployed the US 1st and 9th Corps and then in succession the 1st, 2nd and 3rd ROK Corps, with the US 10th Corps in reserve, bringing it up, as already described, to support the ROK corps in the centre.

Facing Ridgway, Lin Piao, who commanded the whole front, had 21 Chinese and 12 North Korean divisions, amounting to some 485,000 men, before he began his attacks on Seoul and Wonju, in which he suffered heavy casualties. He had also outrun his primitive supply system, which relied very largely on masses of porters moving at night to avoid the attentions of the US Air Force, and his soldiers were even less well-equipped to face the severe winter than Ridgway's. After the line had stabilized in mid-January, the Chinese withdrew out of immediate contact and Ridgway, as soon as he had sorted things out, ordered reconnaissance units to patrol forward. Starting on 15 January in the west, they found no enemy south of Suwon, half-way between the front line and Seoul. Anxious not to walk into a trap similar to that which had been sprung on his predecessor in the advance to the Yalu, he made a personal reconnaissance in a light aircraft on 24 January before finally committing his troops next day to a general advance. With strong air support, his two American corps moved methodically forward, maintaining an unbroken front until, early in February, they reached the Han River, the US 10th Corps and ROK 3rd Corps conforming to their movement in the centre, opposition hardening as they neared Hoengsong, north of Wonju. Here they were fiercely counter-attacked, the ROK 5th and 8th Divisions and the 2nd US Infantry Division, including the Dutch battalion, suffering heavy casualties and being forced back. Lin Paio followed this with another blow between that area and the Han River; but this was held by the 2nd Division, the French

battalion playing a prominent part. East of Hoengsong Lin Piao had penetrated farther, to within ten miles of the line from which the advance had
started; but this was also held, and by the middle of the month Ridgway's
Operation *Killer* was forcing them back everywhere. By this time the spring
thaw had set in and the country was transformed into a morass of mud, over
which Ridgway's troops plodded forward to recapture Hoengsong and close
up to Seoul, Inchon and Kimpo airfield having fallen to them earlier in the
month. Piao's army was suffering heavy losses both from air attack and from
Ridgway's cautious, methodical attacks, delivered with massive artillery support. Lin Piao himself was replaced early in March by Peng Teh-huai, whose
first order to his Fourth Field Army was to hold the 38th parallel at all costs
until a further major offensive, the supplies and equipment for which would be
provided by Russia, could be launched in May.

Ridgway pressed on with Operation *Ripper*, 9th and 10th US Corps being
directed up the centre to Chunchon, their right flank covered by the ROK
corps, hoping that this would force the enemy to withdraw from Seoul. The
advance began on 7 March and succeeded in its aims, Seoul being abandoned
a week later. An attempt was made to intercept the retreating garrison by the
airdrop of an airborne regiment on 23 March, combined with an armoured
drive north from the city; but it was too late, the 20,000-strong North Korean
force already having got away to Kaesong. By the end of March Ridgway's
troops were everywhere up to the 38th parallel and in some cases a few miles
beyond it, and a major controversy had arisen about the next step, as a result of
which Ridgway found himself transferred, on 11 April, to replace his superior.

Since the exchange of signals in January, the argument between MacArthur
and the Joint Chiefs had been in abeyance until he had raised it again on 21
February with a request to bomb the small port of Rashin, just inside the
border of North Korea from the Russian frontier south of Vladivostok, which
the Chinese were using. When this was refused, MacArthur complained of the
'unparalleled conditions of restraint and handicap' imposed on him. Meanwhile Republican political figures, who sympathized with his views, were
agitating for an all-out war against China. On 7 March, the day Ridgway
launched Operation *Ripper*, MacArthur flew to Suwon airfield and read a
carefully prepared statement to the press, in which he maintained that, if
restrictions were placed on the war in Korea, victory could not be achieved: the
Chinese would be able to build up a fresh and stronger army and return to the
attack in greater strength, and so it would go on. He implied that the only way
to ensure a free Korea was to carry the war to China itself. Ridgway was so
concerned at the effect this might have on his troops that he gave a press
conference himself five days later, rebutting the view that victory was not
possible in Korea itself. As the advance to the 38th parallel proceeded, so did
political pressure for a statement of the United States and United Nations
attitude to the terms on which the war might be brought to an end. A draft had

been sent to MacArthur for his comments, to which his only reply was to demand a removal of the operational restrictions imposed on him. While the United States was consulting with its allies, MacArthur issued a statement in which, among other things, he said: 'The enemy now must be painfully aware that a decision of the United Nations to depart from its tolerant effort to contain the war to the area of Korea through expansion of our military operations to his coastal areas and interior bases would doom Red China to the risk of imminent military collapse.' This was interpreted by the State Department as a deliberate attempt to sabotage peace efforts, as it was clearly seen to be when Peking Radio on 29 March described it as 'an insult to the Chinese people'. Truman limited his reaction to a terse reminder from the Joint Chiefs of Staff to MacArthur that he must clear his statements with them and was to report any request from Communist leaders in the field for an armistice. But the last straw to break the patient President's back came when a letter from MacArthur to Congress Representative Joseph Martin was read out by the latter in the House on 5 April. MacArthur congratulated Martin on a speech he had made on 12 February, favouring opening a second front in Asia. He said that his own views had been forwarded in detail to Washington and were well known: they were to 'meet force with maximum counterforce' and said that Martin's proposal to use Chinese forces from Formosa was 'in conflict neither with logic nor with this tradition'. He went on to expound the view that the war in the Far East was World Communism's attempt to gain power and that, in fighting it, the United States was defending Europe. 'If we lose the war to Communism in Asia,' he wrote, 'the fall of Europe is inevitable; win it, and Europe most probably would avoid war and yet preserve freedom. As you point out, we must win. There is no substitute for victory.' After consultation with his colleagues and the Chiefs of Staff, Truman had clear support for MacArthur's dismissal. His decision to do so appeared to be in danger of leaking in a Chicago newspaper before he had transmitted it to MacArthur himself. It was therefore hastily announced to the press at 1 a.m. 10 April Washington time and had been broadcast and picked up in Tokyo twenty minutes before MacArthur received an official signal. The first he heard of it was as he was finishing a luncheon party at his residence at 3 p.m. 11 April Tokyo time. To his wife, who whispered to him the message brought by his aide, all he said was: 'Jeannie, we're going home at last.' And go he did, to stir up a hornet's nest, in spite of posing as a plain soldier, martyred for doing his duty.

Three days later Ridgway replaced him in Tokyo, having handed over Eighth Army to Lieutenant-General James Van Fleet, who had commanded a division and a corps in the North West Europe campaign and had later commanded American forces in Greece. He was a tough, experienced soldier with a penchant for massive employment of artillery and also for amphibious operations. The army he took over from Ridgway was now a formidable one, well-equipped, firmly organized, its US divisions, with their integrated Korean complement, each 20,000 strong, and its tail well up as a result of its successful advances over the previous three months. His immediate concern was the threat of an adverse change in the air situation. In reaction to the overwhelming US air superiority, to which the F104 Sabres had made a significant contribution, General Liu Ya-lou, Commander-in-Chief of the Chinese Air Force, with the help of the Russians, was building up his air force with a sizeable programme of airfield construction east of the Yalu. For fear of American retaliation, he was not allowed to use bases in Manchuria for attacks on targets in Korea. Both the airfield construction and the supply of aircraft from Russia were designed to support a fresh offensive by Peng Teh-huai's army in late April; but the former was frustrated by a carefully planned offensive by the US Air Force, designed to destroy the airfields just as all the facilities were nearing completion, and the latter by delays in the supply of aircraft from Russia.

The air situation was not Van Fleet's only concern, as within a week of his arrival there were signs of an impending Chinese counter-offensive. It opened on 22 April with three main thrusts, the strongest one in the west, attempting to encircle Seoul, another strong one in the east and a weaker one in the centre. In the course of the western thrust across the Imjin River, the Chinese struck hard at a ROK division on the boundary between 1st and 9th US Corps, which collapsed, leaving the British 29th Brigade isolated. After resisting gallantly for three days, the brigade was ordered to withdraw; but one of its battalions, the Gloucesters, was surrounded and fought grimly in the finest traditions of this regiment, which wears cap badges fore and aft in recognition of its stand at the Battle of Alexandria in 1801, until it was overrun. Van Fleet saw that attempts to hold everywhere would only result in large numbers of his men being cut off, and ordered a controlled withdrawal, inflicting casualties with air attacks and artillery, but giving up ground. After a week, when Seoul still had not fallen to them, the enemy's efforts began to flag, and on 7 May Van Fleet counter-attacked from the line which he had started to construct and which he called No Name line, hoping to be able to move his forces forward again to Ridgway's final Kansas line. As they did so, they met increasing resistance, especially in the centre, and on the night of 15/16 May Peng launched a major attack there, which made some progress, but petered out by 20 May, having cost him many thousands of casualties. For the next three weeks Van Fleet fought back and by mid-June had established a line which ran from just south of the Imjin River in the west, crossed the 38th parallel to Chorwon, some twenty miles north of it and south of what was known as the Iron Triangle, then east to the Punchbowl and north-east to the coast just south of Kosong, where it was fifty miles north of the parallel. Van Fleet felt he had his enemy on the run and planned a series of amphibious landings, using the Marine Division augmented with Korean marines, combined with a thrust up the east coast. But the US Government was in no mood to run the risks of another extension of this unpopular war, which had already cost 80,000 American casualties, including 12,000 dead and 10,000 missing. Peace feelers were put out again and on this occasion met with response. At the end of a tirade against the United States and NATO, the Russian representative at the United Nations, Malik, proposed discussions between the belligerents to bring about a cease-fire and armistice 'providing for the mutual withdrawal of forces from the 38th parallel' as a first step towards the peaceful settlement of the Korean question. The offer was taken up and Ridgway was ordered to send a radio message on 30 June, addressed to the Commander-in-Chief Communist Forces in Korea, inviting his representative to a meeting on board a Danish hospital ship in Wonsan harbour. The invitation was accepted, but the site refused and Kaesong proposed instead. Having checked that it was clear of enemy troops, Ridgway agreed. On 10 July the first meeting was held, by which time Kaesong had been turned into a Communist Chinese military encampment and the US negotiators, led by Admiral Joy, found themselves at both a physical and psychological disadvantage.

Those who imagined that the war was quickly going to come to an end were to be bitterly disappointed. Both sides agreed that, until some agreement was reached, hostilities were to continue; but the UN side at least would have been appalled had they realized that negotiations and hostilities were to drag on for another two years, a great deal of the argument centring round what was to happen to the prisoners of war taken by both sides. Until winter set in towards the end of 1951, most of the fighting was concerned with attempts by both sides to establish a permanent defence line which would give them an advantage in observation, fields of fire, security and economy in occupation. This led to some fierce and bitter battles, particularly round the Iron Triangle in the centre. These continued with severe casualties to both sides through 1952, by which time the defences, particularly on the Chinese side, had become extremely elaborate. It was trench warfare of 1914–18 all over again, but with extensive minefields added. While these struggles to improve positions continued, bursting into activity at each breakdown of the talks, the air war became the main conflict as the Chinese Air Force built up its strength and completed the construction of over thirty airfields in North Korea, its principal bases in Manchuria remaining inviolate. Strong anti-aircraft defences were deployed, but the US Air Force continued to maintain its overall superiority, while the US and British Navies, with their allies, totally dominated the sea areas on either side of the peninsula. By the end of the year the Communist forces, still under General Peng, had risen to an overall figure of 1,200,000, of which 270,000 were deployed in the front line in seven Chinese field armies and two North Korean corps, a large proportion of the total being employed on the lines of communication. General Mark Clark, who replaced Ridgway in May 1952, had in Korea 768,000 men, producing sixteen divisions in the front line, four US, eleven ROK and one Commonwealth, formed by joining a Canadian brigade to the two British ones, which included two Australian battalions and a New Zealand artillery regiment. In reserve were three more US divisions and one ROK. General Eisenhower replaced Truman in 1953 and, having paid a visit to Korea as President-elect and concluded that major attacks were a waste of lives, authorized an increase in the ROK Army, for which Syngman Rhee had been pressing, from 460,000 to 525,000. At the same time he did not conceal the fact that he was considering the use of atomic weapons, which were said to have been deployed to Okinawa. Stalin died in March and it was believed that this was one of the main reasons for a change in Chinese and Russian policy to favour an end to the war. The decision appears to have been taken before the explosion of America's first hydrogen bomb in May, which does not therefore seem to have had anything to do with it. The first exchange of prisoners began in May and hard bargaining continued until the final armistice agreement was signed and came into effect on 27 July 1953.

The war had lasted just over three years, two years of which were of static trench warfare, and had cost the lives of nearly 30,000 Americans and 3,143 other UN servicemen (793 from the UK), the total of American wounded and missing being 107,000 and that of other UN nations 15,700 (2,878 from the UK). Accurate South Korean casualty figures are difficult to establish, but appear to have been over 400,000 killed and rather more than that number wounded and missing, and about the same figure for civilian casualties. North Korean casualties were estimated at 520,000 and Chinese at 900,000. Both North and South Korea had been devastated and economically ruined. A quarter of a century later the country remains as firmly divided as it was at the time of the signature of the armistice.

Could a different result have been obtained by different military methods? Given the situation when the war started, there was little chance of the US and ROK forces holding the initial attack farther north than they did, and MacArthur's decision to concentrate on securing a firm base in the south-eastern corner was decisive in saving the country, as was Walker's success in achieving it. Then MacArthur's bold stroke at Inchon was a brilliant example of military leadership. However, had it failed, he would have been condemned for rash imprudence and poor military judgement, accusations which he did more to deserve in brushing aside the risks inherent in his advance to the Yalu. He was not then, as Montgomery would have put it, properly balanced, and was forced to 'dance to the enemy's tune'. His reluctance to have to do so thereafter lay behind his insistence that the war could only be won by extending it to China itself. In pressing for this, he had a strong case. Mao Tse-tung had only recently extended his control over the whole of China and was embroiled in Tibet. With America's dominant nuclear power it is doubtful if Russia would in the event have dared to intervene directly at that time. If she had, the United States was in a better position to face it than she was ever likely to be again.

The risks of extending the war into China were not so much those of Russian intervention as those of getting bogged down in a war without end, as the Japanese in China had been. Both MacArthur and the US Air Force greatly exaggerated the effect that US and Nationalist Chinese military action against the mainland was likely to produce on Chinese policy. Truman's administration and the US Chiefs of Staff were certainly right in taking the view that, for the limited gain of expelling the communists from Korea, it was not worthwhile becoming directly embroiled with China and possibly with Russia as well. In any case neither the American public nor that of its allies in Europe and elsewhere would have supported it. MacArthur and those who thought like him might argue that, if his advice had been followed, the Vietnam War would never have taken place and the whole history of communist expansion, small as it has been in territorial terms elsewhere, would have been different. But other things would have been different too, and the world might have seen a Russo–Chinese alliance facing a divided Western world instead.

As far as the military art is concerned, Korea had few lessons to teach. Second World War methods were used and were, on the whole, successful against a large but primitive army, for most of the time inadequately supported in the air and completely outclassed at sea, the latter ceasing to be greatly significant once the Chinese Air Force had been built up to a degree which increased the risks to major amphibious operations. The treatment of prisoners of war on both sides was an aspect which drew much attention. The North Koreans and Chinese did not observe the Geneva Conventions and subjected their prisoners not only to physical duress, but notably to psychological pressures in the hope of persuading them to condemn the cause for which they had fought, and in this they were in some cases successful. In contrast, the prisoners held by the ROK and the Americans on Koje Island organized themselves politically and were a constant source of trouble and embarrassment to their captors. The brain-washing techniques employed by the Chinese were carefully studied after the war in order that soldiers could be trained to resist them, and the experience was later exploited in the development of techniques of interrogation to be used against terrorists.

The main effect of the Korean War on Britain, coinciding as it did with the build-up of NATO forces, was to impose a rearmament burden on her economy just when she could least afford it, contributing to her inability to re-establish a healthy basis for her economy with effects which, in the opinion of some experts, and certainly in the minds of Treasury officials, have lasted to the time of writing.

Perhaps the most interesting field for speculation is that of the real aims of China. Russia had taken the initiative in encouraging North Korea to start the war; but when her intervention failed to achieve its aim immediately, she appeared to take a back seat, persuading China to take over the driving seat and provide the forces, which she helped to equip, lending political and general military support in reserve. Was China motivated by ideology, by anti-Americanism, by fear that a resuscitated Japan or Chiang Kai-shek, either or both supported by the United States, might threaten her through Manchuria, or was it a fear that Russia might install herself there if allowed a free hand, and thus encircle Manchuria? The security of Manchuria, so close to her capital and so influential throughout her long history, must have been one of the strongest factors in determining Mao's policy. Whatever her motives, the fact is that after the armistice in 1953 and the withdrawal of Chinese forces, the position largely reverted to the initial one, North Korea looking more to Russia than to China.

Chapter Ten

VIETNAM

American direct involvement in Vietnam was a reaction to Mao Tse-tung's establishment of communist supremacy throughout China in 1949. In 1950, as already mentioned in chapter 7, Vietnam qualified for US Military Aid and by 1954, when the French military campaign against the Viet Minh collapsed at Dien Bien Phu, the United States was footing 78 per cent of the bill. The armistice agreement finally concluding the Korean War had been signed the previous July and the policy of the United States in the Far East was influenced by the fear that Chinese communism was now free to break out elsewhere. Her aim had been to stiffen French resolve to fight against it and to persuade France to discard as rapidly as possible the colonial trappings which, in American eyes, were seen to be a prime factor in handing to the communists the trump card of support for independence, nationalism, patriotism and other pillars of xenophobia.

Eisenhower's administration, and John Foster Dulles his Secretary of State in particular, regarded the Geneva Conference in the summer of 1954 as a disaster. They saw it as a capitulation by the French, aided by the Soviet Union and abetted by Britain, to the communists. Eisenhower recorded in his memoirs that there was general agreement among his expert advisers at the time that, if elections were held then, 80 per cent of the population of Vietnam would vote for Ho Chi Minh rather than for Bao Dai, who was then President of Vietnam. The Geneva agreements, signed on 21 July 1954, stipulated that the 17th parallel was merely a provisional military demarcation line and not a frontier between two separate territories, and that general elections by secret ballot should be held in July 1956 under international supervision to determine 'the national will of the Vietnamese people'. The Americans had no faith that this could result in anything but a victory for the communists, and, strong believers then and for long after in the domino theory that it would lead to all the countries of South East Asia falling one after the other into communist hands, they determined to frustrate the clear intention of Geneva and, as the French had intended before them, to build up a viable non-communist state south of the 17th parallel. The crucial decisions were taken in August, but even before then serious consideration had been given to direct US military intervention. The first occasion was early in April 1954 before the situation at Dien Bien Phu had become critical. Dulles and Admiral Radford, Chairman of the US Chiefs of Staff, were in favour of intervention, but the other Chiefs of Staff, notably General Ridgway, were cool. It became clear that Congress would not support it unless Britain at least joined in, and it was evident that she was not inclined that way. But after the fall of Dien Bien Phu, it was raised again on American initiative, the French being persuaded to ask for American help and British participation not being stipulated as a necessary condition. The US Chiefs of Staff wished to limit their intervention to air and naval action by forces based outside the country, pointing out that 'Indochina is devoid of decisive military objectives and the allocation of more than token US armed forces to that area would be a serious diversion of limited US capabilities'.* Their concern was allayed when nothing came of it. The French Government decided that their parliament would no longer support fighting by them, and the situation deteriorated so rapidly that on 15 June Dulles told the French that the opportunity had been missed.

In the light of the Geneva Conference that followed, the Americans decided that France had no further part to play and on 20 August Eisenhower had approved a policy which involved the United States pushing the French aside and dealing directly with their protégé, Ngo Dinh Diem, who had been persuaded to return to Vietnam and assume power as Prime Minister to Bao Dai, who remained titular President. He would be encouraged to broaden his government and make it more democratic. At the same time the activities of Colonel Lansdale, an expert in subversive warfare who had helped Magsaysay to repress the communist Huks in the Philippines, would be stepped up. His team, working under the aegis of the CIA, had been sent to Saigon in June with the dual task of undertaking covert operations, including sabotage, in North Vietnam and of giving support to Diem, including a special force for his personal protection. In October 1954 Eisenhower had publicly committed himself to the support of Diem, stating that 'The United States would supply aid for maintaining a strong, viable state, capable of resisting attempted subversion or aggression through military means', but adding that 'The United States expects that this aid will be met by performance on the part of the Government of Vietnam in undertaking needed reforms', thus impaling America on the horns of a dilemma from which she was not to extricate herself for nineteen years.

The Geneva agreements had prohibited 'the introduction into Vietnam of foreign troops and military personnel as well as of all kinds of arms and munitions' and had stipulated that 'no military base under the control of a foreign state may be established in the regrouping zones of the two parties, the

* *The Pentagon Papers*, p. 45.

latter having the obligation to see that the zones allotted to them should not constitute part of any military alliance and shall not be used for the resumption of hostilities or in the service of an aggressive policy'. The United States was not party to the agreements, but made a unilateral declaration in which she promised to refrain from the threat or use of force to disturb them and stated that she would view any renewal of the aggression in violation of them with grave concern and as a serious threat to international peace and security. In respect of the country-wide elections due to be held in 1956, she declared: 'In the case of nations now divided against their will, we shall continue to seek to achieve unity through free elections supervised by the United Nations to ensure that they are conducted fairly.' Under these agreements US military personnel in Vietnam would be limited to those stationed there as members of the Military Advisory Group at the time of the armistice, a total of 342, although the Americans interpreted this in 1956 as allowing them 685.

Following the Geneva agreements, it was estimated that 90,000 to 150,000 inhabitants of South Vietnam moved to the North and nearly 900,000, mostly from the strongly Catholic provinces in the south-east of the Red River delta, moved to the South. The French finally left the North early in October and a month later General Lawton Collins, former Chief of the US Army Staff, was appointed by Eisenhower as his personal representative with Diem. His first act was to come to an agreement with the French to take over from them responsibility for all assistance to Diem's armed forces. At that time Diem was already faced with the threat of a coup headed by his Army Chief of Staff, General Nguyen Van Hinh, which Lansdale was instrumental in averting, Hinh being spirited out of the country. But Diem's dictatorial methods soon raised opposition in other quarters, and in April 1955 the three private armies, those of the Binh Xuyen, the Cao Dai and the Hoa Hao, were ranged against him. General Collins strongly recommended his removal, but Lansdale equally strongly opposed it and, through his influence with the leaders of the sectarian armies, which the United States had been secretly arming as opponents of communism, he managed to bring about an agreement between them and Diem. Having dealt with these immediate threats, Diem was ready to cast aside his titular superior, Bao Dai, in October 1955 and in a patently rigged referendum received an overwhelming vote to appoint himself as President of the Republic of Vietnam.

By June 1955 Ho Chi Minh was pressing to start discussions on the arrangements to be made for the elections due a year later. Diem, with support from the Americans, had no intention of letting them take place. All his efforts, and those of his American supporters, were concentrated on eliminating communists in the South, and in the process other political opponents also, and building up an anti-communist state south of the 17th parallel. To submit to country-wide elections before this was achieved would gravely prejudice the chances of success. He maintained that, as he had not been a party to the

Geneva agreements, he was not bound by them. Ho Chi Minh and his colleagues had reluctantly given way at Geneva to the advice of both the Chinese and the Russians that, with the French out of the way, they could achieve their aims by political action in the South, and this remained their policy even after it was clear that the 1956 elections were not going to take place. They gave encouragement, advice and covert support to the communist cadres in the South, but did not directly participate in nor control their activities. Meanwhile, as communist activity developed, Diem employed increasingly repressive measures against the population in areas where communists were active, making extensive use of Catholic Vietnamese from the North in imposing his will through the security forces and administration, the activities of his notorious brother, Ngo Dinh Nhu, and his wife adding to the unpopularity which these measures provoked.

When Kennedy became President at the end of Eisenhower's second term in 1961, the situation in Vietnam was highly unsatisfactory. In 1959 Ho Chi Minh, in response to appeals from the communists in the South, had decided that he and his government should take control of the struggle against Diem and give direct support, resuming the armed struggle which, as far as the North was concerned, had been in abeyance since 1954. Their aim was to bring about a general uprising in the South, avoiding overt intervention by the North. This would result in the establishment of a government friendly to the North, leading subsequently to the unification of the country under communist leadership. The classic methods would be used by which intimidation and persuasion would be combined with acts of terrorism designed both to undermine the authority of government and provoke it into retaliatory repressive measures, which would swing the population further towards the communists. Diem's attempts to counter this by tighter control of the population only made him more unpopular.

Kennedy's first concern was to deal with Cuba and he burnt his fingers badly in the Bay of Pigs fiasco. His standing weakened by that affair, he had a highly unsatisfactory meeting with Krushchev in Vienna, as a result of which he felt the need to exert himself and the power of the United States. 'Now we have a problem to make our power credible,' he said to James Reston of the *New York Times*, 'and Vietnam looks like the place.'* By April he had to face a serious situation in South East Asia. Laos was in a state of crisis and it was thought that it might fall at any moment into the hands of the communist Pathet Lao led by Souphanouvong. Eisenhower had seriously considered deploying American troops to Laos to prevent this, and Kennedy found himself under strong pressure to intervene there and to take drastic action to remedy the deteriorating situation in Vietnam. There the communists had virtually established their own rule and ousted that of Diem's government in most of the

---

* David Halberstam, *The Best and the Brightest*, p. 76.

country, murders and other terrorist incidents having quadrupled in the previous year. While Kennedy was on the brink of a decision to threaten intervention in Laos, the crisis there subsided at the beginning of May and the measures proposed 'to save Vietnam from communism' were whittled down to an increase by a hundred men of the US Military Mission, the despatch of a force of 400 men of the Special Forces, designed both to train Vietnamese in their methods and to infiltrate into the north and the areas of Laos which the communists were using as bases and infiltration routes for their activities both in Laos and in Vietnam. Not only was air action over Laos to be carried out by Vietnamese and Thai Air Force aircraft supplied by and sometimes manned by Americans, but approval was given to the employment of civilian American aircraft, mainly the CIA's private airline, Air America. Ambassador Nolting was to initiate discussions with Diem about the possibility of a bilateral defence treaty, on condition that Diem took effective action to introduce reforms and end corruption, broaden his government and generally make it more popular, democratic and internationally acceptable. The possibility of the introduction of US troops, other than the Special Forces who were to be brought in clandestinely, was put aside for the moment and was to be raised with Diem by Vice-President Lyndon Johnson, who was to visit South East Asia immediately after these decisions were taken on 9 May 1961. Johnson found that Diem was not in favour, and in his report said that, at that time, direct involvement of US troops was not wanted by Asian leaders. It was not only not required, it was not desirable. It would be another matter if there was an open attack, but the probability of that at that time seemed small and 'we might gain much needed flexibility in our policies if the spectre of combat troop commitment could be lessened domestically'.*

However by October Diem was asking both for a bilateral treaty and for the commitment of 100,000 American troops, partly sparked off by the refusal of the US Government to agree to his request in June to finance an increase in his army from 170,000 to 200,000. The arguments for it were based on highly suspect figures of greatly increased infiltration from the North, which was said to be the cause of the rise of terrorist incidents to a level of 450 a month, and evidence that the Vietcong were now operating in many areas at battalion strength. The situation in Laos was deteriorating again. Diem's request led to a major reconsideration of policy in Washington. The US Chiefs of Staff were in favour of intervention to secure the borders of Laos, Thailand and South Vietnam, and others made suggestions for forces to be introduced into the Central Highlands, where Diem's writ hardly ran at all, and to the port of Danang. For the first time the suggestion emerged that the aim of the United States was not just to bolster up Diem, so that he could establish a viable non-communist state, but directly themselves to defeat the Vietcong. The

* *The Pentagon Papers*, p. 134.

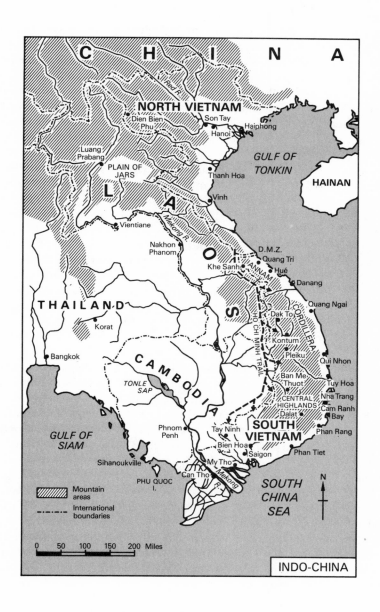

C H I N A

NORTH VIETNAM

Dien Bien Phu
Son Tay
Hanoi
Haiphong
Red R.

GULF OF TONKIN

HAINAN

Luang Prabang

PLAIN OF JARS

L A O S

Thanh Hoa

Vinh

Vientiane

Mekong R.

Nakhon Phanom

D.M.Z.
Quang Tri
Khe Sanh
Hué
Danang

THAILAND

Korat

Quang Ngai

Dak To

Kontum

Pleiku

Qui Nhon

Bangkok

C A M B O D I A

TONLE SAP

Ban Me Thuot

Tuy Hoa

Nha Trang

CENTRAL HIGHLANDS

Cam Ranh Bay

Dalat

GULF OF SIAM

Phnom Penh

Tay Ninh

SOUTH VIETNAM

Phan Rang

Bien Hoa

Saigon

Phan Tiet

Sihanoukville

My Tho

PHU QUOC I.

Can Tho

Mekong R.

SOUTH CHINA SEA

N

Mountain areas

International boundaries

0   50   100   150   200 Miles

INDO-CHINA

178 American Adventures

Chiefs of Staff estimated that 40,000 US troops would be needed to 'clean up the Vietcong threat' and a further 128,000 to deal with the possibility of intervention by North Vietnam or China. There was considerable pressure for strong, decisive action to be taken before the situation got worse. It was hoped that SEATO (South East Asia Treaty Organization) would act, although it was realized that little but token support, if that, could be expected from other members. The intelligence estimates were both pessimistic and more realistic, casting doubt on the effectiveness of the various schemes proposed and pointing out that the bulk of the Vietcong and the resistance to Diem came from within South Vietnam itself.

Kennedy's reaction was to send General Maxwell Taylor, his special assistant, formerly Chief of the Army Staff and Chairman of the Joint Chiefs of Staff, to visit Vietnam and make a special report. His visit coincided with disastrous floods in the Mekong delta and the idea of introducing US troops on the pretext of helping in flood relief appealed both to Diem and to Taylor. When the latter made his report, he came out firmly for the despatch of a force of 8,000 men, primarily for the boost it would give to the morale of the South Vietnamese, especially Diem and his army, which was considered ineffective. It would also show South East Asia 'the seriousness of the US intent to resist a communist take-over'. He said that what he called both 'limited partnership' and 'a massive joint effort' was needed to reverse the downward trend of events, and played down the risk of intervention being the thin end of a wedge leading to a major Asian war. He explained that the force would not be required to 'clear the jungles and forests'. That would be the task of the ARVN (Army of the Republic of Vietnam), which should be organized, trained and stiffened up by a greatly increased number of US advisers, down to battalion level. The 8,000-man force, which would engage in flood relief, would be called upon to protect themselves and their activities, and might also be employed as a general reserve 'against large, formed guerrilla bands which have abandoned the forest for attacks on major targets'. In addition to this task force, the United States should provide airlift for the ARVN, both fixed-wing and helicopter. The US Military Aid Group should be radically increased and become involved in the direction of the campaign against the Vietcong. The report was imbued with the idea that, if only American effort was put into it, the Vietnamese could be brought up to scratch to defeat the Vietcong themselves, but added a cautionary note in saying that 'if worse comes to worst, the US could probably save its position in Vietnam by bombing the North'.

The report led to a flurry of discussion in Washington, in which the intelligence community again cast doubt on whether the remedies proposed would be effective and Kennedy hesitated to commit himself both to the decisive step of openly intervening with US troops and, as his Secretary of State, Dean Rusk, and his Secretary for Defense, Robert McNamara, wished, to the unqualified objective of preventing the fall of South Vietnam to communism.

He authorized the airlift forces, the increase in the Mission and its development to take a significant part in the control of operations. Communication of these decisions to Diem in mid-November was to be accompanied by a further demand for the latter to carry out internal reforms. Diem was disappointed that his requests had been significantly whittled down, and, to alleviate his disappointment, the demand for reforms was not made a condition of the support promised, the latter being made public in December after the first helicopters had already been deployed. From the 948 US servicemen in Vietnam in November 1961, the number had increased to 2,600 in January and 5,500 by June 1962. At that time two army helicopter companies were flying 'combat support missions', the US Air Force was instructing the Vietnamese Air Force by flying on combat missions with them as well as themselves operating from bases in Thailand on reconnaissance tasks over Laos, and in Vietnam were flying six aircraft spraying defoliant. US Navy aircraft were flying reconnaissance missions from carriers of the Seventh Fleet, and five US Navy minesweepers were also operating from Danang along the coast. As US strength increased, so did their casualties, from 14 in 1961 to 109 in 1962 and 489 in 1963, by which time US troop strength had risen to over 16,000.

The 'strategic hamlet' policy was the main feature of the year 1962. This was based on the 'villagization' measures which the British had used in Malaya and Kenya, concentrating the population in defended villages in order to prevent contact between them and the Vietcong. Considerable publicity was given to the implementation of this project and high hopes placed on it by the Americans; but the tight control exercised by Diem's officials and security forces, applied generally in a harsh fashion, alienated the population rather than weaned them away from the Vietcong. The other apparent cause for optimism was the signature in July of the Laotian peace agreement. So favourable did the outlook appear that McNamara instituted planning for US withdrawal, aiming at a reduction to 1,500 US military personnel in Vietnam by 1968.

However this rosy view of the situation did not last long. Early in 1963 a combination of different factors led to major clashes between Diem and the Buddhists, culminating in an incident in the ancient capital of Hué, when Diem's troops fired into a crowd of Buddhists. The US administration pressed Diem to make peace with the Buddhists and threatened to withdraw their support unless he did. Only a week after he had given the departing US Ambassador his assurance that he would do so, his military police raided pagodas throughout the country and arrested 1,400 Buddhist monks, the operation having been directed by Diem's brother Nhu, possibly without Diem's knowledge. The new Ambassador, Henry Cabot Lodge, arrived the following morning and found himself from the start, as he was to remain, in confrontation with Diem. He was immediately involved in discussion about whether or not to support a plot by the senior generals, led by Duong Van

Minh (Big Minh), to force Diem to get rid of his brother and sister-in-law. Lodge was in favour of encouraging them, while General Harkins, head of the Military Mission, and Lodge's predecessor, Nolting, were doubtful if their coup would succeed, Harkins also objecting in principle to going behind Diem's back. The division of opinion was reflected in Washington, the President tending to support Lodge; but, before the decision had been made, Big Minh called off the coup, appreciating that Diem's support in Saigon and in the Mekong delta was too strong for his team, whose support came principally from north of Saigon, to overcome.

These events had instigated a basic reappraisal of the US policy of supporting Diem, even of supporting South Vietnam at all, disengagement being favoured by Robert Kennedy among others; but Lyndon Johnson, Dean Rusk and McNamara were totally opposed, insisting that the United States should not pull out until the war was won and should not get involved in a coup. The President's reaction was the familiar one of sending out a fact-finding mission. The first having failed to agree, a higher level one of McNamara and General Maxwell Taylor was despatched at the end of September 1963. They reported that the military situation 'has made great progress and continues to progress', but that there were serious political tensions and that a number of officers were dissatisfied with the government, although not to the extent of favouring a switch of allegiance to the communists. If Diem and Nhu continued their repressive measures, the situation would deteriorate. Pressure on them could be counter-productive, but, unless it was exerted, they would not change their ways. They did not recommend active steps to change the government, but said that it was urgent to identify and contact an alternative leadership. On the military side General Harkins should try and improve the methods employed by the ARVN and see that the development of the strategic hamlet programme did not get ahead of the availability of the means to defend them. They envisaged that the Vietnamese themselves would progressively take over responsibility for initiating and directing military operations, suggested withdrawing 1,000 US troops by the end of the year and estimated that their task would be completed by the end of 1965.

The ink was hardly dry on this when Big Minh's plot came to the boil again. Through CIA contacts he sought an assurance that he would receive US support. The instructions Lodge received from Washington were that, while the US Government did not wish to 'stimulate' the coup, it did not wish to 'leave the impression that the US would thwart a change of government'. Lodge interpreted this as the green light to go ahead and support a move to get rid of Diem, as well as his two notorious brothers; but Harkins interpreted it differently: that they should not encourage it either. This difference of opinion and interpretation led to vacillation in Washington. Kennedy's main concern seemed to be to ensure that his administration should not be involved in an unsuccessful coup. He did not want another Bay of Pigs, and Lodge's final instructions were based on that consideration. If he thought it would succeed, he should support it: but, if not, he should try and persuade the generals at least to postpone it. The coup was launched on 1 November and, when Diem telephoned Lodge to ask what was the attitude of the US, he was told that, as it was 4.30 a.m. in Washington, the US Government could not have a view. Lodge offered to provide for his physical safety, but would not give any advice as to what Diem should do. Diem and Nhu escaped from the Presidential Palace into the Chinese quarter, but were tracked down next day by one of the armoured units and shot inside the armoured car taking them to army head-quarters. Three weeks later President Kennedy was himself assassinated. Four days after that President Johnson confirmed his support for the late President's policy 'to assist the people and Government of Vietnam to win their contest against the externally directed and supported Communist campaign'. His directive emphasized the importance of concentrating effort in the Mekong delta, of developing popular support for the new Government of Vietnam and on clandestine operations into both North Vietnam and the areas of Laos used by the Vietcong and the North Vietnamese in supporting them.

Lodge's initial optimism that the coup would improve matters by raising the morale of the ARVN and swinging popular support to the government's side was dispelled by a gloomy report by McNamara on his return from a visit just before Christmas 1963. He described the situation as 'very disturbing'. Big Minh and his government were preoccupied with political jockeying and were giving no clear direction to affairs, civil or military. The same situation existed at lower levels. 'Current trends,' he wrote, 'unless reversed in the next 2–3 months, will lead to neutralization at best and more likely to a Communist-controlled state.'* In spite of this he did not recommend any specific measures, concluding his report with the words: 'We should watch the situation very carefully, running scared, hoping for the best, but preparing for more forceful moves if the situation does not show early signs of improvement.'*

A few weeks later General Westmoreland, who had only been in command of 18th Airborne Corps for six months after three years as Superintendent of West Point, arrived in Saigon as deputy to General Harkins, whom he was to succeed in command of the US Military Advisory Group in June, at the same time as General Taylor succeeded Lodge as Ambassador, in order to allow the latter to take part as a Republican candidate in the campaign for President. Westmoreland was surprised to find that there was little sense of urgency among the Vietnamese. They knocked off for week-ends and shut up shop in the afternoon. He found that the ARVN had 192,000 men organized in nine divisions, an airborne brigade and four ranger battalions. There was a

* *The Pentagon Papers*, p. 279.

separate Marine brigade. In addition there were 181,000 men in the militia, divided between the Self-Defence Corps and the Civil Guard, later to be known respectively, taking a leaf out of the communist book, as Regional and Popular Forces. The former could be employed anywhere within their province: the latter were part-time soldiers for the local defence of hamlets and villages. There were also 18,000 men in companies of the civilian irregular defence groups (CIDG), originally raised and controlled by the CIA and later by the US Army Special Forces. They were mainly raised from the Montagnards, the original inhabitants of the country, who lived in the Central Highlands and were employed generally on surveillance of the Laotian border. The country was divided into four zones: I, covering the five northern provinces; II, largest in area but with the smallest population, the twelve central provinces; III, the eleven provinces round Saigon, which itself with its immediate environs formed a separate military district; and IV, the sixteen provinces of the Mekong delta. One army corps was allotted to each zone and its commander was also the zonal governor. American advisers were attached to each formation headquarters down to regiment (British brigade) and additional advisers were in the process of being provided down to battalion level. The Vietnamese Air Force had 190 aircraft, mostly T28 propeller-driven training aircraft, while the US Air Force had 140 fixed-wing, mostly fighter-bombers, and 248 helicopters in the country. The Vietnamese Navy had a small fleet of landing-craft, patrol boats and minesweepers.

Two days after Westmoreland's arrival, General Khanh, commander of I Corps, in alliance with General Khiem of III Corps, seized power and, although leaving Big Minh in titular control, despatched his colleagues to twiddle their thumbs in the hill resort of Dalat. He took the precaution of establishing good relations with the head of the Air Force, Air Vice-Marshal Ky. One of Westmoreland's main concerns was the confusion that reigned in what was known as the 'pacification' programme, all those measures designed to improve the lot of the people and persuade them to support the government. Several different US Government agencies were involved, each reporting to its own head in the United States and inadequately co-ordinated within Vietnam.

Khanh seemed to be no improvement on Minh. Faced with the troublesome Buddhists, he was inclined to make concessions, which led him into conflict with other generals. At the end of June, after Westmoreland had taken over and just before Lodge handed over to Taylor, a conference was held at Honolulu to review the situation. Lodge had taken the line that little more could be expected of the Vietnamese unless the United States itself took more positive action against North Vietnam, which was held to be the cause of all the trouble. At the beginning of the year President Johnson had already authorized a considerable extension of clandestine operations against the North, and in March had authorized contingency planning for further action. At the Honolulu meeting Lodge pressed for a selective bombing campaign against military targets in the North, and William Bundy, who had just moved from the Pentagon to the State Department, produced a plan for graduated pressures culminating in a full-scale bombing campaign. There were differences of opinion among the President's advisers as to whether a Congressional Resolution would be required for this. With the political conventions to choose the parties' presidential candidates for the election in November about to be held, Johnson was not at that stage prepared to commit himself, but authorized planning and preparations so that bombing the North could be ordered at short notice.

The irony of it was that Ho Chi Minh, Giap and their colleagues were at the same time also taking a gloomy view of the situation. In spite of their support of the Vietcong and the considerable extension of their activities, there was no sign of the hoped for 'general uprising'. An intensification of activity after the coup against Diem had failed to produce it and with every month that passed US presence and influence increased, their numbers having then risen to 23,000. Khanh had about 500,000 armed men at his disposal, while the Vietcong could muster little over 100,000, helped by a few thousand from the North. Although the Vietcong were well-established in almost all provinces (they levied taxes in 41 out of 44), denied the government access to about four-fifths of the territory and had almost succeeded in cutting the country in half at the centre, they were not strong enough to gain control of Saigon and the larger towns. It appears that at about this time they decided to increase the effort of North Vietnam in support of the Vietcong in the hope that they could bring about the collapse of South Vietnam while the American presidential election campaign was in progress, judging that in such circumstances the major decision to employ US troops directly in operations would not be taken.

Westmoreland was deeply concerned at the way things were going in the field. The Vietcong were now operating bodies of battalion size, up to 350 strong. The ARVN, and to a greater degree the militia, tended to be split up into smaller bodies scattered all over the country, a large proportion on guard and defensive duties. The Vietcong were successfully pursuing a policy of surrounding their positions and attacking them in greatly superior strength. If they ventured away from their posts, they ran the risk of ambush. As a result morale was low and a feeling of despair was widespread. Khanh tried to counter it by publicly declaring that action would be taken against the North, Ky to the dismay of the Americans revealing that secret planning had been taking place with them for operations into Laos. Under pressure from Khanh, who threatened to resign unless the United States took action, Taylor recommended that joint planning with the Vietnamese Air Force for bombing the North should be secretly undertaken, and was given authority to initiate it 'if the pressure from dissident South Vietnamese factions became too great'.*

* *The Pentagon Papers*, p. 266.

While this was being considered, South Vietnamese naval commandos under Westmoreland's command carried out a raid on 30 July 1964, as part of the stepped-up clandestine operation programme, on two islands in the Gulf of Tonkin off the coast of North Vietnam, while, independently of them, the USN destroyer *Maddox*, on an intelligence-gathering patrol, was heading north into the gulf 120 miles away. On 2 August, having reached the northernmost point of her patrol and turned south twenty-three miles from the coast, she was attacked, although not hit, by North Vietnamese PT boats which had probably mistaken her for a South Vietnamese escort to the raiding force. Two of the PT boats were attacked by aircraft from the carrier *Ticonderoga*, which happened to be at hand, and the third sunk by the guns of the *Maddox*. Next day President Johnson ordered the *Maddox* to return to the area in company with another destroyer, the *Turner Joy*, and a second carrier, the *Constellation*, which was visiting Hong Kong, was ordered to the area. It was also decided that two previously planned clandestine raids in the area should go ahead. That night North Vietnamese PT boats attacked the destroyers. Their intention to do so was intercepted and known in Washington at 9.20 a.m. Washington time 5 August. The Pentagon immediately started planning reprisal air raids on PT bases and their oil supplies in North Vietnam. Confirmation that the attack on the destroyers was taking place (it was unsuccessful) was received at 11 a.m., and at 1.25 p.m. the President authorized the reprisal raids, which were not actually delivered until some ten hours later. By that time President Johnson had organized a Congressional Resolution which resolved to 'approve and support the determination of the President, as Commander-in-Chief, to take all necessary measures to repel armed attack against the forces of the United States and to prevent further aggression' and stated that 'the United States is, therefore, prepared, as the President determines, to take all necessary steps, including the use of armed force, to assist any member or Protocol State of the South East Asia Collective Defence Treaty requesting assistance in defence of its freedom'. The President had announced the air strikes on television at the time they took place, saying 'We still seek no wider war'. Neither publicly nor to the sponsors of the Resolution was any mention made of the clandestine raids, and, when this became public knowledge and was raised when McNamara was testifying to Congress in support of the Resolution, he maintained that there was no connection between the action of the South Vietnamese Navy, which was engaged in countering infiltration in junks, and the routine patrol of the *Maddox* in international waters. On 7 August the Resolution was passed, and on its authority the United States directly entered the Vietnam War.

A month later a further review of policy took place. Emphasis was once more laid on clandestine operations, an arrangement was to be made with Souvanna Phouma of Laos for US Air Force aircraft to operate 'armed reconnaissance' missions in Laos, that is flights on which strikes could be made on targets which the reconnaissance aircraft had found, and bombing the North would still be limited to reprisals for action against US forces or any 'special DRV–VC [Democratic Republic of Vietnam–Vietcong] action against South Vietnam'. Economic and political action would also be taken to bolster Khanh's government. The aim of US military action would be partly to boost South Vietnamese morale and partly as a warning to North Vietnam that the United States 'still meant business'. It was assumed that this would keep the risks to the United States low and under their control, a hope that was to dominate US policy throughout its involvement, gravely affect its conduct of operations and at the same time prove illusory. A week after these decisions had been taken, Khanh survived an abortive coup by Generals Phat and Duc, thanks largely to the support of Ky and his air force and of General Nguyen Van Thieu, Chief of Staff of the Joint General Staff. This was immediately followed by a revolt of the Montagnards which, with American help, was eventually overcome by the end of the month.

Westmoreland realized that, unless a radical change in operations (if they could be graced by that name) took place, the security situation would disintegrate. Rather as Briggs in Malaya had decided to work systematically south to north, combining military and civil action to clear the areas in succession, so Westmoreland, in a programme he called HOP-TAC (Vietnamese for co-operation), planned that the area around Saigon should first be secured and cleared and that operations and 'pacification' working hand-in-hand would spread outwards in concentric circles. If it proved successful, it could then be initiated round other cities, such as Danang, Qui Nhon and Can Tho, until eventually the circles merged. Anxious to push matters forward with urgency and to secure closer co-ordination of all the authorities involved, he had to accept the frustrations of being only an 'adviser', as were all his subordinates. The whole aim of US policy being to make South Vietnam viable on its own, it was essential to avoid either the appearance or the reality of an American take-over. Political intrigues at the top and the reflection of them at lower levels seriously affected the Vietnamese contribution to HOP-TAC, which nevertheless showed some progress by the turn of the year. However Vietcong incidents increased, three aimed at American targets hitting the headlines, two on the Bien Hoa airbase (although one may have been an accidental explosion) and one on a snack bar at the Saigon airbase of Tan Son Nhut. Their most spectacular exploit came on 27 December, when two Vietcong regiments, joining together to form the so-called 9th Division, attacked the village of Binh Gia, only forty miles east of Saigon, where 6,000 Catholic refugees from the North were housed, overran the defences and, over the following few days, almost totally annihilated the Vietnamese Marine and Ranger battalions sent to deal with them. It was now clear to Westmoreland that the ARVN could not afford to operate in only battalion strength, certainly not in smaller bodies. Any question of winning the war by patrolling was out of the question. The enemy had turned over to 'protracted' or even to 'mobile' warfare, and the ARVN would have to follow suit if they were not to suffer further humiliations and defeats which would lower their morale to rock bottom. An immense uphill struggle had to be faced before they would be in a position to handle such a threat on their own. A breathing space would have to be provided by greater active participation on the part of the United States itself.

Washington had been studying this problem while the presidential campaign had been in progress, and by the end of November his advisers recommended to the President a programme in two phases. In the first, which would last a month, air attacks on infiltration routes through Laos and coastal targets from which infiltrating junks were thought to sail would be stepped up, as would raids on the North as reprisals for incidents such as the attack on Bien Hoa. During this period pressure would be brought to bear on Khanh to improve both the appearance and the effectiveness of his government. Provided that he showed some signs of doing so, the second phase would start. It would consist of a crescendo of attacks on the North lasting over six months, designed to persuade Ho Chi Minh to desist from increasing his support to the Vietcong and bring him to the negotiating table, the principal card in the American hand being the threat of further intensifying the air war. When the UN Secretary-General, U Thant, had tried to bring the North Vietnamese and the Americans together in September, the United States had refused, having few cards of any value in their hand at that time and the presidential election being imminent. This graduated programme had three sets of opponents: the military, the intelligence community and those, like George Ball, who wanted the United States to extricate itself altogether. Westmoreland feared that it would provoke rather than limit North Vietnamese involvement, but agreed with the Chiefs of Staff in urging that, if a bombing campaign against the North were to be decided upon, it should be an all-out one. Neither he nor the Chiefs of Staff had any faith in a limited or graduated programme, 'the slow squeeze' as it was dubbed, designed more as a political signalling device than a militarily effective strategy. The intelligence community did not believe that a bombing campaign of either kind would be effective militarily or politically in limiting North Vietnamese support to the Vietcong or bringing them to the conference table, and they were to be proved right. Johnson also had his doubts. However he authorized initiation of the first phase and also all preparations required to make it possible to implement the second immediately, if it were decided upon. The plan was nicknamed *Rolling Thunder*.

In aid of improving the appearance of his government, Khanh established a Higher National Council of elderly and respected figures, headed by a purely ceremonial Head of State, Phan Khoc Suu, who in turn appointed a former Mayor of Saigon, Tran Van Huong, as Premier. Huong appointed a government of technocrats which soon found itself in trouble with students, Catholics and Buddhists. He was forced to declare martial law and rely on the support of Khanh, but the latter had lost the support of the armed forces. Khanh, backed by the Armed Forces Council, dismissed Huong and appointed Dr Phan Huy Quat, a Northerner as Premier. Khanh and Quat tried to do a deal with the Buddhists and faced another coup by General Phat, in the course of which the real wielders of power behind the scenes, who turned out to be Thieu for the army and Ky for the air force, ousted Khanh on 20 February 1965, the day that *Rolling Thunder* was due to start, and installed General Tran Van Minh (Little Minh) as Commander-in-Chief of the armed forces. Quat remained as Premier and Suu as titular Head of State.

The decision to go ahead with *Rolling Thunder* gave Westmoreland concern for the security from both ground and air attack of the bases from which the aircraft operated, the shorter range aircraft from Danang on the coast 100 miles south of the 17th parallel, the longer range ones from Bien Hoa and Vung Tau north and east of Saigon. At the end of February 1965 he obtained authority from Washington to deploy two US Marine battalions to defend the former and on 8 March they stormed ashore in an amphibious landing, disappointed to find no enemy. From that beginning the commitment of US land forces quickly grew. The Army Chief of Staff, General Johnson, was sent out by his namesake, the President, in that same week with the order: 'You get things bubbling, General.'* He returned with Westmoreland's request for more US aid and increased helicopter and fixed-wing air support, the creation of an international force to control infiltration through the demilitarized zone astride the 17th parallel, the commitment of a US division to the Central Highlands, a brigade to defend Bien Hoa and Saigon airfields, and a renewed request for logistic and engineer troops to construct a logistic base to support future deployments. Only the first of these requests was granted. While discussion continued, Taylor put forward a rival proposal for US troops to be restricted to coastal enclaves, his argument being that it would reassure the Vietnamese without tempting them to shift the burden of fighting the war on to the Americans, although the latter would be permitted to engage in offensive operations in the vicinity of their enclaves and act as a reserve for the ARVN out to a range of fifty miles from them. Early in April the President approved Taylor's plan and granted Westmoreland's request for logistic and engineer troops. Later in the month McNamara held a meeting in Honolulu which approved sending nine battalions, three for the Bien Hoa-Vung Tau area, three to establish two coastal enclaves at Qui Nhon and Nha Trang and three Marine battalions for Chu Lai. Australia was to be asked to send one battalion and South Korea three. With the four Marine battalions already ashore, that would total seventeen, bringing US troop strength to 82,000 and that of other countries to 7,250. Although Westmoreland did not get his division for the Central Highlands, deploying the Airmobile Cavalry Division there and

* William C. Westmoreland, *A Soldier Reports*, p. 125.

bringing the South Korean contribution up to a whole division were noted as possibilities for the future.

Definition of the role of these forces was unsatisfactory. President Johnson had banned publication of the authority for them to operate up to fifty miles from their enclaves. Under questioning from the press, the White House maintained that there had been no change in their defensive role, but added that 'General Westmoreland also has authority within the assigned mission to employ these troops in support of Vietnamese forces faced with aggressive attack when in his judgement the general military situation requires it'.* Westmoreland was unhappy at this, both because he wished to be free to employ them in offensive operations without restriction and also because it was a deception practised on the American press and public. He was himself later to become one of the principal targets of criticism, the basic origin of which was the justified resentment, particularly of the news media, that they had been deliberately deceived by successive administrations, which had led the people of the United States up the garden path.

While all this had been going on, and almost certainly before the decisions were made to deploy US land forces to Vietnam, Ho Chi Minh and Giap had also been facing up to fundamental issues. They had decided that only the deployment of units of the North Vietnamese Army to the South could ensure the achievement of their aim, a united communist Vietnam, if not indeed the wider aim of a united communist Indo-China. More realistic than the Americans, taking a longer view and less in a hurry, they allowed for a gradual build-up of two years, expecting victory in 1968. Their overall plan was to step up operations in the Central Highlands, where they were already well-established, in order to divert ARVN and US effort from the Saigon area. While doing this, they would build up their forces in three areas surrounding Saigon from the north, known as War Zone C, astride the Cambodian border round the Cao Dai centre of Tay Ninh, War Zone D, a forested area about fifty miles north of Saigon, and the May Tao Zone north of Vung Tau. In these areas battalions would be expanded into regiments and they in turn linked up to form divisions. From secure and well-protected bases in these zones they would establish control over the links between Saigon and the major towns held by the government. At the appropriate time, planned for 1968, they would cut off Saigon, execute a major assault on it and install a communist government.

It was the early stages of the implementation of this plan which led West-moreland to report in June that he saw 'no course of action open to us except to reinforce our efforts in South Vietnam with additional US or third-country forces as rapidly as is practical during the weeks ahead'.† He made it clear that enclaves were no answer; bombing the North, if it produced results at all,

* Westmoreland, p. 135.
† *The Pentagon Papers*, p. 420.

would not do so quickly, certainly not in time to prevent the collapse of the ARVN which had suffered a succession of defeats in the preceding weeks. If South Vietnam were to survive, he argued, the US had to make an active commitment with troops that could be employed offensively. He asked for an increase from 17 to 44 battalions, stating that this was not enough to gain victory, but only to serve as a stop-gap measure to save the ARVN from defeat. 'It is time all concerned,' he reported, 'face up to the fact that we must be prepared for a long war which will probably involve increasing numbers of US troops.'* While argument raged in Washington about the response to be made to this, he was given authority to commit US forces in support of the ARVN 'in any situation . . . when, in [his] judgement, their use is necessary to strengthen the relative position of the ARVN forces'. Acting on this, he committed 173rd Brigade, sent to defend the Bien Hoa-Vung Tau area, and the Australians, together with a larger ARVN force, on a three-day operation into War Zone D.

Before this operation a further twist had been given to the political scene. Quat and Suu resigned in the course of a row over the dismissal of two ministers who refused to go, and power was taken over by a council of ten generals, Thieu assuming the post of Head of State and Ky of Premier. They were to provide the most stable and effective administration that South Vietnam was ever to experience. This event was closely followed by a fact-finding mission to Vietnam by McNamara, General Wheeler, Chairman of the US Chiefs of Staff, and Lodge, about to resume his post as Ambassador in place of Taylor. In reaction to Westmoreland's estimate that his 44-battalion request would do no more than stave off defeat of the ARVN, the policy planners in Washington posed the question as to how many more would be needed to win. This question was transformed by McNamara into the one he posed to Westmoreland: How many would be needed to convince the enemy that he could not win. He found it difficult to answer, but came up with the estimate that a further 24 battalions, with the necessary supporting troops, would put him in a position to 'begin the winning phase'. He qualified it by saying that Vietcong or North Vietnamese reactions could cause him to revise his estimate, which entailed adding 100,000 men to the 175,000 represented by his initial 44-battalion request. His plan would be a strategy in three phases: the first, to commit US and allied forces to 'halt the losing trend' in 1965: the second, occupying the first half of 1966, to take the offensive with these forces to destroy the enemy and reinstate the pacification programme in high priority areas. If after this the enemy continued to fight, he might be defeated and his forces destroyed a year after the end of Phase II.

While McNamara was still in Vietnam, the President decided to meet Westmoreland's initial request and on 28 July announced publicly that the Airmobile Cavalry Division and other forces had been ordered to move, bringing US strength in Vietnam up from 75,000 to 125,000, and stating that

* Westmoreland, p. 140.

more would follow. On his return McNamara, having been assured by General Wheeler that 'within the bounds of reasonable assumptions, there appears to be no reason we cannot win if such is our will, and if that will is manifested in strategy and tactical operations',* recommended to the President that Westmoreland should get his extra 100,000 men. The aim of US military intervention had now clearly changed from just bolstering up the South Vietnamese to taking it upon themselves to defeat the communists, although there remained a basic difference of outlook between the military, who thought in terms of defeating their forces in the field and destroying the infrastructure of the North from the air, and the civilians in the Pentagon and elsewhere who thought in terms of psychological and political pressure exerted by the use of military force to convince the enemy that he could not win and therefore to desist; not at that stage to negotiate. The conflict between the military and the civilian view of the aim was seen most clearly in the air war. Three pauses in the *Rolling Thunder* programme were made in 1965, one early in the year, one in May and one at the end, all with the intention of giving North Vietnam an opportunity to give up, which they showed no sign of doing. The military, who in any case disliked the concept of a graduated and restricted operation in which every target had to be cleared with the civilians, opposed the bombing pauses as making an ineffective programme even less effective.

Westmoreland's hands were no longer tied by the enclave policy and he named his new strategy 'search and destroy'. His plan was that in principle the ARVN would be responsible for the more densely populated areas, their primary task being to deal with the guerrilla warfare of the Vietcong's regional and popular forces, countering the intimidation and pressure they exerted on the populace. The US and allied troops, while participating in this type of task in the areas surrounding their bases, would be primarily deployed to seek out and destroy the 'main force' units and formations of the Vietcong and North Vietnamese Army, although the ARVN would also participate in this task. It was not long before this strategy was applied, as the Vietcong and North Vietnamese Army reacted to the American build-up. In August the Marines were in action near Chu Lai, and, from the time that the Airmobile Cavalry Division began to establish its base in the heart of the Central Highlands at An Khe, it was almost continuously in action against North Vietnamese troops in Pleiku province to the west. These operations had convinced Westmoreland that the North Vietnamese Army were reinforcing South Vietnam at a rate at least equal to and probably higher than that at which US troops were arriving to reinforce him. If this continued at the same rate, it would be double that planned by the Americans, even with his extra 100,000. From November 1965 into the new year discussions continued between Westmoreland, his immediate superior, Admiral Sharp, C-in-C Pacific, the Chiefs of Staff and McNam-

---

* *The Pentagon Papers*, p. 475.

ara about the implications of this. Matters were brought to a head in a meeting in Honolulu in February 1966. Westmoreland's request, supported by McNamara and the Chiefs of Staff, was to raise the level of troops from the 71 battalions, then planned, to 102, 79 of them US and 23 allied. This would increase the number of US troops from the current 235,000 to 429,000 by the end of the year. Westmoreland hoped that this could be done without calling up reserves, entailing the disadvantage that, once their reserve call-up period was over, a reduction in numbers would be forced on him. The Pentagon however said that they could not produce that number without a call-up, and McNamara recommended a force level of 367,000 for 1966, increasing to 395,000 by mid-1967.

Westmoreland made clear that the probability of a long war had to be faced. The long western frontier of Vietnam with Laos and Cambodia – whose territory was freely used by the enemy, although Westmoreland was not free to do so overtly – imposed on him a war of attrition. This would have remained true even if he had had sufficient troops to extend the land war into those countries, which he considered he had not. He had to fight the enemy within South Vietnam and the most effective way of doing so was to force the enemy to attack his forces, enabling the Americans then to apply their overwhelming superiority in fire-power. These methods laid him open to the criticism of fighting a jungle war by the methods of a European one, but they were fundamentally a product of the geography of the country, the methods employed by his opponents, the peculiar relationship with the South Vienamese and the fact that his political masters were in a hurry. To these factors must be added the habits, training and outlook of the US forces, Marine, Army, and Air Force, who had always believed in the application of as massive fire-power as could be brought to bear. One of the factors tending to support Westmoreland's request for more troops at the Honolulu meeting was the growing disillusionment of all concerned at the effectiveness of the bombing campaign against the North, leading to arguments between those who wanted to give it up and those, like the Chiefs of Staff, who wished to free it of all restrictions and extend it to the areas of Hanoi and Haiphong, to include the oil tanks at the latter. One of the arguments against this was the fear that it would provoke the direct intervention of the Russians or the Chinese or both. However attacks on the oil tanks were authorized in May 1966, and by August they had been completely destroyed with no apparent effect on either the military operations in the South or the determination of North Vietnam to continue the war.

Westmoreland's hopes of making progress received a severe setback soon after the Honolulu Conference, when serious trouble broke out in Danang and Hué, involving the dismissal of the ARVN Corps Commander, General Thi, who was sympathetic to the Buddists of that area, as were many of his troops. From March until May the South Vietnamese were fighting each other there, the Americans doing their best to act as peace-makers and eventually succeeding. Elsewhere operations under Phase II of his plan continued, centred principally on the 'War Zones' surrounding Saigon from north-west to east, reinforced along the Ho Chi Minh trail down the panhandle of Laos. These operations were supported not only by US Air Force tactical aircraft, but also by B52 bombers operating from high altitude. A new development was the increasing activity of the North Vietnamese Army in and near the demilitarized zone astride the 17th parallel. There were signs during the months of the Buddhist troubles that Giap was planning to cut off and try to take over the northernmost provinces south of the demilitarized zone, Westmoreland's reaction to which was to move the Marines to reinforce the area and to obtain authority to lift the restrictions imposed on artillery fire and air operations in and near it. One significant step was the occupation by the Marines of Khe Sanh, a key point on the route which led into the area from across the Laotian border. Westmoreland was concerned that this threat to the north should not divert effort from his main aim of destroying the enemy threatening the Saigon area, and once more requested an increase in the troops allotted to him, asking that they should reach a total of 542,000 in 1967. McNamara's reaction to this was cool. Although he did not turn it down, he demanded a detailed justification and did not in the end approve. He was by now disillusioned about the effectiveness both of the bombing campaign and of sending more and more troops. The enemy, in spite of his estimated losses, seemed to have an inexhaustible supply and showed no sign of giving up. McNamara's mind was turning both to an aim more limited than 'winning' and to the possibility of improving the effectiveness of the American military effort by greater resort to modern technology. He assembled a seminar of distinguished scientists and academics, who met for three months in the summer. Their conclusion was that *Rolling Thunder* had accomplished nothing, that it should be stopped and that an anti-infiltration fence, based on a combination of sensors and minefields, should be built across the demilitarized zone. It would cost $800 million and take a year to build. In October McNamara visited Vietnam and came away depressed at the lack of progress in every field and disillusioned at the prospects of improving matters by stepping up military operations. In his report to President Johnson he proposed to limit US troop strength to 470,000 in 1967; the installation of a barrier south of the demilitarized zone, extending westward into Laos across the Ho Chi Minh trail; stabilization of *Rolling Thunder* at its current level of 12,000 sorties a month; intensification of the pacification programme; and 'steps to increase the credibility of our peace gestures in the minds of the enemy'. This report was hotly opposed by the Chiefs of Staff who wished to extend the bombing, give Westmoreland all the troops he asked for and authorize him to extend his operations into the enemy's sanctuaries in Laos and Cambodia. Johnson held a conference in Manila in October to review these divergent views, after which, in a press statement, to

Westmoreland's surprise he gave an undertaking that the United States and its allies would withdraw their troops from Vietnam within six months after the other side had withdrawn its forces and put a stop to infiltration, and after the level of violence had consequently subsided. During the conference Westmoreland had been persuaded to trim his request to 480,000 men by the end of 1967 and 500,000 by the end of 1968, provided that two divisions were held in reserve for him to meet an emergency. The final decision was to allow him 469,000 by 30 June 1968. The President did not accept McNamara's proposed limit on *Rolling Thunder* and discussion of bombing policy continued into the new year.

While the Americans were beginning to doubt their ability to win the war and achieve their aim of establishing South Vietnam as a viable anti-communist state, their minds turning more and more to how they could limit damage to their own world reputation and standing, Ho Chi Minh and Giap were far from happy at their situation. Although the hold of the Vietcong on the countryside remained strong, the 'general uprising' seemed further away than ever, Thieu and Ky having held an election in June to confirm their position and the Vietcong and North Vietnamese Army having suffered heavy casualties, first at the hands of the Marines and Air Cavalry in the north and later as a result of Operation *Attleboro* in War Zone C. In 1967 there was a continuation of these major assaults on their main forces and bases, Operation *Cedar Falls* in January against The Iron Triangle, a forested area only twenty miles north of Saigon, and *Junction City* in February against War Zone C. Although these operations, methodically executed and supported by massive fire-power, did not succeed in clearing the NVA/VC from these areas, they forced important elements of them to move west of the border into Cambodia in order to reorganize. Westmoreland remained very dissatisfied at the conduct of the pacification programme. It was pointless to inflict casualties on the enemy if his grip on the population could not be loosened. He wanted to assume responsibility for it himself, but found Lodge strongly opposed to handing over responsibility for US contributions to it. In the end a compromise was found by which Robert Komer, one of the President's White House Assistants, was assigned to Lodge as a deputy and also as a deputy to Westmoreland for co-ordination of the pacification programme. A suggestion was made that, when Lodge retired, as he had made clear he wished to do in 1967, Westmoreland should assume his mantle as well, but Rusk opposed this and the veteran Ellsworth Bunker was appointed Ambassador.

The major operations executed in the first half of 1967 and the stability of the Thieu–Ky regime compared to its predecessors led Westmoreland to believe that, if he could increase his effort, there would be a decisive turn in events in his favour which could hasten the prospects of success. In particular he wished to seize the initiative by attacks into Laos and Cambodia, combined with an amphibious landing north of the demilitarized zone. As the optimum for achieving this, he estimated that he needed a reinforcement of four and a third divisions and ten tactical fighter squadrons, an addition of 200,000 men bringing his total strength to 670,000. Realizing that this was probably opening his mouth too wide, he regarded the minimum essential as two and a third divisions and five squadrons, an addition of 80,500 men, bringing him to a total of 550,000. He appreciated that this would almost certainly mean calling up reserves, but he was sufficiently confident of success, if the forces were produced, that he was prepared to accept that his strength could only be kept at that level for a limited period. When he went to the States in April, at the request of the President, to make public appearances to counter the growing opposition to the war, discussions were held in which McNamara pressed him to estimate how long the American commitment would last, assuming that his plan were approved and *Rolling Thunder* continued. With the optimum force, he put it at three years; with the minimum essential, at five. Argument in Washington as to whether or not to accede to Westmoreland's request was fierce, most of the influential civilian ex-hawks, like McGeorge Bundy, coming out against it, as many of them did also against the extension of *Rolling Thunder* to targets in the Hanoi–Haiphong area, which the Chiefs of Staff were pressing for. One of the Chiefs' arguments was that all other targets had been destroyed and only these were left. The consensus of opinion, notably in the intelligence community, was that bombing of the North had achieved nothing, and proposals were made to restrict it to targets closer to the demilitarized zone and on the supply routes through Laos. Reluctant to order a reserve call-up, Johnson chose Westmoreland's 'minimum essential', but that was cut further to a total of 525,000 and his request for authority to extend operations into Laos and Cambodia and north of the demilitarized zone was turned down. Johnson was kinder to the airmen and, after the Arab–Israeli Six-Day War in June, he approved attacks on all but twelve of the fifty-seven targets in North Vietnam which the Chiefs of Staff had requested. After the heavy blows received in the War Zones north of Saigon, Giap switched his effort farther north and the latter half of 1967 saw a succession of engagements, known as the 'border battles'. The first two had been in Phuoc Long province, near the Cambodian border seventy miles north of Saigon, and appear to have been designed to cut off ARVN forces in that area, the US 1st Division also suffering heavy casualties in an ambush. The third was at Dak To in Kontum province, east of the point at which the frontiers of Laos, Cambodia and Vietnam joined. In all these battles the North Vietnamese and the Vietcong suffered considerably heavier casualties than the Americans and the ARVN, but they had the effect of keeping the initiative in Giap's hands.

In 1967 there had been a very significant increase in the public opposition to the war in the United States. It stemmed from a number of different sources.

The two most significant perhaps were the student fraternity and the news media. It must be remembered that 1967 was a time of student protest in various forms world-wide, with a strong anti-establishment, pro-peace, pro-third world and Marxist tinge. Added to this was the influence of deferment of the draft (compulsory military service) for students and a large number of exemptions. This produced a form of class division between those who did not attend college and were not deferred and those who did, which gave the latter a feeling of guilt. The simplest way to escape it was to maintain that the draft and the war for which it was required should not exist at all. The influence of the media, particularly that of television, was great. Almost all resented the duplicity and deception which successive administrations practised as to the extent of the American commitment and the prospects of success in it achieving its aim, and they were intent on discrediting both. All news media, but television more than any other, concentrate on the spectacular. Scenes of horror, devastation and shock were portrayed nightly on American TV screens, distorting the actual state of affairs. Finally, to the servicemen themselves it was an unsatisfactory war. The climate and conditions of life were strange and uncomfortable, the population unresponsive, the enemy treacherous and liable to attack one at unexpected times and places. There was no visible sign of progress, other than the 'body-count': no pushing forward or territory occupied: no cause but the vague one of the fight against communism. There was almost as much resentment at the optimistic statements of politicians and senior officers as there was at the pessimism and lack of patriotism of the anti-war elements. The more troops that were deployed to Vietnam, the higher the casualties and the greater the impact of the war on the public. On top of domestic disapproval, there was little support from other nations, a holier-than-thou type of indifference on the part of most of America's NATO allies and downright disapproval by the great majority of countries. Nobody, not even the Vietnamese, seemed to be grateful to the United States for the sacrifices she was making. All this began to come to a head in 1967 and undoubtedly influenced McNamara and others – the Bundy brothers, John McNaughton and even Walt Rostow – who only two years before had been full of confidence, more so than the Presidents they had served.

Westmoreland's last major operation of 1967 had been *Fairfax*, a joint US Army/ARVN operation in December to clear up the immediate outskirts of Saigon. In January he planned operations in Phuoc Long province to pre-empt enemy attacks from War Zones C and D, and also *York*, a series of four operations designed to clear up the Laotian border area in the four northern provinces, hoping to secure the region for a future attack into Laos, which he hoped would be supported by whatever administration resulted from the 1968 presidential election. None of these had got going before intelligence revealed not only an imminent North Vietnamese attack on the isolated Marine position at Khe Sanh in the extreme north, but also signs of an impending offensive throughout the country. The attack on Khe Sanh, starting on the night of 2 January, was made by two North Vietnamese divisions. It soon became the focus of everyone's attention, Johnson and others in Washington anxious that it should not turn into another Dien Bien Phu, to which its position made it liable. Westmoreland rapidly reinforced the surrounding area and concentrated overwhelming air support in its defence. The fighting was intense for three weeks, by which time it was clear that attacks elsewhere were impending. Westmoreland expected Hué and Quang Tri to be targets, but did not rule out a major effort towards Saigon, and he withdrew troops from his planned operations to strengthen these areas. It appeared that Giap, in spite of his heavy losses in 1967, believed that a major country-wide offensive could bring about the 'general uprising' which had been awaited for so long and which, in 1965, he had planned to bring about in 1968. Although it was clear that the offensive was to be launched in relation to the Tet holiday at the end of January, just before or after, or even during it, nobody foresaw the form it would take.

The enemy's timing went astray, troops in their 5th Military Region in the Central Highlands starting their action in the first few hours of 30 January, twenty-four hours before attacks elsewhere, thus warning the Americans and South Vietnamese both of the timing and of the pattern the offensive was taking. That pattern was to infiltrate armed men in groups of varying size up to battalion strength into the heart of all the main towns and cities, and there to attack the most important installations of the government and the armed forces. Eight towns were attacked on that first night. Many attacks were initially successful, as most ARVN posts and units were only half-manned because of the start of the Tet holiday period. The most dramatic was that of a group of fifteen Vietcong on the new American Embassy in Saigon. They blew a hole in the wall of the compound and attacked the main building, killing five of the guards, but failing to gain entry. The situation was restored at dawn and all the attackers killed, but the immediate reaction of the US press corps was to represent the attack as successful, and even the authors of the Pentagon Papers erroneously recorded that the Vietcong occupied the embassy throughout the day. The main headquarters of the South Vietnamese General Staff was also attacked by three Vietcong battalions, US troops, previously sent to the area as a precaution, helping the ARVN to defeat it. In all some 84,000, mostly Vietcong but with a sprinkling of North Vietnamese in support, attacked 36 out of 44 provincial capitals, 5 out of 6 of the main cities, 64 out of 242 district capitals and 50 hamlets. The most serious attack was on Hué by eight battalions, which penetrated into the old city including part of the citadel. They were not dislodged until 25 days later, by which time a further eight battalions had been involved. The US Airmobile Cavalry Division, three Marine battalions and eleven of the ARVN were involved in its relief, inflicting an estimated 8,000 killed on the Vietcong and North Vietnamese at a cost of

142 US Marines and 384 ARVN killed. In all the operations arising out of the Tet attacks, the Vietcong and North Vietnamese lost 37,000 killed and about 6,000 captured, mostly wounded. The Americans lost 1,001 and the South Vietnamese 2,082.

In the light of these figures it is not surprising that Westmoreland regarded it as a severe defeat for the enemy, who themselves admitted, as captured documents later proved, that they had failed in their principal aims of seizing and maintaining control of the cities and bringing about a general uprising of the people. But, whether it was by design or by accident, they had achieved a major victory over US public opinion, greatly helped by the instant reaction of the American and international news media who reported the initial attacks as almost wholly successful. It was not surprising that the reaction was sharp to a situation in which the Vietcong, with little direct NVA help, could penetrate into the heart of almost every town of any importance, in spite of the fact that the Americans, their allies and the South Vietnamese had between them over a million armed men in the country, backed by overwhelming fire-power. The immediate reaction of Washington was to think in terms of staving off defeat and to ask Westmoreland what he needed for this, General Wheeler offering him the 82nd Airborne Division and half of a Marine division. Their anxiety was increased by the intensification of attacks on Khe Sanh and the evidence of a concentrated North Vietnamese effort aimed at the most northerly provinces. Visions of another Dien Bien Phu, and the possibility of suffering a humiliation akin to that experienced by the French, at the beginning of a presidential election year, caused deep anxiety in the White House and elsewhere. But Westmoreland, although he accepted the events of Tet as a setback, particularly in its disruption of the pacification programme and the creation of a further 600,000 refugees from areas occupied by the Vietcong, was thinking in very different terms. The brunt of the attacks had been taken by the ARVN, and almost everywhere, in spite of temporary setbacks, they had restored the situation. The enemy had staked much on an all-out effort and had failed. Now was the critical time to go on to the counter-offensive and put all available effort into it, casting aside the inhibitions imposed by trying to fight a war while the home country enjoyed the conditions of peace. Operations should be launched into Laos and Cambodia, and an amphibious landing made north of the demilitarized zone to take the pressure off the northern provinces: restrictions on air operations should be removed and reserves called up. To implement that strategy he would need a further 206,000 men by the end of 1968, half of whom could be deployed to Vietnam and the remainder held as a strategic reserve in the United States. The Chiefs of Staff, anxious to create such a reserve and realizing that it could not be done without the call-up of reserves, backed Westmoreland or, if viewed in another light, made use of anxiety about his position to try and persuade the President to take the decisive step.

But the view of the American public, with presidential primaries imminent, and that of almost all the civilian hierarchy in Washington was very different. If all the effort that had been put into Vietnam, and the destruction, disruption and distress that the massive application of fire-power had inflicted on its population and territory, could not prevent events like those of the Tet attacks, it was time to call a halt. McNamara had reached that conclusion some time before and was due to be replaced by Clifford Clark, who had a reputation as a hawk, at the end of March. The President sent General Wheeler out to Vietnam in February to report on what was really needed. Unfortunately for Westmoreland, although he accepted the latter's reasoning, either he realized that such an optimistic line would not wear back home or he genuinely took a pessimistic view of the situation, and it was in the latter sense that he reported and on it that he based his arguments for supporting Westmoreland's requests. Faced with pressure from every direction not to increase the American stake and to seek some other way out, accentuated by a press leak that an increase of 206,000 men was being considered, Johnson, at the end of March, sought the advice of a group of distinguished 'Wise Men'. All but two, George Ball and Alfred Goldberg, had been considered hawks. Not only they, but Clifford Clark also, came out against the advice of Westmoreland and the Chiefs of Staff and recommended a limitation of bombing to the operational area, a refusal of further major reinforcement and an opening of negotiations. President Johnson had already announced his decision, planned in January, that Westmoreland should succeed General Johnson as Chief of the Army Staff when the latter's statutory four years was completed in June and that he would be succeeded by his deputy, General Abrams. On the last day of the month he announced the limitation of bombing to the Laotian panhandle and the area immediately north of the demilitarized zone, and mention of a reinforcement of a further 30,000 troops was overshadowed by the dramatic statement that he would not stand for another term as President.

It was the most powerful nation in the world, the United States of America, not the so-called Democratic Republic of Vietnam, that had been convinced that it could not win. From then on, all its diplomatic and military efforts were concentrated on how to extricate itself from the bog into which it had sunk. The interests of the inhabitants of South Vietnam were secondary, as indeed they had always been. The rationale for involvement had been assertion of the power of the United States to oppose communism, wherever it might raise its ugly head. With the advent of a Republican administration under the direction of that most hard-line of all anti-communists, Richard Nixon, it might have been expected that policy would have been reversed and a hawkish attitude adopted; but, as only de Gaulle could extricate France from Algeria, only a President whom nobody could outflank from the right could extricate the United States from Vietnam. Aided and abetted by that master of *realpolitik*, Henry Kissinger, he attempted to stick out for conditions which could save

America's honour and retain credibility in her support as an ally; but, faced on the one hand with Vietnamese intransigence (or consistency, to paint it in a different colour), three years of negotiations, punctuated by the invasion of Cambodia and periodic renewals of bombing of even the most sensitive targets in North Vietnam, culminated in a straight, pragmatic exchange: total withdrawal of US troops in return for repatriation of US prisoners of war.

Meanwhile the unfortunate US serviceman, whether drafted for one tour or a regular returning for yet another spell of duty, had to face the possibility of death, knowing that his country no longer had any faith in the cause for which he was called upon to fight. Little wonder that morale sank to the lowest depths as troop withdrawals began. A reduction of 100,000, from the total of 541,000, was made between August 1969 and April 1970, and a further 150,000 in the subsequent year. In April 1971 Nixon lowered the total still further to 184,000 and in November of that year to 139,000. In 1972 progressive reductions were made as the presidential election loomed and peace talks in Paris looked like reaching a conclusion. By December the total was down to 27,000 and in that month bombing of the North finally ceased. Peace was signed on 23 January 1973.

Thieu and his colleagues had fought a losing battle for their position to be upheld, but the realities of power were against them. Kissinger had to give way on point after point, and it proved impossible to obtain a commitment from North Vietnam to withdraw their forces, which they maintained were not in the South. After Nixon's resignation over Watergate in 1975, North Vietnam attacks, starting in the northern provinces, combined with a successful Khmer Rouge rebellion in Cambodia, brought about a collapse of South Vietnamese resistance and a total negation of all that the United States had fought for both on the battlefield and in the diplomatic negotiating chamber.

Could any other result have been achieved? One must dismiss the facile arguments of those who maintained that, had the Americans adopted the military and political methods followed by the British in Malaya, they could have achieved their aims. The conditions, both political and military, under which they operated were far more adverse and severe and totally different in scale. In essence they aimed too high, but were not prepared to devote the resources required to achieve that aim, largely because they underestimated what was needed, both in the military and in the political field, much as the British, three-quarters of a century before, had underestimated what was needed to defeat the spirit and the armed forces of the Boers of South Africa. Those who come best out of the sad story are the intelligence community and, strangely enough, the military. The former retained throughout a realistic view of the determination, strength and capability for endurance of North Vietnam and the Vietcong and of the weaknesses of successive regimes in the South. The military stuck to their guns. If they were called upon to fight the other side, no holds should be barred. If the enemy made use of the territory of

North Vietnam, Laos and Cambodia, so should they. If they could not, a long war, involving ever growing application of effort, had to be accepted. The weakness of their arguments lay in a lack of realism in terms of both international and domestic politics and in a failure to envisage what might follow a 'victory' obtained in such a manner. The real culprits were the 'Brightest and the Best', to use David Halberstam's description, the civilian advisers to successive presidents, imbued with 'games theories' and 'signalling', and as ignorant of the political, historical and cultural background of the area as they were of the realities of the battlefield, whether it were a jungle patrol, a conventional all-arms battle or the operation of air forces. Initially they pitched their hopes of the effectiveness of armed force, both as a political and as a military weapon, too high; and, when it did not quickly produce the results expected, they lost heart. Those who saw realities more clearly were labelled as defeatists, as they often are. One must have sympathy for the unfortunate 'Westy', struggling to follow the motto of his beloved West Point, 'Honour, Duty, Country'.

Although it is unlikely that the United States could have achieved her ambitious aim, there were occasions when she could have limited her commitment or withdrawn altogether. Apart from 1954, when she chose to reject the path of compromise with the communists of North Vietnam, 1963 and 1965 were crucial turning-points. In the former, the evident unpopularity of Diem's regime provided a justification for abandoning the self-imposed task of creating a separate anti-communist state south of the 17th parallel, although, once encouragement had been given to the generals who proposed to oust him, it would have been difficult to have deserted them. In the latter year, both the United States and North Vietnam chose to escalate the war to one in which their main forces were engaged, at great cost to themselves and even more so to that of South Vietnam. It was a tragedy that they did so. The communists of Vietnam could probably have achieved their aim by the time they eventually did by a combination of political action and guerrilla warfare, which the Americans would have found just as difficult, if not more difficult to deal with as the 'protracted' or 'mobile' warfare to which Giap turned, bringing down on his forces and on the country and population of Vietnam, North and South, all the destructive fire-power that the US Army, Air Force and Navy could bring to bear. The Vietnamese suffered heavily for their liberation from the imperial yoke.

PART FOUR

Conventional Clashes

Chapter Eleven

INDIA'S WARS

At first sight it appears that the wars in which India has been engaged since gaining independence in 1947 have been caused, either directly or indirectly, by her dispute with Pakistan over Kashmir. But Kashmir has been the symptom rather than the cause of her differences with Pakistan. However, if she had not accepted Kashmir as part of India, her short war with China in 1962 would almost certainly not have occurred. It was the basic incompatibility between the Muslim and the Hindu attitudes to life, and the memories of the former's domination of most of India before the British extended their imperial rule over the country, that was the root cause, its political manifestation being the rivalry between the Congress Party and the Muslim League, after Jinnah deserted Congress in 1928, becoming President of the Muslim League six years later. Until 1937 Congress and the League maintained an uneasy alliance in their demand for independence, but from then on each went its own way, the Muslim League turning increasingly to the demand for a separate Muslim state and finally adopting this as its policy in 1940.

Apart from the practical difficulties of establishing such a state, with Muslims scattered all over India both in the provinces ruled by the British and in states under princely rule, the concept was anathema to Congress and the mass of its Hindu supporters. The rivers which flowed through the country were holy and the land itself was in a sense sacred. If the Muslims were to demand a separate state, where would it end? The Sikhs and all the myriad races and sects that lived in the Indian sub-continent, loosely held together by British imperial rule and power, could demand independence also, and the independent Indian nation which Congress fought for would fall apart. In their eyes, those who demanded a separate state were traitors to the cause of independence.

When the Second World War came to an end and Attlee's Labour government faced the problem of granting independence to India, Jinnah and the Muslim League were adamant in demanding the establishment of a separate state of Pakistan, split into two parts which had little in common between them except that the majority of their inhabitants were Muslim. Britain's proposal, made by a three-man Cabinet Mission in 1946, was for a compromise. A central federal government would control foreign affairs, defence and communications. All else would be the responsibility of provincial governments, which could group themselves with other provinces, if they wished, to form larger states within the federation. Three groups, two Muslim, corresponding to the areas later to become West and East Pakistan, and one Hindu would be established on independence. After ten years the groupings could change according to the wishes of the provinces. A provisional federal government would be formed from Congress and the Muslim League to draw up a constitution on these lines. The British were surprised when both Congress, much influenced by Gandhi, and the Muslim League accepted the plan in principle. However, when Nehru became President of Congress a few months later, he publicly opposed it on the grounds that it would in fact lead to separatism, and he and Jinnah took no pains to conceal their mutual personal hostility. On 27 June 1946 the Muslim League withdrew their support from the plan, and from then on Jinnah publicly agitated for a separate Pakistan. The result was serious rioting in the provinces of Behar and Bengal, culminating in particularly bloody inter-communal fighting in Calcutta on Jinnah's 'Direct Action Day' in August. The inter-communal strife spread to include the Sikhs in the Punjab in 1947, and the country was in turmoil when Mountbatten succeeded Wavell as Viceroy in March of that year, charged with the task of extricating Britain from India as quickly as possible. By May he was convinced that the Cabinet Mission plan would not work, and, after a fateful meeting with Nehru in Simla, he flew to London and persuaded Attlee's Cabinet not only to accept partition but also to advance the date of independence from 1 June 1948 to 15 August 1947, only three months ahead. The Punjab and Bengal were to be divided between India and Pakistan, the boundaries being determined by Sir Cyril Radcliffe (as he was then), the boundary commissions set up to define them being unable to agree. As the date for independence approached, the civil war intensified. Britain neither could nor would keep order, and there were horrific scenes of inter-communal slaughter on a shameful scale, which accentuated the animosity between Muslim and Hindu and left scars that have not healed to this day. The speed with which the drastic surgical operation was carried out, and the confusion it led to, inevitably created a host of differences and conflicts between the newly established states, overshadowed by fear on the part of Pakistan that India had not accepted separation and would work actively to destroy the new state, and on the part of India that Pakistan would subvert the Muslims remaining in India and encourage other acts of separatism, especially among the princely states.

At independence there were 562 of these, varying in size from tiny estates to the huge state of Hyderabad, where a population of sixteen and a half million, 87 per cent non-Muslim, 81 per cent Hindu, was ruled over by the Muslim

Nizam and Muslim ruling class. Independence left the princely states free to accede to either dominion, which Mountbatten advised them to do, or technically to declare total independence. The vast majority were within India and Nehru made it clear that his government would not recognize the right of any princely state to become independent. If their borders were contiguous with Pakistan, they could opt to join her, but otherwise they must accept incorporation in India. The Nizam of Hyderabad refused to accept this, and in November 1947 signed an agreement with India to preserve their existing relations until final agreement was reached. However a communist insurrection within the state in 1948 and an apparent alliance between communist terrorists and the Nizam's private army, combined with the continued refusal of the Nizam to sign a final agreement, led to the Indian invasion of Hyderabad on 13 September, its occupation being completed within a few days and the state thereafter being dismembered and divided among neighbouring provinces.

Jammu and Kashmir was another state with a predominantly Muslim population, especially in the Vale of Kashmir itself, and a Hindu ruler, complicated by the fact that Jammu, down on the plains, was predominantly Hindu. Kashmir's wild mountainous country had been invaded from every direction over the centuries: from Sinkiang, from Tibet and, in the eighteenth century, from Afghanistan, shortly after it had declared its independence from the weakened Mogul empire. To escape from the cruelties of Afghan rule, the Kashmiris in the nineteenth century had appealed to the Sikhs to help them. One of their generals, Gulab Singh, the Rajput ruler of Jammu and a devout Hindu, conquered it in 1819 and, in 1826, when the Sikhs had been defeated by the British, bought it and annexed it to his own state, encouraged by Britain as a counterbalance to Sikh power and a buffer against the unruly men of the mountains. His descendant, Hari Singh, an irresponsible playboy, was Maharajah at the time of independence. His autocratic and irresponsible ways were opposed by a Muslim movement, led by 'Sheikh' Abdullah, which demanded independence and therefore found itself at odds with the Muslim League's demand for its accession to Pakistan. Hari Singh could not decide what to do. Of his population of 4 million, 77 per cent were Muslim and 20 per cent Hindu, the former concentrated in the Vale, where the capital, Srinagar, lay, and the latter in Jammu. Mountbatten had advised him to join one dominion or the other, but apparently did not suggest which. If he chose India, he was advised to accede before independence, Pakistan not at that stage being in existence; but the Congress leaders had assured Mountbatten that, if he chose to accede to Pakistan, they would not object. While the Maharajah dithered, hoping to maintain his independence, an armed rebellion broke out in the western part of the state round Poonch, declaring a free (Azad) Kashmir government, at the same time as the area known as the Gilgit Agency, which had been administered by the British, was handed back by them to Hari Singh.

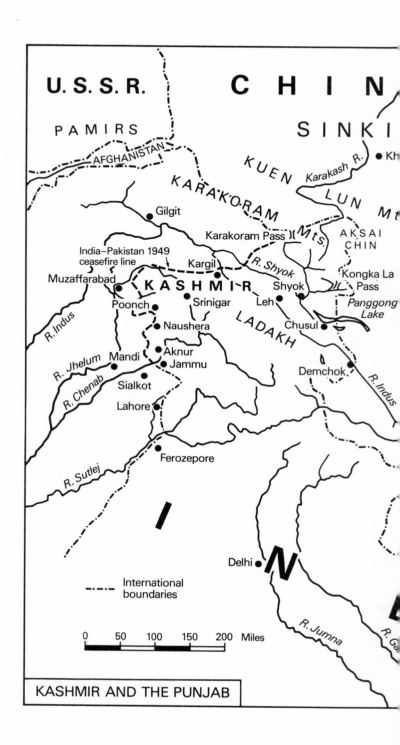

U.S.S.R.

CHIN

PAMIRS

AFGHANISTAN

SINKI

KUEN

Karakash R.

Kh

LUN Mt

KARAKORAM Mts.

AKSAI
CHIN

Gilgit

Karakoram Pass

India–Pakistan 1949
ceasefire line

Kargil

R. Shyok

Kongka La
Pass

Muzaffarabad

KASHMIR

Shyok

Panggong
Lake

Poonch

Srinigar

Leh

LADAKH

Chusul

Naushera

R. Indus

Aknur

Jammu

R. Jhelum Mandi

Demchok.

R. Indus

R. Chenab

Sialkot

Lahore

Ferozepore

R. Sutlej

N

Delhi

- · - · - International
boundaries

R. Jumna

R. Ga

0   50   100   150   200   Miles

KASHMIR AND THE PUNJAB

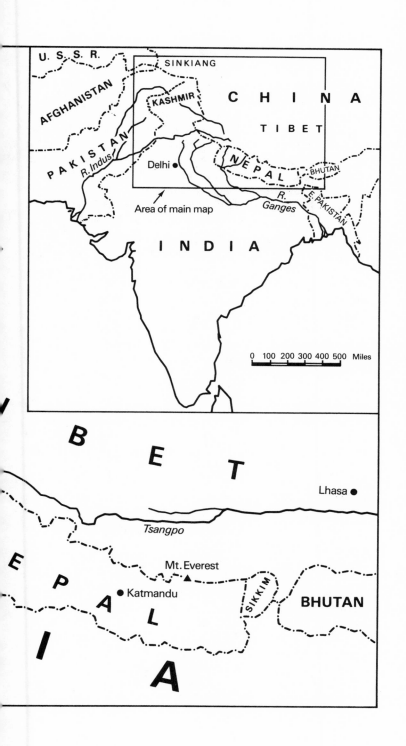

This was quickly absorbed into Pakistan, while anti-Muslim riots in Jammu in August drove Muslims from that area to take refuge farther west. By October 1947 Pakistan was supporting and co-ordinating the Muslim-based movements in Western Kashmir to overthrow the Maharajah's rule, and on 24 October the latter appealed to India for help. Mountbatten was still Governor-General of India and took the line that, before India could intervene, the Maharajah must accede to India, but that his state's accession must be subject to his agreement that a plebiscite should be held to decide the wishes of the people after the rebellion had been suppressed. Nehru, himself a Kashmiri Brahmin, and his ministers agreed, as did Hari Singh who signed on 26 October. Next day an Indian infantry battalion flew into Srinagar. Jinnah ordered his British Commander-in-Chief, General Gracey, to send in troops from Pakistan, but was persuaded to cancel this by Field-Marshal Auchinleck, who was still presiding over the problems of distributing the former Indian Army between the two dominions.

The Indian troops secured Srinagar and cleared the area of the Vale, as well as securing the high mountain area of Ladakh, but did not attempt to recapture the area farther west, where the rebels, whose numbers of fighting men they estimated at 5,000, had established the capital of Azad Kashmir at Muzaffarabad. Their principal problem was their communications. Although they had brought armoured cars in across the 9,000 foot Banihal Pass, they could not rely on that route for supply, and were dependent on a newly built narrow road which ran along the southern edge of the hills from Jammu, through Akhnur and Naushera to Jhangar. This ran parallel to and not far from the border with Pakistan and was the target of 'rebels' all through the winter, a fierce battle taking place at Naushera on 6 February, in which the Indians estimated the attacking force at 15,000. By this time Pakistan had moved her 7th Division up to the frontier as a backstop in case the Indians drove the Azad Kashmiri forces back over it. Some of the Pakistani Army undoubtedly crossed to support the rebels and were in action in an attack on the isolated Indian garrison of Poonch in March. This was followed by an Indian counter-offensive, their forces in Kashmir having now been increased to two divisions, and by the end of May General Thimmaya had captured Tithwal on the Kishen Ganga River and his forces were only eighteen miles from Muzaffarabad. This threat to Azad Kashmir's capital brought more Pakistani forces into action, and the armies of the two dominions, so recently members of the same army, were now firmly face to face. Stalemate in the Uri area ensued, Pakistan in the summer launching a counter-offensive farther north in Ladakh. They attacked near Kargil, cut the Srinagar–Leh road and threatened Leh itself, while irregular forces moved towards Srinagar, but were held at the Zoji Pass. By November Pakistan had the best part of two divisions in Kashmir, having weakened the force protecting Lahore in the Punjab in order to do so. At the end of the previous year India had referred the dispute to the United Nations and a Security Council resolution on 21 April 1948 had called upon India, Pakistan and 'tribal forces' to withdraw, allowing an interim coalition government to be established in Kashmir. Nothing came of this until, on 31 December 1948, a truce was brought about by the British generals, Gracey and Bucher, Chiefs of Staff respectively of the Pakistani and Indian Armies, to be supervised by the United Nations, and a cease-fire line was agreed on 20 January 1949, based on the positions that the forces of both sides occupied. Since then it has become a *de facto* international frontier, watched over by a small UN observer force. India never ceased to accuse Pakistan of having instigated and supported the so-called rebellion of Azad Kashmir, while the latter maintained that it was a spontaneous movement of the Kashmiri people to free themselves from the tyrannical yoke of a corrupt Hindu Maharajah, and that they had only directly intervened when he had invited Indian troops to support him in suppressing the people. There is little doubt that the Kashmiris themselves wished to be independent, a view which both the Maharajah and Sheikh Abdullah shared.

The UN resolution of 5 January 1949 left Azad Kashmir with 5,000 square miles and about 700,000 people under the control of Pakistan, the rest of the state with 81,000 square miles and 3½ million people under the control of India, provided for further steps of demilitarization, once the cease-fire had been stabilized, and then a plebiscite to be held under UN supervision. However attempts to progress beyond the cease-fire came to naught, primarily on the status of Azad Kashmir. India insisted that, before a plebiscite was held, Pakistan should withdraw her forces from that area and that the whole of the original state of Jammu and Kashmir be reunited under the state government, of which Sheikh Abdullah, having been released from jail, had become Prime Minister in 1948. Pakistan regarded Abdullah as a tool of India and refused to agree to the demilitarization of Azad Kashmir unless the Indians withdrew their forces from the rest of the state. Tension remained high for the next few years and the United Nations finally despaired of being able to put their resolution into effect.

Sheikh Abdullah continued to work for an independent Kashmir and the end of the Maharajah's rule. In spite of objection by the United Nations, an election was held in the autumn of 1951 for a Constituent Assembly to decide 'the future political affiliation'. Abdullah's party, the National Conference, won an overwhelming victory, as a result of which the Maharajah abdicated in favour of his son, who was elected Chief of State. Abdullah negotiated a special status for Kashmir in which it retained responsibility for all matters except foreign affairs, defence and communications, which the Indian Government would control. He then proceeded to implement a drastic policy of socialism which met with considerable opposition, especially in Jammu. In August 1953 his deputy, Bakshi Ghulan Mohammed, with Hindu support, arrested the Sheikh, whom he accused unjustly of plotting with Pakistan, and within six months brought Kashmir constitutionally within the Indian Union. A new constitution based on this was adopted in November 1956 and its accession was formalized by India in January 1957, although the legal processes were not completed until 1960. Abdullah remained in prison or house arrest for the rest of his life, apart from a few brief periods of liberty in 1958 and 1964.

All of this was naturally bitterly opposed by Pakistan and, when John Foster Dulles was looking round the frontiers of the communist powers in 1954 to find allies to join in a ring to contain them, he was as glad to rope in Pakistan as she was to seize the opportunity it might provide for her to build up her forces to redress the balance with India. So in 1954 she joined both the Central and the South East Asia Treaty Organizations, East Pakistan providing the justification for the latter, and signed a bilateral alliance with the United States under which she received US Military Aid. This was to have a profound effect on the relations between India and Pakistan and between both of them and the major world powers. The sensible and rational policy for both of them would have been to accept the existence of the other and to unite in coping with their very severe political and economic difficulties and in resisting the pressure of Russia, China and the West, particularly of the United States, to become involved in their cold war rivalries. But their initial enmity and mutual suspicion, fanned by events in Kashmir, persuaded first Pakistan and then reluctantly India to exploit cold war rivalries between East and West and the internecine quarrel between Russia and China in the hope that this would help them in their quarrel with each other. Nobody was to gain from this and the results remain a monument to human folly.

Pakistan's alliance with the United States led Nehru, in spite of his emphasis on non-alignment, to flirt with Russia, the visit of Krushchev and Bulganin to India in 1955 demonstrating this, by which time tension between the Soviet Union and China over several matters, including activity near the border of Sinkiang, was rising. Kashmir was therefore a sensitive area for Russia, and Krushchev in 1955 declared that he supported India's view that it had become part of India by the free decision of its own people. There was therefore no case for a further plebiscite as Pakistan consistently demanded. Mikoyan, however, visiting Pakistan in March 1956, took a different view and stated that a final decision still awaited the verdict of the people. In that year Nehru made it clear that the offer of a plebiscite no longer stood, and Pakistan brought the issue before the United Nations in January 1957, the Security Council resolving that 'the final disposition of the state of Jammu and Kashmir will be made in accordance with the will of the people expressed through the democratic method of a free and impartial plebiscite conducted under the auspices of the United Nations', the Soviet representative abstaining. As we have seen, this was quickly followed by India formally incorporating the state into the Indian Union, and there matters rested while other events occupied India's attention and relations between India and Russia cooled, partly as a result of Nehru's attitude to Russia's intervention in Hungary in 1956.

One such event, which heightened Pakistan's suspicion that India would eventually try and eliminate Pakistan as a separate state, was India's invasion and occupation of the Portuguese colony of Goa in December 1961. It could hardly be called a war, as there was no resistance, and it was undertaken primarily for domestic political reasons, to rally support to the government which, at this period, was under constant attack from the right; but it had an adverse effect on the moves that had been made to patch up the quarrel between the two countries and hopefully unite them against external threats, as Pakistan's military President, Ayub Khan, had publicly suggested that they should in 1959.

While in public being principally concerned with domestic problems, Nehru was secretly facing a troublesome difference of opinion with China over their mutual frontiers. There were three areas of dispute: the north-east corner of Ladakh in Kashmir, known as the Aksai Chin (see map on page 212); an area west of Nepal where the frontier of Uttar Pradesh province joined that of Tibet; and that between Assam and Tibet, east of Bhutan up to the border with Burma, the province known as the North East Frontier Agency (see map on page 214). The one that mattered most to China was the Aksai Chin, as it was China's main route from Sinkiang to Tibet. India, apart from doubts about its position in Kashmir at all, had inherited the frontiers which the British had claimed. China's case, with much justification, was that no Chinese government had ever agreed to nor signed any treaty delimiting these frontiers. In the late nineteenth century and the first decade of the twentieth, the threat of Russian encroachment on the frontiers of India preoccupied the Government of India. At that time China was weak and quiescent. Her claim to Tibet was recognized, but not thought to pose any danger. Expeditions penetrating the uninhabited frozen wastes of the mountains north of Kashmir found that the choice lay between the Karakoram range of mountains, which formed the watershed, and the Kuen Lun range, some seventy miles farther north. In the fatal manner in which defenders, in order to secure the high ground, are tempted to push their defences down the forward slope, so the British Director of Military Intelligence, Sir John Ardagh, urged in 1897 that the line of the Kuen Lun should be claimed, as had been recommended by an officer of the Indian Survey, Johnson, who had led an expedition to the area in 1865 and stated that they formed the northern frontier of Kashmir. It was therefore known as the Johnson–Ardagh line. But the Viceroy, Lord Elgin, objected that this would lead to difficulties with China in an area in which it would be very difficult to maintain India's claim. He preferred the line proposed by his representative in Kashgar, George Macartney, who had discussed the matter

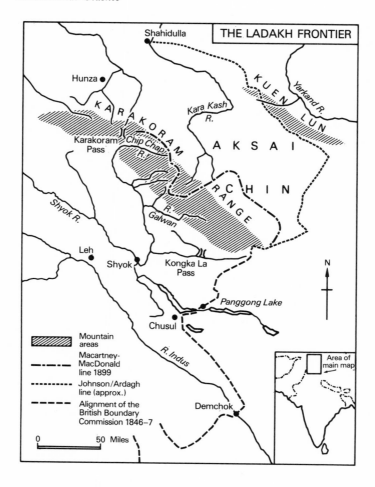

with both the Russians and a Chinese official from Sinkiang. This skirted the northern edge of the Karakoram mountains, but left the plateau between them and the Kuen Lun to Tibet, and therefore to China. This line, known as the Macartney–Macdonald line, was proposed to the Chinese Government in 1899 by the British Minister, Sir Claude Macdonald. The Chinese never replied, but the British adopted it. In 1911 the revolution in China and fears that Russia would extend her influence led the Viceroy of India, Lord Hardinge, to propose claiming the Johnson–Ardagh line, but nothing was done about it. In 1927 the Government of India decided to readjust their version of the frontier, making it follow the Karakoram range from the junction with the frontier of Afghanistan to the Karakoram Pass, following the Macartney–Macdonald line, and then pushing out to join the Johnson–Ardagh line across the plateau of the Aksai Chin to the Kuen Lun; but official Government of India maps at the time of independence showed the original Johnson–Ardagh line as the frontier, although it had never been openly claimed nor discussed with China or Tibet.

The status of Tibet was naturally a significant factor in this case and in that of the eastern disputed area. In 1904 Francis Younghusband had penetrated to Lhasa and signed an agreement with the Dalai Lama by which the latter undertook not to admit representatives of any other foreign power but Britain, China's suzerainty however being recognized. This was followed by an agreement in 1907 between Britain and Russia that both countries would keep out of the country and only enter into negotiations with the Tibetans through the Chinese. At that time the boundary between Assam (occupied by the British in 1826) and Tibet was assumed to run along the southern edge of the Himalayan foothills, parallel to the course of the Brahmaputra River from the south-east corner of the independent princely state of Bhutan. But the aggressive attitude taken by the Manchu Emperor in 1910, the murder in 1911 of a British official, Mr Williamson, who was investigating the degree of Tibetan influence in the foothills, and the internal collapse of China in the revolution of 1911–12, persuaded Hardinge to change his policy, as he had in Kashmir, to a forward one, dealing directly with Tibet behind the back of China. An expedition was despatched to avenge Williamson's death and survey a frontier based on the watershed, although there had never been any doubt that the area immediately east of Bhutan, known as the Tawang Tract, owed allegiance to Tibet. To advance the frontier to the mountain passes, but leave the Tract in Tibetan hands, would have been nonsensical in military terms. From its southern border, a short advance to the Brahmaputra would have cut off all of Assam east of that point. Under the guise of mending relations between Tibet and China, who were fighting each other, Britain called a conference at Simla in 1913, at which she tried to persuade China to divide Tibet, as China had agreed with Russia to divide Mongolia, into an Inner Tibet, which she would administer, and an Outer Tibet, over which her suzerainty would be recognized but she would have no administrative control. China did not accept, but neither did she reject this proposal, arguing about the boundary between the two, disagreement on which brought the conference to an end, but not before Sir Henry McMahon had persuaded the Chinese representative to initial the draft of the treaty which would have resulted, attached to which was a map showing the proposed frontier between Tibet and Assam running along the mountain passes, although the monastery of Tawang itself (just south of them) remained a Tibetan enclave. The Chinese Government immediately repudiated even their representative's provisional initialling of the draft. Following the break-up of the conference, direct discussions between Tibetan representatives and the Government of India in February 1914 led to agreement on the McMahon line as the frontier, China being neither consulted nor

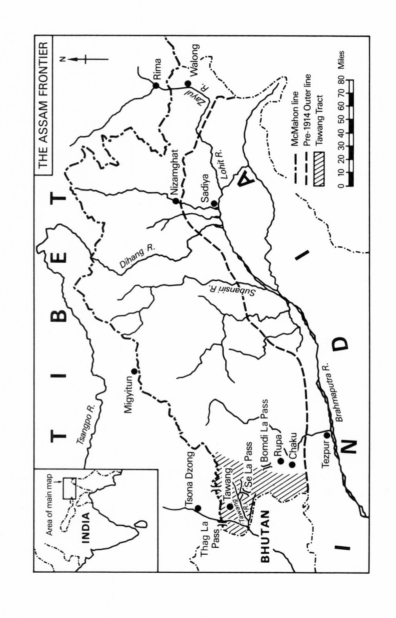

THE ASSAM FRONTIER

N

Rima

Walong

Zayul R.

Nizamghat

Sadiya

Lohit R.

Dihang R.

A

Tsangpo R.

T I B E T

Subansiri R.

Migyitun

Area of main map

INDIA

Tsona Dzong

Thag La Pass

Tawang

Tawang R.

Se La Pass

Bomdi La Pass

Rupa

Chaku

Tezpur

Brahmaputra R.

BHUTAN

I N D I A

McMahon line
Pre-1914 Outer line
Tawang Tract

0 10 20 30 40 50 60 70 80   Miles

informed. However the Government of India made no attempt to administer the area north of the originally accepted frontier nor to make a public claim to authority over the area, until the question as to where the frontier lay came to the fore in 1935, when a British botanist, Kingdon Ward, was accused by the Tibetan authorities of entering Tibet without their permission. This led to pressure by officials of the Government of India for the McMahon line to be accepted as the frontier, and the Survey of India began to show it as such, although not on all maps. An Indian Army officer, Captain Lightfoot, was sent with a small escort in April 1938 to Tawang 'to examine the country, get in touch with the inhabitants, and form some estimate of its revenue possibilities' before the government made up its mind whether or not to agree to the Governor of Assam's request that his administration should be extended up to the McMahon line. The decision went against him, and, when the Second World War distracted peoples' attention, things stayed as they were, the Tibetan authorities maintaining that their agreement to the McMahon line as the frontier with Assam had been dependent on China agreeing to the independence of Outer Tibet, in other words that the draft treaty proposed at the Simla Convention of 1913 had to be accepted as a whole.

India's independence in 1947 was followed by Mao Tse-tung's victory in establishing his authority over all of China, which in 1950 was extended to Tibet. Although India had reacted sharply to China's declaration of intent in 1949 to do this, Nehru accepted it. India had already regulated her relations with Nepal, where she had supported the King in overthrowing the power of the Rana clan; had sent troops into Sikkim, when riots threatened disorder there; and signed an agreement with the Ruler of Bhutan. Nehru's acceptance of Chinese authority over Tibet brought on him severe criticism from the right wing of the Congress Party, and his reaction was to show determination in asserting Indian authority up to the McMahon line. In 1951 an expedition set out to implement it over the whole of the Tawang Tract, including Tawang itself, in the face of protests from Lhasa, but surprising silence from Peking. However, in September of that year Chou En-lai, China's Prime Minister, suggested that discussions between India, Nepal and China should take place to 'stabilize the frontier of Tibet', stating that 'there was no territorial dispute or controversy between India and China', a fairly clear indication that the McMahon line was accepted; but, although India said that negotiations would be welcome, there was no follow-up, and, when negotiations took place in 1954 about trade and representation issues in Tibet, no mention was made by either side of boundary questions. One of India's most distinguished civil servants, Sir G. S. Bajpai, had suggested that India should raise the issue in order to avoid future misunderstandings, but Nehru decided that there should be no negotiation about any part of India's frontiers and issued a directive that they should be decided upon unilaterally and clearly shown on all maps as firmly delimited frontiers. In the eastern sector the McMahon line was shown as such. In the west, it followed the Macartney–Macdonald line from the Afghan border to the Karakoram Pass (the area of Kashmir in fact controlled by Pakistan), and then bulged out to the Johnson–Ardagh line to include the Kuen Lun range. In March 1956 the Chinese began to build a motorable road through the Aksai Chin to link Sinkiang and Tibet, where they were having trouble with the Khampa rebellion, and the first India knew of this was when the Chinese press reported its completion in September 1957, its reports accompanied by maps showing both the Aksai Chin and the foothills south of the McMahon line as part of China. Nehru's reaction was to send patrols to see where the road actually went. They had to wait until winter was over and set off from Leh in July 1958. In December, before they had returned (one of them was arrested by the Chinese), Nehru wrote a friendly letter to Chou En-lai about the Chinese maps, recalling the latter's statement that there was no boundary dispute between them, and going on to say that there could be no question of 'these large parts of India', shown as Chinese on their maps, 'being anything but India, and there is no dispute about them'. Chou En-lai replied in an equally friendly manner, pointing out that the frontier had never been officially delimited or agreed between the Chinese and Indian Governments; that those shown on Chinese maps had been shown as such for many decades; that he did not claim that they everywhere represented the *de facto* situation on the ground, and proposed that discussions should take place leading to a mutually agreed survey; but that meanwhile they should provisionally and temporarily 'maintain the *status quo*'. In the use of that Latin phrase lay the seed of all the future difference or misunderstanding (if it ever really was a misunderstanding) that bedevilled the issue. *Fowler's Modern English Usage* (1926) defines the *status quo* as 'the position in which things (1) are now, or (2) have been till now'. Chou En-lai meant the former, while Nehru insisted on the latter. In all the exchanges that were to follow, Nehru, under increasing criticism for being prepared to give way to China by discussing frontier problems, maintained that there could be no negotiation about the frontiers claimed by India. He was prepared to have talks about minor details of their delimitation, but, before they could start, China must withdraw from and renounce her claim to the Aksai Chin. Chou En-lai was consistent in refusing to accept any of India's claims, but proposing that negotiations start from the basis of the actual position of control on the ground, a fairly broad hint, consistently maintained, that if India withdrew her claim to the Aksai Chin and remained content with the Macartney–Macdonald line along the Karakoram range, China would accept the McMahon line in the east; but that, if she persisted in her claim to the Aksai Chin, China would maintain hers to the foothills of Assam.

What appeared at the start to be a genuine difference of opinion between friends soon began to acquire more sinister tinges in the imagination of both sides. The rebellion in Tibet, the flight of the Dalai Lama to India, the welcome Tibetan refugees received there and the anti-Chinese feelings it aroused both in India and in the Western world, led China to suspect India of trying once again to separate Tibet from China and of playing the anti-communist game in collusion with the West. Eisenhower's visit to Delhi in 1959 appeared to confirm this. India's increasingly close relations with the Soviet Union gave her no reassurance either. A visit by Chou En-lai to New Delhi in April 1960 did nothing to improve relations, and after it Nehru, who in August 1959 had for the first time made public the existence of the Aksai Chin road and his exchanges of view with Chou, gave directions to implement a forward policy to assert Indian claims.

Incidents in which Indian and Chinese troops had clashed had already occurred. In the east, the Indians had attempted to occupy the hamlet of Longju in the Tawang Tract, north of where it had long been accepted that the McMahon line lay, and exchanged fire with Chinese border guards. At almost the same time, August 1959, a more severe clash had occurred at the Kongka La Pass south of the Karakoram range. Designed to counter political criticism, India's forward policy, whatever the rights or wrongs of the frontier issue (and China's case must be considered a strong one), was militarily nonsensical. The state of communications in both eastern and western sectors was in favour of China. She normally maintained forces north of the mountain passes and could more easily reinforce them than the Indian Army, which hitherto had deployed none in the area south of them. Once moved there, Indian troops, who were not equipped nor normally trained for mountain warfare at those heights, would be entirely dependent on air supply, which, even if suitable aircraft had been available at that time, was precarious on account of both the country and the weather.

The Indian Army was in a poor state, starved of funds, as her anti-military political leaders saw no threat to the country, in spite of Pakistan's growing military strength, nurtured by US military aid. Senior officers who objected to the forward policy on sound military grounds were replaced by more subservient men, prominent among whom was Nehru's favourite General Kaul. The policy proposed was to thrust forward patrols and establish posts behind those already set up by the Chinese, in the touching faith that the latter would not actively oppose this, but withdraw their forces as their supply was interrupted. The belief that China would back down was based on the political view that she would not stand up against India, when the latter was backed, as she expected to be, both by the Soviet Union and the West. Chou En-lai gave several clear warnings to India of the dangers of pursuing this policy, which was only made possible by the supply by Russia to the Indian Air Force of AN12 transport aircraft and helicopters capable of operating at high altitude; but, hoist by his own petard of describing Chinese occupation of the Aksai Chin and resistance to Indian encroachments on the McMahon line as aggression, aimed at further expansion into India, Nehru not only continued, but attempted to intensify, the forward policy against the advice, and at times the deliberate delaying tactics, of sensible military commanders.

By the latter half of 1961 the Indian Army had established some forty posts on the Ladakh frontier in territory claimed by China, all the way from the Chip Chap River near the Karakoram Pass down to the Panggong Lake east of Chusul. Chinese countermeasures in the Chip Chap Valley had led to a decision by Nehru, taken at a meeting on 2 November, for the immediate intensification of the forward policy, in spite of protests by General Daulat Singh of Western Command and others that it was necessary to build up the forces near the border and their logistic support before embarking on more aggressive moves. Kaul, now Chief of the General Staff, played a prominent part in pressing for immediate action. This decision immediately preceded India's occupation of Goa, and aggressive assertion of her rights was the order of the day. In the spring of 1962 China reacted to the implementation of this policy in the Aksai Chin, and, as soon as the Indians set up a new post, would surround it with superior forces. Matters came to a head when a platoon of Gurkhas penetrated up the Galwan Valley in July and took up a position threatening an important Chinese post at Samzungling. When the Chinese surrounded them, a reinforcing force was sent to relieve them, but was turned back by the Chinese in August. The post remained, supplied by air, until 20 October, when it was attacked and overrun as part of China's general reaction to events on the McMahon line.

The Assam border had been quiet for three years since the Longju incident, Chou En-lai and Nehru having agreed then that neither army would patrol within two miles of the border. But the directive resulting from the meeting of 2 November 1961 stirred it up, Kaul issuing orders personally in February 1962 to General Umrao Singh, Commander of xxxiii Corps, who was reluctant to embark on such operations, to establish twenty-four new posts along the McMahon line. The one which sparked off the war was at Dhola Post in the valley of the Namka Chu River south of the Thag La ridge in the Tawang Tract. From the north-east corner of Bhutan the ridge ran eastward immediately north of the McMahon line as originally drawn on the map. It was the highest ridge in the area and since 1959 the Indians had decided that they preferred to observe it as the frontier in preference to the lower ridge to the south, along which the McMahon line was drawn. They had then established a post at Khinzemane at the eastern end of the Thag La ridge. The Chinese had reacted strongly at the time, but, after exchanges between New Delhi and Peking, the Indian post had been allowed to remain there. Now Kaul's orders were for the Thag La ridge to be occupied in order to assert India's claim. The local commanders were strongly opposed to it, but were overruled. The new post was established on the south side of the river on 4 June 1962 instead of, as originally intended, at the junction of the frontiers of Tibet, Bhutan and Assam at the western end of the ridge, which was inaccessible. A proposal was then made that it should be moved up to the 14,500 foot high Thag La Pass itself, and this was approved by Delhi. It was not until 8 September that the Chinese reacted, a party of about sixty (reported by the post commander as 600) moving over and down the Thag La ridge and establishing themselves in positions from which they totally dominated the Indian position at Dhola Post. They then proposed that local political officers of the two sides should meet and discuss just where the border lay. This was referred to Nehru, who was in London, and refused. Instead the army was told to relieve the garrison of Dhola Post and force the Chinese back behind the ridge. As in Ladakh, the realities of military operations made this a nonsensical order, and the local commanders, Brigadier Dalvi commanding 7th Brigade, Major-General Prasad, the 4th Division and Lieutenant-General Umrao Singh, xxxiii Corps, were not slow to point it out. So Umrao Singh was replaced by a more compliant officer, fatally by Kaul himself.

As in Ladakh, it was assumed by the politicians, supported by Kaul, that the Indian Army would easily overcome the Chinese, who would not react, in spite of the fact that hitherto they had always been able to produce superior numbers on the spot. In fact Chou En-lai had by now despaired of getting sense out of Nehru, who he considered had given way to pressures from pro-American, capitalist bourgeois influences, intent on involving India in an anti-Chinese bloc. If Nehru could not see sense, he would have it knocked into him, and Chou made his preparations accordingly. His aim was unchanged: to negotiate the delimitation of frontiers which left China with the Aksai Chin in the west, accepting the McMahon line in the east.

Meanwhile pressure was exerted for early action to capture the Thag La ridge, while Nehru was once more hoist with his own petard. The more he described China's reaction as aggression and encouraged press exaggeration of it in order to whip up domestic and international support (as it was very successful in doing), the greater the pressure for immediate military action to restore the situation, although all sensible military advice was that, if it were to be attempted at all, adequate forces and logistic support should be built up first. Air strikes were precluded, as running the risk of retaliation on India's crowded cities. On 26 September, when Kaul assumed command of xxxiii Corps, Dalvi's 7th Brigade had one battalion, 9th Punjab, with one company of 2nd Rajput, on the Namka Chu, their sole heavy weapon support being two medium machine-guns, spread out over seven miles of river. Several days' march away at Lumpu were the brigade headquarters, the other two companies of 2nd Rajput and 1/9th Gurkhas. 4th Grenadiers were on their way there. Farther away still, at Tawang, were two more battalions and some mountain artillery. Kaul himself went up to the Namka Chu on 7 October to hurry things up, forcing the Rajputs and the Gurkhas to move up there also, although supplies were insufficient to maintain them and they had no winter clothing. On 9 October he ordered Dalvi to send the Rajputs across the river and up the Thag La ridge to secure the Yumtso La Pass at 16,000 feet on the top of the ridge, outflanking the Chinese. Dalvi and Prasad protested that, without artillery support, they would be mown down by the Chinese fire and that, even if they did get there, they could not be supplied nor survive at that height. Kaul compromised by agreeing to a preliminary move of a fifty-man patrol of the Punjabis to Tseng Jong, a point half-way there, to test the route. Kaul felt he had been justified when the patrol reached their objective without incident shortly before dark, the Chinese having done nothing to interfere with them. But at dawn on 10 October the whole Chinese battalion facing the Namka Chu attacked Tseng Jong, but were held off by the Punjabis, who were then allowed to withdraw south of the river, having suffered twenty-five casualties to the Chinese thirty-three. Kaul now realized that capturing the ridge was out of the question, and there is much disagreement about what he recommended to his superiors. After a confused meeting in New Delhi, Nehru left for a visit to Colombo, telling the press as he left that his orders were 'to free our territory', but that it was for the army to determine when it could be done. For nine days, while Kaul retired to his house in Delhi, ostensibly because he was suffering from pulmonary trouble, not having been acclimatized to the heights, 7th Brigade remained on the Namka Chu and was even ordered to extend its posts to the western end of the ridge. By then, 18 October, it was clear that the Chinese were making preparations to attack, and on the night of 19/20 October they deployed to do so. By 9 a.m. on 20 October they had overwhelmed all 7th Brigade's troops in the Namka Chu area, their total force there being estimated at three regiments. At the same time they attacked Indian posts in the Aksai Chin, overrunning those in the Chip Chap Valley, the Galwan and the Panggong Lake area.

That their action in the Tawang Tract was not merely a local counter-attack became clear in the next two days as three columns converged on Tawang, which could not easily be defended. A decision was needed as to whether to try and hold them at the 14,600 foot Se La Pass, ten miles east of Tawang, or at the Bomdi La Pass, twenty-five miles farther back. The first decision, after one, quickly rescinded, to hold Tawang 'at all costs', was to go back to Bomdi La, the northernmost point at which the corps staff judged that the Indians could build up their forces more quickly than could the Chinese; but army headquarters reversed the order and insisted that Se La be held. This split the forces of 4th Division between Se La, Bomdi La, where a little-used track, known as the Bailey trail, joined the road from the north, and the road in between.

Meanwhile in Ladakh minds were clearer. With less interference from New Delhi, General Daulat Singh at Western Command withdrew small posts from Chinese-claimed territory and concentrated on defensible positions west of the Karakoram range, moving additional forces up from Kashmir, until he had built up a whole division in Ladakh. By mid-November he had the situation firmly under control. The same could not be said about the situation in Assam.

There a wholesale change round of commanders, formations and units took place, some of it apparently for no better reason than that the officers did not like each other. Kaul returned from his sickbed, and on 14 November flew to the extreme eastern end of the North East Frontier Agency, where the newly appointed commander of the newly-formed 2nd Division, General M. S. Pathania, had persuaded him that he could drive back a Chinese incursion from Rima, over the border, to celebrate Nehru's 73rd birthday. It was a total failure, and, when the Chinese counter-attacked two days later, they overran the Indian positions, in which the soldiers fought to the last man and round, survivors making their way down the Lohit Valley, command having broken down. This Chinese counter-attack at Walong preceded by one day the resumption of their operations in the Tawang Tract. By then the Se La Pass was held by 62nd Brigade with five battalions. 48th Brigade was at Bomdi La with three, and 65th Brigade with two was with 4th Division Headquarters (General Prasad having been replaced by General A. S. Pathania) at Dirang Dzong, ten miles to the west on the road to Se La. Pathania had begun to be concerned at the threat of a Chinese move down the Bailey trail and successively weakened 48th Brigade by ordering it to send companies out to block routes from the north, until its strength at Bomdi La had been halved. On 17 November, at the same time as the first Chinese attack was made on Se La, one of 48th Brigade's battalions was attacked at the junction of the Bailey trail and the road between Bomdi La and Dirang Dzong. For three hours they fought the Chinese off, but ran out of ammunition, and, withdrawing in the dark to Bomdi La, lost control and broke up. With the road now cut behind him, Pathania asked permission to withdraw 62nd Brigade from Se La, join them with the weak 65th Brigade protecting his headquarters, and break through to Bomdi La to concentrate all of his division there. This led to a prolonged discussion among his superiors, the result of which was an order from Kaul to hold on to his present positions 'to the best of his ability', but, when any position became untenable, he could withdraw at his own discretion to 'any alternative position you can hold'. The depleted 48th Brigade had been ordered, in the face of protests from its commander, to counter-attack to clear the road, and another brigade with two battalions would reach Bomdi La on 18 November. The result was as might have been expected. 62nd Brigade was attacked by the Chinese as it withdrew. 65th Brigade and 4th Division Headquarters broke up as Pathania told them to make their own way back to the Plains, and 48th Brigade had to face the Chinese alone. They were successively outflanked at Bomdi La, Rupa and Chaku, and by 20 November no organized Indian Army force was left either in the North East Frontier Agency or in the area of the Aksai Chin claimed by China.

Nehru's reaction was totally to abandon his policy of non-alignment and dislike of foreign military aid, appealing to the United State and Britain, as well as to Soviet Russia, to come to his aid. The two former acted rapidly, offering air support and arms and, in the case of the United States, ordering an aircraft-carrier into the Bay of Bengal. But the imagined Chinese invasion of India did not materialize. On 21 November Chou En-lai announced that from midnight the Chinese 'frontier-guards' would cease fire everywhere, and then, starting on 1 December, they would withdraw twenty kilometres behind 'the line of actual control which existed between China and India on 7 November 1959'. The Indians would be expected to keep their forces at the same distance from that line also, although civilian police posts could be established up to it. Officials should then meet on the border to discuss where those posts should be and arrange for the exchange of prisoners. He and Nehru could thereafter meet to discuss an amicable settlement.

General Chaudari had now replaced General Thapar as Chief of the Army Staff and could see no alternative to agreement. He gave orders to his troops accordingly; but Nehru could not publicly admit defeat and, while privately letting Chou En-lai know that in practice Indian forces would conform, he continued in public to prevaricate and to refuse to accept China's terms. The Indian Army was lucky to get away with casualties of 1,383 killed, 1,696 missing and 3,968 captured. Kaul was replaced in command of his corps by his rival Manekshaw and resigned from the army.

This very limited war had significant effects on the relations between India and Pakistan. The weaknesses it had revealed in the Indian Armed Forces led to the initiation of a major programme of rearmament and reorganization, partly with foreign help, but principally by building up India's own potential for production of military equipment. This alarmed Pakistan, although it gave her confidence that, until the programme had produced results, she was in a comparatively favourable military position, particularly if she allied herself, as she did, with China. If the Kashmir issue was to be solved, the sooner the better. Attention in any case was drawn to Kashmir by both events within the state itself and outside pressures. Pakistan had signed a border agreement with China in 1963, covering China's frontier westward from the Karakoram Pass, in which the Chinese received a small bulge of territory south of the mountains round Hunza. At the end of the year there were serious riots in the Vale arising out of the disappearance of a relic, the Hair of the Prophet, from the Mosque in Srinagar. Disturbances continued throughout 1964, coinciding with agitation for independence by a movement known as the Action Committee. Britain and the United States had attempted to make renewal of negotiations about the future of Kashmir a condition of their military support for India, Nehru's response to which was to offer a permanent division on the existing cease-fire line. Pakistan referred the problem once more to the United Nations, claiming for herself the whole state except for 3,000 square miles of eastern Jammu. Nehru was anxious for a settlement, and, when he died in May 1964, his successor, Shastri, was not thought to carry sufficient weight to be able to make any concessions to Pakistan, where Ayub Khan, in spite of a willingness to meet Shastri, was compensating for his increasing domestic political difficulties by constant rattling of the sabre in his attitude to India, especially over Kashmir. He faced a presidential election, the first ever, in January 1965, and was run very close by Jinnah's daughter, much of her support coming from East Pakistan, which was increasingly dissatisfied with the subordination of its interests to those of West Pakistan and the latter's obsession with the Kashmir issue.

It was in this atmosphere that a minor incident occurred in an area of apparently no importance to either country, although a disputed one, the Rann of Kutch, an almost uninhabited region east of the mouths of the Indus, mud flats in the dry season and covered in water when the south-west monsoon starts blowing in May. In January 1965 Indian Police found their Pakistan counterparts using a track a mile and a half inside territory claimed by India. They expelled them and set up posts to prevent a repetition. Pakistan retaliated, and in April both sides sent troops, access from Pakistan being much easier than that from India. On 24 April Pakistan attacked Indian positions with the best part of a division and forced India, who had no wish to commit a large force to this useless territory just before it was due to be flooded, to withdraw. Their reaction was to strengthen their forces in the Punjab facing Lahore. At the Commonwealth Conference in London in June an agreement over the Rann of Kutch was arrived at between Shastri and Ayub Khan, but shortly before that the latter had initiated preparations to launch a major subversive campaign in Kashmir. This was to be carried out by a force of some 30,000 men under General Malik, Commander of Pakistan's 12th Division. It was divided into some ten 'forces', each of six units of five companies each, the commanders being regular officers of the Pakistan Army, lower echelons of command being provided by the Azad Kashmir Army, itself part of the Pakistan Army, and the rank and file recruited from Mujahid and Razakar irregulars. As this force was being trained in Pakistan, incidents on the cease-fire line increased daily, while the political situation in Kashmir remained tense. Sheikh Abdullah, who had been released from prison by Nehru shortly before his death, was arrested again in May, the Action Committee was causing trouble and the repercussions of the Hair of the Prophet affair had still not died down.

On 5 August 1965 General Malik's force infiltrated across the cease-fire line on a wide front in four main areas: one near Kargil in the north, where they tried to cut the road to Leh; a second, the approaches to Srinagar on a wide front; the third in the Poonch region, where they succeeded in capturing Mandi; and the fourth aimed at the road through Jammu, the last supported by Pakistani artillery fire from across the border. It was the action of regular forces of both sides in this area that sparked off the subsequent war, rather than that of the irregulars, who failed to achieve their objective of sparking off a 'general uprising' and were for the most part soon confined to within ten miles of the cease-fire line.

At this time India's Army of about 800,000 men formed seventeen divisions, of which there were three in Kashmir, one of them committed to the Chinese border with Ladakh. Five were committed to the defence of the Himalayas elsewhere and one to watch East Pakistan. Of the remaining eight, five were in the Punjab facing West Pakistan and three in reserve. Her total tank strength was 1,450, her one armoured division being equipped with British Centurions, the remainder being Second World War Shermans and light tanks. The Indian Air Force had 500 combat aircraft, their only high performance fighters being a few Russian MIG21s. The Pakistan Army totalled about 230,000 men, forming eight divisions, including one armoured division fully equipped with the modern American Patton M60 tank, the second in process of formation. This imbalance in numbers was more than compensated for in that she could concentrate her whole army in the only area that really mattered to her, the Punjab. Her Air Force had some 200 combat aircraft, which included a high proportion of the modern American F104 Sabres.

On 14 August Indian positions north of the cease-fire line at Bhimbar, near its junction with the Indo–Pakistan frontier west of Jammu, were attacked and overrun by a force which included a regular Pakistan battalion, supported by Pakistan artillery. Next day Indian forces crossed the cease-fire line near Kargil and reoccupied positions they had vacated in May. A series of actions then followed near Tithwal, Uri and Poonch, some limited to exchanges of artillery fire, while the United Nations tried to bring the two sides together and prevent escalation. The threat posed to Azad Kashmir's capital, Muzaffarabad, by India's capture of the Haji Pir Pass on 29 August may have been what prompted Pakistan to attempt a diversionary attack in strength on 1 September in the Bhimbar–Chamb area, in which she employed an infantry brigade supported by two battalions of tanks against Indian positions totalling 1,000 men with only 15 tanks. In the operations which followed, Pakistan's newly raised 6th Armoured Division penetrated as far as Jaurian, only six miles from Akhnur, the capture of which would have severed India's main supply route to her forces in Kashmir. She, in her turn, launched a major diversionary attack in the Punjab, threatening Lahore, on 6 September, nicknamed Operation *Grand Slam*. Lahore was protected from the east by the Ichhogil or B.R.B. (Bambansala-Ravi-Bedian) Canal. Built after independence, it ran parallel to the Indo–Pakistan border three to nine miles west of it. One hundred and forty feet wide and fifteen feet deep, with concrete walls higher on the western side and heavily fortified, it served as a formidable anti-tank ditch, and the first aim of the attacking Indian forces was to secure crossings over it. At dawn on 6 September India attacked with a corps of three divisions under General Dhillon. The northern, under General Pershad, advanced on the line of the Grand Trunk Road to the Dograi bridge over the canal, which they had captured and had crossed by 10 a.m. However a Pakistani counter-attack recaptured and demolished it. The central thrust, under General Sibal, was aimed at Burki, a Pakistan position east of the canal, which was resolutely defended and took the Indians four days to subdue. The southern thrust, under General Gurbaksh Singh, launched from Khem Karan, was to establish a firm base at Kasur before crossing the canal and turning north towards Lahore. The Pakistan defences were strong in this area and reacted firmly, counter-attacking Gurbaksh Singh and forcing him on to the defensive, while they moved up their strong 1st Armoured Division, commanded by General Nazir Ahmed. Over the next four days fierce but inconclusive fighting took place in the northern and central sectors, Indian troops making little or no progress, while the Pakistani forces dominated the southern sector, keeping the Indians on the defensive and anxious about the whereabouts of Pakistan's armour. The operation of the opposing air forces was limited to battlefield strikes, both sides refraining from attacks on civilian targets or ones deeper within the enemy's territory from a mutual fear of the effect of air attacks on their crowded cities. In these operations the Pakistan Air Force's F104s were unable to take advantage of their technical superiority over the Indian Gnats, operating at low altitude. On 10 September Pakistan's 1st Armoured Division launched a major attack in the southern sector near Khem Karan, but their tanks were not well handled, were not supported by infantry and found themselves operating in high crops of sugar cane and cotton, often in boggy ground. The Indians had prepared their defences well and inflicted heavy casualties, 100 Pakistani tanks falling into Indian hands, fifty of them knocked out.

It is not entirely clear what the aim of Indian operations at this stage was, whether it was to capture Lahore, which they later denied – its occupation would certainly have presented them with major problems – or merely, by threatening it, to draw Pakistani forces away from Kashmir and inflict such casualties on them that they would abandon their aggressive intentions. Unlike India, Pakistan was almost wholly dependent on external sources of military supply and therefore less able to face heavy expenditure of material. Whatever may have been her aim, and it appears more likely that each side was merely reacting to the other without any very clear aim, India's next move was another diversionary threat farther north, aimed at Sialkot, to relieve pressure on the Jammu sector and threaten Pakistan herself in that area. India had built up a corps of four divisions there, three infantry and one armoured, under General Dunn. Two days before Pakistan launched her counter-attack at Khem Karan, India's armoured division, commanded by General Rajinder (Sparrow) Singh, crossed the frontier south-east of Jammu, aimed at Phillaura, where it would cut the road from Sialkot to Zaffarabad. It had almost reached its objective on 8 September before it met opposition, which then built up over the next two days as Pakistan's 6th Armoured Division concentrated against it. The tanks of the two sides clashed on 11 September, and fighting continued in this area for the next two weeks, in which some 400 tanks altogether were involved, each side losing about fifty. While the tanks fought each other round Phillaura, the infantry divisions attempted to clear the approaches to Sialkot on both flanks, coming up against determined opposition which kept them from approaching nearer than 4,000 yards from Sialkot itself. The only other area of operations was the desert of Rajasthan, where some inconclusive skirmishing took place which had no effect on the main battles.

Meanwhile international pressure for the fighting to cease was mounting, the most effective being the British and American Governments' decision to cut off all military supplies to both sides. The Soviet Union did not follow suit, although it added its pressure for a cease-fire. The military of both sides realized that they could not afford to continue to lose equipment at the rate that operations of this nature involved, and that neither had the degree of superiority over the other to make it possible to reach a quick decision. On 6 September the UN Security Council had passed a resolution calling for a cease-fire and the withdrawal of forces to the 1949 cease-fire line, and U Thant, the Secretary-General, had been active in trying to persuade both sides to implement it. It was only when a position of stalemate had been reached in the Sialkot sector that both sides were prepared to consider it. On 19 September Krushchev had invited Shastri and Ayub to meet within the Soviet Union, probably at Tashkent. Next day the Security Council passed another resolution demanding a cease-fire on 22 September and subsequent withdrawal to the positions that had been occupied before 5 August, after which the Council would consider 'what steps could be taken to assist towards a settlement of the political problem underlying the present conflict'. India accepted the resolution for a cease-fire and withdrawal, but not for the political settlement. Anti-American riots in Pakistan protested against acceptance, and it was not until the very minute that the Council's ultimatum expired that her Foreign Minister Zulfikar Ali Bhutto, at the end of a long impassioned speech, unexpectedly announced Ayub's acceptance 'in the interests of international peace', protesting that the resolution was 'unsatisfactory'.

Casualties on both sides, of which the figures are unreliable, appear to have been about the same, a total of 12,000, of whom about 3,000 were killed. Both sides appear to have lost about 200 tanks each, with another 150 out of action but repairable, although Pakistan's losses may have been slightly higher. India lost about seventy aircraft and Pakistan twenty, their navies hardly having been engaged at all. In terms of their total populations, these losses were of course very small, the effect on their armoured forces and on their stocks of ammunition and spare parts being the most significant. Although both sides accepted the cease-fire, it was some time before they withdrew their forces, both being subject to considerable internal pressures and neither wishing to abandon a bargaining counter, the United Nations appearing helpless to enforce its resolution and China stepping up pressure in late November and early December by activity in the Tawang Tract and in Ladakh. Krushchev renewed his invitation to a meeting in Tashkent, which, after considerable pressure had been applied, both Ayub and Shastri accepted. From 4 to 10 January 1966 Krushchev worked hard to force them into an agreement which accepted withdrawal to the pre-5 August positions, promised that their relations with each other would be conducted on a 'good neighbourly' basis and that disputes would be settled by peaceful means. The central problem, that of Kashmir, was covered by the anodyne phrase: 'It was against this background that Jammu and Kashmir was discussed, and each of the sides set forth its respective position.'

That very night Shastri died of a heart attack, his place being taken by Mrs Gandhi. The effect of the war had been to strengthen the right-wing element of the Congress Party and to reinforce those who supported the strengthening of India's military position. The embargo on arms supplies, imposed by Britain and America while hostilities lasted and maintained until the UN resolution was complied with, had already encouraged Pakistan to turn more to China for arms and India to accelerate her own arms production and turn more also to the Soviet Union. While in many ways the war strengthened India, it weakened Pakistan. In 1965 she had been on the crest of a wave, militarily, economically, but less so politically, based primarily on the results of ten years of military and economic aid from the United States, the great bulk of it applied for the benefit of West Pakistan. The failure of her attempt to solve the Kashmir problem, and the estrangement from the United States which it brought about, produced a reaction against Ayub and his government, particularly in East Pakistan, which saw its interests, among them good relations with India, sacrificed to Ayub's military ambitions and obsession with Kashmir. These tensions grew and led in 1969 to Ayub's supersession by another general, Yahia Khan, and to the mounting popularity in East Pakistan of Sheikh Mujibur Rahman and his Awami League, who demanded a greater degree of independence from Rawalpindi.

Matters came to a head as a result of the elections which Yahia, in response to popular pressure, had agreed to hold in December 1970. The Sheikh won an overwhelming victory in East Pakistan, giving his Awami League a majority in the Pakistan National Asembly, Bhutto's People's Party coming second. The implications of this for West Pakistan were more than Yahia could face. When Bhutto announced that his party would boycott the Assembly, Yahia, on 1 March 1971, postponed its opening indefinitely. This predictably led to violent demonstrations in East Pakistan, Yahia's reaction to which was to declare martial law and reinforce the army there, until it reached a strength of forty-two battalions, organized in three divisions, in addition to para-military forces of 25,000. The repressive regime which first General Tikka Khan and then General Niazi Khan imposed, including a deliberate campaign of eliminating the educated Bengali from all positions of influence, if not from life itself, started a movement of refugees into India, which developed into a flood. It also swelled the ranks of the Awami League's militant resistance organization, the Mukti Fouj, later renamed the Mukti Bahini.

The Awami League and its militant supporters had for some time received help from fellow Bengalis in India. In May Mrs Gandhi decided that, if Yahia Khan could not be persuaded by political pressures to remove his stranglehold on East Pakistan, with the serious implications it had for Indian Bengal, invaded by a flood of refugees, she must be prepared to use military force in support of the Mukti Bahini; but the time for it was not then ripe. India's armed forces, which normally looked primarily westward and secondarily northward to fight in very different terrain from that of East Pakistan, would have to be prepared and redeployed for a very different campaign from any for which they had hitherto planned: the Mukti Bahini would have to be built up and trained to prepare the ground and spearhead action, if they could not carry it off entirely by themselves; and the threat of Chinese intervention would have to be minimized, partly by diplomatic action and partly by waiting until winter had set in on the mountain passes, which would also be the most suitable weather for operating in East Pakistan.

The Indian Army in 1971 had about 825,000 men, organized into one armoured, thirteen infantry and ten mountain divisions and a number of independent brigades. Her tank strength had been increased since 1965 by the acquisition of 450 Russian T55 and T56 tanks and the production of 300 of the Vickers Vijayanta tank, less thickly armoured but carrying the same powerful 105 mm. gun as their British Centurions. The Air Force had increased its combat strength to 625 aircraft, including seven squadrons of Russian MIG21s, the rest being Russian Sukhoi 7s, British Canberras and Hunters and Indian-produced Gnats. The Navy had also been strengthened, built around the aircraft-carrier *Vikrant*. Pakistan had two armoured and twelve infantry divisions and one independent armoured brigade, two other divisions being in the process of formation to replace in the west those deployed to East Pakistan. Her air force had fourteen fighter and three bomber squadrons, but only one squadron of Sabre fighter-bombers was deployed to East Pakistan, as was one regiment of fifty tanks, all of them light.

As Yahia's repressive policy took effect, most of the 70,000 locally recruited armed men in the army and the para-military police and border forces deserted to the Mukti Bahini and had to be replaced by soldiers from West Pakistan, so that by October, with the exception of some men from non-Bengali minorities, mostly Bihari, all the armed men acting for the Pakistan

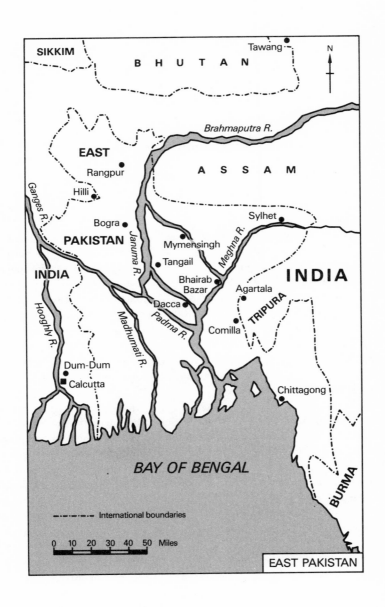

SIKKIM

B H U T A N

Tawang

N

Brahmaputra R.

EAST

Rangpur

A S S A M

Hilli

Ganges R.

Bogra

Sylhet

PAKISTAN

Janurna R.

Mymensingh

Meghna R.

Tangail

INDIA

Bhairab
Bazar

INDIA

Agartala

Dacca

TRIPURA

Hooghly R.

Madhumati R.

Padma R.

Comilla

Dum-Dum

Calcutta

Chittagong

BAY OF BENGAL

BURMA

International boundaries

0   10   20   30   40   50   Miles

EAST PAKISTAN

Government in East Pakistan came from the West. The Mukti Bahini hoped to achieve their aim of an independent Bangladesh by bringing the economy to a halt and killing Pakistani soldiers. In the early months most of their activities took place near the frontier with India and were carried out by small groups. By July they had increased their numbers and operated in larger bodies well into the heart of the country, the forested area north of Dacca playing the same part for them as the 'War Zones' north of Saigon had for the Vietcong. Meanwhile refugees poured over the borders into India, particularly into West Bengal. By August, the month in which Indira Gandhi signed a treaty with the Soviet Union, the total had risen to six million out of a population of seventy-five, and was eventually to rise to fifteen. This posed an intolerable problem to the Indian Government. By November it was leading to frequent incidents on the border in West Bengal as more and more Pakistani troops were deployed to deal with the Mukti Bahini. As a result of incidents in that month at Boyra and Hilli, both sides announced that their forces would be authorized to cross the frontier 'in self-defence'.

Yahia Khan's reaction to Indian support of the Mukti Bahini and the deployment of her forces not only to the areas surrounding East Pakistan, but also to strengthen their army in the Punjab, was to embark on a rash repetition of previous threats to the Indian position in Kashmir. At 5.45 p.m. on 3 December the Pakistan Air Force made a number of ineffective attacks on seven Indian Air Force airfields, the Indian Air Force retaliating that night and next day on eight Pakistan Air Force airfields with more effect. At the same time an Azad Kashmir force crossed the cease-fire line and attacked Poonch, while regular Pakistani forces attacked in the Chamb sector to cut the Kashmir road at Akhnur and also a post covering the Hussainiwalla bridge over the Sutlej River west of Ferozepore in the southern Punjab. None of these attacks were successful, and a few days later the Indians retaliated in a series of operations both in Kashmir and in the Punjab which were limited to straightening and securing the frontier positions, making them more economical to defend. The attack at Chamb led to a fierce battle which lasted for a week, by which time Pakistan had deployed four brigades and three tank battalions in a fruitless frontal attack, losing 3,000 men and nearly fifty tanks in the process. India's reaction to this had been to counter-attack farther east at the point where the border of Jammu joins that of the Punjab. This led to another tank battle on 15 and 16 December, as the Indian attack approached Zafarwal, Pakistan losing forty-five Pattons and India fifteen Centurions.

While these operations of limited aim and scope had been taking place on the borders of West Pakistan, more dramatic events had occurred in the East. The problem facing Pakistan's General Niazi Khan was a difficult one. The country was entirely surrounded by India, except for the sea area of the Bay of Bengal, in which the Indian Navy was dominant. Almost all of the forces available to him were widely deployed, mostly near the frontiers, attempting to suppress a subversive movement which was supported by the overwhelming majority of the people as well as from across the borders by India, who could concentrate much superior forces to his on land, in the air and at sea. His main strength was concentrated in the west, because both the Mukti Bahini and the Indian Army were strongest there. Next in priority came the south-east, the vital communication links between the capital, Dacca, through Comilla to the port of Chittagong, threatened by the build-up of Indian forces in the adjacent Tripura area of southern Assam. This left very little to guard the long northern frontier and the area between the rivers which flowed southward through the length of the country.

The Indian forces surrounding East Pakistan were under General Aurora of Eastern Command in Calcutta. They were organized into three corps, II under General Raina in West Bengal with two divisions, XXXIII covering the northern frontier under General Thapar with the equivalent of two divisions, and IV under General Sagat Singh in Tripura with three. With the responsibility also of guarding the frontier of the North East Frontier Agency with China, General Aurora had 500,000 men under his command. Indira Gandhi was in Calcutta when Pakistan launched her attacks on 3 December. This gave her the justification she needed for military intervention in East Pakistan, and orders were given that night from New Delhi, to which she had returned, for Aurora to put his plan into effect. It is possible that she had already decided on action, and that Pakistan had information of this and decided herself to attack from West Pakistan to forestall it. Aurora's plan was an imaginative and bold one. The accent was to be on speed, and Pakistani positions were to be by-passed and left to be contained either by the Mukti Bahini or by follow-up troops. With the mass of water obstacles, large and small, emphasis was laid on independence of roads, troops and their supporting arms making their way across country, guided and helped by the Mukti Bahini and the local populace. Every unit of army engineers that could be spared was made available. They would concentrate on providing essential bridges and ferries, movement of the material for which would be the top priority task for Indian Air Force helicopters. II Corps' objective was to advance as quickly as possible to the Padma River, and from there thrust on to the Madhumati, thus cutting off the Pakistani division in the south-west of the country. XXXIII Corps had two tasks. The bulk of its forces were to invade the north-western bulge north of Hilli and cut off the other Pakistani division west of the Januma River in that area. A smaller force of one brigade would cross the frontier from Western Assam, heading for Mymensingh, and then south between the Januma and Brahmaputra Rivers. IV Corps was to invade the east in three widely separated divisional thrusts, the northern to Sylhet, turning south from there, the central from Agartala, taking the shortest route to Dacca, crossing the Meghna River at Bhairab Bazar, and the southern cutting off Chittagong from the north. All these corps attacks were successful, the strongest resistance being made to the xxxiii Corps attack in the north-west and the iv Corps invasion in the north-east; but this did not hold up the advance of their spearheads. Enthusiastically provided by the local population with information and willing hands to help move their supplies and weapons across the fields, and never in danger of a counter-attack, they were able to take risks which would have been military folly in a more conventional setting. The Indian Air Force had also established total air superiority and gave unrestricted transport and strike support to the army on the ground. Meanwhile the navy attacked Chittagong with its aircraft and sealed off access to the ports, turning away shipping of all natures.

On 6 December Mrs Gandhi announced that India recognized the independence of Bangladesh, while President Nixon blamed her for deepening the crisis and broadening hostilities, despatching the 90,000-ton nuclear-powered aircraft-carrier *Enterprise*, with a naval task force from the Pacific Fleet, towards the Bay of Bengal. But the progress of Indian forces was too swift to be influenced by such gestures. By 11 December 11 Corps had reached the Madhumati, but had to wait there before they could cross. On 9 December iv Corps reached the Meghna, where two spans of the rail bridge over the mile-wide river had been destroyed, and by 11 December had sufficient troops on the far side to resume the advance to Dacca. xxxiii Corps had made less dramatic progress and was still some way from its two main objectives of Rangpur and Bogra; but it was on the operations of the small force under General Nagra in the northern sector that Aurora had his eye. The Pakistan brigade at Mymensingh, which his force, reinforced by a second brigade, was in the process of attempting to surround, was the only one that might now be able to escape, making its way south to join the garrison of Dacca. Aurora therefore decided to employ a parachute battalion to drop at Tangail, half-way down the road to Dacca, to prevent this. Taking off from Dum Dum airfield at Calcutta, they dropped in the afternoon of 11 December just in time to cut off the Pakistani brigade retreating from Mymensingh. After several attempts to fight their way through, the Pakistanis gave up, some surrendering, others disappearing into the countryside. Nagra decided to exploit the situation and pushed his forces rapidly southwards. Delayed for a time at Joydepur, they by-passed it by a new road not marked on their maps, and by the early morning of 16 December were in the western outskirts of Dacca, twelve days after the war had started. By this time Pakistani troops were surrendering all over the country and Niazi realized that the game was up. He had already asked for a cease-fire on 14 December through the American ambassador, and General Manekshaw, now Chief of the Indian Army Staff, on 15 December broadcast a message to say that only a surrender would be accepted. The US Government said that they would not act, unless Yahia Khan agreed to Manekshaw's demand. In the early hours of 16 December he did so, and, having given orders that there would be no air operations against the city,

General Aurora, with his naval and air force colleagues and the Chief of Staff of the Mukti Bahini, flew by helicopter to Dacca racecourse and there, at 4.31 p.m. received Niazi's signature to the surrender document, which his Chief of Staff had flown in three and a half hours before and presented to Niazi to initial. At 3 p.m. Nagra had entered Dacca with four battalions and received the surrender of General Ansari's 9th Pakistan Division.

This *blitzkrieg*, as it could truly be called, was a classic example of the application of Liddell Hart's theory of the expanding torrent, first pioneered by the German Army with its tactics of infiltration in the Ludendorff offensive on the Western Front in March 1918. It was a very differently conducted affair from other operations carried out by the Indian Army since 1947. The standard of professionalism in all three services had improved immensely since the débâcle of 1962, and considerable credit must be given to the heads of the three Indian armed services at the time, General Manekshaw of the army, Air Chief Marshal Lal of the air force and Admiral Nanda of the navy. They had done much personally in the preceding years to bring their forces up to the standards they had then reached; they worked well together; gave Indira Gandhi sound advice, receiving clear, firm decisions in return; and, having provided their subordinates with more than adequate tools with which to do the job, they did not interfere with the planning or the execution of their tasks. General Niazi in East Pakistan had all the odds weighted against him, and the morale of all ranks of his forces was in a poor state before operations began, as a result of being employed to impose a harsh, military regime on an alien and hostile population.

This last (at the time of writing) of India's wars solved one problem in the emergence of Bangladesh as a separate state, although that in itself has not lessened significantly the immense difficulties faced by that country. The previous wars could surely be said to have been totally unnecessary, unless they are seen as a purging process through which both countries had to go before they could accept the existence of the other as a fact of life, which had to be lived with and made the most of. To persist in an attitude of mutual hostility, leaving them both open to exploitation by outside interests, can only be regarded by an outsider as signal human folly. The recent outburst of extremist Islamic movements in Iran and Pakistan does not augur well for the future.

Given their populations and the size of their armed forces, their wars were very limited, although the forces employed were large in terms of other wars since 1945. They produced few important lessons in the strictly military field, but provided many cautionary tales about how not to behave in the politico-military sphere. In this story China came out best.

Chapter Twelve

ARAB–ISRAELI WARS

THE WAR OF INDEPENDENCE

There are those who would say that war between the Arabs and Israel has never ceased and that one cannot describe it in terms of separate wars. There is some truth in that, but there is a distinction between periods of open fighting and the times in between, when activity has been limited to the operations of terrorists and to retaliatory raids. Chapter 1 has already described what went on in Palestine, as it then was, before the United Nations resolution brought the British mandate to an end in 1948, leading to the establishment of the State of Israel. The first Arab–Israeli war started as that process got under way in the early months of the year. Israel refers to it as the War of Liberation or Independence. It opened with a series of unco-ordinated attacks by Arabs on isolated Jewish settlements, on Jewish buses and other vehicles on the roads and in areas where Jews and Arabs lived close to each other in the towns, as in Haifa and where Jaffa joined Tel Aviv. The Jewish military organization, Haganah, under David Ben Gurion and Israel Galili, with its mobile spearhead Palmach, under Yigal Allon, and the two extreme organizations, Irgun Zvai Leumi, directed by Menachem Begin, and LHI, the most militant leader of which was Zettler, had to decide how to react. Ben Gurion's policy was for Haganah to concentrate on protecting vulnerable and isolated settlements, while he built up support from outside the country, especially in the United States. Irgun wished to continue their campaign against the British, widening it to include the Arabs. They believed that the two were in collusion to bring about such a state of chaos that Britain would be persuaded to keep her forces in the country, while *de facto* handing it over to the Arabs. LHI went further and wished to fight against the concept of partition itself, widening its target to include the United Nations. As they reviewed their position, they had to consider their strength in armed men. It was not as great as their opponents often made it out to be. Haganah had a total strength of some 36,000, but only 400 of them were full time and there were not, at that time, arms for them all. It had 700 light and 200 medium machine-guns, 600 two-inch and 100 three-inch mortars; no armour, no air force, no artillery and not much ammunition. This figure included the 3,000 men of Palmach, but not all of them could be fully mobilized at the same time. Irgun had about 1,500 men and LHI perhaps half that. But they were not united, and up till March 1948 Haganah and Irgun were at times fighting each other.

If they were not united, neither were the Arabs, who were much less well prepared for hostilities. Here the main division was between the Emir Abdulla of Transjordan and the rest; but there were subsidiary divisions among the latter also. Abdulla already had his forces in the country. The Transjordan Frontier Force, a force raised by the British in Transjordan, was part of the British occupying forces stationed in Galilee, and the Arab Legion, Jordan's own army under Glubb, was also employed on guard duties in Arab areas. Abdulla, with the tacit agreement of Britain's Foreign Secretary, Bevin, assumed that, when the British forces left, his army would occupy the area allotted by the United Nations to the Arabs. This was not to the taste of the Mufti of Jerusalem nor of Egypt, Syria, the Lebanon and the Arab League which supported them. Egypt wished to secure southern Palestine for herself; Syria and the Lebanon both cast envious eyes on Galilee; the Mufti wanted to rule not only Jerusalem and the Arab area in the Judaean hills and Samaria, but an Arab state covering the whole of Palestine. Initially three forces were involved: a force led by Abdul Kader Husseini, a cousin of the Mufti and a respected Arab fighter, based on the area round Jerusalem, calling on all armed Arabs in the region; a motley force called the Arab Liberation Army, based in Galilee, led by a disreputable Lebanese soldier of fortune called Fawzi el Kaujki, based partly on Arabs living in the area and partly on volunteers from surrounding countries; and the Arab Legion, which, although under the orders of Abdulla, had to maintain correct relations with the British on whom they relied for supply. The British themselves initially tried to keep the peace between the two sides, but, as the date of their departure, 15 May, approached, they tended to stand aside and concern themselves only with their own security. The principal areas of tension, in which both sides sought to improve their positions at the expense of the other, were round Jerusalem, the road leading to it from Tel Aviv, especially where it entered the hills at Latrun, and in the plain of Esdraelon and Galilee. April 1948 saw fighting break out in all these areas. It was particularly fierce round Jerusalem, where the Jews were determined to maintain not only their position in the city, including the Jewish quarter of the Old City, but also in their settlements round it, particularly Neve Yaakov on the road leading in from the north and the Kafr Etzion group between Bethlehem and Hebron to the south, on Jordan's road link to the British in Egypt. There were hard fought battles at Kastel, in which Abdul Kader was killed, and at Deir Yassim, an attack by Irgun and LHI which resulted in the deaths of all the inhabitants, including women and children. Although Haganah had agreed to the attack, they dissociated themselves from what was widely regarded as a massacre. The fighting took place as Haganah managed to fight convoys through to Jerusalem and up to Kafr Etzion, although the Arabs held Latrun. Two days before the final departure of the British, the Arab Legion, who the British insisted must leave the country, attacked Kafr Etzion in order to clear the road to ensure the passage of their last supply convoy from the British base in Egypt. The Legion returned to Palestine on 16 May and occupied the area of Judaea and Samaria. Its

strength at that time was 4,500, but it had no reserves and no administrative backing, the latter having been provided by the British. Under the Arab League's arrangements Egypt sent 10,000 men to occupy southern Palestine, that is the Negev, which had been allotted by the United Nations to the Jews, and the Gaza strip, allotted to the Arabs; Syria sent a force of 3,000 and Lebanon one of 1,000 to reinforce Kaujki's Arab Liberation Army in the north, the Arabs having already been evicted by the Jews from Haifa and Tiberias and defeated at Acre and Safed, all of which the Jews now controlled, as they did Jaffa after a fierce battle in the last week of April. Iraq sent a force of 3,000 men who tried but failed to force a crossing of the Jordan at Beisan, close to where Moshe Dayan was defending the settlements of Degania against Syrian attack. Eventually the Iraqis took over northern Samaria from the Arab Legion, who were fully committed in and around Jerusalem and at Latrun.

The total of organized Arab forces was therefore only 21,500, much less than generally supposed. In addition the local Arabs were almost all armed, although they could not be relied upon to defend themselves against an organized Israeli attack. The Arabs themselves estimated the forces available to the Jews at 65,000, which was almost certainly on the high side, as they, like the Arabs, had a large proportion of their strength tied up in direct protection of their settlements and the areas they had occupied. But they had received considerable reinforcements both of men and even more so of weapons since the beginning of the year. The main source was Czechoslovakia and the supply route was organized through Austria and Italy.

The main battle, as soon as the mandate ended, was centred on Jerusalem and it raged for almost two weeks, all the Jewish fighting organizations, Haganah, Palmach, Irgun and LHI, being involved under the leadership of Haganah's Shaltiel, the Arab Legion opposing them in support of Arab irregulars. By the end of it the Arabs held the Old City, having evicted the Jews from their quarter of it, the approaches to it from the north and the area to the east, except for a Jewish enclave on Mount Scopus. By this time the Egyptian Army had occupied Hebron and reached Bethlehem, not at all warmly welcomed by the Jordanians. The centre of interest in the fighting then switched to the road from Tel Aviv to Jerusalem. In a succession of fierce engagements at Latrun the Arab Legion had clung on to this vital point, blocking access to Jerusalem from the coastal plain and forcing the Israelis to construct a new route by-passing it to the south.

While the fighting had been going on, the United Nations had been trying to bring about a cease-fire. They had appointed the Swedish Count Bernadotte as a mediator, and on 29 May the Security Council passed a resolution calling for a four-week truce to start on 11 June, the intention being that neither side should in any respect improve its position during that period. Both sides tried hard to do so before it came into effect and indeed afterwards, although both were glad of a breather.

The introduction of the cease-fire led to one remarkable incident. Irgun had organized a shipment of arms and ammunition from France. This was viewed with suspicion by Ben Gurion, who had wanted Irgun to be merged with Haganah into the new army, *Zahal*, to prevent them from setting themselves up as a rival force in the new Israel. Delays in the departure of the ship, the *Altalena*, meant that it would arrive during the truce – a clear breach of it. When Ben Gurion discovered that Begin was proposing to land the stores near Kafr Vitkin between Tel Aviv and Haifa on 20 June, Zahal was ordered to prevent it. Moshe Dayan's 89th Battalion was one of those involved in dealing with the Irgun force unloading the ship, which was then switched to Tel Aviv itself where Irgun was stronger. This led to a battle between the Palmach, led by Yigal Allon in Tel Aviv, and Irgun, in which the ship was set on fire and Begin only escaped by being thrown overboard.

The situation the truce had crystallized was that the Jews had roughly the area allotted to them under the UN partition plan, except for the Negev, and had established a very narrow corridor to the New City of Jerusalem, which they held. Half-way through the truce Bernadotte proposed a new plan: that the Arab areas should be united with Jordan and that Jordan, with them, should form a federal union with Israel. The union would handle economic affairs, foreign policy and defence, but in all other matters the two separate parts of the union would run their own affairs. Even if this plan had been acceptable to the Jews, which it was not, it was considered too favourable to Jordan to be acceptable to Egypt, Syria and Saudi Arabia. It was therefore rejected by the Arab League.

As soon as the truce ended on 9 July, the Palmach attacked Lydda and Ramleh, two Arab towns between Tel Aviv and Latrun. The Arab Legion had infiltrated a company into Ramleh two days before the truce had come into effect. The Legion could not however afford to reinforce the two towns sufficiently to defend them against a direct attack without endangering its position in the hills and thus risking its hold on Jerusalem, a decision for which Glubb came under sharp criticism from the Arabs. Moshe Dayan, commanding Zahal's 89th Commando Battalion, took a prominent and dramatic part in these operations. Having captured a Jordanian armoured car, he used it to take part in a daring dash through Lydda and Ramleh, which was instrumental in bringing about their rapid surrender. Zahal quickly followed up their success by attacking eastwards into the edge of the hills to try and capture or outflank Latrun, but were held by the Arab Legion at Latrun and at Beit Sira farther north. While this was going on, the Arabs improved their position slightly in Jerusalem. On 18 July Bernadotte managed to negotiate a further cease-fire, which lasted until shortly after he was murdered in Jerusalem by LHI on 17 September, an act which led to the disbandment of both Irgun's and LHI's forces and their absorption into Zahal. At the time he was murdered, the United Nations was preparing to consider his report, which recommended that the Negev, as primarily an Arab area and then occupied by the Egyptian Army, should be handed over to the Arabs rather than to the Jews, as had been proposed in the UN partition plan. Although the Egyptians had established a continuous defensive line from the coast, half-way between Gaza and Tel Aviv, eastward through Falluja to Hebron, several Jewish settlements had held out in the area to the south of them, maintained partly by air and partly by Zahal patrols which got through the Egyptian lines at night. During the truce supplies had been allowed to pass under United Nations supervision. As both the date for discussion of Bernadotte's plan and that of the American presidential election approached, Zahal began to concentrate forces in this area, and on 15 October, when the Egyptians fired on a convoy of supplies, the Israelis attacked. It was not until 20 October that they managed to break through. Once they did, they dashed on regardless of the risk to their flanks and rear. On the twenty-first they captured Beersheba, and next day they cut the road and railway just north of Gaza, forcing the Egyptians to withdraw. They then occupied all of the Negev except for a triangle in the south, where the Arab Legion held them fifty miles north of Eilat and the Gulf of Aqaba. A few days later the Israelis switched their effort to the north and drove the Lebanese and Syrian forces out of Galilee. At the end of the month the truce was renewed, an attempt by Britain and Chiang Kai-shek having failed to get the Security Council to authorize sanctions against both Egypt and Israel if they did not withdraw from positions they might occupy as a result of breaches of the truce. It held until 22 December when fighting flared up again between Falluja, where an Egyptian garrison was isolated, and their main position near Gaza. Inconclusive fighting went on for two weeks, after which negotiations began in Rhodes under the presidency of Dr Ralph Bunche of the United Nations. While these were going on, the Israelis attacked the Arab Legion in the southern Negev and secured the whole area up to the Egyptian frontier, including the port of Eilat. Syria was in the throes of a revolution and the Iraqis had already announced that they would leave Samaria on 13 March 1949. In return for agreement to the Arab Legion replacing the Iraqis, the Israelis extracted the cession of a small but significant strip all round the area. The final armistice with Jordan was signed on 3 April 1949, Israel having enlarged the area originally proposed for it under the UN partition plan by the whole of Galilee west of the Jordan and a corridor some five miles wide leading to Jerusalem, the proposal for the international control of which had foundered. The Arabs – in practice Jordan – were left in control of Judaea, Samaria and the Old City of Jerusalem. In May Israel and Jordan were recognized by the United Nations as independent states.

In this first of the Arab–Israeli wars, Israel had been fighting for her very existence, and her forces had shown remarkable qualities of determination, endurance, ingenuity, boldness and courage, qualities which they were to display in subsequent campaigns. Among their opponents only the Jordanian Arab Legion could claim any credit. At the start it numbered only 4,500 men, and by the end had no more than 10,000, by which time the strength of its allies in the field had risen to about 45,000. The idea that they greatly outnumbered the Israeli forces at that time is mistaken. The latter initially probably had about 50,000 men under arms and double that number by the end, but a large proportion of them was tied up in direct defence of their settlements. In spite of attempts by Glubb to paint a realistic picture before 15 May 1948, the Arab League had seriously underestimated the military capability of the Israelis and overestimated that of their own contingents and of the Arab irregulars in Palestine. In the end the Jordanian Arab Legion was left to face the Israelis alone. Neither side had much in the way of heavy or sophisticated weapons – a little field artillery, a few armoured cars and, at the end, a few aircraft also. The Israelis had acquired a number of half-tracked thinly armoured personnel carriers, of which they made good use; but it was primarily an infantry war, waged with infantry weapons.

A feature of the war that was to recur in future campaigns was that the fighting took place under international pressure for a cease-fire. In any case neither side could afford prolonged hostilities. The campaign therefore tended to consist of attempts both to secure what one had and rapidly to seize something more as bargaining counters when the cease-fire was agreed or imposed, a politico-military form of the game of Grandmother's Steps. This also was to be a feature of future campaigns.

THE SUEZ WAR

Peace was to prove elusive. While immigration doubled the Jewish population of Israel in a few years, the surrounding Arab countries and the Palestinian Arab refugees were not prepared to accept the state of Israel as a *fait accompli*. Their protest took the form of acts of terrorism and sabotage against Israel's settlements and individuals. Israel's reply was to carry out retaliatory raids over the border. Meanwhile she was turning her forces into a more conventional, professional body, particularly her air force. From 1953 onwards, when Moshe Dayan became Chief of Staff, the scale and ferocity of her retaliatory raids increased. This had the effect of strengthening the defences against them, so that she began to suffer casualties herself, and the value of such raids as a solution to the problem was questioned. At the same time it was becoming clear that Egypt at least was preparing for full-scale war. As long as Britain had kept her forces in the Suez Canal zone, Egypt was inhibited from this. But early in 1955 they left, and in September of that year Egypt concluded a large arms deal with Czechoslovakia and imposed a blockade of Israeli shipping in the Straits of Tiran, the southern end of the Gulf of Aqaba, as well as in the canal itself. Dayan wanted to respond by an operation to seize Sharm el Sheikh and establish control over the Straits, but Ben Gurion and his Cabinet would not agree. The latter feared that Egypt would retaliate with air attacks on Israeli cities and that Israel would be isolated internationally. Tolkowsky, Commander of the Israeli Air Force, was confident that he could prevent Egyptian air attacks, if he were allowed to carry out a pre-emptive strike against their airfields, but Ben Gurion was not prepared to initiate war without an ally. Nasser's announcement in July 1956 that he proposed to nationalize the Suez Canal provided the ally in the form of France, who had already supplied aircraft and other arms in March. In September the French informed the Israelis of the proposals that were being made for an Anglo–French operation, if other attempts to regain control over the canal failed. Almost continuous contact was maintained between the French Ministry of Defence and the Israelis through their military attaché in Paris, as the date for the

Anglo–French operation, known as *Musketeer*, was successively postponed, while negotiations continued over Dulles's abortive proposal for a Suez Canal Users Association. At the beginning of October Dayan appears to have suggested that Israel might make the first move, and Anglo–French discussions and plans were henceforward based on that assumption and that their D-day would be 31 October.

On 21 September Ben Gurion, Dayan and Shimon Peres went to France to finalize the plan, with the British also present for the first time. They firmly rejected the British proposal that, Israel having started the war, Britain and France would demand a cease-fire and send troops to intervene under the guise of peacemakers. Ben Gurion saw no reason why Israel should be branded as the aggressor and take all the risks. Dayan proposed a compromise which was accepted. Israel's initial action would take the form of an enlarged retaliatory raid. The fact that it would involve a parachute drop not far from the canal, at the Mitla Pass, would be regarded by Britain as an act of war threatening the canal, entitling her, under her recent agreement with Egypt, to occupy her civilianized base there. France meanwhile would allay Ben Gurion's fears by guaranteeing Israel against air attack and would also provide a naval bombardment to support Israeli attacks on Egyptian positions on the northern coast of Sinai. If the British and French failed to play their full parts initially, the raiding troops, one parachute battalion, could be withdrawn and the other operations, timed to coincide with the Anglo–French landing at Port Said, could be cancelled.

These were the considerations that lay behind Dayan's plan. He relied on the surprise and shock of his initial deep penetration, combined with first the threat and then the actual deployment of Anglo–French forces to bring about the complete collapse of the Egyptian position in Sinai. A second paratroop battalion, moving over land with supplies, was to join the first at the Mitla Pass, if possible within twenty-four hours, but certainly within forty-eight. Motorized columns would then drive west to the canal and south to Sharm el Sheikh, by-passing the Egyptian defences. Tanks were to be relegated to a secondary role as too slow and cumbersome and requiring too much logistic support. Their task would be to support the infantry attacks, where these were necessary, in the third phase of the operation, which was not due to be launched until the Anglo–French attack had started. This relegation of armour to a secondary role brought him into conflict with Laskov, the commander of the armour, who was not alone in thinking that Dayan's plan ran too great a risk. Dayan stuck to his plan, and at one minute to five o'clock in the afternoon of 29 October 1956 Sharon's paratroopers dropped at the eastern end of the Mitla Pass, over 100 miles into Sinai. At the same time two mobile columns, each 500 strong, crossed the frontier well to the south, one at Kuntilla, to drive west and join up with the parachute drop, the other at Ras el Nakeb near Eilat, to drive south for some 200 miles along the western shore of

the Gulf of Aqaba to Sharm el Sheikh. This action was announced to the world as engaging *fedayeen* units in Sinai in retaliation for what was described as 'Egyptian military assaults on Israeli transport on land and sea'. Egyptian reaction appeared to accept this and was limited to sending one brigade to occupy the Mitla Pass. Having done so, it made no attempt to advance beyond its eastern end for two days. They made no other move. Dayan's carefully designed plan now began to go astray as a result of the keenness of his subordinates. He had intended not to take any further offensive action until the night of 30 October and to leave the Egyptian positions on the north coast until the night after that, so that, if anything went wrong with the Anglo–French plan, he was not too far committed. However Colonel Simhoni had already launched his 7th Armoured Brigade on the morning of the thirtieth in an attack on the strong Egyptian position of Um Katef in the defensive complex of Abu Agheila. Dayan chased after it to stop it, but changed his mind when he caught up with them in the afternoon. Deciding to exploit the situation which had arisen as a result of disregard of his orders, he told the brigade to break off its attack, by-pass Um Katef and drive westward towards the canal opposite Ismailia. The armour was to be used in its primary role after all. At the same time he decided to bring forward by twenty-four hours the attack by the 10th Brigade against the Abu Agheila positions and by the 4th Brigade against those about twenty miles to the south of them at Kusseima. These two sets of Egyptian positions commanded the roads by which the 7th Armoured Brigade would have to be supplied. Having done so, he went back to see Ben Gurion and learnt from him that the Anglo–French attack had been postponed for twenty-five hours – a misunderstanding, as it had in fact been postponed for thirteen. Dayan was not as concerned as he might have been, as he was now confident that he could defeat the Egyptians in Sinai even without the help of the Anglo–French attack.

His optimism received a setback next morning when he found that the 10th Brigade had not achieved much. However the 4th had done better and captured its objectives. Dayan ordered it to move off south-west and open up the track to Nakhl in order to secure a supply route for Sharon, who now had two battalions at the east entrance to the Mitla Pass. It was Sharon's turn now to disobey orders. He had been told very firmly and clearly that he was not to try and capture the pass itself; but, wishing to improve his position and make it easier to defend against an attack by Egyptian tanks, and also feeling that his paratroopers could not just sit tight while others were advancing and gaining glory, he attacked the eastern end of the pass on the morning of the thirty-first and drove straight into a trap. A fierce battle ensued in which the whole brigade became involved and suffered 150 casualties, more than half of the total received in the whole campaign. There was little to show for it except for the 200 casualties inflicted on the Egyptian brigade.

Meanwhile both the 10th Brigade and the 37th Armoured Brigade, which had been sent to support it in its attack on Um Katef, were in a muddle and had not overcome the strong resistance being put up by the Egyptian garrison. While they continued their attempts to reduce it, Dayan began the assault on the Egyptian positions on the coast by a direct attack on Rafah with Bar-Lev's 27th Armoured Brigade, concentrating all his tanks to effect a breakthrough on the morning of 1 November. He was successful, and was ordered to move straight on westward to El Arish, which was captured early next day as the Egyptians withdrew. On the same day, 2 November, Israeli troops entered the

Gaza strip and on the following day completed the occupation of this area with its 60,000 Arab inhabitants and 200,000 Palestinian refugees. Two days later, early in the morning of 5 November, the Israeli column at last reached Sharm el Sheikh, the Egyptian garrison withdrawing northwards soon after they had been attacked, a few hours after British and French paratroopers dropped at Port Said. The Israelis had finished their war just as the British and French were starting theirs.

The latters' first move had been to issue an ultimatum to Israel and Egypt at 4.15 p.m. on 30 October to withdraw to ten miles each side of the canal within the next twelve hours, failing which Britain and France would establish themselves there. Israeli forces, of course, were not within ten miles of the canal at that time. Egypt predictably refused to comply. Israel therefore expected the British to start bombing Egyptian airfields at 4.30 a.m. on the thirty-first, but this was postponed as the RAF had planned night attacks. They started that night on twelve Egyptian airfields and went on for the next forty-eight hours. Nasser's reaction was to sink forty-seven old ships, filled with concrete, in the canal. Little but feverish diplomatic and political activity followed, while the Anglo–French armada steamed slowly on its way from Malta and Algiers. Fears that American and other political pressures would frustrate the whole operation before it had started, led to a change of plan by which the parachute drop would be brought forward and precede the seaborne landing by twenty-four hours. By this time the aim of the operation, which had originally included occupying Cairo, was limited to occupying the canal zone as rapidly as possible. Britain and France had been embarrassed by the speed of Israel's victory. The latter was inclined to accept a United Nations cease-fire before they had even got into action and secured the canal, the grand object of all their plotting, although the main aim of Eden and Mollet had been wider, to topple Nasser and teach Egypt a lesson; from Eden's point of view for his behaviour in the Middle East, from Mollet's for his suspected aid to the Algerian rebels.

At dawn on 5 November 600 British and 487 French paratroops dropped round Port Said, and twenty-four hours later, preceded by a naval bombardment, the amphibious landings began. There was little opposition and Port Said was fully secured by the afternoon. An armoured column immediately set off south down the west bank of the canal, preceded by patrols which were already only twenty-five miles from Suez. The column had reached a point the same distance south of Port Said when the commander heard the BBC news that Eden had accepted a UN cease-fire to be effective from midnight, although the French were keen to keep going.

The war had come to an end, in terms of casualties a cheap one. Egyptian dead totalled something between 2,500 and 3,000; Israeli, 200; British, 22; and French, 10. But in political terms it was disastrous for the British, serious for the French, negative for Israel; only positive for the loser in military terms,

Egypt. Under pressure from the United States and the United Nations, Britain and France left Port Said in December and Israel all of Sinai, except the Gaza strip and Sharm el Sheikh. Under further pressure and in return for a guarantee both of the security of her southern border by the presence of a United Nations force and of free access to the Red Sea through the Straits of Tiran, she withdrew in March 1957 from the Gaza strip and Sharm el Sheikh back to the frontiers from which she had embarked upon the adventure.

THE SIX-DAY WAR

For close on ten years the presence of the United Nations force in Sinai preserved peace on Israel's southern border. During that time the Arab world had been in turmoil with revolutions in Iraq, Libya, Syria and the Yemen, while Hussein in Jordan, at odds with his neighbours, had also to face internal troubles, chiefly caused by Palestinian refugees in his country. Yasser Arafat's Palestine Liberation Organization and its armed force, *Fatah*, had been gaining strength and support and had multiplied their acts of sabotage and terrorism in Israel, who retaliated by raids into Lebanon, Syria and the West Bank, defended by Jordan. As Nasser's political ambition to lead a union of all the Arab states met with successive setbacks, he turned increasingly to the idea of military victory to boost his standing. He received very large quantities of arms from Russia as well as advice and training. In spite of America's virtual intervention on his side in 1956, her influence with him was small. His intervention in the Yemen proved an embarrassing burden to him; but by the latter half of 1966 he felt himself strong enough to begin flexing his muscles and provoking a clash with Israel which he thought he could win, although it is doubtful if he expected it to develop into a war proper. Since the Ba'ath regime had come to power in Syria in February of that year, incidents between Israel and Syria had intensified and Fatah had also stepped up its activities. A particularly fierce Israeli retaliation against the village of Sanur, south of Hebron, in November was exploited to stir up Arab resentment, although none of his neighbours had any real sympathy for Hussein. It was after the visit of the Soviet Foreign Minister, Gromyko, to Egypt in March 1967 that war clouds really began to gather. In April there were serious clashes on land and in the air between Israel and Syria, and the Russians actively spread rumours that Israel intended to develop a full-scale attack on that country. Both Egypt and Iraq made public show of promising their support. On 16 May Syria mobilized her forces and Nasser insisted that the UN force, commanded by General Rikhye, should abandon its posts in Sinai, including Sharm el Sheikh, and concentrate in the Gaza strip. When Rikhye refused to withdraw his posts, Egyptian troops just pushed them aside, until two days later U Thant, the UN Secretary-General, ordered him to comply, although a detachment was left at

Sharm el Sheikh. These events naturally caused consternation in Israel, which began its mobilization, as Egypt did also, Libya and the Sudan having now promised their support.

On 23 May, with U Thant actually in Cairo, Nasser, his troops now at Sharm el Sheikh, declared a blockade of the Straits of Tiran, free passage through which the United Nations and America, Britain and France separately had assured Israel would be maintained when she was forced to withdraw from Sharm el Sheikh ten years before. Although various schemes for joint action by Britain and the United States were mooted, other nations were not prepared to become involved, and it soon became clear to Israel that nothing was going to be done. While Russia was adding her own private warnings to Nasser not to take military action and the United States was saying the same to Israel, pressures mounted on the Israeli Prime Minister, Eshkol, to take a firmer line and to accept Moshe Dayan as Defence Minister. Dayan had resigned as Chief of Staff in 1958 and turned to politics as a supporter of Ben Gurion. From 1959 to 1964 he had been Minister of Agriculture under Eshkol, but had then resigned. He had remained in the political wilderness and for a time, in 1966, had been a war correspondent in Vietnam.

On 1 June Jordan reluctantly joined the Arab military alliance and agreed to allow an Iraqi division into her country. This may have provided the final spur to Eshkol to agree, as he did next day, to Moshe Dayan taking over defence. To everyone's surprise Dayan's first announcement on 3 June made it appear that he favoured a continuation of the diplomatic dialogue; but that evening he told his colleagues that he believed that Egyptian forces in Sinai could be defeated at a probable cost of a thousand dead, and that a preemptive strike against the Arab air forces would knock them out and guarantee Israel against air attack. Arab provocation had been such that striking the first blow would not antagonize the United States, and he was confident that Russia would not intervene directly. Within the frontiers to which she was limited at that time, Israel could not afford to let her adversaries strike the first blow. Having listened to him and to reports by the Chief of Staff, General Rabin, the Chief of Intelligence, General Yariv, and the Commander of the Air Force, General Hod, his colleagues agreed to go to war.

The first and the most decisive blow of the war was the air strike against the Egyptian airfields, simultaneously executed at a quarter to eight in the morning of Monday 5 June 1967. That time was chosen because the Egyptian dawn alert would have stood down, the Israeli pilots would have been able to have a decent night's sleep and the early morning mist in the Nile delta would have cleared. In successive attacks lasting for nearly three hours, the Israeli Air Force destroyed some 300 out of about 340 of Egypt's serviceable and 450 total combat aircraft, including all of her long-range bombers. It was then free to go for the other Arab air forces. By the end of the second day, 6 June, the Israeli Air Force with some 250 combat aircraft, of which about 150 were modern

fighters, in more than a thousand sorties, had destroyed 60 Syrian, 29 Jordanian, 17 Iraqi and 1 Lebanese aircraft in addition to the 309 Egyptian, most of
them destroyed on the ground, for a loss of 26 aircraft of their own, some of
which were lost attacking army targets. They had also knocked out 23 Egyptian radar stations and several surface-to-air missile (sam) sites, 16 of them in
Sinai. Nasser could not believe or did not wish it to be thought that these losses
had been inflicted only by the Israeli Air Force, and fabricated allegations that
the United States and Britain had participated.

We must now turn to what the army was doing. Egypt had reinforced her
army in Sinai in the last weeks of May, bringing it from a strength of 35,000 to
one of 80,000 men. General Murtagi, its commander, had five infantry
divisions, one armoured, the 4th, and an additional light armoured division,
known as Shazli Force. One was the so-called 20th Palestine Division which
defended the Gaza strip north of Khan Yunis. West of it was the 7th Infantry
holding Rafah and El Arish, while the 2nd held the important defences round
Abu Agheila and Kusseima, covering the routes into Central Sinai, leading to
Ismailia and the Bitter Lakes. Some twenty to thirty miles behind it the 3rd
Division held reserve position at Jebel Libni and Bir Hassana. The 6th
Division covered the Pilgrim's Way, leading from Aqaba and Eilat to Suez,
with positions at Kuntilla and Nakhl. The two armoured divisions were in
reserve, the 4th, a strong division equipped with the newest Soviet tanks,
between the 7th Division on the coast and the 2nd farther south, while Shazli
Force of some 200 tanks was north of the 6th Division and had the task of
moving rapidly east into the Negev to cut Israel off from Eilat and link up with
Jordan at Aqaba. Including the tank units incorporated in infantry divisions,
the Egyptians had some 950 tanks in Sinai.

The Israeli troops in its Southern Command under Brigadier-General
Gavish were formed into three groups or *Ugda*. The most northerly was
commanded by Brigadier-General Tal, the commander of the armoured
corps. He had two armoured brigades totalling some 300 tanks, but only one
battalion in each had modern tanks, one of them British Centurions and the
other American Pattons. Tal also had a parachute brigade. His task was to
deal with the Egyptian defences near the coast. Sharon's Ugda, of one
armoured brigade with some 200 tanks and one infantry brigade, was to deal
with the defensive complex round Abu Agheila, while Yoffe's Ugda, of two
armoured brigades, each of 100 tanks, all Centurions, was to advance through
an area of sand dunes between Tal and Sharon and be prepared to help out
either of them by outflanking their opponents. An infantry brigade in the north
and two armoured brigades farther south would be available in reserve.

When Dayan took over as Defence Minister, he found two alternative plans
prepared. The first, favoured by Eshkol and Rabin, envisaged little more than
an extended raid as far as Jebel Libni and Bir Hassana, some fifty miles into
Sinai, the territory being held as a hostage in return for lifting the blockade of

the Straits of Tiran. The other, proposed by Gavish, was more ambitious, but still limited to an advance only as far as the Gidi and Mitla Passes. Dayan supported the latter, but opposed pressure from some officers for an advance right up to the canal. He thought that to go as far as that would not only arouse international opposition, but would make it impossible for Nasser to come to terms. The general expectation was that the war would last about three weeks. Only when the situation in Sinai had been secured, was Dayan prepared to release resources to his Central Command to improve the position in Judaea and Samaria and around Jerusalem, and he did not wish to complicate matters by getting involved in hostilities with Syria. However, greatly helped by the overwhelming victory of the Israeli Air Force, events turned out more success-fully and moved more rapidly than expected, and he was swept forward on the tide of victory.

At 8.15 a.m. on the morning of 5 June, half an hour after the attacks on the Egyptian airfields, Tal attacked the Gaza strip at Khan Yunis, a few miles east of Rafah, with his tanks leading. His plan, once he had penetrated, was to turn the defences from the north and then advance westward along the roads used by the Egyptians themselves in order to avoid minefields. Although his initial break-in cost him dear, it was successful, and he was soon into the Egyptian artillery positions and pushing westward along the coast. By the end of the day he was already in contact with Egyptian positions defending El Arish.

Nearly forty miles farther south Sharon's Ugda crossed the frontier at 9 a.m. Optimistic as always, Sharon thought that by a rapid direct assault he could bounce the Egyptians out of Um Katef, which had proved a hard nut to crack in 1956. He should have known better and he had to revise his plans. Leaving his artillery in position, he moved his force round the northern flank of the defences and attacked Abu Agheila from the north without success. Sharon had to think again, which he did quickly. Flying in a battalion of his own beloved paratroopers by helicopter after dark, he launched an attack from the rear shortly after midnight. By dawn on 6 June the position was in his hands and the route open for an advance westward on the roads leading to the Gidi and Mitla Passes.

While Tal and Sharon had been battling against the Egyptian defences, Yoffe had slipped between them and his leading brigade, making slow progress through the sand dunes, reached the road leading from El Arish to Abu Agheila at Bir Lahfan by the end of the day, thus blocking any movement of Egyptian reserves between their two main positions. This brigade spent the night uncomfortably close to the much stronger Egyptian 4th Armoured Division, but fortunately the latter made no move. Yoffe had to wait for his second brigade to join up until Sharon had secured Abu Agheila and cleared the route through it. However Tal was able to divert one of his brigades from the southern outskirts of El Arish to attack the Egyptian position at Bir Lahfan from the north, where it had secured El Arish airfield.

Although fighting was still going on at the important Jeradi Pass east of El Arish and in the Gaza strip east of Rafah, Tal's forces had surrounded El Arish itself. By 11 a.m. Tal's and Yoffe's situation was good enough for the decision to be taken for Yoffe's brigades, with one of Tal's and a second in reserve, to thrust farther west along the Central Route leading to Ismailia to deal with the reserve Egyptian position at Jebel Libni. They were in contact with this in the early afternoon and captured the airfield, but not the main Egyptian positions to the north of it. Yoffe's brigade was ordered to by-pass the defences and drive on south-west to Bir Hassana on the Southern Route, leaving Tal to deal with Jebel Libni later.

Back at Abu Agheila Sharon, soon after dawn, had captured the main position of Um Katef and cleared it sufficiently to let Yoffe's second brigade through, although, even by the end of the day, all resistance had not ceased. However Sharon's tanks were free to be switched south to deal with the Egyptian defences at Kusseima, covering the Southern Route. His men were tired and in need of reorganization and replenishment. By 5 p.m. he had still not attacked and was waiting for a second armoured brigade to reinforce him, when he received orders to move off to the south-west instead in order to deal with Shazli Force. By this time the Israelis had intercepted the order given by the Egyptian commander in Sinai, General Murtagi, to all his forces to withdraw to a line about fifty miles east of the canal, covering the passes leading to it. He had now realized that all hope of air support had vanished, while his positions were being heavily attacked by the Israeli Air Force, whose support had greatly helped the Israeli operations in Sinai that day.

Although Israeli prospects in Sinai looked good, they had problems elsewhere. Dyan and Rabin therefore had some reservations about immediate exploitation. They centred round the battle for Jerusalem. At the outbreak of the war they had hoped to persuade Jordan to keep out of it, in spite of Hussein's pact with Nasser, his agreement to the entry of an Iraqi division into his country and to a joint command, under the Egyptian General Riad, of his own, the Iraqi and the Syrian forces involved. But after the initial Israeli air attacks on Egypt, Riad gave orders for his forces to go into action against Israel, and Jordanian artillery began to shell Israeli areas of Jerusalem and other areas farther north. After further messages to Hussein and an appeal by the UN General Odd Bull for a cease-fire round Jerusalem, the shelling continued and by mid-day on 5 June the Israelis decided to retaliate. One of their earliest and most effective blows was that by the Israeli Air Force which wiped out the Jordanian Air Force and neutralized the Iraqi brigade which had arrived in Jordan as the advanced guard of its division.

The Israeli commander in the Jerusalem area was Brigadier-General Narkiss. His first concern was with the isolated Jewish area of Mount Scopus and the UN area round Government House just to the south of it. The forces available to him were an infantry brigade and an armoured brigade in the plain, and he was later given the parachute brigade which had been earmarked for the capture of El Arish. By the end of the second day, after some fierce fighting in which the Israelis suffered significant casualties, Narkiss had cut the roads leading into Jerusalem from the north and south, had captured Latrun and therefore cleared the main route from the west, and, at the very end of the day, had also taken Ramallah farther north. However he had still not secured the important Augusta Victoria ridge between Mount Scopus and Government House, which commanded both of them as well as the Old City from the east, and the noise of tanks had been heard moving on the Jerusalem–Jericho road, which it was assumed was the 60th Jordanian Armoured Brigade coming into action. Farther north in Samaria Brigadier-General Peled, with a force initially of one infantry and one armoured brigade, later to be increased to two of each, had made some gains round Jenin, but had been brought to a halt by the Jordanian 40th Armoured Brigade, which, on General Riad's orders, had on the first day been moved down to Jericho, but then ordered back north again.

If Dayan and Rabin had known what was going on on the other side of the Jordanian hill, they need not have worried. The total lack of air cover had persuaded the Syrians that they were not prepared to invade Galilee. The Iraqis' one brigade had been virtually knocked out by air attack and the rest of the division had not arrived. Jordan's two armoured brigades had wasted the first day and most of the second in a fruitless manoeuvre based on General Riad's optimistic plan to send one of them south to Hebron to link up with an Egyptian force, which he had assumed would be advancing to meet it, while the other moved south to replace it near Jericho. This was on the assumption that its place would have been taken by the Iraqi brigade and that Syrian pressure would remove a threat to northern Samaria. This plan had collapsed, the situation round Jerusalem looked serious and that in Sinai worse still; so General Riad, after consulting the Egyptian Chief of Staff, Field-Marshal Hakim Amer, decided that all Jordanian forces should be withdrawn to the east bank of the Jordan. Hussein, seeing this as depriving him of the West Bank, which he was unlikely to be able to recover, and suspecting that there were political motives behind it, was reluctant to agree. At 10 o'clock that night Riad gave the order, and the Jordanian brigades had started to implement it when a cease-fire call by General Odd Bull, ignored in fact by both sides, caused some Jordanian units to stay where they were.

The situation therefore at the beginning of the third day, 7 June, was more favourable to the Israelis than they appreciated. It was to be a day of decision on all fronts. At dawn the force at Jebel Libni, one armoured brigade of Tal's and one of Yoffe's under Tal's command, attacked the main position and, supported by strong air attack, soon had it in their hands, the Egyptian garrison making off to the west. Tal pressed on westward down the Central Route, intent on gaining the Khatmia Pass. By half-past three that afternoon his leading brigade had reached Bir Gifgafa, another airfield and an important military base not far from the pass. An hour and a half later Tal reached the eastern approaches to the pass just as the remnants of the Egyptian 4th Armoured Division did so from the south. A fierce tank battle ensued, in which both sides suffered significant casualties, the bulk of the Egyptian division succeeding in getting away through the pass. Farther north the Israeli Northern Force had entered El Arish and was speeding westward along the Northern Route, meeting no opposition. The Egyptian forces they did come across just got out of their way. In the Gaza strip a brigade of the Palestinian Division held out in Khan Yunis for some time, but by the end of the day the whole area was in Israeli hands.

South of Tal, Yoffe was heading for the Gidi and Mitla Passes with the principal aim of cutting off Shazli Force, if it escaped the clutches of Sharon. As he did so, his brigades found themselves mixed up with Egyptian forces acting on Murtagi's orders of the previous day to withdraw, the situation being further confused by the fact that the tanks of both sides were often the same, British Centurions. There was little organized resistance. Both his brigades had a brief battle in the middle of the day with an Egyptian force at Bir Hassana, twenty miles south of Jebel Libni; but thereafter fuel supply was the main problem. With that and mechanical problems his tank strength was falling very low. Fortunately an Egyptian fuel dump was found at Bir Thamada, twenty miles from the Mitla Pass, which his leading tanks reached, some of them out of fuel, just as an Egyptian column, mainly from their 6th Division which had been defending the Southern Route, reached it, most of the column getting away down the pass. While Yoffe was reorganizing his forces during the night in order to have enough tanks at both the Mitla and Gidi Passes to hold them securely, a considerable number of Egyptian vehicles managed to get through the latter.

While Tal and Yoffe had had a good day, Sharon had not been so fortunate. Having by-passed Kusseima and set off south to find Shazli, Sharon stopped for the night to rest his weary troops. In the morning he was held in case his force might be needed after all to help in the attack on Kusseima, due to be launched by another brigade. It was some time in the morning before it was realized that Kusseima had in fact been evacuated during the night, and Sharon was told to set off again after Shazli. The going was not good and progress was slow. At one stage his tanks were fired on by some of Yoffe's that were farther east than they were meant to be, and after dark his leading troops hit a minefield and were fired on twenty miles north-east of Nakhl, his objective on the Southern Route. Unable to find a way round the minefield, he decided to stop for the night, refuel and start again at dawn. While he had been moving south, Shazli had slipped away behind him, heading for the passes. Farther south still an airborne attack had been planned to capture Sharm el Sheikh, but it was cancelled when air reconnaissance showed that the 1,000 strong Egyptian garrison had evacuated it. The first Israeli troops there were sailors from three motor torpedo-boats, who landed at dawn, followed up later by a force which landed on the airfield. The Egyptian withdrawal had been occasioned primarily by shortage of water, as the UN force had destroyed the desalination plant when they had left. In the afternoon a small Israeli force was taken on by helicopter to occupy the oilfield area at Al Tur and Abu Durba in the Gulf of Suez.

The war was still not over in Sinai, but the withdrawal of Jordan's forces to the east bank meant that there was nothing to stop the Israelis from occupying the whole area west of the river, which they quickly proceeded to do, the scene at the Wailing Wall as they entered the Old City of Jerusalem being one of deep emotion. In Sinai action centred on the frantic attempts of Murtagi's forces to escape through the passes and across the canal. At the start of 8 June, the fourth day of the war, Israeli troops on the Northern Route were at Romani only forty miles from the canal at Kantara. At first they were quite severely attacked by the Egyptian Air force, while they fought a battle lasting until 10 o'clock against an Egyptian blocking position which included Russian T55 tanks. Then the Israeli Air Force came to help them and they pushed on until they came up against the next position, twelve miles from Kantara. With strong air support, the parachute brigade leading the advance managed to overcome the opposition, and, surviving a counter-attack by tanks when they were only four miles from the canal, they reached it soon after dark, moving north during the night to try and prevent the Egyptians from getting their tanks away over the El Firdan bridge.

Tal's main concern was to block the Khatmia Pass on the Central Route. His forces at the eastern end were not strong enough to stop a considerable number of Egyptian vehicles from getting through during the night, and, when he advanced towards the pass in the morning, he found the Egyptians strongly posted, supported by about a hundred tanks sited in depth on either side of the road, so that they could bring enfilade fire against any advance into the pass. The Israeli tanks carried out a methodical fire-fight against each successive position throughout the day until, after some six hours, they had destroyed forty Egyptian tanks for a loss of only two of their own, a remarkable tribute to their superior skill in tank gunnery. As it got dark, the Egyptians began to withdraw and, in so doing, their vehicles became jammed head to tail in the pass, where they were slaughtered by the Israeli Air force, whose attacks were largely responsible for the congestion. Tal now wished to race for the canal. His problem was no longer organized opposition, but clearance of wrecked vehicles from the road. As bulldozers were set to work, Tal sent a battalion of Patton tanks, with headlights blazing, crashing straight down the road. The only opposition came from an infantry company and four tanks two miles from the canal, and, when they had brushed that aside, they reached the east bank soon after midnight, the Egyptians on the west bank at first assuming that they were their own tanks retreating. By dawn Tal's reconnaissance unit had joined up with the Northern Force at the El Firdan bridge.

South of Tal, Yoffe had sorted out his force during the night. One of his brigades spent all day attempting to capture the Gidi Pass, which, with the help of air attacks, it had succeeded in doing just as the news was heard at 7 o'clock in the evening that Egypt was seeking a cease-fire. Farther south Yoffe had secured the Mitla Pass where his problem was how to handle the increasing number of prisoners falling into his hands. The threat of an Egyptian attack from the west was dealt with by the air force, after which Yoffe sent a detachment off to help helicopter-borne troops from the oilfield at Abu Durba, who had been landed at Ras Sudar, forty miles south of Suez, and were in difficulties in trying to deal with an Egyptian force there. The tanks reached them in the early afternoon and a successful attack was delivered soon afterwards, resulting in the capture of 100 prisoners. When Yoffe heard the news at 7 o'clock of the Egyptian call for a cease-fire, he ordered all the Centurion tanks he could muster to race for the canal, which they reached at half-past two in the morning of 9 June, the fifth day, capturing Port Tewfik, opposite Suez, at dawn.

Farther east on the Southern Route, Sharon had had an eventful day. The position at Jebel Karim, which had held him up the night before, had been abandoned during the night, the Egyptians leaving over fifty perfectly fit tanks there. They had tried to get away in wheeled vehicles through the Mitla Pass, but when they found it held by Yoffe, some of them, including the brigade commander, had returned and given themselves up, while others took to the desert in an attempt to make their own way westward. While Sharon was dealing with the remnants and pushing on to Nakhl, he heard that the Egyptian brigade, which had been defending Kuntilla on the frontier, was trying to make its way west along the Southern Route. They were pursued by an Israeli armoured brigade while Sharon blocked their escape at Nakhl and the Israeli Air Force harried them in between. A confused battle took place round Nakhl which went on until 5 o'clock in the afternoon, none of the Egyptian force managing to escape. Sharon then sent his Centurion tank battalion along the Southern Route to join Yoffe at the Mitla Pass.

The cease-fire requested by Egypt to the United Nations was supposed to come into effect at 5.20 a.m. local time on 9 June, and was accepted also by Syria. It appears that Dayan was not aware of this until 3 a.m. He was determined that, before it came into full effect, his forces should evict the Syrians from the positions on the Golan Heights from which they overlooked and shelled the Israeli settlements in the Jordan valley (for a map of the Golan Heights, see page 259). The Israeli Air Force had been delivering heavy air attacks on them during the previous day and General Elazar, at Israel's Northern Command, had been pressing to be allowed to attack them. Without consulting either the Prime Minister, Eshkol, or the Chief of Staff, Rabin, who was asleep at his home, Dayan at 7 a.m. ordered Elazar to attack and clear the Syrian positions on the Golan Heights, knowing that it would be 11.30 before the attack could start. There would be time to stop it, if the Cabinet did not approve; but they did. The initial attack was made in the extreme north close to Mount Hermon, where it would be least expected as the escarpment there rose sharply from the valley. The Syrian troops put up a stout resistance in spite of heavy and prolonged air attacks. By the end of the day Elazar had driven a wedge five miles wide into the positions in the north, while making subsidiary attacks farther south designed to draw away Syrian reserves. He expected counter-attacks during the night and was prepared to receive them, but none came. He resumed his attacks before dawn, including assaults farther south, and had made general progress by 11 a.m. when a series of explosions throughout the area made him realize that the Syrians had decided to withdraw. It was now a race between all his brigades to reach the important road centre of Quneitra, which his tanks entered at half-past two, half-an-hour after the original deadline of another United Nations cease-fire. By then Dayan had persuaded General Bull to extend it until half-past six. By that time the whole of the Golan Heights was in Israeli hands.

Israel's victory was complete. Egyptian army casualties alone were well above 10,000 killed, perhaps 15,000, and possibly over 50,000 wounded. 11,500 were taken prisoner, of whom about half were almost immediately released. She had lost 700 tanks and her air force had been virtually wiped out. Israeli had lost 778 soldiers and 26 civilians killed, 2,586 soldiers and 195 civilians wounded. Twenty-one men were taken prisoner of whom five were killed by an infuriated Egyptian mob. Elated as Israel was by her victory, which gave her frontiers that were easier to defend, victory nevertheless brought with it serious problems. The basic one was what policy to adopt about the areas she had conquered, and it embraced the problem of administering a million more Arabs, including nearly 200,000 refugees; that is, a total Arab population of 1,385,000, a million less than her Jewish population at that time. The problem is still unresolved.

THE WAR OF ATTRITION

Victory in the Six-Day War did not bring peace for long. While America and Russia both within and outside the United Nations tried to reach some agreement on the basis of a solution on which a lasting peace could be based, the military on both sides began to consolidate their respective positions. The fundamental question for Israel was one of security: for the Arabs, of what they saw as the just rights of the original inhabitants of the country. The essence of all the proposed international solutions was that Israel's pre-Six-Day War frontiers should be recognized by the Arabs and guaranteed both by a United Nations presence and by the assurance of physical support for the solution from the major powers, in return for which Israel would evacuate the areas she had captured. To some in Israel on whose support the government depended, and certainly to the harder-line opposition, it was unacceptable to return to the vulnerable pre-1967 borders, trusting only in international guarantees and the word of the Arabs. In any case the Arab countries were not prepared to recognize Israel on these terms and insisted on a solution which met the demands of the Palestinians, whether refugees or inhabitants of the country. So, while the politicians argued, the soldiers got on with building defences where the fighting had stopped, notably on the Golan Heights and on the east bank of the Suez Canal. The defence of the latter posed a particularly awkward problem for Israel. She could only maintain a small army permanently in being. To have maintained one in Sinai capable of meeting an all-out Egyptian assault was out of the question. The answer was the construction of the Bar-Lev line, a series of defended posts strung out all along the east bank of the canal to serve the political purpose of continuing to hold the canal as a hostage and the dual military one of observing activity on the west bank and forcing the Egyptians to make a major military effort to cross it. The preparations for and the execution of such a crossing would, it was assumed, give Israel sufficient warning to mobilize and deploy her forces behind the line, as well as to oppose it with air strikes.

Egypt's reaction was two-fold: to carry out commando raids and heavy artillery bombardments to interfere with its construction and, with Russian help, to erect an air defence system, based on the SAM2, to counter Israeli Air Force retaliation. Israel's reply was to carry out a series of devastating air raids on Egyptian air bases, missile complexes, as they were brought into action, and military installations. In 1969 this so-called War of Attrition was in full swing. In September it was extended by an amphibious raid by Israeli troops disguised as Egyptians, using captured equipment, across the Gulf of Suez, destroying radars and capturing valuable modern Russian equipment recently delivered to Egypt. By 1970, in order to deal with the SAM2, Israel had obtained from the United States Phantom F4 aircraft and electronic countermeasure pods. In response Egypt acquired the SAM3 from the Russians, who sent their own aircrews to Egypt to fly the MIG21J as a counter to the Phantoms, while they began the deployment of an anti-aircraft system covering the whole area from the canal to the Nile. This was under way in the first half of 1970, when in June President Nixon launched a peace initiative to start with a three month cease-fire. This was accepted by Israel at the end of July, and under its cover Egypt completed her air defence system, moving its forward edge right up to the canal, so that it threatened Israeli aircraft flying on their side of it.

Nasser died on 28 September of that year and was succeeded by Sadat, after a brief struggle for power with the more pro-Russian Aly Sabry. In February 1971 Sadat made an offer to accept a partial withdrawal by Israel in return for the right of passage through the canal and settlement of the Palestinian question, immediately followed up by a proposal by the United Nations mediator, Gunnar Jarring, that, as usual, Israel's withdrawal from the territory occupied in 1967 should be exchanged for recognition by Egypt, freedom of access through the canal and the Gulf of Aqaba and 'satisfactory arrangements' for demilitarized zones. Mrs Meir would not accept this. The extended cease-fire ended on 5 March and Sadat began to contemplate war instead. The rest of the year was largely taken up by arguments between the Arab countries themselves or visits by them to Moscow, including an important one by Sadat, from which he came away in the belief that the Russians approved resort to a military solution and would provide him with the offensive arms by the end of the year to enable him to launch it. By the end of the year the arms had not arrived and Sadat went to Moscow again in February 1972 to try and get things moving. He found the Russians more concerned with avoiding a clash with the United States than in helping him. They were expecting a visit by Nixon to Brezhnev in May and they had their eyes on the American presidential election in November. As soon as Nixon's visit to Moscow was over, Sadat sent a virtual ultimatum to Brezhnev, saying that, if he did not receive the arms he felt he had been promised, he would expel the Russian advisers from Egypt, of which there were more than 10,000. Brezhnev's reply was unsatisfactory and harped on the theme of avoiding a clash between the major powers. Sadat carried out his threat, and in October 1972 made the definite decision that he would go to war against Israel, ordering General Ismail, his Minister of Defence, and Shazli, his Chief of Staff, to plan it.

They set about this in a thorough, deliberate fashion, determined to avoid the type of war in which the Israelis excelled – a swift, mobile one in which tanks and aircraft would play the dominant part. They planned to neutralize the Israeli Air Force by the full deployment of a complex anti-aircraft missile system, and they would not move their army out of its cover. By secrecy and deception they would hope to avoid the danger of a pre-emptive Israeli strike. The Israelis would be forced to fight on two fronts by co-ordinating action with Syria and Jordan, and Egypt would be prepared for a fairly long war of attrition, which Israel would not be able to afford. They gave detailed attention to the problems of crossing the canal, and all troops sent over would be well provided with anti-tank missiles as defence against Israeli tanks.

General Ismail went to Moscow in February 1973 and it was perhaps because the Russians were impressed by the thoroughness of his plans and the fact that Egypt clearly meant business that the flow of arms and equipment both to Egypt and to Syria began again. Hitherto the failure of the Arab countries to agree among each other and the suspicion that, if they supplied arms, they would not be effectively used, appear to have been factors making the Russians hesitant over their supply. While Ismail proceeded with the military planning, Sadat set about building up the political support to ensure that Egypt would not be on its own. Both Syria and the Palestinians had been inclined to rely on a prolonged and expanded terrorist campaign to undermine Israel. This had caused difficulties both to the Lebanon and to Jordan, from whose countries the terrorists operated. In 1971 it had posed a serious threat to Hussein's regime and he had acted decisively to suppress them in his country. But their activities had the effect of concentrating the attention of the Israelis on this threat and leading them to believe that the development of Syrian and Egyptian defences was designed to protect them against attacks which Israel might make in retaliation for terrorist activity. Sadat managed to persuade President Assad of Syria to run the risk of deliberately courting war, based on the assurance of Russian support. His task with Hussein was more difficult. With the help of Hussein's old friend and adviser, Zaid Rifai, and of King Faisal of Saudi Arabia, Sadat persuaded him to accept the risk of remaining neutral on his own border with Israel and giving help to Syria. Sadat's policy, both of deception as to his intentions and of binding Syria firmly to him, was strengthened in May 1973 when the assassination of three well-known Palestinian leaders in Beirut by Israeli commandos in civilian clothes led to the fall of the Lebanese Government, rumours that Syria was going to intervene and Israeli mobilization in reaction to what proved to be a false alarm.

As both the military and the political preparations were well advanced, Sadat and his advisers chose 6 October as the day, although they kept the knowledge of this to a very small circle until the last moment. September or October were favoured as by then the nights would be long enough; but it would not be so late in the year that rain or snow in Syria would limit the mobility of the forces. There would be enough moon to see by, but not so much that the tidal flow in the canal would complicate the crossing. These factors narrowed the choice to four days in either month, October being preferred. The sixth was the tenth day of Ramadan, when Mahomet started to prepare for the Battle of Badr, forerunner of all his victories. It was also *Yom Kippur*, the Jewish Day of Atonement, when the Egyptians thought that Israel would be at a low state of alert, overlooking perhaps that, if they were, everyone would be at home and easy to recall.

By September it was clear to Israeli intelligence that both Egypt and Syria were building up their forces in the forward areas considerably, but their actions were interpreted as either defensive or mere bluff. It was thought that Egypt would not initiate war until her air force could neutralize that of Israel, which it was not yet in a position to do, and that Syria would not attack without Egypt. The threat of the development of a terrorist campaign still seemed greater. Towards the end of the month Israel's attention was distracted by an incident in Austria, in which the Austrian Government had yielded to the demands of two Arab terrorists to close the transit centre at Schonau for Jews leaving Russia for Israel, in return for the release of hostages.

THE YOM KIPPUR WAR

On 1 October Egyptian so-called manoeuvres began and, with some notable exceptions, they were interpreted as no more than that; until 3 October when Dayan, Minister of Defence, and Elazar, the Chief of Staff, began to be seriously alarmed. By the following day the air force was convinced that Egypt and Syria were planning to go to war, and Dayan was swinging round to that view also. On 5 October there seemed little doubt, and the argument revolved around whether or not full mobilization should be ordered and a pre-emptive air strike authorized. Both would incur the accusation that Israel had pro-voked or started the war, which would not only affect international political support, but could prejudice the supply of military material from the United States once hostilities had started. With her frontiers farther away from her vital centres than at the outbreak of war in 1967, Israel could better afford to run the risks involved in not being the first to strike; but, when clear informa-tion reached Israeli intelligence early on the sixth that Egypt and Syria were going to launch their attack at 6 o'clock that evening, demands from the army and the air force to strike first became more insistent. Golda Meir, with the support of Dayan, refused, one of the arguments being that, given the state of the enemy's air defences, it would not achieve a great deal, but could cost much in terms of international support. Four hours before the time predicted, the Egyptian and Syrian Air Forces struck and their armies began to move.

The most immediate danger to Israel came on the Golan Heights. In normal times this area, captured by Israel in 1967, was defended by two infantry battalions of the Golani Brigade, occupying eleven fortified positions running south from Mount Hermon, high up on which there was an observation and electronic warfare post manned by fifty-five men, including the operators. These defences were backed up by the Barak Armoured Brigade of two tank battalions, one normally in the line with its tanks widely distributed in pre-selected and prepared positions: the other in reserve, training. At the end of September these forces, under Brigadier-General Eytan, himself under Major-General Hafi at Northern Command, were reinforced by the 7th Armoured Brigade, increasing the number of Israeli tanks in the area from about 60 to 177, and the artillery from four batteries to eleven. This small force faced three Syrian infantry divisions, each of two infantry, one mechanized and one tank brigade, totalling some 540 tanks, backed up by two armoured divisions, each of 230 tanks, bringing the total to 1,000. In addition to this, the Syrians had 200 tanks sited in static defences, and three additional tank brigades, bringing the grand total to 1,500. All three infantry divisions in the line advanced with their tanks leading, backed by massive artillery support, shortly after the initial air strikes a few minutes before 2 p.m. Israeli time on Saturday 6 October. Hafi had been called to GHQ for a conference with the Chief of Staff, and was there when the attack started. Soon after he had

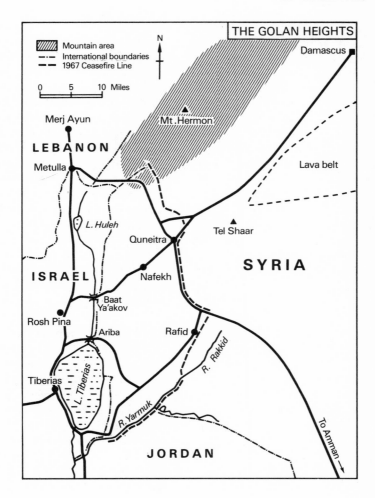

returned and realized that attacks were taking place in strength along the whole width of the front, he ordered Colonel Avigdor's 7th Brigade to hand over one of its tank battalions to Colonel Ben Shoham's Barak Brigade and assume responsibility for the northern sector from the southern slopes of Mount Hermon to Quneitra, a front of some fifteen miles, while the Barak Brigade looked after the area south of that down to the frontier between Syria and Jordan, nearly double the width.

The Syrian tanks advanced in close order as if on parade, preceded by bridge-laying tanks to get them over the anti-tank ditch. These became the prime target of the Israeli tank gunners, who shot with deadly accuracy at long range. The Israeli Air Force came to their support, but suffered heavy casualties from anti-aircraft missiles. One of the early losses was the Israeli post on Mount Hermon, which was attacked by a Syrian commando battalion landed by helicopter, overwhelming the post in under an hour's fighting. The defences in the plain however held firmly in 7th Brigade's area. By the end of the day it was clear that the 9th Syrian Division had achieved a breakthrough in the Barak Brigade's sector astride the oil pipeline in the area of Rafid. This was particularly dangerous as it was the shortest route to both the vital Baat Ya'akov and Ariba bridges over the Jordan. Three of the defensive posts had to be evacuated and confused fighting took place in this area all through the night. At dawn on the morning of 7 October it was clear that a considerable force of several hundred Syrian tanks was in the area overlooking Lake Tiberias, the Sea of Galilee. The breakthrough had been made by the tank brigade of the Syrian's southern 5th Division, and during the night they had begun to pass through it their 1st Armoured Division, commanded by Colonel Jehani. As the tanks of this division began to come into action, some of them only six miles from the River Jordan, the first tanks of the Israeli reserve brigades, formed on mobilization, began to cross the river to meet them and back up the remnants of the Barak Brigade, which had fewer than a dozen tanks left.

Meanwhile Avigdor's 7th Armoured Brigade held a succession of attacks by the 7th Syrian Division, reinforced during the night by their 3rd Armoured Division. All through the night of Saturday, the day of Sunday 7 October and, with hardly a pause until the assault died down as daylight faded on Tuesday 9 October, the 7th Brigade, later reinforced by the remnants of the Barak Brigade, as its place was taken by the reserve brigades in the south, fought one attack after another, while subjected to intense artillery bombardment. When daylight came in the morning of the tenth, they could count some 500 enemy armoured vehicles, half of which were tanks, lying knocked out all round them. It was an epic story of courage and determination, linked to a high degree of professional skill, assisted by familiarity with every detail of the ground.

While the 7th Brigade held firm, two reserve brigades, grouped as a division under General Laner, were fighting a desperate battle all through 7 and 8 October to hold the Syrian armoured division's thrust towards the important centre of Nafekh and the vital bridge at Baat Ya'akov, from which at one stage they were only a few miles away. The fighting was fierce and casualties heavy on both sides. But the tide began to turn on 9 October as Major-General Peled, with three armoured brigades, fought his way slowly forward in a hard-fought counter-attack, coming up from the south, east of Lake Tiberias. As he did so, he began to drive into the southern flank of the Syrian penetration and to link up with some of the southern Israeli fortified defences that were still holding out south of Rafid. As he developed his pressure, Laner from the north began

to make progress also against the Syrian incursion. By mid-day on Wednesday
10 October Peled from the south completed the closing of the pincers between
them, the Syrians withdrawing eastward, having left behind them 867 tanks
and thousands of guns and vehicles of all sorts. At a heavy cost, much of it
because they had not been prepared, the Israeli Army, against all odds, had
restored its original position on the heights.

While this desperate struggle on the Golan Heights had been going on,
Israel was also facing a serious situation in Sinai, although it did not threaten
the heart of the country as did the attack in the north. The Israeli forces in
Sinai formed a division under General Mandler, who himself came under
General Gonen at Southern Command, who had only just relieved General
Sharon. The latter had retired to enter politics and took over command of a
reserve division. Mandler had three armoured brigades, each of a hundred
tanks. Their first task on the outbreak of war was to move up to the canal to
support the fifteen fortified posts spaced at about eight-mile intervals along the
110 miles of the canal's east bank. These posts were manned by a reserve unit
doing its annual training, at this time a brigade from Jerusalem, with a
strength of under 500 men. They were supported by only seven artillery
batteries. Opposing this covering force, for that is all it could be called, the
Egyptians had two armies, the Second with three divisions in the line covering
the canal north of the centre of the Great Bitter Lake, the Third, with two,
stretching south from there to Suez. These five divisions, each of three
brigades, every one of which included a tank battalion, were backed up by
three mechanized divisions, each of two mechanized and one armoured
brigade, and two armoured divisions, each of two armoured and one mechanized brigade. There were also some additional independent brigades. Each of
the infantry divisions had 120 tanks, the mechanized 160 and the armoured
250. Altogether the Egyptian Army had over 2,200 tanks, 2,300 pieces of
artillery and 150 anti-aircraft missile batteries. It was supported by 550
first-line aircraft.

The Egyptian plan was to cross in strength along the whole length of the
canal in the sectors between the Israeli fortified posts. Gaps were to be made in
the bank on the eastern side by very high pressure hoses, pontoon bridges then
being erected at each gap. The Israeli tanks, as they came to the defence of the
fortified posts, would be picked off by anti-tank missiles fired from the west
bank, which had been built up to a height of 130 feet, double that of the east
bank which it therefore overlooked. By the end of the first day the assaulting
infantry were expected to have established a line about two miles east of the
canal, while special parties dealt with the fortifications which they would have
by-passed. During the following day the infantry divisions would complete the
crossing and push forward to a depth of about five miles, consolidating there in
anticipation of Israeli counter-attacks. During the second night one armoured
brigade would cross to support each division and the bridgeheads would be

linked up and further expanded to a depth of about eight miles. In that position, well-covered by the anti-aircraft defences west of the canal, they would deal with counter-attacks, while over a period of four days the two armoured divisions would cross over. When this movement was complete, which was expected to be ten days after the first crossing, they would advance in a pincer movement to capture the important Israeli military installations at Bir Gifgafa, on the Central Route sixty miles east of Ismailia, a very deliberate operation which appeared to run no risks at any stage.

When the Egyptian Air Force launched its first attacks on many different targets in Sinai and their army's artillery began to bombard the Israeli fortifications at 2 p.m. on 6 October, Mandler's tanks had not been deployed forward. Acting on the information that H-hour was to be 6 p.m., they had been held back for fear of being accused of provoking hostilities. As they moved forward to take up their positions, they came under fire both from missiles sited west of the canal and from shorter-range weapons with which the assaulting infantry had been liberally supplied. By the end of the day they had suffered heavy casualties, few had reached their designated positions and the fortified posts were under intense fire, including that from tanks on the west bank. There were therefore few Israeli weapons capable of bringing any fire to bear on the canal crossing sites. Information was scanty and the seriousness of the situation was not realized at General Gonen's headquarters until the following morning. By this time Mandler's three armoured brigades had lost two-thirds of their tanks and he was being pressed by Colonel Dan, commanding the southernmost brigade, for a decision as to whether the tanks, of which by that time Dan only had twenty-three, were to continue to try and support the fortified posts or to concentrate on dealing with the Egyptian bridgeheads, the posts being abandoned or withdrawn. He did not get a decision until 11 a.m., when it was decided to evacuate the posts where possible and devote all available effort to the containment of the bridgeheads. The natural reaction of all commanders had been to ask for air support, but they were told that this was being concentrated on the Golan Heights, which had a higher priority.

By this time two reserve divisional headquarters were available, and Gonen divided up the front between them, Bren in the north, Sharon in the centre and Mandler in the south. The principal matter for decision was on what general line should the enemy be held, as reserve formations became available. When Dayan visited Gonen shortly before mid-day, he advised a withdrawal to a line on the western edge of the central mountains, east of the Khatmia, Gidi and Mitla Passes, in order to reduce the width of the front. Neither Gonen nor Elazar agreed. The latter, in a meeting with Dayan and Golda Meir at 4 p.m., argued for a line west of the passes, from which a counter-attack could be launched next day, although he turned down Sharon's suggestion for an attempt to cross the canal. He received permission to make his own decision when he got to Gonen's headquarters, which he did, accompanied by his predecessor Rabin, at 7 p.m. to meet Gonen and his divisional commanders. His plan was for Bren to attack the Egyptian Second Army from the north and, if this was successful, Sharon would do the same to the Third Army east of the Bitter Lakes, while Mandler suported him. If Bren's attack was not successful, Sharon would not attack the Third Army, but would attack the Second from the south, while Bren pressed them from the north. He did not want to attempt to return to the canal at this stage, and, when Gonen asked for permission to cross the canal if the counter-attacks were successful, Elazar agreed that, if Egyptian bridges were captured, this might be allowed; but not without his personal approval. There was certainly nothing defeatist about his attitude.

Early on 8 October Bren began his attack southwards from Romani with three brigades. At first all seemed to be going well and he was encouraged by Gonen to aim for bridges over the canal. Unfortunately the two leading brigades initially moved southward too far to the east. Instead of slicing into the flank of the Egyptian Second Army's positions, they were moving across its front. When this was realized, they changed direction westward. This, combined with the objective of reaching bridge sites, turned their attacks into direct frontal ones heading straight for the canal. As they progressed, they suddenly found themselves surrounded by infantry who had been hidden in the dunes and who attacked them from all sides with anti-tank missiles and rockets, while their leading tanks also came under fire from longer range missiles on the canal banks. They were subjected to intense artillery fire, while they themselves had very little artillery support or accompanying infantry. By the early afternoon the attack had ground to a halt and Bren's brigades were all in grave difficulties. However, acting on the earlier optimistic reports, Gonen had ordered Sharon at 11 a.m. to move through the passes and turn south to attack the Third Army. At 2 p.m. he cancelled this and told him to turn north and help Bren, but Sharon said that he could not develop an attack before dark, which fell at 6 p.m. Before then the Egyptian 16th Division had launched a counter-attack against Bren's southern brigade and had captured several important positions about fifteen miles east of Ismailia after heavy fighting in which both sides suffered severe casualties. Although the Israeli attack had failed and the opportunity to deliver a telling counter-attack had been missed, the attack had at least largely frustrated the Egyptian plan to expand the bridgeheads on this day.

Gonen's intention for Tuesday, 9 October was to contain the bridgeheads, but undertake no offensive action until he had built up his forces further. He was therefore angry when, in the afternoon of that day, he found that Sharon, determined to link up with the garrison of one of the fortified posts that had got stuck in the middle of the battlefield while trying to withdraw, had authorized attacks to regain some of the ground lost to the Egyptian attack the previous afternoon. The attack proved expensive and, as he developed it further, Gonen ordered him to stop it. Even after he had personally flown by helicopter to insist on his orders being obeyed, Sharon continued and his tank casualties mounted. Gonen therefore telephoned Elazar, requesting Sharon's dismissal. The reaction to this at GHQ was a compromise. The retired General Bar Lev, who had already helped to co-ordinate the counter-attacks in the north which had restored the situation on the Golan Heights, was sent to Southern Command to act as a sort of extra commander or adviser to Gonen, in much the same position as O'Connor was with Neame in Libya in the spring of 1941. He was soon to find himself also at loggerheads with Sharon. Meanwhile Bren and Sharon had been successfully resisting Egyptian attacks designed to expand the Second Army's bridgehead. These took place all along the front and were successfully held by the Israeli armoured brigades which inflicted heavy casualties on the attackers. These attacks continued on 10 October, but made no progress. Sharon now proposed to Bar Lev that his two brigades should carry out an attack southward against the Third Army's positions east of the Bitter Lakes on 11 October, but Bar Lev refused to agree. He thought it would produce little in the way of decisive results and wished to preserve the armoured brigades for a decisive counter-stroke when the Egyptians attacked again. Gonen was now coming round to the view that only a counter-offensive across the canal could be decisive and turn the war from one of attrition into one of manoeuvre.

The general situation by 10 October was therefore that the initial massive assaults by both the Syrian and Egyptian armies had been held and, in the case of the former, thrown back to its start line. The air situation was also improving for Israel. Initially her air force had had to devote much of its effort to ground attack in order to help the desperate situation on the Golan Heights and to try and destroy the bridges over the Suez Canal. They had suffered heavy casualties from low-level anti-aircraft missiles and guns in doing so. They had also not immediately developed countermeasures to the new Russian surface-to-air missiles supplied both to Syria and to Egypt. By 10 October they could turn their effort both to countering the enemy air defence systems operating at higher altitudes, to which they were acquiring appropriate countermeasures, and also to destroying enemy aircraft in air-to-air combat.

10 October was a turning point and a day of decision. If the full strength of army and air force was to be available for a counter-offensive against Egypt, the threat from Syria had to be disposed of. Elazar was for a counter-offensive into Syria, which would deal them such a blow, in the air and on land, that they could not intervene while Egypt was being dealt with. An immediate and decisive blow against Syria would affect the attitude of Jordan, hitherto sitting on the fence for fear of retaliatory air attack. In addition Iraqi reinforcements were on their way. The blow should be delivered before they could arrive. Against these arguments Dayan hesitated, fearing that the defeat and humiliation of Syria might force the Russians to intervene to save their protégé and

their own reputation as her supporter. But when they went to see Golda Meir some time before midnight, he had been won over and she approved Elazar's plan for a counter-offensive to start next day, 11 October.

Hafi's plan was to attack in the north, resting his left flank on the southern slopes of Hermon. It was the shortest and most direct route to Damascus and provided good observation over the area to the south. He attacked at 11 a.m. with two divisions, Raful on the left, led by the heroic 7th Brigade, patched up and reinforced, while to the south of him Laner, with two of the reserve brigades which had turned the tables on the Syrian 1st Armoured Division, attacked two hours later on the axis of the main Quneitra–Damascus road. In two days of dogged fighting Raful beat back the Syrian and Moroccan brigades opposing him and occupied the important area between Mount Hermon and the lava belt, penetrating ten miles behind the Syrian defences. It had been decided that no attempt should be made to threaten Damascus itself more directly for fear of the repercussions it could have.

To the south Laner's brigades had an even tougher time forcing their way forwards past Quneitra south of the lava belt, but on the second day Syrian resistance began to weaken significantly and he felt that he had them on the run. As his weary but determined brigades were thrusting eastward and were already over twenty miles beyond Quneitra, and he himself was scanning the area from the dominating height of Tel Shaar some ten miles north-east of it, he saw to his dismay a force of between 100 and 150 tanks only six miles away to the south, advancing towards his open right flank. At first he thought it might be Peled's division, one brigade of which was being sent to join him; but a quick check on the radio proved that it was not. To the protests of his brigade commanders, who were intent on pushing on, he stopped them and made them face south to meet the threat, which in fact was the leading brigade of the 3rd Iraqi Armoured Division. A brief clash took place before dark, in which seventeen Iraqi tanks were knocked out. Laner rapidly readjusted his brigades to form a three-sided box open to the south, and in bright moonlight he awaited an Iraqi attack. It came at 3 a.m. when the division, reinforced by its second armoured brigade, drove straight into the trap, its mechanized brigade being almost totally destroyed in a matter of minutes, while Laner did not lose a single tank. During the next two days Raful and Laner, in spite of the exhaustion of their troops and a shortage of artillery ammunition, improved their positions in a series of limited attacks. On Tuesday 16 October Laner was attacked again, this time by the Jordanian 40th Armoured Brigade which Hussein had sent north in response to a desperate plea from Assad. Their attack was supposed to have been co-ordinated with a simultaneous attack by the Iraqis on their right, but the Iraqis were late in moving and then advanced only hesitantly. The Jordanians lost twenty-eight tanks and withdrew. Over the next few days, during which Peled's division relieved Laner's, the Iraqis and Jordanians tried again with no success. By 20 October the former had lost

100 and the latter fifty tanks and had nothing to show for it. Two days later the Golan Brigade, at a cost of fifty-one killed and 100 wounded, recaptured their post on Mount Hermon, and in the evening Syria accepted a cease-fire proposal by the United Nations Security Council.

In Sinai also 10 October had seen the Egyptians held, and a decision had to be made about the next step. The choice lay between three courses of action: to try and throw the Egyptian armies back to the canal by a major counter-attack on their bridgeheads; to try and cross the canal in order to throw them off balance; or to await a major attack by them, which was expected once their two armoured divisions had crossed to the east bank, and, when it had been dealt with, then to strike across the canal. The first course was likely to be costly and not decisive: the second ran considerable risks. To reach one of the preselected crossing points would involve a battle in itself, and, as long as the two Egyptian armoured divisions were still on the west bank, there could be great difficulty in developing the bridgehead. After some discussion Gonen's choice of Deversoir, at the northern end of the Great Bitter Lake, was agreed as the point at which to make the crossing. Special equipment and arrangements for a crossing there had been prepared; it was near the boundary between the two Egyptian armies, and there was only one irrigation canal and a narrow strip of cultivated land to cross before reaching open desert on the far side, in which mobile forces could be freely deployed. Bar Lev accepted Gonen's plan and on 12 October went to GHQ to discuss it with Elazar. The latter wished to wait until after the Egyptians had launched their expected attack. Dayan was not enthusiastic about a crossing at all, and at a meeting with members of the Cabinet no decision was reached, the news that the Egyptian armoured divisions were crossing the canal and that they were expected to attack next day appearing to pre-empt the need for a decision.

During 13 October the Egyptian Second Army carried out a series of probing attacks all along their front, while Gonen reorganized his dispositions to prepare to receive them, Bren's division, less one of his brigades, being held in reserve as a counter-attack force. The major Egyptian assault started at dawn on 14 October with massive attacks. In the north their 18th Infantry Division, reinforced by an armoured brigade of the latest Russian T62 tanks, tried to push east from opposite Kantara towards Romani. In the centre their 21st Armoured Division, reinforced by an additional brigade, drove east astride the Central Route opposite Ismailia, clashing with Amnon's brigade in Sharon's division. In the south their 4th Armoured Division attempted a flanking move east of Suez, bringing them up against the Mitla Pass, held by Dan's brigade, formerly of Mandler's division, now commanded by Magen, Mandler having been killed. In all some 2,000 tanks must have been involved in battle that day, the biggest tank battle since that of Kursk in 1943. The Egyptians found their opponents well prepared and made little or no progress. The skilled Israeli tank gunners, assisted by infantry with wire-guided anti-tank missiles and supported by the Israeli Air Force, took heavy toll of the Egyptian tanks. For a loss of only six themselves, they knocked out 264. The shock of failure gave the Egyptian Army Commander, General Mamoun, a heart attack, and he was succeeded by General Halil. The time for the counterstroke had arrived, and Elazar gave orders that it should take place the following night, that of 15/16 October.

The plan was for Sharon's division to secure the approach to the canal on the southern edge of the Egyptian Second Army's bridgehead, allowing Matt's parachute brigade to cross in rubber boats to cover the construction of a pontoon bridge and the deployment of a specially prepared preconstructed bridge. Ten tanks to support them would cross on rafts. Sharon, having widened the corridor of approach, would then move his division over during the night and expand the bridgehead westwards. Bren's division would cross the following day and turn south down the western edge of the Great Bitter Lake to destroy Egyptian anti-aircraft sites. Finally Magen's division would follow through to complete the encirclement of the Third Army. The operation was to start at 5 p.m. on 15 October, just as it was beginning to get dark. With only an hour and a half to go before H-hour, Sharon came to the conclusion that, as the bridging equipment was not ready, the plan should be changed. Either the whole operation should be postponed for twenty-four hours or, while the operation to clear the approaches should go ahead, the crossing itself should wait until the following night. The only other possible course was to go ahead and adjust the timing according to events as they developed. After discussion with Bar Lev, the last course was adopted.

Sharon's plan was for Amnon's armoured brigade, which had borne the brunt of defeating the Egyptian 21st Armoured Division the day before, to move round the southern flank of the Egyptian position, based on what was known as the Chinese Farm, and attack it from the rear, while Matt's parachute brigade moved immediately on its left to a specially prepared area, known as the Yard, from which the assault crossing would be launched at the point where the canal enters the Great Bitter Lake. Amnon reached the shore of the lake without meeting any opposition, but, as his three battalions moved north into the Egyptian positions, they stirred up a hornet's nest. They were penetrating into the main administrative and reserve centre of the Egyptian 16th Division, into which their 21st Armoured Division had withdrawn to lick its wounds. While an intense and confused battle raged in this area all through the night, Matt, under heavy shelling and losing many of his vehicles, including a whole company of tanks, reached the Yard and launched his men across the canal, meeting no opposition on the far side. By 5 a.m. all his infantry were over, the first tank crossed at 6.45 and by 8 a.m. he held a bridgehead extending three miles from the shore of the lake. But the situation east of the canal meant that there was no follow up. Indeed such was the gloom at Gonen's headquarters that Dayan, who was there, suggested bringing Matt's paratroopers back again; but Gonen would not hear of it. Not only was the situation of Sharon's division critical, but, to make matters worse, the preconstructed bridge had broken down. Sharon however was in favour of exploiting the crossing immediately and suggested that Bren's division should cross on rafts and that the force on the west bank should push on. But Bar Lev and Gonen decided to ensure that bridges could be built and the approaches to them cleared before any more troops were sent over, and Matt was told to sit tight. Bren was ordered to be prepared to help Sharon to clear the approaches and was made responsible for getting the bridging equipment to the site. The battle to achieve this raged with great ferocity all through 16 and 17 October, the Egyptians making repeated attempts to close the corridor which Sharon had established. In addition to attacks from the north, they moved an armoured brigade up from the south on the afternoon of 17 October. Bren rapidly redeployed his brigades to meet it, and, as it moved up the eastern shore of the lake and neared the corridor, it ran into what amounted to a large ambush and lost eighty-six of its ninety-six T62 tanks. While this battle was going on, the pontoon bridge was completed and most of the principal positions round the Chinese Farm, covering the approaches to it, had been secured and cleared of the enemy. By this time, however, the Egyptian command had finally woken up to the presence of the Israeli bridgehead on the west bank and begun to subject it and the crossing itself to heavy bombardment. On the morning of 18 October Amnon's gallant brigade launched a final attack on the Chinese Farm from the rear and succeeded in occupying the area, littered with bodies and shattered equipment. The fight for it must have been one of the fiercest in history.

Meanwhile another argument had erupted between Sharon and Gonen. The former wanted to transfer Amnon to join the rest of his division on the west bank and to push north to Ismailia, instead of leaving Amnon to secure the corridor and himself turning south from the bridgehead to the west of Bren. Bar Lev supported Sharon and ordered that Magen's division should lead the break-out west of Bren, while Sharon secured the bridgehead. Gonen accepted this decision with some relief. The preconstructed bridge, after many breakdowns, was finally in position shortly after midnight on 18 October, and a second pontoon bridge was completed the following night. During the eighteenth the bridgehead was expanded northward against increasing opposition and under heavy artillery bombardment and the occasional air attack, and on that day also Bren started to break out on his southward move. By the end of the day his leading troops had reached the Geneifa Hills west of the southern end of the Great Bitter Lake, an advance of some twenty miles which brought them halfway to Suez. On 19 October Magen's division passed through him, initially pushing out westward and then turning south parallel to Bren. Fighting in this area went on for the next two days, as Bren's troops neared Suez itself and Magen's had almost cut the routes leading to it from

Cairo, thus encircling the whole of the Third Army. By this time moves to bring about a cease-fire were in hand.

Kosygin arrived in Cairo on 16 October, but, in spite of the failure of their attack on 14 October and the Israeli crossing of the canal, the Egyptians painted a moderately optimistic picture of the situation, and were proposing a cease-fire, guaranteed by the Russians, which would involve Israeli withdrawal to its pre-1967 borders. By the time Kosygin left two days later, he at least had no illusions about the need for a cease-fire to save Egypt from disaster. Brezhnev asked Nixon to send Kissinger to Moscow, where he arrived on Saturday, 20 October and met Brezhnev that evening, the latter insisting that Egyptian terms be met. Kissinger did not even discuss them, but, when they met next morning, put forward his own proposals. By that evening they had agreed a draft resolution to the Security Council calling for an immediate cease-fire and standstill to come into effect twelve hours after the resolution was passed; for an immediate start to the implementation of the long contested Resolution 242 of 1967; and finally that talks between the parties to the dispute should also start immediately 'aimed at establishing a just and durable peace in the Middle East'. The second clause, calling for implementation of Resolution 242, with its demand for withdrawal from the occupied territories, although vague as to whether it meant total withdrawal, unpopular with Israel, was intended to be balanced by the call for direct talks, which Israel had always demanded, but which to the Arabs involved recognition of Israel and acceptance that she had a future as a state. A meeting of the Security Council was fixed for 10 p.m. New York time that day, 21 October, 4 a.m. Monday, 22 October by Israel and Egypt time. They were first told about it, Golda Meir by the Israeli Ambassador in Moscow and Sadat by the Russian Ambassador in Cairo, at 9.30 p.m. their time on Sunday evening with six and a half hours to go before the Security Council meeting. Neither of them liked it, but both accepted, Mrs Meir on condition that Kissinger came straight to Tel Aviv. The Security Council approved the resolution as number 338, and it was due to come into effect at 6.52 p.m. Egypt time on 22 October. Urged on by Dayan and Bar Lev during the day, Bren had reached the southern end of the Little Bitter Lake fifteen miles north of Suez, and Magen, although there is some argument about this, had cut the main Cairo road at Kilometer Post 109, the same distance to the north-west of Suez. What with the speed of events and the disorganization of the Egyptian Third Army, it is hardly surprising that many of its units west of the canal, in spite of the standstill, moved west to escape the net and get home. When they found themselves blocked by Israeli troops, it is certainly not surprising that both sides regarded such action as a breach of the cease-fire. Fighting started up again almost immediately and Israel took advantage of it to complete the encirclement, attacking Suez itself from the rear and reaching the coast south of it before a second cease-fire came into effect on the evening of 24 October as a result of Security Council

Resolution 339, which demanded a return to the positions occupied on 22 October and the despatch of a United Nations observer force to supervise its implementation.

The failure of the first cease-fire and Israel's apparently blatant disregard of it caused an international crisis of major proportions. Kissinger was anxious that Russia should not think that America had connived at Israel's action. Egypt demanded that Russia and the United States should together impose the cease-fire on Israel. Brezhnev sent a message to Nixon, who was preoccupied with Watergate, which reached Kissinger at 10.45 p.m. Washington time on 24 October. It said: 'We strongly urge that we both send forces to enforce the cease-fire, and, if you do not, we may be obliged to consider acting alone.' Some accounts represent the message as being considerably tougher. There were already indications that Russian airborne forces had been alerted and the transport aircraft, which had been shuttling between Russia and both Syria and Egypt, recalled. Kissinger regarded this as a grave development and, in little over an hour, having consulted President Nixon and conferred with Defence Secretary Schlesinger, the Chairman of the Joint Chiefs of Staff, Admiral Moorer, and the head of the CIA, William Colby, the order was given to place all United States forces world-wide on Alert State 3, that is troops placed on standby and awaiting orders: all leave cancelled.

When the Security Council met in the morning, the tension had eased. The cease-fire was observed and a UN force agreed to, excluding the forces of the major powers. It was however not until January 1974 that an agreement was finally reached by which Israeli forces would be withdrawn behind the passes in Sinai in return for a limitation on Egyptian forces east of the canal and an arrangement under the auspices of the United Nations by which, with the help of American equipment and technicians, both sides would receive early warning of any move by the other. The intervening months had seen a confrontation between the Middle East oil-producing countries and the West, as the former used both the threat of denial of supplies and a drastic rise in price as means to try and force the United States, Western Europe and countries linked to them to bring pressure on Israel to meet Arab demands. This had widened a breach between the United States and some of her European allies, whom she accused of failing to support her during the war for fear of the effect on their oil supplies. A further side-effect of the war was a growing disillusionment on the part of both Israel and Egypt with their normal backers, respectively the United States and the Soviet Union. Both felt that they had been let down during the war and in its aftermath, and that their supporters could and should have done more for them. The repercussions of the war were to go on reverberating long after.

It had been one of the fiercest and most intense struggles in the history of warfare. Both sides had been equipped with the most modern weapons, although their inventory also included a considerable number of older ones.

Egypt and Syria started with some 2,200 and 2,000 tanks respectively. Of these they lost about 2,000, most of them, in spite of the publicity given to the anti-tank guided missiles, to the gunfire of Israel's 1,700 tanks, of which she lost about half. Egypt and Syria each lost about 250 aircraft out of their combined total of about 800, mostly in air-to-air combat, while Israel lost only 115 out of her 500, almost all from surface-to-air guns or missiles, a large proportion incurred on ground support missions. Egypt and Syria each lost about 8,000 men killed, Israel 2,500. In terms of population, even in the case of Israel of which it had now reached three million, it could not be called high; but at an average of 115 men killed a day, it seemed so. It was the very high rate of expenditure of equipment and munitions on both sides, for which neither was prepared, that caused alarm to them both. The result was an urgent plea to their respective sponsors for immediate supply, to which both responded with massive airlifts, Russian and American transport aircraft carrying them, crossing each other's routes in the Eastern Mediterranean from 15 October onwards. The rate of expenditure made logisticians on both sides of the Iron Curtain revise their estimates of their own requirements. If half one's inventory could be lost in less than three weeks, how was a long war to be sustained? The lessons of the war were studied with great care and interest as the first example of the use of many of the most sophisticated and modern weapons produced both by the Western powers and by Soviet Russia in action against each other. This applied particularly to the tank and anti-tank and the aircraft and anti-aircraft fields, although the latter had been tested in the Vietnam war, where the US Air Force had encountered the Russian Surface-to-Air Missiles, except the SAM6. An interesting feature of the war was the continuing importance of tank *versus* tank and air-to-air combat.

Israeli victories in all three wars seemed to be a vindication of the theories of those apostles of mobility, Fuller and Liddell Hart. Liddell Hart himself regarded the Six-Day War as 'the best demonstration yet of the theory of the indirect approach'.* They had shown that a small, highly trained and skilled army, equipped for mobile operations and commanded from the front by men of high intelligence and speed of thought, could defeat much larger armies, more ponderous in thought and action. They had also shown that the combination of speed and surprise produced its own momentum and that operations aimed to upset the enemy's equilibrium, psychologically as well as physically, were more fruitful than direct assaults. But, unlike Fuller and Liddell Hart, the Israelis never hesitated to engage in such assaults if they thought them necessary, often when they could have avoided them. They did not recognize any short cuts to victory by avoiding action, nor could they afford to play for time. At their backs, for both political and military reasons, they always heard time's winged chariot hovering near. Unlike their opponents, they knew that they were fighting for their very existence, and this spurred them on. Although

* Liddell Hart, 'Strategy of a War', *Encounter* (February 1968).

very sensitive about casualties, much more so than their opponents, they took risks which few other soldiers would have been prepared to face, and, although boldness did not always pay, more often than not it did.

Their opponents, Jordanian, Egyptian, Syrian and Palestinian Arab, often fought with dogged and determined courage in defence, as they did also in advancing to attack; but their overall command was ponderous and hesitant in its reaction, as well as being disunited. Syria and Egypt received a poor return for the vast resources devoted by them and by their Russian supporters to their armed forces. Their resort to war has so far achieved nothing. Israel, by her own defence effort, with significant help from the United States and some others, has survived. To her there is no doubt that security comes first.

Chapter Thirteen

CONCLUSION

To some the wars that have been waged since 1945 are seen as part of a world-wide struggle between communism and the political, economic and cultural heritage of European civilization which embraces democracy as a political system, capitalism as an economic one and the fusion of Ancient Greek civilization and Christianity as their cultural base. However most of the wars that have been described in the preceding chapters were not directly concerned with the struggle between these opposing systems or ideologies, unless the fight against colonialism or imperialism is considered as having been instigated, as opposed to merely supported, by communism. The principal causes of these wars were either the contest between imperial authorities, attempting to maintain that authority, and the nationalist movements which challenged it, or the struggle for power between rival elements of the population as the imperial authority withdrew, willingly or under duress. These rivalries were at times based on differences of political outlook, but almost all were heavily influenced by racial, historical and cultural differences, some, as in the case of the Arab–Israeli and Indo–Pakistan wars, being primarily based on that difference. The imperial or ex-imperial powers themselves, and in particular the United States of America, were concerned to ensure that, in the process of removal of the colonial yoke, the communists, whether of Russian or Chinese origin or home-grown, did not enjoy the advantage derived from their ideological commitment to the overthrow of imperialism and step into the shoes of the receding imperial power. Their concern was to find and establish as firmly as possible, both in power and in popularity, regimes which would be sympathetic to the Western political, economic and cultural system. They were faced with two rival theories as to how this could best be accomplished. One was rapidly to withdraw imperial authority and the military force which supported it, and grant freedom and independence in the hope that the political leaders to whom it was granted would gain in popularity and therefore in power, and that both they and their people would be favourably inclined to the West and perhaps agree to military arrangements designed to deter communists, and others who were not so well disposed, from subversion in that area. The opponents of this policy argued that this would create a power vacuum which opponents of the West would exploit, particularly where, as was more often than not the case, there were rival aspirants for the power that the imperial authority might relinquish. Even if the aim of eventual withdrawal was accepted, their argument ran that it should not be contemplated until a solid foundation for future stability had been laid. The supporters of the first policy often found that in practice such a foundation could not be laid: Palestine, India, Aden and Cyprus were examples of this. The advocates of the second policy were reinforced by the interests of those of European stock who had settled in or had extensive commercial interests in the territory, as was the case in Kenya, Indo-China and Algeria, and, to a lesser extent, in Malaya. The irony of the situation lay in the fact that the basic objections to colonial rule derived from the culture of the imperial powers themselves, and notably from that of France and the ideas which lay behind the French Revolution. To preach and teach *liberté*, *égalité* and *fraternité*, and in practice deny all three to the people whom they ruled, was as blatant a paradox as that of British imperial rule buttressed and supported by the Church of England.

In this struggle, were the wars fought in vain or did they achieve the aims of those who took up arms? Clearly the answer must be different in different cases. In many of them the imperial authority had no alternative, at least initially, but to meet force with force, if it were not to abandon all authority in the face of intimidation by what was in most cases believed to be a minority, and in the initial stages probably was so. Subsequent events have shown only too clearly that there was no hope of Britain finding a solution to the rivalry between the Jews in Palestine and the Arabs, not merely of Palestine itself but of the countries surrounding it. There was no solution acceptable to both sides which she could enforce, however great a military effort she might make, and her problem quickly became how to escape from the commitment with the least dishonour. Malaya, in contrast, was a success story, owing as much to the good sense of the majority of its inhabitants of all races as to the skill and judgement of Britain's political and military handling of the problem. A nice balance was achieved between the need to assert the authority of the imperial government and concessions to the political aspirations of the people. Nevertheless it took a very long time and the deployment of large security forces of all kinds to defeat a small subversive movement, almost entirely confined to the non-indigenous element of the population which received almost no direct and very little indirect help from outside the country. The methods employed were sound and their general pattern was to be followed by almost every country faced with a similar problem, although not always with success. Their essence was to combine incentives to the population at large to support the government with military and other measures of enforcement which were intended to reinforce the authority of the government, reassure the populace that the government could and would provide for their security, and persuade them that it was more likely to win and remain the governing authority than those who sought to subvert it. The principal difficulty lay in achieving the best balance between measures designed as incentives and the others which were bound to restrict the freedom of the individual and perhaps cause him hardship, loss of earnings and certainly inconvenience. If the government was a colonial one and aiming sooner or later to withdraw and hand over to an indigenous one, it was difficult to persuade the populace that they should not reinsure with its opponents. When the Americans in Vietnam picked up the colonial burden which had been dropped by the French, they did so in the worst possible conditions. They were not the governing authority: that had been totally discredited; the indigenous one which they attempted to create and support had no real popular base and was opposed by an efficient and implacable foe, buttressed by the prestige derived from its victory over the French. Methods that had succeeded in Malaya failed, as the essential bases for them could not be established.

Britain's least successful little wars were in the Middle East. Palestine was a hopeless case. The Suez affair was an ill-conceived intervention which misjudged the international political atmosphere at the time of an American presidential election and revealed the inappropriateness of a Second World War military machine as a method of applying political pressure in the mid-twentieth century. Its impact on the Arab world had much to do with the sorry story of Aden, which suffered from sharp changes of policy, varying within a few years from determination of the imperial power to create a military base and maintain it there indefinitely to a rapid scuttle reminiscent of Palestine. Kenya and Borneo can be called success stories, but the effort involved to achieve success was high in relation, in the case of Kenya, to the size and sophistication of the opposition, and, in the case of Borneo, to the British interest involved. In the latter Britain was fortunate in that the internal revolution in Indonesia solved the problem for her, although it is true that the success of her campaign in Borneo may have contributed to, even been the main cause of, Sukarno's overthrow. Cyprus can also be claimed as a success story, although it did not solve the island's problems, and to achieve it the British Government had to concede much of what it had initially insisted on. There again the military effort involved to defeat a small subversive organization was considerable.

Although in all these wars the military effort deployed seemed large in proportion to that of the opposition, the contrast between Britain's colonial conflicts and those of France is stark in terms of scale, as it is compared with the two American adventures. Once the British Army had left Palestine, where it had been built up to 100,000 men, it never deployed anything like that number of soldiers from the United Kingdom again, except in the Suez affair. The maximum strength of the British Army in Korea was 16,000. Although the army in Malaya numbered 45,000 at its peak, 20,000 of these were Gurkha or Malay. Of the 10,000 in Kenya, half were from Britain. In 1966 and 1967 some 9,300 British soldiers and 5,700 airmen were deployed in Aden. At its peak at the end of 1956 Cyprus absorbed 20,000, while the infinitely larger area of Borneo was covered with 17,000 men, 10,000 from the United Kingdom. These figures compare with a French army of 152,000 in Indo-China, of whom 65,000 were French, and 200,000 in Algeria; and American armies in Korea and Vietnam of over 500,000 each. With the exception of the Suez affair, Britain's wars since 1945 made very little impact on the daily life of her people, until her army became involved in Northern Ireland in 1969.

The other wars described here were much more serious affairs. The French wars in Indo-China and Algeria had major domestic repercussions, as had the Korean and Vietnamese for the United States, particularly the latter. India's wars, although short and cheap in terms of manpower losses, notably so in relation to the large populations of the countries involved, had highly significant domestic and international repercussions, while Israel's were concerned with the very survival of the state itself, truly life and death struggles.

In the case of Britain's wars, the aim of defeating a subversive movement was achieved in Malaya, Kenya, Cyprus and Borneo, failing in Aden, although there is no doubt that, in the first three, the fact that a subversive movement had resorted to violence undoubtedly hastened the withdrawal of colonial rule, which at the start had not even been contemplated. To a degree, therefore, the defeated insurgents could nevertheless claim partly to have achieved their aims, although not to the extent nor in the fashion that they had intended. Malaya did not become communist; Kenya did not totally expel the European and Asian; nor did Grivas achieve *enosis*, while Britain continued to maintain military bases in Malaysia and Cyprus as long as she wished to.

For France it was a different story. In spite of a very considerable military effort in both Indo-China and Algeria, none of her aims were achieved. Her own political and economic stability were seriously affected as a result, and the countries in which and for which the wars were fought suffered severely. Could other results have been achieved? Would France have been better off if she had not attempted to resurrect her empire in order to re-establish herself as a major power? Was the bitter experience of Indo-China and Algeria a necessary purging process before she could regain her self-respect? It is impossible to give a definite answer to those questions: to say what either France herself or Indo-China and Algeria would be like in 1980, if de Gaulle's Brazzaville Declaration in January 1944 – 'To lead each of the colonial peoples to a development which will permit them to administer themselves and later to govern themselves' – had been the mainspring of his policy as the war ended, instead, as it was in fact, to re-establish French imperial authority. In Indo-China she certainly overreached herself, making a fatal error in attempting to reoccupy Tonkin, the Red River delta. If she had limited her aim, at any rate initially, to re-establishing her presence in the Mekong delta and concentrated on establishing the basis for a pro-French indigenous government there, leaving Annam, Tonkin, Laos and Cambodia to look after themselves, it is possible that she might have succeeded, and the whole sad story of her Indo-China War and the American Vietnam War avoided. On the other hand, if Ho Chi Minh had been able at that stage to establish a communist regime without opposition, he might, with support from communist China, have rapidly extended communist sway over the rest of Indo-China. This would undoubtedly have had major repercussions farther afield in the Far East, and the history of Thailand, Malaysia and Indonesia, and perhaps of the Philippines also, might have been different.

Although it seems clear in retrospect that America's chances of succeeding where France had failed were based on such slender foundations that success was never on the cards, her aims initially were strictly limited. It was only when even achievement of these limited aims seemed to be slipping from her grasp that she took a forward step into the bog to pull out the sinking Government of South Vietnam, only to be dragged deeper and deeper into the morass herself. It seems clear now that she was foolish to have become so involved and should have taken the opportunities which, at certain stages, were presented to her to extricate herself. But, as in the case of France's Indo-China War, for her to have done so could have had wide repercussions in the Far East at the time. While the United States, Vietnam, Russia and China had their attention and effort concentrated on the Vietnam War, the threat was lifted off other areas. The development of Malaysia, Singapore, Indonesia, the Philippines and, to a lesser extent, Thailand could go forward, while the poison, as it were, was drained out through the abscess of Vietnam. If anybody gained from the Vietnam War, they did. Neither the United States nor any of the countries of Indo-China can be said to have done so. Ho Chi Minh and Giap may have gained political and military victory, as they did, which they could claim justified their initial resort to the armed struggle; but the countries over which the regime in Hanoi now holds sway were ruined in the process. By what criteria could anybody claim that violence had paid? Only by that which maintains that the imposition of a particular ideological pattern of society is more important than a pleasant life.

It might have been thought that the bitter lessons France had learnt in Indo-China would have persuaded her not to repeat those errors in Algeria. Her reaction was indeed that; but her interpretation, certainly that of the military, was to be even more insistent on the need to maintain her authority over that country, which, fatally, she insisted on regarding as part of France herself. The presence of the *colons*, and the important commercial interests in France linked to them, made it difficult for her to follow any other policy. Only the adoption of an active political policy to treat all Algerians as equal and to press forward with implementation of the Brazzaville Declaration as soon as the Second World War ended might have averted the Algerian War. It would have been bitterly opposed by the *pieds noirs*, and there is no certainty that, in the event, the result would have been different. However, had such a policy been followed and had the French security forces of all kinds been able to initiate earlier a programme to win over the sympathy of the people to an indigenous regime, it is possible, although unlikely given the harsh character of so many of the country's inhabitants, that the story of Algeria could have been less grim. As in Indo-China, although Boumedienne and his associates appear to have gained political and military victory as the result of a resort to violence, it was a victory gained at the expense of the ruin of the country. In the event de Gaulle was right in seeing that France would gain by extricating herself.

Frustrating as was the course and the result of the Korean War, it must however be regarded as a significant victory for the United States of America, assisted by the fortuitous chance that the Soviet Union had chosen, at the time it started, to absent herself from the United Nations. If America, backed by many different nations of the Western world, had not committed herself at that particular juncture of time and place, the world, and particularly those emerging from imperial rule, European and Japanese, could have decided that communism was inevitably going to win the struggle, and would have trimmed their sails accordingly. But in this case, in spite of the intense frustration it imposed on the world's greatest military power, recently emerging victorious from a global war, the United States acted wisely in refusing to allow herself to become more deeply involved in a major war with China or Russia or both. The fact that Korea has remained divided to this day is not too high a price to pay for the generally beneficial results of the policy pursued at that time. Japan certainly has cause to be grateful.

Of India's wars there is little to add. Those with Pakistan over Kashmir were surely unnecessary. If one accepts that they were instigated by Pakistan, she gained nothing from them, and would certainly have been wiser to have accepted the 1949 cease-fire line in Kashmir as her frontier with India. Nehru's pursuit of his 'forward' policy over his frontier with Tibet was foolish in the extreme, and China's politico-military response to it a model of restrained, limited use of military force to achieve a clearly thought out and limited political aim. India's invasion of East Pakistan falls into the same category, and who can doubt that Pakistan herself gained from having forced on her the end of a political unreality, which could not be maintained by military means.

The Arab–Israeli wars were in a different category from all the others. Whatever views may be held of the rights or wrongs of the establishment of the state of Israel in Palestine, there can be no doubt that the frontiers proposed by the United Nations in 1948, and those which resulted from the War of

Independence, left Israel virtually indefensible against enemies equipped with modern weapons, especially if all her Arab neighbours combined against her. The Golan Heights, the central mountain range of Samaria and Judaea, and to a lesser degree the southern desert of Sinai, are essential geographical features for her defence. She has had to fight for them in the knowledge that her survival is at stake, that she cannot afford a long war and that, in any case, the major powers, including her sponsor, the United States, would not permit hostilities to continue to a point which threatened world peace. In contrast to all the other wars described, hers have been ones in which the whole nation has been mobilized and everything has been at stake. On the Arab side, only Jordan has had as much at stake, although at times the involvement of Egypt and Syria has been almost total. Neither side can be said to have won these wars, although, in military terms, Israel has come out best in all of them. She at least has survived and has recently achieved a major aim of her policy, recognition by Egypt and a removal of the military threat from that quarter, neither of them the result of a war, although they could be said to have stemmed from Egypt's failure in the Yom Kippur War. The Arab countries themselves have little to show for the immense effort some of them, notably Syria, Iraq and Egypt, have poured into their military machines, greatly assisted at times by the Soviet Union. Resort to war for them has been an unrewarding policy.

The hopes placed on the United Nations at San Francisco in 1945, when its charter was drafted, that it would prevent such wars as these, would provide a forum in which such disputes would be peacefully settled, and that its trusteeship would 'develop self-government, take due account of the political aspirations of the peoples, and assist them in the progressive development of their free institutions', have certainly not been fulfilled. Its organization has only been effective in very limited circumstances: as a channel through which an armistice or cease-fire can be brought about and thereafter supervised. Even in this limited field, its effectiveness has been dependent either on pressure being applied by the major powers in support of its aims or by the mutual, if reluctant, consent of the opposing parties. It has hardly ever itself been able to find, and certainly not to impose, a political or military solution. Korea was a peculiar exception, entirely dependent on employing the power of the United States under the theoretical flag of the United Nations. The result of its 'peace-keeping' activities has been to preserve the existing situation, postponing the application of political or military pressures, which could produce a solution that, however repugnant it might be to one side, could be maintained by the actual balance of power between the two sides in the dispute. It can be argued that preservation of such a situation is better than an outbreak of war to put an end to it. In some cases, this is clearly so; but it produces a tendency to allow sores to fester, instead of taking surgical action to cure them.

What lessons do these wars teach us? It is difficult to disentangle the political from the military. In the purely military field, the development of air transport for light military forces, notably the helicopter, lagged behind the need. The pattern of armed forces for all the major powers in the 1950s was based on the apparent need to meet a major conventional war of the 1939–45 pattern, in spite of the fact that, in that period, the balance of nuclear power was firmly in favour of the United States. Nevertheless the 1939–45 pattern of war, up-dated with developing technology, was found appropriate in Korea, the Indo-Pakistan and the Arab–Israeli Wars, each in succession bringing home to the military the logistic and procurement implications of the high rate of expenditure of munitions and equipment, a lesson obscured by the short period in the Second World War in which all the forces of Britain and America were fully engaged. Had helicopters of sufficient power been available in adequate numbers in Malaya, Kenya, Cyprus and Borneo, the campaigns there might have been brought to a successful conclusion with less effort in a shorter time. It would also have helped the French in Indo-China, although it is doubtful if it would have made a significant difference to the outcome. Neither they nor the Americans after them found the right military solution to defeat the combination of 'guerrilla', 'protracted' and 'mobile' warfare practised by Giap. Dealing with it involved fighting major units and formations in addition to widespread low-level terrorist or guerrilla warfare. 'Sweeps', fighting patrols and ambushes were not effective against bodies of that size. The British were beginning to face a similar situation, but on a much reduced scale, in Borneo, when the Indonesian Army operated in company or greater strength across the border of Kalimantan; but neither the strength nor the fighting effectiveness of the Indonesian forces posed a threat that could not be met by rapid concentration of battalions, normally widely deployed. This would not have sufficed in Vietnam.

In the politico-military field, certain lessons stand out. Foremost, the importance of 'intelligence', or accurate and timely information, both in the political and the military field. In almost all these wars, even in Israel's intelligence about her neighbours' intentions and dispositions, politicians and soldiers were surprised, not only at the outbreak of hostilities, but also by their nature and extent. In almost every case the threat and the force required to meet it was underestimated. Because the intelligence on which to act was not available (or not disseminated when it was) and the forces themselves either not available or not provided, the time taken to build up an effective organization and force to defeat the enemy was longer than it need have been. In almost every case it is true to say that, had much greater force been applied at the very start, either the outcome, where it was a failure, might have been different – Aden is an example – or success might have been achieved in a much shorter period, with an overall reduction both in effort and in the hardship or inconvenience imposed on the people. This could have been true of Malaya, Kenya and perhaps Cyprus also. In Borneo there were always adequate troops, but the availability of helicopters for them and their supplies was the limiting factor.

The importance of accurate and timely intelligence at every level, particularly of the enemy's intentions, cannot be over-emphasized. This is of course not easy to achieve: the enemy may not himself be clear about his own intentions, nor have decided on how he is to achieve them. Even if he has, his subordinates may not fit in with them. Penetration of the enemy's organization at every level and interception of his communications are far better sources of information than guesswork, based on an assessment of the probabilities. Many soldiers are reluctant to prefer action based on such information to their own ideas about what they wish to do, and the danger of ignoring information based on intelligence sources in favour of political judgement is clearly demonstrated by the sad stories of Indo-China and Vietnam, as well as of Nehru's frontier quarrel with China.

The outstanding politico-military lesson is an old one: that one should clarify one's aim before one embarks upon a military operation; ruthlessly and objectively dissect and analyse where it will lead one, what is to be gained from it, and what one will be faced with when it is over. The Suez affair is the supreme example of failure to subject policy to such an examination. Once embarked upon, many factors make it very difficult to extricate oneself, as the history of all these wars proves only too clearly. Chou En-lai's wisdom in extricating China at the first opportunity in December 1962 illustrates this well.

These wars were not, for the most part, easy for the soldiers who fought in them. The territory – jungle, desert, swamp or mountain – and the climate posed severe physical strain; but that could be cheerfully borne by those who were physically fit, often indeed regarded as an adventurous challenge. The greater challenge was to the soldier's morale. Except in the case of Israel, and perhaps in some cases in the Indo-Pakistan Wars, he was not supported by the feeling that his home country was in danger and that he had the full support of the nation and its leaders behind him. In the worst case, as with the French in Indo-China and Algeria and the Americans in Vietnam, the reverse was the case, especially in the later stages of all three campaigns, when it was clear that their nation had despaired of victory and was actively seeking means of extricating herself. The British soldier was subject to the same depressing influence in the later stages of the operations in Palestine and Aden. There, and even more so in Cyprus – to a lesser degree in Malaya and Kenya – he also faced the unpleasant experience of the hidden enemy, the terrorist who could not be distinguished from the peaceful citizen, a threat harder to endure when the soldiers' or airmen's families were present in the territory, attempting to live a normal peacetime life. Since 1969 he has faced a similar challenge in Northern Ireland.

Are wars like those the world has seen in the past thirty-five years likely to recur in the next quarter of a century? The colonial conflict must be almost a thing of the past, so few are the relics of empire still in existence. At the time of writing Africa appears to be the most likely scene for what one might call an ex-colonial war. America's experience in Vietnam provides a grim cautionary tale in that field. While the great powers are inhibited from war between them by the fear of escalation to nuclear war, the possibility remains that wars between lesser powers, which do not pose too high a risk of that, may break out and may not be contained. There is certainly no lack of actual and potential disputes which could give rise to them, all over Asia and Africa as well as in Central and South America. New fears will be introduced into the picture if attempts to prevent the spread of nuclear weapons fail. There certainly seems to be no reason to take an optimistic view and to run risks in letting either one's warning system or one's ability to react rapidly to a threat to one's interests wither or rust. All these wars show that a quick reaction with sufficient force at the start may save a load of trouble later.

To the final question – does war, the resort to force or violence, achieve its aim, 'the continuation of state-policy by other means' (to translate Clausewitz correctly) – there can be no definite answer. In some cases, it clearly has done; in others, it has achieved its political or military aim, but at a cost to some or all of the participants, or to the inhabitants of the country over which it was fought, that calls into question whether it was worth the effort. In few of the countries involved can one say that the majority of the population lead a better life as a result. But, if the alternative is to give in without a fight to whomever threatens or uses violence to obtain power for himself or for those with whom he is associated, society would collapse into anarchy. It is as well to remind those who quote the injunction in the Sermon on the Mount to 'turn the other cheek also' to him who 'shall smite thee on the right cheek', that, in the version in Saint Matthew's Gospel, this is preceded by the words 'I say unto you that ye resist not evil'. The sad fact of life is that, if evil is not resisted, it will prevail. That is the justification for the use of force to deter, and if necessary, defeat those who turn to it to further their own ends, the justification for maintaining in the service of the community and the state, forces who are trained, skilled and well-equipped to meet that challenge when and wherever it arises. Their profession is an honourable one.

CHRONOLOGY

1945

March	*Indo-China*	Japanese confine French troops to barracks: execute General Lemonnier and Governor Auphelle, when they resist.
May		May 8: Germans surrender. Victory in Europe Day)
	Algeria	Break-up of demonstration at Sétif leads to savage inter-communal fighting.
July	*Korea*	Potsdam Conference reaffirms commitment to an independent Korea, and fixes boundary between Russian and American occupation zones at 38th parallel.
August		After US had dropped atom bombs on Japan, latter collapses and Russian troops enter Korea.
	Palestine	Jewish United Resistance Movement formed. 6th British Airborne Division deployed.
September	*Korea*	September 8: Victory over Japan Day. US troops land at Inchon.
	Indo-China	September 12: British troops under General Gracey land at Saigon. September 23: Free French seize public buildings in Saigon and are disarmed by British.
October		General Leclerc with French colonial troops replaces British in Saigon.
	Palestine	Start of Jewish United Resistance Movement bombing campaign. General Cunningham arrives as High Commissioner.
November	*Indo-China*	Admiral d'Argenlieu arrives as High Commissioner.

1946

January		General de Gaulle resigns.
February	*Indo-China*	Leclerc re-establishes French authority up to 16th parallel, and in Laos and Cambodia. Giau joins forces with Ho Chi Minh. French negotiate Chinese withdrawal from Tonkin.
	Palestine	Jewish attacks on RAF bases.
March	*Indo-China*	French occupy Haiphong and Hanoi; accept in principle independent Vietnam, part of Indo-China Federation within French Union. Ho Chi Minh agrees to French troops manning Chinese frontier.
	Palestine	Irgun attack on British Army camp at Sarafand.
April		Irgun attacks on railway. LHI attack 6th Airborne Division car park at Tel Aviv.
June		Irgun men sentenced to death. British officers kidnapped in retaliation. Operation *Agatha*.
July		July 22: King David Hotel, Jerusalem, blown up.
August		Fontainebleau Conference starts and continues till October without result.
November		French occupy Red River Delta against Viet Minh resistance. Ho Chi Minh and Giap withdraw to mountains.
December	*Palestine*	Irgun kidnap British officers in retaliation for sentence on Irgun men of 'the cat'.

1947

January	*Palestine*	British 3rd Division deployed. Service and civilian families evacuated. Irgun kidnaps in retaliation for death sentence on Dov Gruner.
March		Irgun and LHI attacks on British Army installations and personnel. Martial law introduced. Irgun attack Haifa oil refinery.
April		Britain requests special session of UN General Assembly. Dov Gruner and three others hanged.
May		Break-out from Acre prison.
July		LHI kidnap two British Army sergeants in retaliation for death sentences imposed by military court, and later hang them. *Exodus 1947* refugee ship turned back.

August	*India*	August 15: independence and partition.
October		In response to appeal from Maharajah, Indian troops enter Kashmir.
November	*Palestine*	UN General Assembly votes to establish partition.
	Indo-China	French forces under General Valluy increased to 100,000. Bollaerts replaces d'Argenlieu as High Commissioner. Attempts to base a nationalist government on Emperor Bao Dai.

1948

February	*India*	Azad Kashmir attacks at Naushera.
March		Attack on Poonch. India counter-attacks in Kashmir.
April	*Palestine*	Fighting breaks out between Jews and Arabs.
	Indo-China	French agree to provisional government of Vietnam under Bao Dai.
	India	UN Security Council calls on India and Pakistan to withdraw from Kashmir.
May	*Palestine*	May 15: British leave. Jordan, Egypt, Syria and Iraq intervene. May 29: UN Security Council resolution for a truce. Count Bernadotte appointed as mediator.
	India	Indians, capturing Tithwal, face Pakistani troops, who reinforce Kashmir.
June	*Palestine*	First UN cease-fire. Attempt of *Altalena* to land arms.
	Malaya	June 16: State of Emergency declared. Sir Edward Gent, High Commissioner, dismissed and on June 28 killed in air crash.
July	*Palestine*	Israeli attacks on Lydda, Ramleh and Latrun. Second UN cease-fire.
	Malaya	Major-General Boucher produces British Army plan.
	India	Pakistan attacks in Ladakh.
August	*Korea*	Following elections, Syngman Rhee becomes President of Republic of Korea.
September	*Palestine*	Bernadotte murdered. Second UN cease-fire ends. Irgun and LHI disbanded.
	India	India occupies Hyderabad.
	Korea	Kim Il-sung proclaims Peoples' Democratic Republic of Korea with himself as President.

October	*Palestine*	Israeli attacks result in occupation of Negev and eviction of Lebanese and Syrian forces from Galilee. Third UN cease-fire starts.
	Malaya	Sir Henry Gurney arrives as High Commissioner.
December	*Palestine*	Israeli attacks at Falluja and Gaza. Dr Bunche holds peace negotiations in Rhodes.
	Korea	Russian occupation troops leave.

1949

January	*India*	Cease-fire in Kashmir, supervised by UN.
April	*Palestine*	Israel signs armistice with Jordan.
May		UN recognizes Israel and Jordan as independent states.
	Indo-China	French National Assembly approves union of Vietnam, Laos and Cambodia. Pignon replaces Bollaerts as High Commissioner. General Revers reviews situation, with 150,000 troops in country.
June	*Korea*	US occupation troops leave.
July	*Malaya*	General Harding succeeds General Ritchie as British Army C-in-C Far East.
October	*Indo-China*	Mao Tse-tung establishes authority over all China; proclaims Chinese Peoples Republic.

1950

January	*Indo-China*	Ho Chi Minh claims his is the only representative government of Vietnam: recognized by China and Russia. USA recognizes government of Bao Dai and grants US Military Aid.
	Korea	US Secretary of State, Dean Acheson, defines US defence commitment in Pacific.
February	*Indo-China*	Giap starts attacks on isolated French garrisons, now under command of General Carpentier.
March	*Malaya*	Additional Gurkha brigade deployed from Hong Kong.
April		Lieut.-General Sir Harold Briggs appointed as Director of Operations; produces Briggs Plan.

June		Chin Peng's MRLA's attacks running at average of 400 a month. Operations under Briggs Plan start.
	Korea	June 25: North attacks South. US forces intervene under UN Security Council Resolution. Fall of Seoul.
	Cyprus	Michael Mouskos elected Archbishop Makarios III and Ethnarch.
July	*Malaya*	3 Commando Brigade Royal Marines deployed from Hong Kong.
	Korea	US forces increased to 47,000. HQ Eighth Army deployed with General Walker in command.
August		Pusan bridgehead established. British forces deployed.
September		September 17: MacArthur lands two divisions at Inchon; link up with Eighth Army advancing from Pusan. September 27: US Chiefs of Staff authorize MacArthur to move north of 38th parallel, but not over Yalu River.
October	*Indo-China*	Giap's attacks force French to abandon most of Red River Delta.
	Korea	MacArthur meets Truman. Fall of Pyongyang, followed by mass North Korean surrenders. October 26: ROK troops reach Yalu River.
November	*Indo-China*	Marshal Juin's visit leads to replacement of Carpentier and Pignon by Marshal de Lattre as High Commisioner and C-in-C.
	Korea	Chinese counter-offensive across Yalu River.
December		MacArthur's forces, under pressure from Chinese, withdraw to 38th parallel. December 24: General Walker killed in accident and succeeded by Ridgway.

1951

January	*Korea*	Arguments between MacArthur and Washington over future strategy. January 24 Ridgway launches counter-offensive to Han River.
March		Ridgway launches Operation *Ripper*, recapturing Seoul and all territory south of 38th parallel.

	Indo-China	Battle of Mao Khe: Viet Minh defeat.
	Cyprus	Makarios visits Athens and confers with Grivas and brothers Loizides.
April	*Korea*	April 11: MacArthur dismissed; succeeded by Ridgway, who hands Eighth Army over to Van Fleet. April 22: Chinese counter-offensive across Imjin River.
May		Major fighting in area of 38th parallel.
	Indo-China	Battle of Phat Diem.
	Malaya	General Keightley succeeds General Harding as C-in-C British Army Far East.
July	*Korea*	July 10: First meeting of Armistice Commission at Kaesong. Fighting continues on 38th parallel.
	Cyprus	Grivas arrives and prepares plan of campaign.
September	*India*	China suggests discussions 'to stabilize the frontiers of Tibet'.
October	*Indo-China*	Battle of Nglia Lo.
	Malaya	High Commissioner, Sir Henry Gurney, killed in ambush by MRLA.
November	*Indo-China*	De Lattre captures Hoa Binh; returns to France; succeeded by General Salan.
December	*Malaya*	Briggs retires; replaced by General Sir Rob Lockhart. Police Commissioner Gray replaced by Sir Arthur Young.
	Indo-China	Giap counter-attacks Hoa Binh. Salan orders withdrawal.

1952

January	*Malaya*	Alliance Party formed.
February		General Sir Gerald Templer arrives as High Commissioner and Director of Operations.
June	*Kenya*	Sir Philip Mitchell retires as Governor.
September		Sir Evelyn Baring arrives as Governor.
October		October 9: Chief Warukiu murdered. October 20: State of Emergency declared; Kenyatta and 182 others detained. Garrison reinforced by one British battalion.
	Indo-China	Giap renews offensive at Nglia Lo. Salan counter-attacks in Clear River valley.

November		Salan withdraws to de Lattre line and concentrates on clearing Annam and Mekong Delta.

1953

January	*Kenya*	Ruck family murdered. Settlers march on Government House.
February		Major-General Hinde arrives as Chief Staff Officer to the Governor. First visit by CIGS, General Harding.
March		Stalin dies.
		Lari massacre.
April		Hinde becomes Director of Operations. 39th British Infantry Brigade deployed.
	Indo-China	Giap invades Laos and then withdraws.
May		General Navarre succeeds Salan; plans period of consolidation and development of Vietnam National Army.
	Korea	Exchange of prisoners starts.
June	*Kenya*	General Sir George Erskine arrives as C-in-C.
July	*Korea*	July 27: final armistice agreement signed.
October	*Indo-China*	Navarre's attack on Phu Ly held by Giap.
November		Navarre decides to construct base at Dien Bien Phu. Giap invades Laos again.

1954

February	*Kenya*	Colonial Secretary, Oliver Lyttelton, visits with CIGS to negotiate Lyttelton Constitution. Establishment of War Council. Baring goes on leave; Sir Frederick Crawford Acting Governor.
March	*Indo-China*	Giap begins attack on Dien Bien Phu.
April	*Kenya*	Henderson and Ruck contact Mau-Mau leaders on Mount Kenya. Operation *Anvil* on Nairobi. Development of pseudo-gangs and forest operating companies.
	Algeria	CRUA formed by the 'neuf historiques'.
June	*Kenya*	Baring returns. Sir Arthur Young arrives as Commissioner of Police. Resigns later and replaced by Catling.
	Cyprus	Announcement that British Headquarters in Suez Canal Zone would be moved to Cyprus.

May	*Indo-China*	May 7: Dien Bien Phu falls. First Geneva Conference starts.
July		July 21: Armistice signed at Geneva. Agreement stipulates 17th parallel only a provisional military demarcation line and general elections to be held under international supervision in July 1956.
August	*Vietnam*	US President Eisenhower approves policy of giving direct support to Diem in South, by-passing French – announces it in October.
October	*Algeria*	CRUA meeting in Switzerland plans campaign to start November 1 and changes its name to FLN.
	Vietnam	French troops leave North.
	Middle East	Agreement between Britain and Egypt for withdrawal of British troops from Suez Canal Zone and maintenance of civilian-manned base there.
November	*Malaya*	Templer hands over as High Commissioner to Sir Donald McGillivray.
	Cyprus	Greece raises Cyprus question in UN General Assembly. Grivas smuggled in in caique *Siren*. Caique *St George* intercepted, attempting to smuggle in arms.
	Algeria	FLN campaign of violence starts with limited success. French 25th Airborne Division arrives and launches offensive in Aures Mountains.
	Vietnam	General Lawton Collins appointed Eisenhower's Special Representative with Diem.

1955

January	*Kenya*	Operation *Hammer* in Aberdare Mountains.
February		Operation *First Flute* on Mount Kenya. Negotiations with Stanley Mathenge.
	Algeria	Soustelle succeeds Léonard as Governor-General.
April	*Kenya*	General Lathbury succeeds Erskine as C-in-C.
	Cyprus	April 1: EOKA campaign starts with bomb attacks.
May		EOKA attempt to blow up Governor, Sir Robert Armitage, fails.
June		British invite Greek and Turkish Governments to Conference.

	Vietnam	Ho Chi Minh's pressure for discussions on election meets with no response.
July	Malaya	First Federal elections held. Sweeping victory of Alliance Party, led by Tunku Abdul Rahman.
	Kenya	Operation *Dante* in Kiambu District.
	Cyprus	Detention introduced. Evangelakis and Drakos arrested. Grivas moves from Nicosia to Troodos Mountains. Colonial Secretary, Lennox-Boyd, and CIGS, Harding, visit.
August		EOKA bomb attacks increase. Constable Poullis killed. Caraolis arrested and Georgadjis detained.
	Algeria	Philippeville massacres lead to severe reprisals by French *paras*.
September	Cyprus	Garrison reinforced. Georgadjis, Evangelakis and Drakos escape from Kyrenia Castle and join Grivas.
	Middle East	Egypt imposes blockade of Israeli shipping and concludes arms deal with Czechoslovakia.
October	Cyprus	Field Marshal Harding arrives as Governor and C-in-C. Meetings with Makarios.
	Vietnam	After referendum, Diem replaces Bao Dai as President of Republic.
November	Cyprus	EOKA bomb attacks increase. First British serviceman murdered. November 26: bomb explosion in Ledra Palace Hotel, Nicosia.
December	Malaya	Meeting of Tunku Abdul Rahman, David Marshall and Chin Peng.
	Cyprus	Operation *Foxhunter* in Troodos Mountains. Search of monasteries. Haralambos Mouskos killed in ambush of Major Combe.

1956

January	Cyprus	Five more battalions and armoured car regiment deployed, bring total of British soldiers to 17,000. Harding holds several meetings with Makarios.
February	Algeria	Soustelle replaced as Governor-General by Lacoste. General Lorillot replaces General Cherrière and Major-General Massu arrives with his 10th Parachute Division.

March	*Cyprus*	March 1: Makarios meets with Lennox-Boyd and Harding, while Grivas explodes 19 bombs. March 5: EOKA attempt to blow up RAF Hermes fails. March 9: Makarios, Bishop of Kyrenia, Ioannides and Papastavros deported to Seychelles. March 20: EOKA attempt to blow up Harding fails.
	India	China starts to build road in Aksai Chin. Khampa rebellion in Tibet.
May	*Cyprus*	First EOKA men, convicted of murder, hanged. Grivas announces death of two British Army deserters held by EOKA. Operation *Pepperpot* in Troodos Mountains.
	Algeria	Palestro incident: ambush and mutilation of French reservists. Massacre by FLN at Melouza.
June	*Cyprus*	Operation *Lucky Alphonse* round Kykko. Grivas narrowly escapes capture; moves to Limassol.
	Algeria	Execution of FLN men, convicted of murder, leads to fighting in Algiers.
July	*Cyprus*	Lord Radcliffe starts constitutional inquiry.
	Middle East	July 6: Nasser announces nationalization of Suez Canal.
August	*Cyprus*	EOKA offers to suspend operations to enable discussions to start. August 23: Grivas rejects terms. Nicos Sampson rescues Georgadjis.
	Algeria	FLN conference in Soummam valley forms CCE and CNRA, tightens up organization and plans future campaign.
September		FLN under Yacef increase violence in Algiers, culminating in murder of Mayor on December 28.
	Middle East	September 21: meeting at Villacoublay between French, British and Israelis to co-ordinate action on Suez Canal.
October	*Kenya*	Dedan Kimathi killed. Army withdrawn from operations.
	Cyprus	EOKA increase murders. Operation *Sparrowhawk* in Pentadactylos Mountains. Lefkoniko incident. Further operations in Troodos Mountains. 16th Parachute Brigade removed to take part in Suez operation.

	Algeria	Massu's 10th Parachute Division withdrawn to take part in Suez operation. Ben Bella and others seized in aircraft and imprisoned in France.
	Middle East	October 29: Israel invades Sinai. October 30: Anglo-French ultimatum to Israel and Egypt to withdraw ten miles from canal. October 31: RAF attacks Egyptian airfields. Egypt sinks ships in canal.
November		November 5: British and French paratroops land at Port Said. Israelis occupy Sharm el Sheikh. November 6: British and French amphibious landing at Port Said. November 7: cease-fire.
December	*Algeria*	General Salan succeeds Lorillot.
	Middle East	British and French forces leave Port Said. Israelis withdraw from Sinai, except for Gaza strip and Sharm el Sheikh.

1957

January	*Cyprus*	Operations in Troodos Mountains result in death of Drakos and Afxentiou and recapture of Georgadjis. Sampson captured in Nicosia. Publication of Radcliffe's proposals.
	Algeria	In reaction to FLN-called general strike, Massu moves 10th Parachute Division into Algiers.
February		Defeat of FLN in Casbah of Algiers. CCE leave Algiers and split up, Ben Bella and Belkacem Krim escaping to Tunisia.
March	*Cyprus*	Grivas announces EOKA ready to suspend operations if Makarios released. Britain accepts, provided he does not return to Cyprus until Radcliffe constitution implemented.
May	*Algeria*	Fierce battles in Wilaya II.
June		Renewed FLN bomb attacks lead to return of paras to Algiers.
July		FLN meeting in Cairo forms new CCE of five colonels and five politicals.
August	*Malaya*	August 31: independence granted.
September	*Algeria*	Final defeat of FLN in Casbah of Algiers. General strike by *pieds noirs* in Algiers, protesting at Lacoste's 'loi-cadre',

		suppressed by Massu. Loi-cadre fails to pass French National Assembly.
	India	China completes road through Aksai Chin.
November	*Cyprus*	Sir Hugh Foot replaces Harding as Governor.
December	*Algeria*	Abane murdered in Morocco on orders of Boussouf.

1958

February	*Algeria*	French bombing of Sakiet in Tunisia in retaliation for FLN raids across Morice line.
April	*Cyprus*	EOKA renews campaign of violence. Georgadjis escapes again. New British proposals associating Greece, Turkey and Cypriot ministers with Government. Inter-communal riots.
May	*Algeria*	FLN execution of three French soldiers leads to crisis and threatened coup by Salan and Massu. President Coty calls on de Gaulle, who assumes power in France.
June		De Gaulle visits and states that there is only one category of inhabitant of Algeria: 'Français, à part entière.'
July	*India*	Indian expedition to Aksai Chin leaves Ladakh.
September	*Algeria*	De Gaulle's constitutional referendum receives a 96 per cent *Oui* from 80 per cent of Algerian electorate.
October		De Gaulle visits again: announces major concessions and, three weeks later, announces 'paix des braves', with offer of amnesty to FLN.
December		Salan removed; succeeded as Governor-General by Delouvrier and as C-in-C by General Challe, who plans systematic clearance operations from west to east.
	India	Exchange of letters between Nehru and Chou En-lai over Tibetan frontier.

1959

	Vietnam	Some time early in the year, Ho Chi Minh's government decides to assume control of opposition to Diem in South and renew armed struggle.

February	*Cyprus*	Agreement reached in London for proposals for independent republic with British Sovereign Bases.
March		Makarios returns. Grivas leaves. EOKA campaign ends.
July	*Algeria*	Operation *Jumelles* starts in Kabyle Mountains and continues till October.
August	*India*	Clashes between Indian and Chinese troops on disputed frontier in Ladakh and Assam.
September	*Algeria*	FLN bombing campaign resuscitated; declaration of government in exile. September 16: de Gaulle announces new policy, leading to self-determination. Challe protests, and elements in French army begin to plot with *pieds noirs* to resist it.

1960

January	*Algeria*	Massu sacked for opposing de Gaulle's policy. Crisis in Algiers, led by Ortiz and Lagaillarde, defeated by de Gaulle.
February	*Aden*	Formation of Federation of Arab Amirates of the South, with British Defence Treaty.
April	*Algeria*	Challe replaced by General Crépin.
	India	Chou En-lai visits Delhi. Nehru orders forward policy on Tibetan frontier.
June	*Algeria*	Operation *Tilsit*, de Gaulle's abortive negotiation with Si Salah. Meeting at Melun between French Government and GRPA.
October		Salan goes to Spain and starts plotting coup.
November		De Gaulle announces new policy, leading to Algerian Republic. Delouvrier resigns: his functions assumed by Joxe in Paris and Morin in Algiers. Crépin replaced by Gambiez.
December		Coup, planned to coincide with de Gaulle's visit, fails.
	Vietnam	Civil war in Laos reaches crisis. Pressure for US intervention to counter Russian.

1961

April	*Algeria*	Coup, led by Challe, fails.
May	*Malaya*	Tunku Abdul Rahman proposes formation

		of Malaysia, incorporating Singapore, North Borneo, Brunei and Sarawak.
	Vietnam	Cease-fire in Laos becomes effective. Second Geneva Conference. Vice-president Lyndon Johnson visits South East Asia and advises Kennedy against introduction of US troops.
October		Pressure from Diem leads to visit of General Taylor, coinciding with Mekong floods. Taylor recommends despatch of 8,000 US troops and strengthening of Military Aid Group above current level of 900.
November		Kennedy approves despatch of airlift, increase of MAG to over 2,000 and extension of its role; but rejects provision of US troops in active role. Diem disappointed.
	India	Chinese incursion in Chip Chap valley leads Nehru to intensify forward policy.
December		India occupies Goa.

1962

February	*Aden*	Britain announces that forces would be stationed in Aden permanently.
	India	India establishes new posts on McMahon line.
	Vietnam	Start of Strategic Hamlet policy.
March	*Algeria*	Cease-fire signed at Evian.
June	*India*	China reacts to Indian attempt to occupy Thag La ridge.
July		Indian patrol in Galwan valley surrounded by Chinese.
	Vietnam	Total of US servicemen increased to 5,500. Peace agreement signed at Geneva ending Laos Civil War.
September	*Aden*	Death of Imam of Yemen, followed by revolution, supported by Egypt.
	Borneo	First elections in Brunei lead to victory of Partai Ra'ayat.
	Algeria	September 15: independence granted.
October	*India*	India's further attempt to occupy Thag La ridge coincides with Chinese offensive in Assam and Ladakh. Indians withdraw.
November		November 21: war between India and China ends. Chinese start withdrawal.

| December | *Borneo* | December 8: Azahari launches TNKU revolt against Sultan of Brunei. British troops, flown in from Singapore, defeat it by December 12. December 19: General Walker assumes command in North Borneo, Brunei and Sarawak. |

1963

January	*Aden*	Aden Colony joins Federation.
April	*Borneo*	Indonesian attack on Tebedu police station.
May	*Vietnam*	Incident at Hué leads to further clashes with Buddhists. Henry Cabot Lodge replaces Nolting as US Ambassador. Threatened coup against Diem by Big Minh. Reappraisal of US policy.
August	*Borneo*	Indonesian raids in First and Third Division of Sarawak.
September		September 16: Malaysia formed from Malaya, Singapore, North Borneo and Sarawak. British Embassy at Djakarta attacked and burned. Indonesian attack on Long Jawi.
	Vietnam	US Defence Secretary McNamara and General Taylor on fact-finding mission.
October	*Aden*	NLF launches violent revolutionary struggle.
November	*Vietnam*	Big Minh's coup against Diem succeeds. Diem and Nhu killed. President Kennedy assassinated. Succeeding him Johnson confirms US policy to 'assist people and government of Vietnam to win their contest against the externally directed and supported Communist campaign'. US troop strength reaches 16,000.
December	*Aden*	Bomb attack on Governor, Sir Kennedy Trevaskis, at airfield. State of Emergency declared in Federation.
	Borneo	Indonesian attack on Kalabakan.

1964

| January | *Aden* | Operation *Nutcracker* in Radfan. |
| | *Borneo* | Cease-fire during abortive talks in Bangkok. |

March	*Aden*	Cross-border air attacks. Further operations launched in Radfan.
	Borneo	Battle on Kling Klang ridge.
May	*India*	Nehru dies; succeeded by Shastri.
June	*Aden*	Operations in Radfan end.
	Vietnam	Taylor succeeds Lodge as US Ambassador. General Westmoreland succeeds Harkins as commander of US Military Aid Command. General Khanh seizes power from Big Minh.
July	*Aden*	Britain announces intention to maintain a military base in Aden, but to grant independence to South Arabia not later than 1968.
August	*Borneo*	Indonesian naval and airborne attacks against Malayan mainland.
	Vietnam	Gulf of Tonkin incident leads to US Congressional Resolution giving President wide authority to use armed force.
September		UN Secretary General U Thant's attempt to arrange meeting between US and North Vietnam rejected by US. Abortive coup against Khanh. Revolt of Montagnards.
November	*Aden*	NLF steps up campaign of violence. Visit of Colonial Secretary, Anthony Greenwood.
	Borneo	Operation *Claret*, operations across Indonesian border, authorized.
December	*Aden*	British 24th Infantry Brigade completes move from Kenya to Little Aden.
	Borneo	British reinforcements bring Walker's command to 14,000.
	Vietnam	Increase in Vietcong attacks, including USAF bases. Reconsideration of US policy. Johnson decides on Operation *Rolling Thunder*, bombing campaign against North.

1965

January	*Aden*	Sir Richard Turnbull succeeds Trevaskis as High Commissioner. Mackawee appointed Chief Minister of Aden State.
	Vietnam	Ho Chi Minh and Giap decide plan of major intervention by NVA to concentrate round Saigon, aiming for victory in 1968.
	India	Elections in Pakistan. Clash between Indian and Pakistani police in Rann of Kutch.

February	Aden	Alliance formed between PSP and SAL, known as OLOS.
	Vietnam	Generals Thieu and Ky oust Khanh. Bombing of North starts. Westmoreland obtains authority to use US troops to defend air bases.
March	Borneo	Walker hands over command to Major-General Lea.
April		Indonesian attack on Plaman Mapu.
	Vietnam	Johnson approves increase in US troop strength to 82,000, but limits their activity to fifty miles from 'enclaves'.
	India	Pakistan attacks Rann of Kutch. Indians withdraw.
June	Aden	Turnbull declares State of Emergency in Aden State and proscribes NLF.
	Vietnam	Intervention of NVA leads Westmoreland to request increase in US troop strength from seventeen to forty-four battalions 'to save ARVN from defeat'.
	India	Agreement over Rann of Kutch reached between Ayub Khan and Shastri in London.
July	Vietnam	Johnson authorizes deployment of US Airmobile Cavalry Division and other troops, bringing total to 125,000. Later he agrees to total increase of 100,000 and lifts restrictions on their use.
August	Aden	Murder of police superintendent and Speaker of Assembly.
	Borneo	Singapore leaves Malaysia.
	Vietnam	US troops engaged in major operations in Central Highlands and coastal strip.
	India	Pakistan attacks in Kashmir. India counter-attacks.
September	Aden	Grenade thrown at British schoolchildren at airfield. Turnbull dismisses Mackawee and assumes direct rule of Aden State.
	India	Indian counter-offensive in Punjab. War ends with cease-fire, called for by UN, on September 22.
October	Aden	Federal troops brought in to support British in Crater. PSP leaders arrested.
	Borneo	Pro-communist coup in Indonesia leads to fighting between communists and their opponents.

1966

January	*Aden*	OLOS combine with NLF to form FLOSY, SAL breaking away.
	India	Russian-sponsored conference in Tashkent leads to withdrawal of Indian and Pakistani troops to pre-August 5 positions. Shastri dies, succeeded by Mrs Gandhi.
February	*Aden*	Britain announces that she no longer intends to station British forces in South Arabia after independence in 1968.
	Vietnam	Honolulu meeting to review US troop strength. Westmoreland's request to raise total to 429,000 by end 1966 reduced by McNamara to 367,000, rising to 395,000 by mid-1967. Westmoreland warns of long war.
March	*Borneo*	General Suharto replaces Sukarno as ruler of Indonesia.
	Vietnam	Internal fighting within ARVN round Danang and Hué lasts till May. Westmoreland launches attacks on NVA in 'War Zones' round Saigon. Increased NVA activity near 17th parallel demilitarized zone.
May	*Borneo*	Discussions between Malaysia and Indonesia start, leading to meeting in Bangkok in June.
	Vietnam	Extension of *Rolling Thunder* to include oil tanks near Hanoi and Haiphong authorized.
July	*Borneo*	Suharto finally strips Sukarno of all powers.
	Vietnam	US Marines occupy Khe Sanh.
August	*Borneo*	August 11: peace agreement between Malaysia and Indonesia. 'Confrontation' ends.
October	*Vietnam*	Johnson holds conference in Manila to review US troop strength. Westmoreland's original request for 542,000 by end 1967 trimmed to 480,000, rising to 500,000 by end 1968. Johnson offers to withdraw US troops six months after NVA had done the same and ceased intervention in the South. Operation *Attleboro'* launched against War Zone C.
December	*Aden*	NLF breaks with FLOSY.

1967

January	*Vietnam*	Operation *Cedar Falls* launched against 'Iron Triangle'.
February	*Aden*	Major riots and violent incidents. NLF and FLOSY fight each other, notably in Sheikh Othman and Al Mansoura.
	Vietnam	Operation *Junction City* against War Zone C.
March	*Aden*	Commonwealth Secretary, George Thomson, proposes independence brought forward to November 1967. Rejected by Federation.
	Middle East	Gromyko visits Cairo.
April	*Aden*	Visit by Lord Shackleton, proposing independence in January 1968, receives non-committal reply. Visit by UN Mission greeted by increased violence.
	Vietnam	On visit to USA, Westmoreland requests increase in troop strength to 670,000 and authority to extend operations into Laos, Cambodia and North Vietnam. Request reduced to 525,000 and extensions refused.
	Middle East	Land and air clashes between Israeli and Syrian forces.
May	*Aden*	Turnbull replaced as High Commissioner by Sir Humphrey Trevelyan.
	Middle East	Syria mobilizes. On demand of Egypt, UN Force withdrawn from Sinai, except Sharm el Sheikh and Gaza strip. Israel and Egypt mobilize. Egypt declares blockade of Straits of Tiran.
June		June 1: Jordan joins Arab military alliance and agrees to Iraqi division entering Jordan. June 5: Israel attacks Egyptian airfields and invades Sinai. Jordan shells Israeli areas of Jerusalem; Israeli Air Force attacks Jordan. June 7: Israeli forces capture Gaza strip, El Arish, Mitla and Gidi Passes in Sinai. Jordanian forces withdrawn to East Bank. June 9: Israeli forces reach Suez Canal and attack Syrian positions on Golan Heights. June 10: cease-fire comes into effect.
	Aden	June 16: mutiny in South Arabian Army leads to fighting between British troops and Aden Police in Crater, in which some

		British killed. June 30: British troops occupy Crater.
November		November 29: last British troops leave. November 30: South Arabia becomes independent.
December	*Vietnam*	Operation *Fairfax* in area round Saigon.

1968

January	*Vietnam*	January 31: Tet Offensive: widespread Vietcong attacks all over the South pre-empt Westmoreland's planned offensive.
February		General Wheeler visits and reviews strategy after Tet Offensive; supports Westmoreland's request for further 206,000 troops.
March		Clifford Clark replaces McNamara as US Defence Secretary. Johnson consults 'Wise Men', who recommend limit to bombing of North and to troop reinforcement; also advise opening negotiations. March 31: Johnson announces he will not stand again for President. Discussions start on procedure for negotiations in Paris.
June		General Abrams replaces Westmoreland, who becomes Chief of US Army Staff.
November		In response to halt in US bombing, North Vietnam indicates it will not infringe demilitarized zone nor attack major cities.

1969

January	*Vietnam*	Nixon becomes President. Procedure for negotiations in Paris agreed.
February		NVA and Vietcong renew offensive throughout South.
March		Vietcong rocket attacks on Saigon. In retaliation Nixon orders bombing 'sanctuaries' in Cambodia.
May		Nixon publicly offers 8-point peace terms, proposing simultaneous withdrawal of US and North Vietnamese forces.
August		Nixon starts troop withdrawals. 100,000 out by April 1970 and further 150,000 by April 1971.
September		Ho Chi Minh dies.

1970

May	*Vietnam*	US and ARVN troops enter Cambodia. Bombing of North Vietnam resumed close to DMZ.
June	*Middle East*	US proposes cease-fire in War of Attrition between Israel and Egypt accepted in principle.
September		Nasser dies, succeeded by Sadat.
December	*India*	Awami League victory in Pakistan elections.

1971

March	*India*	Riots in East Pakistan lead to martial law and reinforcement of garrison from West Pakistan.
	Middle East	War of Attrition cease-fire ends.
July	*Vietnam*	Dr Kissinger secretly visits Peking.
December	*India*	December 3: Pakistani air attacks on Indian airfields and invasion of Kashmir. Fighting spreads to Punjab. December 4: India invades East Pakistan. December 16: Dacca falls. Army in East Pakistan surrenders. Bangla Desh proclaimed.

1972

February	*Middle East*	Sadat visits Moscow.
March	*Vietnam*	Major NVA offensive across and round DMZ. Nixon resumes full-scale bombing of the North.
May		US bombs Hanoi and mines Haiphong harbour. Nixon visits Moscow.
October	*Middle East*	Egypt expels Russian military advisers and decides to plan war against Israel.

1973

January	*Vietnam*	Nixon's second term as President starts. January 23: peace agreement between USA and North Vietnam signed.
February	*Middle East*	General Ismail, Egyptian Chief of Staff, visits Moscow.

October

October 6: Egypt and Syria attack Israeli forces in Sinai and Golan Heights. October 7: Syrian forces overlook Lake Tiberias and capture Mount Hermon. October 8: Israel counter-attacks Egyptian forces east of Suez Canal. October 9: Israel holds Syrian advance. October 10: Israeli counter-attacks restore position on Golan Heights and contain Egyptian forces east of canal. October 11: Israeli forces advance into Syria. October 14: Egyptian Second Army's major attack fails. October 16–18: fierce fighting round Chinese Farm as Israeli forces cross canal. October 19: Israeli break-out west of Bitter Lakes. October 20: Kissinger visits Moscow. October 21: UN Security Council calls for cease-fire on October 22. October 22: Israeli forces cut Cairo–Suez road. October 23: Israeli forces complete encirclement of Egyptian Third Army. October 24: cease-fire effective.

1974

January	*Middle East*	Agreement reached between Israel and Egypt for withdrawal and limitation of forces in Sinai.
April	*Vietnam*	Talks between North and South broken off.
August		Nixon resigns as President of USA; replaced by Ford.
December		NVA launch offensive in Mekong Delta.

1975

| March | *Vietnam* | NVA launch offensive in Central Highlands. Thieu orders withdrawal. |
| April | | Collapse of South Vietnam. April 30: Saigon falls. Fall of Phnom Penh to Khmer Rouge. |

BIBLIOGRAPHY

Bell, J. Bowyer, *Terror out of Zion* (St Martin's Press, New York, 1977).

Blundell, Michael, *So Rough a Wind* (Weidenfeld and Nicolson, London, 1964).

Brines, Russell, *The Indo-Pakistan Conflict* (Pall Mall, London, 1968).

Burchett, William, *Grasshoppers and Elephants* (Urizen, New York, 1973).

Byford-Jones, W., *Grivas and The Story of EOKA* (Hale, London, 1959).

Carver, Michael, *Harding of Petherton* (Weidenfeld and Nicolson, London, 1978).

Churchill, Randolph and Winston, *The Six Day War* (Heinemann, London, 1967).

Clayton, Anthony, *Counter-Insurgency in Kenya 1952–60* (Transafrica Publishers, Nairobi, 1976).

Clutterbuck, Richard, *The Long, Long War* (Cassell, London, 1966).

Cooper, Chester L., *The Lost Crusade* (Dodd, Mead, New York, 1970).

Corfield, F. D., *Historical Survey of the Origins and Growth of Mau-Mau* (HMSO, London, 1960).

Darby, Phillip, *British Defence Policy East of Suez* (Oxford University Press, 1973).

Douglas Home, Charles, *Evelyn Baring* (Collins, London, 1978).

Fall, Bernard, *Street Without Joy* (Pall Mall, London, 1964).

Foley, Charles, and Scobie, W. I., *The Struggle for Cyprus* (Hoover Institution Press, Stanford, California, 1975).

Giap, Vo Nguyen, *Big Victory, Great Task* (Pall Mall, London, 1968).

Gilbert, Martin, *The Arab–Israel Conflict* (Weidenfeld and Nicolson, London, 1974).

Glubb, J. B., *A Soldier with the Arabs* (Hodder & Stoughton, London, 1967).

Halberstam, David, *The Best and the Brightest* (Randon House, New York, 1972).

Hammer, Ellen J., *The Struggle for Indo-China* (Stanford University Press, 1960).

Herzog, Chaim, *The War of Atonement* (Weidenfeld and Nicolson, London, 1975).

Horne, Alistair, *A Savage War of Peace* (Macmillan, London, 1977).

James, Harold, and Sheil-Small, Denis, *The Undeclared War: Confrontation with Indonesia* (Leo Cooper, London, 1971).

Kaul, B. M., *Confrontation with Pakistan* (Vikas, Delhi, 1971).

Kitson, Frank, *Gangs and Counter-Gangs* (Barrie & Rockliffe, London, 1960).

Leckie, Robert, *The Korean War* (Putnam, New York, 1962; Barrie & Rockliffe, London, 1963).

Majdalany, Fred, *State of Emergency* (Longmans, London, 1962).

Mankekar, D. R., *Pakistan Cut to Size* (Indian Book Co. New Delhi, 1971).

Maxwell, Neville, *India's China War* (Cape, London, 1970).

Middleton, Barry J., *The Compact History of the Korean War* (Hawthorn Books, New York, 1965).

Millett, James, *A Short History of the Viet Nam War* (Indiana University Press, Bloomington and London, 1978).

New York Times, *The Pentagon Papers* (as published in the *New York Times*) (Routledge & Kegan Paul, London, 1971).

O'Ballance, Edgar, *The Indo-China War* (Faber, London, 1964).

Korea 1950–1953 (Faber, London, 1969).

The Algerian Insurrection (Faber, London, 1967).

Malaya. The Communist Insurrection (Faber, London, 1966).

The Third Arab–Israel War (Faber, London, 1972).

O'Neill, Robert J., *The Strategy of General Giap since 1964* (Australian National University Press, Canberra, 1969).

Paget, Julian, *Last Post* (Faber, 1969).

Palit, D. K., *The Lightning Campaign* (Compton Press, Salisbury, 1972).

Pocock, Tom, *Fighting General* (Collins, London, 1973).

Short, Anthony, *The Communist Insurrection in Malaya* (F. Muller, London, 1975).

Stephens, Robert, *Cyprus* (Pall Mall, London, 1966).

Sunday Times Insight Team, *The Yom Kippur War* (Deutsch, London, 1975).

Taylor, Maxwell D., *Swords and Plowshares* (Norton & Co., New York, 1972).

Teveth, Shabtai, *Moshe Dayan* (Weidenfeld and Nicolson, 1972).

Thomas, Hugh, *The Suez Affair* (Weidenfeld and Nicolson, 1966).

Trevaskis, Kennedy, *Shades of Amber* (Hutchinson, London, 1968).

Trevelyan, Humphrey, *The Middle East in Revolution* (Macmillan, London, 1970).

Westmoreland, William C., *A Soldier Reports* (Doubleday, New York, 1976).

Wilson, R. D., *Cordon and Search* (Gale & Polden, Aldershot, 1949).

INDEX